HARVARD EAST ASIAN MONOGRAPHS

59

DIVIDED KOREA

THE POLITICS OF DEVELOPMENT

1945–1972

DIVIDED KOREA: THE POLITICS OF DEVELOPMENT,
1945–1972

by
Joungwon Alexander Kim

Published by
East Asian Research Center
Harvard University

under joint sponsorship with
Research Institute on Communist Affairs
Columbia University

Distributed by
Harvard University Press
Cambridge, Massachusetts
and
London, England
1976

The East Asian Research Center at Harvard University
administers research projects designed to further
scholarly understanding of China, Japan, Korea,
Vietnam, Inner Asia, and adjacent areas. These studies
have been assisted by grants from the Ford Foundation.

Library of Congress No. 74-24936
SBN 674-21287-8

To
the people of Korea, both
South and North, and the
fulfillment of their hope
for the unification of Korea

CONTENTS

PREFACE

This study has been written under the co-sponsorship of the Research Institute on International Change of Columbia University (formerly the Research Institute on Communist Affairs), and the East Asian Research Center of Harvard University. The bulk of the research and writing was completed while I was a Senior Fellow at the Research Institute on International Change during 1969–1970. I would like to express my deep appreciation to Professor Zbigniew Brzezinski, Director of the Research Institute on International Change at Columbia, and Professor Ezra Vogel, Director of the East Asian Research Center at Harvard, for their assistance. I should also like to thank Professor Jerome A. Cohen, Director of East Asian Legal Studies, the Harvard Law School, for providing the facilities to complete the study as well as for his invaluable advice and assistance. Many thanks are due the Council on East Asian Studies of Harvard University, including Professor John K. Fairbank and Professor Edwin O. Reischauer, for recommending the publication of this book.

Much appreciation is owed to those who have read the manuscript, or parts thereof, in various stages of its preparation, and have given encouragement and advice. I would especially like to thank Professors Zbigniew Brzezinski, W. Howard Wriggins, Jerome A. Cohen, A. Doak Barnett, Dankwart Rustow, and Donald Zagoria.

Many friends in South Korea have been of great help, but unfortunately there are too many to name each individually. Among the many in the academic community, special mention should be made of Professor Kim Ke Soo. The many prominent journalists who have generously given their time to keep me filled in on much background information include Choi Chiwhan, Cheon Kwan-wu, Yi Hyung, Chin Chul Soo, Bong Duhwan, and Kim Kyung-rae, among others.

ix

I have been most fortunate in receiving the full cooperation of government officials and members of both major political parties in the South. In particular, I have had personal interviews during the undertaking of this study with President Park Chung Hee, Prime Minister Kim Jong Pil, former Prime Minister Chung Il Kwon, president of the opposition New Democratic Party, Kim Young Sam, and other leading members of the opposition party, Kim Dae Jung and Lee Chul Seung. All of the above, with the exception of President Park, whom I met in a formal interview in Seoul, have talked with me informally not only in Seoul but also during visits to the United States. Much of what has been said in these conversations was not intended for direct quotation, and has not been quoted on the pages which follow.

Others in the South Korean government who have rendered assistance in gathering research materials, some of which are not otherwise available, include Chief Presidential Secretary Kim Jong Nyom, former Home Minister Hong Sung Chul, former CIA Director Kim Hyung Wook, Minister of Commerce and former Vice Minister of the Economic Planning Board Chang Ye Chun, member of the South-North Coordinating Committee and CIA Bureau Chief for North Korean Affairs Kang In Duk, former Assistant Chief of the Presidential Protective Force Kim Un Yong, and former Minister of Health and Social Affairs Chung Hi Sup.

Although I have received no direct assistance of a similar nature from persons in the North, I have continued to receive, over the years, valuable unsolicited resource material from the North via Japan, Hong Kong, the U.S.S.R., and other outlets, which have been most helpful. In this respect, I am also most grateful to Professor Jerome A. Cohen and his wife, Joan LeBold Cohen, for their valuable insights into contemporary North Korea gained during their visit to the North in 1972.

Much helpful library assistance was given me by Mr. Key P. Yang and Dr. Sung Yoon Cho of the Library of Congress, Mr. Sungha Kim of the Harvard-Yenching Institute Library, Mr. Joobong Kim of the East Asian Library of Columbia University, and Mr. Chu

Chin Kang of the National Assembly Library of the Republic of Korea.

Thanks are also due those who have assisted in the preparation of the manuscript, including Quee Young Kim, who worked as research assistant, Sophia Sluzar, Administrative Assistant at the Research Institute on International Change of Columbia University, and especially my wife, Carolyn Campbell Kim, who typed the many drafts of the manuscript, helped with transliteration, checked footnotes, and generally assisted with the routine and time-consuming aspects of manuscript preparation. I would also like to express my deep appreciation to Mrs. Olive Holmes and Mrs. Sheila Merwin Marian of the East Asian Research Center of Harvard University for their valuable editorial work.

For the most part, Korean words appearing in this book follow the McCune-Reischauer system of transliteration from the Korean phonetic alphabet into the Roman. One departure from the McCune-Reischauer system has been the use of the letters shi in place of si where such would more accurately render the correct pronunciation. A difficulty has arisen in the case of proper names which are well known in the Western press under different forms of spelling, however. In such cases, the names of the most familiar figures appear in the more familiar Westernized spelling, which is generally based on the personal preference of the individual Korean—for example, Syngman Rhee rather than Yi Sŭng-man, Kim Il Sung rather than Kim Il-sŏng, and Park Chung Hee rather than Pak Chŏng-hŭi. It has been difficult to draw the line between the more and less well-known figures, and sometimes the writer has had to be arbitrary in the choice of forms. Since the writer is not familiar with the personal choice of spelling of all of the figures in the book, the use of the McCune-Reischauer transliteration system has had to be the standard, from which departures are occasionally made. Other exceptions occasionally appear. For example, the *Dong-A Ilbo* has been favored with its own choice of spelling because this famous newspaper has used this form in print since 1920, and it seemed somewhat irreverent to force upon it a new romanization

derived from a system invented much later. This view is perhaps
due to the idiosyncrasies of the writer. It should be noted that
Koreans themselves (except for those scholars working in the
United States) do not employ the McCune-Reischauer system.
Without it, however, the transliteration of Korean words in this
study would have been a great deal more difficult.

Joungwon Alexander Kim

East Asian Research Center
Harvard University
Cambridge, Massachusetts

Introduction

THE POLITICS OF DEVELOPMENT

In 1945, Korea was divided into two parts, and two experiments in nation-building began, one following a Communist pattern, one attempting to model itself after "Western democracy," the one initially sponsored by the U.S.S.R., the other by the U.S.A.

During the nearly three decades since the decision was made by the United States and the Soviet Union to temporarily separate Korea into two halves for the purpose of receiving the surrender of Japanese troops in the peninsula, the two new political systems have passed through the process of development to form separate, functioning systems. This study is concerned with the introduction of both systems under the sponsorship of the two different foreign powers, through the efforts of different leadership groups, from the moment of collapse of the Japanese government in Korea on August 15, 1945, to the time of writing. In comparing the developments in the two Koreas, we shall be concerned with the roles played by leaders, the contrasting uses of political tools, the relative influence played by factors from both within and without the society, and the contrasting processes of consolidation of power by the new political elites and the institutionalization of two distinct political systems.

The term "developmental" is used to refer to a political system which is in the process of being "developed"—i.e., created.[1] This is in contrast to an "established" system in which the patterns of political order are routinized, or regularized. Thus any new political system goes through a developmental (creational) process until the patterns of political order have become established, or institutionalized, in the society. This would apply to the creation of a new political order in postwar Germany, Japan, or France, for example, as well as to Korea and other nations gaining their independence in the postwar era, and the term "developmental" implies no hierarchy of cultural or social superiority. If the development

1

of a new political order in the two Koreas has involved a longer process than in some other societies, this is largely because virtually all of the pre-existing organizations and patterns of order had been demolished by the prolonged disintegration of the traditional political system. The negative impact of Japanese rule (which is briefly examined), and the continued input of dysfunctional external influences also played a part.

One of the basic distinctions between the developmental system and the established system is the creative role played by leaders in formulating and shaping a new political order, and thus we shall be looking closely at the available political leadership in Korea in the postwar period. Because there are no existing "channels" through which to operate when a new system is being created, and no political tools are ready at hand, the leadership in the developmental system has to forge its own tools from the materials available. The nature of these materials, and of the potential leaders, are therefore important questions in the Korean situation.

To create a viable political system, a leader or leadership group makes use of four basic instruments of politics: guns, funds, organization, and ideas—first to consolidate political power, and second to institutionalize the system which has been created. Since the leader in the developmental system must create these tools, he must employ methods quite dissimilar from the leader who is working within an established system. The leader in the established system comes to power by institutionalized means and hence becomes legitimate in the very act of achieving power; in the developmental system, this leader must create a claim to legitimacy within the national political mythology. Much of the early developmental phase involves a contest between contending leadership groups to determine which will ultimately initiate the new political system and determine its form.

The tools of politics are so obvious they may be taken for granted by political observers; yet no contestant in the developmental system can take them for granted and survive politically. The success of a political leadership will depend upon its ability to use these tools to consolidate a permanent power base to support its advocated system. Because there is no institutionalized source of these political tools in the developmental system, those provided from external sources—from other nations and from international groups or organizations—may be important in determining the outcome of the political contest. Developmental systems have historically been viewed as "political vacuums," tending to draw in external forces from other nations to assist various contenders in determining the outcome of the contest for control. The two Koreas have certainly been prime examples of this absorption of external forces into a political vacuum.

The sources of tools are determined by internal, external, and extrinsic (or nonpolitical) factors—that is, those internal to the society, those external to the society, and those factors which are extrinsic to politics, for example, geography, technology, and literacy. The sources of the tools of politics within the society are those which have developed out of previous political systems, or in opposition to previous systems, and which have not since disintegrated. For example, the distribution of wealth in a previous system may well determine the locus of funds which will influence the outcome of a political contest. In a developmental system, many of the old sources of political tools may have disintegrated or been discredited by the same circumstances which brought the fall of the pre-existing political system. In this case, the political instruments must be created anew. In such circumstances, external assistance in creating these new tools may be sought by different leadership contenders, and it is because of this that the role of external factors in the developmental system takes on such great significance, and has had such a great impact in the contemporary international arena.

Factors internal to the society include the "political culture." This culture encompasses both the political behavior patterns of the society that have developed out of previous systems, and the national political mythology relating to political values and political legitimacy, on which the leader may draw to reinforce his image as a legitimate leader as well as to augment support for the new system.

The political behavior patterns that have developed in previous systems have come as a response to the way in which individuals and groups could maximize their objectives within that particular system. Although these behavior patterns originate as the result of some functional need, they may persist long after the original cause has ceased to exist. Thus, the political behavior patterns in the society may be totally irrelevant to the new system the leadership would seek to introduce, or may be highly dysfunctional within the system, yet they tend to be perpetuated, and will gradually die out only when it becomes clear that they fail to secure, or positively deny, the achievement of participants' goals. In Korea, leaders of quite diverse political persuasions in both the North and the South have repeatedly asserted that the behavior patterns which developed from the traditional system during the Yi dynasty are dysfunctional in a modern society and must be changed if the Korean political system is to survive in the modern world. The national political mythology is the sum of the political values and legends which have developed in the society's political history. A leadership wishing to change political behavior patterns and establish a new institutional system may nonetheless successfully draw on the values and legends in the old political mythology to support this change, and indeed may seek to legitimize the change by means of the old myth system.

Although the interests of other countries in the outcome of the internal contest may well affect how the external actors will behave, the influence they will actually exert upon the power struggle will be restricted to the concrete political tools they provide to, or withhold from, the various political contenders. Frequently, as we shall observe in tracing the actions of both the United States and the Soviet Union with respect to their protegé systems in Korea, the external actors may be blinded by their own myth systems to the extent that they are unable to recognize the realities of the internal situation within the system to which they are supplying external inputs, and thus they tend to take steps which are irrational or simply not suitable within the framework of the subject system.

The nonpolitical, or extrinsic, factors which affect the outcome

in the developmental system include those conditions in the environment which, though extrinsic to politics, nonetheless determine the
effectiveness of the political tools. Education, technology, communications facilities, and so on, are all extrinsic to politics but
will influence the tools of politics available to the contestants.
Because of the relation of these nonpolitical factors to the ability
to create effective political tools (for example, a more economically
developed system may have more funds to influence the outcome
of a political contest and hence may rely less on the coercive use
of guns), these nonpolitical factors have often been used as measures of development. However, they provide only the raw materials
of the political tools to be utilized by the participants.

Political consolidation is the drawing together by a leadership
group of sufficient power within the society to oblige the remainder
of the society to accept it as the political elite, and hence to accept
its political system. The process of consolidation takes place because in order to create an effective new system, one basic concept
of the desired form and its goals must prevail among the political
participants. The result of this consolidation will be the determination of not only who will be the leaders in the new system,
but more significantly, what form the new system will take. It is
thus more than a mere power struggle: the contest will decide not
simply a temporary leadership for the society but the institutional
forms which will shape the political behavior of the society for an
indefinite future.

Consolidation by a leadership group which seeks to bring
about a particular political order has occurred in every historical
society in which a new political system has been successfully introduced. For example, in nineteenth-century Japan, this group was
the Meiji samurai, in Russia, the Bolsheviks, in Turkey, the military
followers of Attaturk, and in the United States, the "Founding
Fathers." All of these shared a basic consensus within the leadership on the form of the system they sought to introduce, and excluded those who opposed that view, whether their opponents were
labeled "Tories," or "enemies of the people," or some other
epithet.

Consolidation is completed when the leadership group has secured sufficient control over the society so that a group offering an alternative system cannot find the means to challenge it successfully. Obviously, if external resources of political tools much greater than those available within the society remain accessible to alternative groups, the group can remain in control only if (1) it too can secure external resources sufficient to heavily offset those available to the alternative group(s), or (2) it can *create* internal resources of tools so strong that the cost to any external power which may seek to influence the outcome will be greater than its interest in the contest would warrant. It is for this reason that countries which seek independence from external control feel compelled to expand their internal economic base, to construct large armies, to create organizations which are so powerful as to dominate the society, and to develop idiosyncratic ideological systems. This defensive development is the compelling force which leads the so-called emerging nations to follow such similar patterns. They are responding to external factors which otherwise may alter the internal power structure (even irrespective of the conscious intent of the external powers) because foreign nations have control over sources of political tools within the subject society.

Institutionalization is the process by which the system introduced by the group which has consolidated control becomes routinized in the society. The new system is then accepted as both "normal" and "legitimate." It has become "normal" when behavior patterns within the society have adjusted to the system in such a way that persons have come to behave in a manner which can rationally be expected to fulfil their goals within the particular system. It is accepted as "legitimate" when persons have come to accept this form of behavior as "right"—that is, when there is no longer a conflict between the values of the individual and the way in which he must act to secure what he considers to be at least a minimum of his own goals within the system.

Consolidation is an ad hoc establishment of power; to institutionalize, this must be transformed into a permanent base of support for the system in each of the political tools. The society must then be resocialized in such a way that the behavior patterns and values of the populace will conform to the framework of the new system. Here the leadership must expand political institutions to penetrate those fundamental areas of society which shape human behavior—for example, the family and educational systems. Of course, the extent to which the new institutions require a change in behavioral patterns will determine the extent of resocialization needed. The more heavily traditionalized the society and the less responsive it has been to the challenge of modernization, the more its modernizing leaders may perceive a need for a "cultural revolution" to create a receptiveness to change.

Institutionalization does not imply a freezing of the system. Change may take place within an institutionalized system in the form of exchange—for example, an alternation of leadership groups which support the system within a regularized process—or development (growth)—for example, the expansion of the scope of available political tools to allow the participation of greater proportions of the populace.

It is within this framework that we examine the two experiments in nation-building in South and North Korea since 1945. We shall be looking at the relative success of the leadership groups in carrying out consolidation and institutionalization, using the political tools available. We shall examine what sources of leadership and political tools existed and how they were combined, in the two areas, to bring about different results.

Chapter I

THE BASES FOR DEVELOPMENT IN KOREA, 1945

On August 15, 1945, the Japanese surrendered to the Allied Powers, ending World War II in the Pacific, and bringing to a close forty years of Japanese rule in Korea.[1] To the Korean people, this was the long-awaited day of independence. "Independence," however, was to be only an illusion for some time to come, for into the peninsula came the armies of two of the victorious Allies, the United States and the Soviet Union, who would seek to shape the course of post-1945 politics in Korea. Ultimately, out of the dual occupation, came two new Korean governments, each laying claim to being the only legitimate "Korea," and each seeking to build its own political system, under the auspices of one of the two sponsoring powers.

When the period of Japanese rule came to an abrupt end, Korea possessed certain unique bases for development, from which a new political system, or systems, might emerge. The internal, external, and nonpolitical factors existing at this time, as well as the available leadership, would shape the systems which would be produced, and would provide the fundamental materials out of which Koreans could build new forms of political order after 1945.

The Internal Factors

The two political systems resulting from the dual occupation were constructed out of virtually identical cultural bases, for Korea prior to its division in 1945 possessed a homogeneous society, with a single language and national heritage, and a single political culture whose roots in the peninsula extended back more than 4000 years. As a political entity, Korea had not been divided for any extended period since its unification under the Silla dynasty nearly 1300 years before, in A.D. 668. Prior to that time, three kingdoms had coexisted in the peninsula (two of which were ultimately conquered and absorbed by the third, Silla). Indeed, Korean society had

8

become one of the most homogeneous of the major world societies (as the thirteenth most populous nation in the world, Korea qualifies as a major world society), for even regional variations in traditional dress had become insignificant, and dialect variation had become no greater than in the English language. Other than the Japanese who had entered Korea during the forty-year occupation, and who departed from the peninsula rapidly upon the surrender in 1945, there were no ethnic minorities.[2] Religious divisions in the society were likewise of no major significance for political cleavage; 1944 statistics indicated that more than 95 percent of the population belonged to no organized religion at all.[3] Korean historians since the division have been hard put to cite any evidence of major differences between the people of North and South Korea, vainly searching for surviving distinctions from the period prior to A.D. 668, nearly one and one-third millennia before. Prior to that time, the kingdom of Koguryŏ had boundaries similar to those of current North Korea, while the two kingdoms of Paekche and Silla were nearly coterminous with contemporary South Korea.

The two new political systems that emerged in Korea after 1945 were constructed on the same cultural base; thus, the differences in post-1945 development could not in any way be attributed to diverse cultural influences. Although the traditional political culture of Korea must be considered a constant factor, it is nonetheless important to have some familiarity with it in order to understand how the two systems sought to meet similar challenges presented by the same traditional behavior patterns, as well as how they sought to utilize similar elements in the traditional political mythology for developmental ends.

The period of the Yi dynasty (1392–1910) is most relevant for an understanding of the behavioral carry-overs from traditional Korea. The previous dynasties obviously were the source of some behavior traits which extended into the Yi period and beyond. Also, the forty-year period of Japanese rule introduced some new strains into the pre-existing patterns of behavior established during the 518-year reign of the Yi dynasty. Still, the half-millennium of

Yi rule can be pinpointed as the source of most of the behavior patterns lamented by Korea's post-1945 political leaders.

The Yi dynasty governmental system was consciously patterned after the Ming dynasty of China (1368–1644).[4] Like the Chinese system, Korean government rested on the ideology of Confucianism, and was headed by a monarch and a bureaucratic system of administrators selected by an examination system. In Korea the monarch was a king, rather than an emperor, as in China, and the lesser title reflected the lesser power of the Korean king. (The king did take the title of emperor in 1898, to emphasize Korea's independence, but it did not reflect any increase in his potency.) The Korean king was not considered to have a "mandate of heaven" as was the Chinese monarch, but on the contrary was invested by the emperor of China, making the latter the ultimate legitimizer of rule and of succession in Korea, though in fact Korea governed itself as an autonomous state.

China did not actually rule Korea, nor did it seek to challenge the actual succession of Korean kings whom it nominally invested; China's attitude might indeed seem a benevolent imperialism, if given that label at all. But since ideology and legitimacy were externally derived those fundamental elements of the Chinese system which made it operate so well for the Chinese were absent in Korea. Western observers have noted that the concept of "the mandate of heaven" created the two essentials of stable rule in China interspersed with periodic regeneration of the system. As Lucian Pye has pointed out, "The formula was necessary to justify the replacement of one dynasty by another while ensuring that both in their time had divine sanction."[5] The Korean king had no divine mandate: his authority was derived from the Chinese emperor, and he could well be challenged for misinterpreting doctrine, which likewise came from Chinese sources. Thus, his internal power was never fully stabilized. At the same time, however, the Korean king could never be legitimately overthrown; the Chinese emperor had confirmed his succession, and to thus challenge the Chinese emperor while he maintained his mandate was unjustifiable in Confucian doctrine. Thus no formula existed for regenerating the Korean political system.

The operational results of this combination of factors were clearly observable. Chinese dynasties averaged 200 to 300 years in length before their decadence brought about an overthrow and re-generation of the system;[6] the Yi dynasty survived for 518 years, though it was ripe for regeneration at least 250 years before it was given the final *coup de grace* by the Japanese in 1910.

Two hundred years of increasing decay is a heavy weight upon a society. In a decadent system, inequalities tend to become magnified, and the abuse of wealth makes the system less and less efficient. A traditional agricultural system is usually thought to be static, but the Korean economy at the end of the nineteenth century was at the end of a long period of spiraling decline. During the last two hundred years of the dynasty, Korea closed itself into rigid isolation and entered a period of extreme decadence: "Rural poverty, exploitation by landlords, removal of land from taxation, nepotism, corruption among officials, weak government, famine, pestilence, and banditry—these became the Korean way of life."[7] Peasant uprisings, the most obvious harbinger of the end of a dynasty, occurred in the eighteenth century, and by the nineteenth had become a constant facet of political life. There were major revolts in 1812, 1813, 1816, 1862, 1863, and the great Tonghak rebellion broke out in 1894, involving perhaps 400,000 partici-pants.[8] Yet even the Tonghaks oddly refused to challenge the king, addressing the monarch in terms of respect and protesting the mis-rule of his underlings of which he was "obviously" unaware.[9]

Population statistics illustrate the rise and decline of the dynasty:[10]

Official Census of Korean Population, Yi Dynasty

1404	360,929	1753	7,304,232
1648	1,531,401	1777	7,238,522
1657	2,290,083	1807	7,566,406
1669	5,018,644	1852	6,918,826
1678	5,246,972	1904	5,665,128
1717	6,846,568		

The population decline at the end of the dynasty represented not only actual loss of lives due to famine, disease, and rebellion, but also the number of people who had taken to wandering as vagabonds and bandits, and hence could not be counted because they had no domicile.[11]

By the end of the fifth century of Yi rule, even the wealthiest persons in Korea, at the apex of the political system, were impoverished to the extent that they had to be concerned about their day-to-day subsistence. Yet Korean agricultural land was rich; within the next half century it proved able to sustain a population which tripled in size at the same time that 35 percent of agricultural produce was exported. The system, not the resources, had created Korea's politics of scarcity.

Western observations of Chinese culture had first been made at a high point in one of the dynastic cycles; Japanese civilization was developing at the time of Western intrusion. But Westerners first observed Korea when it was at the ugly end of a long period of decline, which obscured the fact that Korea had been the bridge for Sinitic culture into Japan. This view of traditional Korea as a decadent society has been picked up by Korean intellectuals, with the result that the objective of Korean leaders in the twentieth century has been a total remolding of Korean civilization to erase the heritage of national shame.

Korean leaders of every degree in the political spectrum, South and North, have agreed on the need to reshape the culture and the behavior of the Korean people. They have also agreed that this culture and behavior *can* be changed through the medium of altered institutions, and that the undesirable behavior patterns existing in Korea today are a direct outgrowth of the Yi institutional system. They have also agreed on the specific aspects of Korean behavior which require alteration if Korea is to exist as a viable, self-governing nation in the modern world. They concur on the kind of change they wish to see; "developmentalism" is an ideology now common to both South and North. Their only disagreement has been about the institutional system best suited to bring about the desired change.

Korean leaders generally agree upon the aspects of Yi dynasty culture that have behavioral carry-overs into the contemporary era and that are dysfunctional for a developing system. These carry-overs include: (1) family-centrism, (2) "factionalism" of a nature peculiar to Korea, (3) an authority paradox which renders the masses always subservient and the elite always hostile to government authority, (4) competition for foreign support ("flunkeyism"), and (5) "bureaucratism," of a nature peculiar to the Sinitic tradition of bureaucratic rule. The writings of Syngman Rhee in 1904, of Kim Il Sung of North Korea since 1945, and of Park Chung Hee who seized power in the South in 1961, have all identified these as the behavior patterns that require alteration.[12]

Because of the extreme sanctity of the family promoted under the Confucian system, political leaders for a long time avoided direct verbal attacks upon the system, although North Korea has recently begun an attack on "familyism." Instead of a direct challenge, however, both governments have sought to promote programs which will, in the long run, undermine the powerful influence of family-centrism in Korean society.

South Korea's first President, Syngman Rhee, found the bitter factional struggles that had developed out of the peculiar patterns of rule of the Yi period to be the most serious threat to national unity in Korea and he insisted that this factionalism would have to be overcome if the Korean nation were to survive. Kim Il Sung, North Korea's president, also found factionalism threatening to an effective political system. He blamed the failure of the Communist movement in South Korea, not on "U.S. imperialism alone," but on traditional Korean factionalism among the various sectarian elements which had torn the party apart internally. For a time, he said, this "sectarianism" infected the North as well:

Sectarianism is a product of petty bourgeois self-glorification, vain glory and careerism, whose ordinary 'methods of work' are the scramble for position, mutual estrangement, cunning 'diplomacy' and calumny . . . No sectarians of our country ever fought each other on the ground of different theories or political views of their own. All of them formed themselves into factions as a means of their scramble for position aimed at winning the 'hegemony' . . . We should . . . clearly understand that without fighting sectarianism uncompromisingly, eradicating it relentlessly, and thoroughly removing the idea of the cult of the individual, our Party will never be able to consolidate its ranks, and fulfil the revolutionary tasks confronting it.[13]

Park Chung Hee, following his military coup d'etat in South Korea in 1961, asserted the same need for the elimination of factionalism:

Unless we eradicate such special privilege consciousness . . . the creation of political parties and resuscitation of parliamentary institutions will only result in the repetition of the former errors and blunders. In such a situation, it would be foolhardy to expect a political party to adhere to any concrete ideals and political platforms . . . Instead, it is bound to split into new and old factions, junior and senior groups . . . each pursuing its own private interests and ambitions. Our factionalism, exclusionism, and special privilege consciousness which abet national disunity, all are direct derivatives of the feudal caste system and mandarin bureaucracy of the Yi dynasty.[14]

On the subservient nature of Korea's common people, her modern leaders have been in general agreement. In 1904, Syngman Rhee wrote in anguish that: "They [the Korean people] simply sit down, making no effort to change the system . . . [and] give away everything of their land and fields and their homes to the people in the parlor [in power], and simply meekly borrow one room at the end of their own house [country] and humbly be thankful if they do not receive too much pressure from their ruler."[15] Kim Il Sung pointed out that "in the case of some of our Party functionaries, the masses seem to follow them not out of sincere respect, but for fear of losing their jobs [and] Party members show such tendencies as to follow blindly whatever instructions their superiors may issue, no matter whether these are correct or not."[16] Park Chung Hee, bemoaning the heritage of mass subservience, attributed it to the Yi system of rule: "The exclusion of the general populace from direct or indirect participation in government [fostered] among them . . . typical Oriental political apathy and indifference . . . the commoners became resigned to their fate, without willpower, incentive, or ability to overcome their abject misery and poverty."[17]

While concerned with the extremes of mass subservience, modern leaders in Korea have been no less disturbed by the other side of the authority paradox, the unrelenting elite resistance to all political authority as illegitimate, when not derivative of one's own political faction. This attitude of the elite has been illustrated by the unwillingness of those out of power to judge the actions of government on its merits, or for those in power to give any serious consideration to views not put forward by members of their own faction. Kim Il Sung put it this way: "When someone advances constructive ideas on a matter, there are people, who although they have been utterly unconcerned with the matter and have not studied it, claim to know all about it and ignore the good ideas of others, instead of taking due notice and putting these ideas into practice . . . There are some people who are only greedy for higher positions although they have neither ability nor enthusiasm for their work."[18] Park Chung Hee wrote of this tendency: "The view that everything one himself does is right while every act of others is wrong; that while one's own undertaking is eminently proper and in conformity with the national interest and benefit, that every enterprise of others is illegal and harmful to the country and the people—such a one-sided, egocentric way of thinking is the greatest psychological cause of social confusion and disorder."[19]

Korea's contemporary leaders have universally declaimed against the tendency of Korean factions to seek foreign support. Syngman Rhee wrote in 1904, before the Japanese annexation: "Those people who hold the sovereignty of our country in their hands sometimes depend too much on foreigners, and for the sake of their own private interests they seek protection from them . . .

Instead of cultivating the energies of the people, and establishing a
firm independent foundation here, these people ignore the rights of
the people and lower themselves to others simply to retain their
own positions for another day. Oh, this is our country's great
shame!"[20] Kim Il Sung, threatened in 1956 by an appeal over his
head to the Soviet leadership, made by his internal opposition
within the Party, later fumed:

> In our country . . . at one time there were persons among
> the leading personnel who had been infected with dogmatism
> and flunkeyism . . . they . . . slid down in the end to the
> position of national nihilism, from which all that is their own
> is disparaged and everything foreign is praised. [In 1956-1957]
> . . . the anti-Party revisionist elements within the Party came
> out to attack the Party . . . banking on the support of outside
> forces. The anti-Party elements within the Party and their
> supporters abroad, revisionists—big-power chauvinists, lined
> up as one in opposition to our Party and resorted to subver-
> sive activities in an attempt to overthrow the leadership of
> our Party and Government.[21]

Calling the tendency to rely on external assistance "vassalage,"
Park Chung Hee likewise denounced its pernicious influence upon
Korean politics in his political tract.[22]

On Korean bureaucratism, Syngman Rhee wrote in 1904,
". . . the so-called officials of our country, thinking not of their
country but only of their own greed and for their selfish motivations ignore the people . . . the people who have power sit in the
comfortable parlor [i.e., seat of government] and order other
people around."[23] Kim Il Sung described a clear outcropping of
traditional-style bureaucratic behavior in North Korea when he
said in 1955:

> Quite a few functionaries are oblivious of the fact that the
> duty of our people's state and Party organs is to serve the
> people. They mentally associate our people's state and Party
> organs with the government offices in the days of the Yi

dynasty. . . . They regard their work in these organs not as serving the people but as holding a post in a government office . . . they have degraded themselves into bureaucrats. Bureaucratism is a manifestation of the survivals of rotten and outmoded ideas left over from . . . the Yi dynasty . . . the method of getting things done [simply] by giving orders is, by its very nature, not the method of Party work.[24]

Park Chung Hee noted in 1962 that:

There are many irresponsible persons among our people, particularly in higher positions, who take for granted that what they say will be the law, and they think they can act as they please, particularly toward subordinates.

As part of our efforts to carry out the imperative tasks of administrative reform and democratization of administration, an organization for making an end to bureaucracy [bureaucratism] should be developed and the control over that machinery rationalized . . . We must create a sound and fresh atmosphere among public officials in which they can work actively and creatively for the benefit of the people.[25]

No studies have been undertaken which have clearly illustrated the persistence of these behavior forms among the Korean people, but all three of the major contemporary leaders of the two Koreas, who are very unlikely to have read each others' works, have identified these same elements as the most serious behavioral obstacles to modernization. The fact that these leaders agree in identifying these problems seems strong evidence of the persistence of these behavior forms in contemporary Korea.

Inherent in all of the contemporary criticisms of traditional society is an assumption by modern Korean leaders that the behavior patterns prevalent in Korea developed out of the Yi dynasty political system, as a result of the nature of that system. This assumption implies that human behavior is a product of social institutions, a philosophical assumption of immense importance for understanding the contemporary Korean political milieu. No contemporary Korean leader seriously believes that simply "releasing the energies" of the Korean people, as some have suggested was the method of modernization in the United States,[26] would result in anything but chaos, given the behavioral traits which developed in Korean society during the half-millennium of Yi dynasty rule. However, such change would not require an alteration of "human nature" itself. Human behavior patterns are malleable, as Korean expatriots demonstrated in readily adapting themselves as immigrants in the United States, China, Russia, Japan, and European nations during the period of the Japanese occupation.

The political behavior patterns which developed out of the old Yi dynasty period of rule were not significantly altered by the forty-year period of Japanese rule. As few Koreans were taken into the Japanese ruling bureaucracy, new elite behavior patterns were not established.[27] While foreign rule legitimated a new peasant resistance to authority, the practical circumstances of Japanese rule, which was backed by many times the force-in-being of the traditional regime, made overtly hostile acts against the government dangerous to the security of the peasant. Thus, the traditional pattern of submission was perpetuated, if no longer on a consensual basis. When conditions became intolerable, the result was not rebellion but emigration, with nearly 15 percent of the Korean population emigrating to other countries during the occupation, only to return home after liberation from Japan.

The traditional resistance to authority by elite educated group not given a role in the government was reinforced by the presence of alien rulers, while traditional factionalism generally prevented Korean opponents of Japan from being able to unite in their endeavors. Thus, while prisons became familiar abodes of the numerous leaders who sought to resist Japan, the 1919 nonviolent uprising was the only unified national resistance movement. The lack of a unified resistance movement could be attributable as much to the overwhelming power and efficiency of the ruling Japanese as to Korean factionalism. The fact remains that the traditional elite behavior patterns, as well as the peasant relationship to authority, were not significantly altered by Japanese rule. When Korea emerge from forty years of Japanese control, traditional behavior patterns remained largely intact—indeed, even exaggerated by the frustration of this period of foreign domination.

If traditional behavior patterns were not significantly altered during the period from the end of the Yi dynasty to 1945, this does not mean that the content of the political mythology remained intact. On the contrary, the symbolism of politics, and the political world view of Koreans in 1945 were vastly different from the outlook four decades previously. The general political awareness of the most humble peasant was certainly affected by the collapse of the old Yi system and forty years of an alien rule which deeply penetrated the entire society. The presence of large clusters of Japanese in every city and town, Japanese police in every village, the mobilization for World War II, large-scale temporary emigration, all accentuated the peasant's awareness of the influence of political happenings upon his daily existence. The helplessness of the peasants in the face of the power of the ruling Japanese was dramatized by the officiousness of those who came to rule by fiat in province and village alike. Though a sense of Korean nationality had been present in the country for centuries, the modern zealous sense of nationalism which was apparent in 1945 had grown out of the period of Japanese rule.

The question that Korean political leaders in 1945 would face was how any regime could seek to draw on traditional criteria of legitimacy—or, if tradition were to be discarded, what criteria could be substituted? The old monarchy had ceased to exist; the last king (who had assumed the title "emperor" in the last years of his reign) had abdicated in 1907, in favor of a mentally retarded son, who died without heir in 1929. The former king's son by a concubine was married by the Japanese to a Japanese princess in 1920, negating any legitimacy he might have claimed in the eyes of the increasingly nationalistic Koreans. There were, however, other competing sources of legitimacy.

Prior to Japanese annexation, movements had arisen in an attempt to bring about political reform, and hence to ward off subjection to Japan. The Kaehwa movement of 1884, which involved only a handful of reformist leaders, and the Independence Club movement of 1896-1898, which was an outgrowth of these former efforts and involved a few hundred members of Seoul's educated classes, and which managed to mobilize several thousand persons in reformist protest demonstrations in the capital, were elitist attempts to secure rapid reforms through the central government as a prelude to modernization. The Tonghak rebellion of 1894-1895, involving perhaps as many as 400,000 participants,[28] and the "Righteous Uprising" of 1907-1912, which the Japanese estimated at 70,000 participants,[29] were peasant uprisings, the first aiming at reforming the government in terms of traditional values, and the second at resisting Japanese domination. Many leaders would seek to trace their associations to these pre-annexation movements in order to bolster claims to legitimacy.

After the Japanese annexation, other sources of legitimacy came from the independence movement. The uprisings of 1919, which came at the time of the funeral of the monarch whom the Japanese had forced to abdicate in 1907, resulted in a declaration of independence and the establishment of a Korean Provisional Government in exile in Shanghai, which many Koreans considered a legitimate successor government to the old monarchy. This government continued to exist in name and personnel, if not always in activity, up through 1945. Besides this uprising and the government it fathered, other resistance movements against the Japanese could be considered fonts of legitimacy. Among these were armed resistance movements against the Japanese by bands with bases in Manchuria and North China, and the nationalist and Communist movements within the peninsula. These achieved negligible results, but the paucity of other sources of legitimacy elevated them to relative prominence after 1945.

Because of the heavily repressive nature of the Japanese occupation, the Koreans had had no opportunity to create an internal organizational base to take over and build a new government when the Japanese surrendered in 1945. Few organizations of any significance existed in the peninsula at all as of 1945. The national groups of political orientation which did exist within the country

were the gradualist nationalists and the Communists, neither of
whom were well organized, but rather maintained relationships
on the basis of past activities which had developed mutual friend-
ships and loyalties among the leaders within each group. Participation in resistance activities, which had taken many forms, had built
up personal ties and mutual commitments among individuals which
would tend to bring them together after independence, but specific
organizational bases were lacking for both groups at the time of
the Japanese surrender. Many of the leaders—and an overwhelming
number of the Communists—were in prison on August 15, 1945.[30]
Even if organized, the groups would have been small. After several
months of recruitment, the Communists were able to claim only
7,000 members by early 1946.[31]

Only religious organizations had nationwide bases in 1945.
With the exception of the Tonghak organization (originally founded
in 1860) which had spurred the rebellion of 1894-1895, religious
groups had not been of significant size prior to the Japanese
annexation. Foreign rule had brought a growth in religious organizations as a rallying focus for nationalists. It was the Ch'ŏndokyo
(the Tonghak organization under a new name) and the Protestant
Christians who planned and brought about the 1919 nonviolent
uprising. According to Japanese statistics, membership in religious
organizations during the Japanese rule changed as follows·[32]

Membership in Religious Organizations, 1911 1944
(In Thousands)

Year	1911	1928	1939	1944
Buddhists	340	270	194	187
Christians	201	340	500	621
Ch'ŏndokyo	109	111	80	72
Others	119	83	50	52
Total	769	804	824	932
Percent of population	5.7	4.3	3.8	3.7

Though religious organizations had more membership than any other politically-oriented group, by 1944 all of them together involved under 4 percent of the total population.

The only other significant organized Korean grouping within the peninsula seemed in a poor position to play a role in post-1945 politics. These were the 45,919 Korean civil servants and 7,968 Korean police who were employed in the Japanese administration in Korea.[33] Because the Japanese had recognized the danger of employing the nationalistic Koreans in their bureaucracy, the percentage of Koreans employed by the Japanese administration in Korea had declined sharply from 65.3 percent of the high officials and 58.1 percent of the middle-level officials in 1910, when Korea was changed from a protectorate to an annexed territory of the Japanese empire, to 29.4 percent of the high-level officials and 33.4 percent of the middle level as early as 1914.[34] This percentage had continued to decline, so that by 1942, Koreans made up only 18 percent of high-level officials in Korea, and only 32.2 percent of middle-level bureaucrats.[35] The more the Koreans had been demeaned in the official bureaucracy, the more resentment had been directed at the remaining Korean "collaborators" in the government by the general populace. Likewise, in the police force, the percentage of Koreans had declined from 35.3 percent of the officers and 61.7 percent of policemen in 1910, to 12.4 percent of the officers and 36.8 percent of the policemen by 1943.[36] Despised by most of the population, these police and bureaucrats appeared more likely to suffer retaliation from their countrymen than to play a constructive role after independence.

Not only were organizational resources weak in Korea as of 1945, but the only instruments of force held by Koreans in the peninsula as of August 15, 1945, were in the hands of the 7,968 Korean members of the Japanese police force. (When the old Korean police had been disbanded in 1910, its members had totaled 8,054;[37] by 1941, the Japanese police force in Korea, including plainclothesmen, totaled 60,000.[38]) There were some armed groups of Koreans outside the peninsula—in China, Manchuria, and the U.S.S.R., in addition to the Korean draftees into the Japanese army (18,000 in 1942[39]). Thus there was a vacuum of guns in the peninsula which could only be filled by the incoming Allied troops.

Sources of funds among Koreans were extremely limited. Although some industrial development had taken place during the Japanese rule, 88.7 percent of all capital investment was Japanese. Japanese held a virtual monopoly in every area of the economy, as illustrated by the following table:[40]

Distribution of Paid-up Capital Investment in Korea
Under Japanese Rule, as of 1938

Type of Investment	Percent of Capital	
	Korean	Japanese
Banks	7.7	92.3
Other financial institutions	30.5	69.5
Insurance	9.1	90.9
Manufacturing	12.3	87.7
Trade	26.2	73.8
Electric Power	--	100.0
Agriculture-Forestry	20.7	79.3
Fisheries	6.3	93.7
Mining	6.8	93.2
Transportation	7.5	92.5
Real Estate	40.6	59.4
Others	14.9	85.1
Total capital	11.3	88.7

These Japanese assets would be assumed by the ruling powers which would take responsibility in the two Koreas after World War II.

The concentration of wealth in Korea in the hands of the Japanese had actually impoverished the Koreans below the low economic level of the pre-Japanese period. The number of tenant farmers had risen from 36.8 percent of the total number of farmers in 1916 to 53.8 percent in 1942.[41] This general impoverishment was also evidenced by the fact that the per capita rice consumption of Koreans declined steadily from 3.62 bushels per year in 1915–

1916 to 2.03 bushels in 1934–1935, at the same time that rice exports to Japan grew to 35 percent of total production (and rice consumption in Japan proper remained constant over the period).[42] This reduction in Korean rice consumption was not offset by a significant increase in the consumption of other staples. Other evidence of the same decline in the economic well-being of the Koreans to the relative benefit of the Japanese was the decline in the average Korean savings account deposit from ¥6.89 in 1909 to ¥3.41 in 1933, while the average Japanese deposit in Korea increased from ¥20.79 to ¥56.01 over the same period.[43]

While Koreans had been progressively impoverished, the accumulation of financial resources by the Japanese Government-General had vastly expanded. Tax income from internal Korean sources had increased from ¥11,347,000 in 1913 to ¥71,485,000 in 1938, while income from "government undertakings" in the peninsula had risen phenomenally from ¥13,047,000 in 1913 to ¥258,214,000 in 1938. The total value of industrial production in Korea in 1939 was said to be ¥1,498,300,000, nearly 90 percent of which was owned by the Japanese.[44]

Sources of ideas in the peninsula as of 1945 are more difficult to pinpoint than other political tools. The Japanese had practiced strict censorship, yet ideas from abroad did manage to penetrate Korea through students who had gone abroad, and through the Christian missionaries, most of whom were Americans. To categorize idea systems is to grossly oversimplify them, but for the purposes of this study five distinct idea systems shared by various groups in Korea as of 1945 may be identified.

The first idea system we might simply call nationalism. This was the sense that the Korean people had shared a common, unique, and tragic experience. This nationalism did not have, or require, any specific formulation as an ideological system. It was intuitively felt by virtually the entire population. Japanese rule had penetrated the society so deeply that this reaction to foreign rule touched the most remote villages. The political group which could mobilize this vibrant strain of nationalism would have an immense advantage in moving the society against any political opponent.

This "modern" nationalism coexisted side-by-side with the traditional Confucianism of the society, which, like nationalism, was without specific codification in the minds of the people. The traditional prescriptions of the Confucian ethical system continued to shape the everyday life—marriages, funerals, family relationships— of even the urbanized Koreans. Respect for scholarship, elders, and traditionally legitimized authority was not disrupted. Indeed, this was one thing which the people distinguished as "Korean" as opposed to the insulting, militaristic, and officious Japanese police who were the face of the foreign ruler to the people in the local towns and villages.

Three other idea systems were less pervasive in the society, being confined to specific groups of a more elite nature. These included the Ch'ŏndokyo political doctrine, an idea system we might call "Christian-Wilsonianism," and Marxism.

The Ch'ŏndokyo political doctrine had influenced attitudes far beyond the membership of this indigenous religious organiza- tion, founded in the 1860's. Its concept of egalitarianism had been a revolutionary philosophy in the 1890's, mobilizing people against an increasingly venal *yangban* (aristocratic) class. Ch'ŏndokyo was a unique co-mingling of the three traditional beliefs of Korea— Confucianism, Buddhism, and Taoism—with the concept of human equality, and it claimed that truth was to be found in "Eastern Learning" alone. True equality could be reconciled with a hier- archical society, because all men contain God, but they realize their potential for godliness unequally. Hierarchy could not, however, be based on heredity, but only on true moral worth.[45]

"Christian-Wilsonianism" was a fusion, in the political thought of Korean Christians, of the traditional concepts of Christianity with the concepts of the "self-determination of peoples" enunciated by the Christian American president, Woodrow Wilson. This phi- losophy, along with a conviction that Wilson would indeed become the savior of the oppressed nations at the Versailles Peace Confer- ence in 1919, infused the 1919 uprisings with conviction and led to the collapse of the movement when Wilson did not respond to the pleas of Korean envoys of the independence movement who managed to arrive in Paris in 1919. The Christian organizations maintained communications with Koreans abroad, coordinated the sending of envoys to Paris, and assisted in the contacts with Koreans in Shanghai who set up the Korean Provisional Government there in response to the March 1 (Sam-il) uprisings in Korea in 1919. Christianity, like Ch'ŏndokyo, became in the minds of its native adherents a religious sanction for self-determination.

In the 1920's, after Wilsonianism had proved itself ineffectual as a means of achieving independence, Marxist theory began to circulate in intellectual circles. Young students studying abroad in China and Japan brought back with them the tenets of Marxist thought. Marxist study groups developed and a Communist Party was founded in Korea in 1925. Within a short time, the Japanese had arrested all of the core members. The party re-formed, only to have its new membership arrested. In all, the party re-formed, under completely new leadership, four times between 1925 and 1928, yet it never succeeded in becoming a permanent organization.[46] The Japanese system of informants and police intelligence was so effective that no Communist-led independence movement could be established. Nonetheless, Marxist thought had become the "vogue" among the intelligentsia. One had to be adept in arguing the problems of "class struggle" and the need for the removal of the "capitalists and imperialists," in order to exhibit intellectual manliness. Thus, a deep chasm developed between those intellectuals educated during the period prior to the 1920's, largely influenced by evangelistic Wilsonianism, and those who reached maturity later.

It would be a difficult task indeed for a political leadership to appeal to, and to reconcile, the holders of these diverse political idea systems present in liberated Korea.

Although Korea in 1945 possessed a unified pattern of political culture, the political tools available from internal sources were extremely weak at independence. Organizational bases, instruments of force, and sources of political funding were almost totally lacking, while diverse elite idea systems seemed more likely to prevent cohesion than to reinforce any efforts at consolidating a political leadership. These factors augured poorly for the introduction of a new political system, or, as events developed, of new political systems.

The External Factors

Though not apparent at the time, certain external developments during the period of Japanese rule in Korea were ultimately to have a great deal of influence on Korea's post-Liberation politics. The negative impact of Japanese inputs on Korean political tools is apparent from the weak nature of the internal factors in Korea as of 1945. What is not so apparent is the influence which American and Soviet policies during the pre-1945 period were to have on the post-Liberation situation in Korea.

The American policy of encouraging the missionary activities of Christians in Korea (there were 400 missionaries in Korea in 1938, mostly Americans)[47] had an obvious effect both upon the presence of a relatively important source of organization and of political ideology when the Japanese rule came to an end. Despite internal divisions, Korean Christians were in 1945 the largest existing organized group of any kind. One reason the Christians had succeeded in organizing so well was the relatively large inputs of funds during the Japanese occupation period, from sister organizations in the United States. These funds permitted an expansion of Christian propaganda, education, and organization. Especially after being infused with the zeal of Wilsonianism, the Christian political ideology had at one stage become so pervasive that it seemed to many Koreans to be the "wave of the future."

Soviet input into Korea proper during the period of Japanese rule was, in contrast, of minor significance. Communism could send no protected missionaries in nonpolitical guise. Korean Communists were rapidly arrested. Some Soviet funds were transferred into Korea in the 1920's, to send some twenty-one Korean students to study in the U.S.S.R.,[48] but in comparison to the educational and financial efforts of American Christians this effort was of little significance. The U.S.S.R. was apparently unwilling to commit large amounts of money to the development of organization in Korea, where it could not supervise and control the party in the presence of tight Japanese rule.

Missionary efforts were, of course, the work of private American citizens; the public efforts of the United States during the Japanese occupation operated in the opposite direction. As early as the opening of Korea's treaty relations with Western powers, the Korean government had sought American support to bolster its strength vis-à-vis Japan. This was, in fact, the rationale for concluding the treaty with the United States in 1882—Korea's first treaty with a Western power.[49] The American "guarantee" to use its "good offices" should "other Powers deal unjustly or oppressively" proved but empty rhetoric, however, when Koreans attempted to appeal to Theodore Roosevelt in 1905, as Japan was imposing its protectorate on Korea following the Russo-Japanese War of 1904–1905.[50] In like manner, Woodrow Wilson's appeal for self-determination seemed to promise Koreans far more support than was forthcoming, when the Korean "envoys" then resident in the United States could not even get traveling papers to go to Paris to make their plea for independence, and those arriving in Paris to seek Wilson's help were rebuffed.[51] Finally, the 1943 Cairo Declaration in which the United States promised Korean independence "in due course" did not deter the United States from suggesting at Yalta in 1945 that Korea be placed under a prolonged joint trusteeship, to last perhaps as long as twenty or thirty years.[52] The result of American public policy toward Korea from 1882 to 1945, which seemed to make pious promises for public consumption but to ignore them in actual practice, was to make many Korean nationalists suspicious of real U.S. intentions and inclined to discredit public statements of American policy.

On the other hand, the Soviet Union was officially more sensitive to the feelings of the Korean nationalists. Kim Kyu-sik, an American-educated nationalist who managed to plead Korea's cause at Versailles in 1919 (having arrived from China after the Korean nationalists in the U.S. were unable to secure travel documents), was also one of the unsuccessful lobbyists for an audience for Korean independence at the Washington Conference

of 1922. Disillusioned by continued American rebuffs, he traveled
to Moscow to attend the First Congress of the Toilers of the Far
East in 1922, and there found a more sympathetic reception. This
induced him to write an article in the *Communist Review* condemning the United States for pretending to be altruistic while really
ignoring the rights of small nations. He stated that "Korean independence must be achieved with the assistance of Russia."[53]

Another factor in American policy which was to greatly influence postwar Korea was the restriction of Korean immigration to
the United States and Hawaii (then a U.S. territory), during the
period 1905 to 1945. While Koreans emigrated from Korea in
large numbers after the Japanese annexation, the flow to the
United States was cut off almost immediately after it began. The
Japanese reported as early as 1912: "Koreans furnished with pass-
ports and going abroad are increasing, especially to Russia . . .
On the contrary, those proceeding to the United States have decreased and even practically ceased, as the United States regulation
limiting Asiatic immigrants is being strictly observed."[54]

During the period of Japanese rule, emigration continued to
climb, as indicated in the following table:[55]

Total Koreans Resident Abroad, 1912-1944
(In Thousands)

| Year | Japan | China | | Russia | Other | | TOTAL |
		Man-churia	Total		U.S.-Hawaii Mexico	Total	ABROAD
1912	n.a.	200	n.a.	50	10	n.a.	n.a.
1920	40.7	300	n.a.	n.a.	10	n.a.	n.a.
1925	40.7	400	500	160	10	20	720
1930	419	n.a.	620	170	10	25	1,234
1935	600	n.a.	775	n.a.	10	30	1,580
1940	950	n.a.	1,162	180	n.a.	34	2,306
1944	1,550	n.a.	1,500	185	9	57	3,292

By 1944, the number of Koreans temporarily resident abroad was
more than three million, or nearly 15 percent of the population in

the country. The temporary nature of this emigration was evidenced by the fact that by April 1946, just eight months after the Japanese surrender, half of the Korean emigrés had been repatriated to South Korea alone, and by December 1948, 2,485,286 had returned to South Korea.[56] Koreans returning from abroad brought with them new ideologies, skills, and personal contacts acquired from their years of residence in other lands.

Although the United States acquired the predominant influence within Korea through Christian missionary activity, particularly during the early years of Japanese rule, the Soviet Union nonetheless held an advantage in 1945. This advantage was acquired by organizing and training the Soviet-Koreans resident in the U.S.S.R. for a return to the homeland. The Russians had been training Soviet-Koreans in separate military units for some time, apparently with the thought of using them as a "liberating" force in Korea.[57] Indeed, American intelligence reported the existence of approximately two full divisions of Korean troops in the regular Soviet Far Eastern Army in 1943.[58] This source of armed Koreans was important, for Koreans in the peninsula (with the exception of the Korean members of the Japanese police force) were completely unarmed. In June 1945 Japanese intelligence reported that these forces were to be used to "liberate" Korea in August of that year,[59] and in July 1945, U.S. Ambassador to the Soviet Union W. Averell Harriman reported to President Truman that the Russians had trained an emigré force to take over Korea, having received this information from the Chinese through their intelligence sources.[60] In 1941, a small group of Korean guerrillas from Manchuria, who had been operating in the Chinese Communist guerrilla forces there, disappeared into the Soviet Union. Japanese intelligence pinpointed several of them in a "field school" there,[61] and when they returned to Korea in 1945, they held ranks in the Soviet Army. Together with the Soviet-Koreans, they formed an organized, indoctrinated, and armed group, the total estimated at between 10,000 and 30,000. They were capable of wielding tremendous power in the disintegrative atmosphere of Korea in the vacuum of the collapse of Japanese power.[62]

The United States did not adopt an official policy of assistance to any Korean political group prior to 1945. Syngman Rhee, representing the Korean Provisional Government in the United States, appealed for recognition of his government. He asked for lend-lease aid to the Provisional Government, which had declared war on Japan, to finance a Korean army and an uprising in Korea during World War II. He was denied any assistance, and his government received recognition only from the similarly-situated exile government of Charles de Gaulle of France. The War Department did provide some funds and advice directly to the Provisional Government in China, however, and a very small military unit of about 500 men was equipped and trained.[63] The War Department and State Department conflicted over Korea policy during the war, as they were to conflict even more strongly during the period of American occupation which followed. While the Office of War Information (the predecessor of the Voice of America) advised Koreans in radio broadcasts in their native language throughout the war to "prepare yourselves for your independence," Franklin Roosevelt and Joseph Stalin reached agreement on a four-power trusteeship for Korea at the Yalta Conference in February 1945.[64]

The one external action which was to affect Korea's postwar politics most was the reportedly impromptu military decision made by the United States (and its carrying out by the armed forces of the United States and the Soviet Union) to divide Korea at the 38th parallel into two zones of occupation in accepting the surrender of the Japanese forces in Korea. The division would have an immediate impact on internal politics. Seoul, the national capital, and the intellectual and administrative hub of the country, was in the South, where more than two-thirds of the population were concentrated. Nonetheless, membership in the religious organizations was greater in the North, where both the Christian and Ch'ŏndokyo religions had their largest followings. Korean members of the Japanese administration were concentrated in Seoul; absentee landlords and others who had made some economic gain during the period of Japanese rule were primarily resident in the South; scholars and political contenders had always

centered their activities around Seoul. In short, the national
division created a different balance in the internal politics of the
two areas of Korea than would have existed had the nation been
liberated as a united land.

The Nonpolitical Factors

Japan had succeeded in bringing about some development in
Korea, primarily as a consequence of the necessities involved in
Japan's expansion for war on the Asian mainland. (This development is of course negligible when contrasted with what Koreans
themselves have been able to accomplish since the Japanese occupation came to an end.) Urbanization had advanced in Korea so that
in 1940, 9.1 percent of the population lived in cities of over
100,000 and 11.6 percent in cities of over 50,000 people, as
compared with only 2 percent and 2.6 percent, respectively, in
1910.[65] Most of this urbanization came with rapid mobilization
after the Marco Polo Bridge incident in 1937 opened the Sino-
Japanese conflict, for in that year the figures had been only 5.8
percent and 8 percent, respectively.[66] (By contrast, both areas of
Korea were 50 percent urban by the mid-1960's, with more than
30 percent residing in cities of over 100,000.[67])

Similarly, the expansion in education which the Japanese
reputedly undertook in Korea increased school enrollment from
0.7 percent of the total population in 1910 to 7.4 percent in 1941.[68]
Illiteracy in Korea in 1944 was 86 percent according to Japan's own
figures.[69] (By 1970 both areas of Korea had raised literacy levels
to above 90 percent.) Furthermore, the increase in the number of
students in school in Korea during the Japanese occupation was in
large part due to the growth of Christian mission schools, sponsored
by Americans, of which there were thirty-six in 1935, including four
colleges and ten secondary schools, which generally provided a
higher quality of education than the government-sponsored
institutions.[70]

Rapid development did take place between 1910 and 1945 in
areas directly related to the necessities of Japan's political control
over Korea, and to Japan's military needs. Thus, communications

facilities were installed rapidly throughout the country so that police stations could communicate with one another. Also, transportation to China was essential to the war efforts, and consequently roads, railroads, shipping, and air traffic expanded considerably. Mining and industry likewise grew rapidly in the late 1930's and early 1940's.

The expansion of industry and mining, though marked in the war years, was integrated with the Japanese economy. Machinery and spare parts came from Japan; raw materials were sent to Japan for processing; and virtually all managerial and technical personnel were Japanese. The last years of the war brought their toll. Machinery was overworked, parts were often not replaced, stockpiles were used up. Without personnel trained to operate these facilities, parts and machinery to keep them operating, and the processing facilities of Japanese factories to which the Korean industry was wedded, the industrial facilities left behind by the Japanese had a far smaller value for an independent Korea than they represented within the framework of the Japanese war economy.

The division of Korea by the United States and the Soviet Union at the 38th parallel was even more damaging to the value of remaining Korean economic enterprise than the severance from the Japanese economy, for the two areas had been totally interdependent, both in agriculture and industry. While 86 percent of heavy industry production had been concentrated north of the 38th parallel, 75 percent of light industry was in the southern sector;[71] 88 percent of textiles were produced in the South.[72] While 64 percent of rice and 63 percent of other grains, the carbohydrate staples, were grown in the South, beans of various kinds and peanuts, the source of vegetable protein which sustained a population with a very minimal animal protein intake, grew almost exclusively in the North.[73] Machines necessary for the industries of the North were produced in the South; fertilizer necessary for the rice production in the South was produced in the North. Power resources were heavily concentrated in the North, with 85 percent of electricity and gas originating in North Korea, though two-thirds of the population were concentrated in the South. Thus, even the economic resources left by the Japanese were of questionable, and unequal, value to the two separate political systems which were to emerge from the division.

The Potential Leadership

The political resources were so scarce in Korea in 1945 that even a political leader highly skilled at recognizing, acquiring, and utilizing the tools of politics would be faced with overwhelming prospects of failure in an attempt to consolidate a political base for a new political system. Given the conditions of Japanese rule, the likelihood that even one leader might emerge who had had an opportunity to learn by experience the essential nature of politics was quite slim, for political resources had all been held securely in the hands of the Japanese. Therefore, it was not surprising that virtually every serious contender for political power in Korea in the days following the Japanese surrender was a member of that enormous group of Koreans who formed the repatriating emigrés.

The contenders who finally emerged to become dominant in the two Koreas in 1948 were Syngman Rhee and Kim Il Sung, who returned from the United States and the Soviet Union, respectively. Rhee, born in Korea in 1875, left for the United States in 1904, and remained there for forty years, with only a brief return to Korea in 1911-1912. Kim Il Sung, born in Korea under the name Kim Sŏng-chu in 1912, emigrated with his family to Manchuria in 1926, where he remained until 1941, when he went to the Soviet Union to stay until 1945. Both of these men, who had spent the greater part of their lives outside of Korea, nonetheless sought with some success to latch on to claims to legitimacy within the Korean mythology. Both also had had opportunities to experience political activity in environments more open to "trial runs" than the oppressive system at home.

Syngman Rhee had accumulated several claims to legitimacy. First of all, he claimed to be a member of the old *yangban*, or ruling class, though this was disputed on the grounds that his ancestors had followed the familiar path of downward mobility, that comes of failure to gain access to the bureaucracy for several generations. More important was the fact that Rhee (Yi) was a direct descendant of the Yi dynasty founder, making him a very distant relative of the last monarch.[74] This relationship, under the traditional system, would have rendered him eligible for the throne had the last monarch chosen to designate (adopt) him. While this family relationship was publicly known, Rhee himself never put forward the claim, but almost too dramatically sought to disassociate himself from the others he termed *yangban*, noting that he believed in the "common man." Thus he was able to draw on an aura of legitimate authority in traditional terms, without appearing to advocate a restoration of the traditional class system or monarchy.

More important to Rhee's popularity in Korea, however, were his reputed contributions to the reform and independence movements. In the late 1890's, Rhee, who had studied the Confucian classics but failed to pass the examinations for public office, began attending a Christian missionary school, run by Americans.[75] There he learned English and Western history, and was swept up in a reform movement started by a Korean who had just returned from receiving an education in the United States. This Korean, Sŏ Chae-p'il (who changed his name to Philip Jaesohn and became the first Korean to become a U.S. citizen), had been associated with the Kaewha reform coup of 1884. The Independence Club formed among these young Christians in Seoul began staging public demonstrations in the city in an effort to pressure the king into bringing about reforms.

In March 1898, Rhee apparently led a demonstration of 8,000 people, demanding that the government remove Russian advisers, because they interfered with the exercise of national sovereignty.[76] The government yielded to the "public" request. Later that same year, however, the Independence Club movement was crushed by the "pro-Russian faction" in the government, and Rhee was put into prison, where he remained for seven years, from the age of 23 to 30.[77] While in prison he wrote a political tract, entitled *The Spirit of Independence*, predicting the Japanese takeover and seeking to arouse popular resistance.[78]

In 1904, Rhee was released from prison in a general amnesty, and came to the United States as a foreign student in November of that year. According to his unsubstantiated claims, he carried instructions from Korean government ministers Prince Min and General Han to appeal to the United States to intervene, at the Emperor's request, against Japan on Korea's behalf under the good offices clause of the 1882 treaty between the United States and Korea.[79] Rhee's former secretary, in a private interview, confirmed that Rhee considered these "instructions" so important to his claims to legitimacy that he kept them in his desk throughout his presidency, half a century later.[80] Rhee did present an appeal to Theodore Roosevelt at the Portsmouth Conference in New Hampshire, which ended the Russo-Japanese War in Korea in 1905, but without effect.[81]

After coming to the United States, Rhee remained to study, receiving a B.A. from George Washington University in 1907, an M.A. from Harvard in 1908, and a Ph.D. in international law from Princeton in 1910, at the age of 35.[82] Rhee was thus one of the few leaders to have received an extensive classical education followed by an advanced Western education. Since education had traditionally been the channel to high position, Rhee's educational credentials gave him a distinct advantage.

After completing his doctorate, Rhee returned to Korea to work with the Christian youth movement. The Japanese quickly began arresting Christian leaders, however, and he managed to escape from the country and return to the United States, where he remained for the remaining four decades of the Japanese occupation. He managed to keep in touch with the leadership of Christian organizations in Korea, however, through friends among the American missionaries.

When the 1919 uprisings occurred in Korea, organized by the Christian and Ch'ŏndokyo religious groups, Rhee's name figured prominently despite the fact that he was in the United States. He had been a student at Princeton when Woodrow Wilson was president of the university, and pictures of Rhee with Wilson were circulated in Korea. Since one of the aims of the movement was to appeal to international sentiment through Wilson at Versailles, it was not surprising that the leaders of the underground movement in Korea and the exile leaders in Shanghai, both meeting to form a Korean Provisional Government, should each name Rhee head of government, though they acted independently.[83] The government claimed true legitimacy not only because it arose as a response to, and was supported by, a genuinely mass-supported nonviolent uprising in Korea, but also because it marked the occasion of the death of the last ruling monarch (whose funeral arrangements had provided a cover for the organization of the movement), and hence stood to replace the king as the central focus of legitimacy.[84]

How much Rhee was known in Korea as of 1945 has been questioned. Immediately after the Japanese surrender, and before the arrival of the American forces, both major political clusters *within* Korea—the Communists and the gradualist-nationalists—named Syngman Rhee head of their political group, reinforcing his claim to be the legitimate leader of Korea.[85] An American information officer, gathering information in Korea during the U.S. occupation of Southern Korea, noted, despite his own distaste for Syngman Rhee, that: "Rhee . . . had one big advantage; either through design or historical accident, his name was the most revered and respected name among the Korean villagers. In the minds of the people he occupied a place somewhat akin to that of a legendary hero."[86]

Rhee was aware of the importance of proving his legitimacy, and kept in his possession a notebook that contained a tracing of his genealogy back to the Yi dynasty founder, the instructions from the members of the Korean cabinet in 1904, newspaper clippings about his activities on Korea's behalf at numerous international conferences, photographs of himself with Woodrow Wilson—indeed, every piece of evidence he could accumulate to demonstrate his claim to be the leader of the Korean people.[87] He even claimed to have secured the original wooden print offset from which the 1919 declaration of independence was produced, apparently in an effort to prove his own association with the movement within Korea.[88]

In the United States, Rhee published and spoke on behalf of Korean independence, and took every opportunity he could to lobby for Korea at international conferences. These activities, of course, required money, for Rhee had to live, travel, and publicize the cause. To raise this money, Rhee formed two organizations, a Korean Christian Church in Hawaii, and an organization known as the Tongji-hoë (Comrades' Society).[89] The Korean Commission of the provisional government in the United States levied taxes on Koreans (at first given enthusiastically, but later ignored when prospects for independence waned), sold government bonds (Rhee sold $250,000 worth of Korean government bonds in 1919), and raised money through voluntary contributions ($21,219 was collected in 1919, for example, to establish a Korean embassy in Paris, and $12,000 for publicity for the Korean cause at the Washington Conference in 1922). Rhee's Christian church members donated regularly to the "cause," as did members of the Tongji-hoë.

There were, however, only 10,000 Koreans in the United States during the period from 1910 to 1945, so most of Rhee's financing had to come from sympathetic Americans. In the United States, Rhee quickly learned the technique of fund-raising. Capitalizing on American sympathy for the Christian cause, he began collecting money for Christian projects, both for the mission activities in Korea and for Christian organizations in the Hawaiian Islands. He had become so adept at attracting contributions that a Korean who went to Hawaii in the 1930's as a missionary tells the following tale:

> When I told Dr. Rhee I was going to Hawaii, he gave me letters of introduction to his American friends. They turned out to be the wealthiest and most influential people in the islands, from the most influential missionary to people in business and in the government. When I met them, they all said, "Oh, yes, I have heard all about you. You are a friend of Dr. Syngman Rhee." Whenever I needed money for my work, all I had to do was to pay a friendly call upon these friends of Dr. Rhee, and, without mentioning money,

casually tell them about how badly Korean children in the
islands needed a new school building, or some more books,
or whatever their current need. Then I would go home, and
within a week my mail box would be full of checks: $1,000,
$5,000, even more.[90]

Indeed, Rhee's financial sources aroused the curiosity of the American Military Government in Korea after 1945; intelligence materials
indicated that he was even able to secure contributions from some
American businessmen to whom he had promised advantageous
investment opportunities in Korea after independence.[91]

Kim Il Sung's background is much less well known than
Rhee's. While Rhee had been building an image as a national leader
for a full half-century, Kim Il Sung, the man who appeared in
Pyongyang to be proclaimed by the Russians as a national leader
in late 1945 at the age of 33, was relatively unknown. He did, however, possess one advantage: the name of Kim Il Sung was a very
famous one, tracing back to a leader who apparently participated
in the resistance movement against the Japanese begun in 1907,
and possibly was even involved in the Tonghak rebellion of the
1890's. The man who appeared in Pyongyang under that name in
1945 was born in 1912, under the name Kim Sŏng-chu, just outside Pyongyang, North Korea.[92] He adopted the name of Kim Il
Sung at about the age of 20, while living in Manchuria.[93]

Kim Il Sung had some experience in "politics" prior to 1945.
As a guerrilla leader in Chinese Communist forces in Manchuria
for several years, he knew how to use the instruments of force. To
hold his band together, even though at peak strength it probably
did not exceed 300, took a well-developed capacity for persuasion,
in view of the fact that the members of the group were all volunteers, fighting against immense odds.

The young Kim Il Sung of 1945 had himself participated in
anti-Japanese activities, and in 1932 had joined the Chinese Communist guerrilla bands operating in the area across the Yalu from
Korea. Kim had succeeded in leading a few forays across the border
to harass the Japanese in Korea. These incidents have been documented

from the files of the Japanese police.[94] The most famous incident was the "battle" of Poch'onbo in 1937, in which Kim led a band of men which caught the Japanese off guard and successfully destroyed much of that little border town.[95] Although Kim had been a genuine participant in the independence movement, he was not listed on the roster of great independence leaders by either the Communist or the non-Communist groups forming at the time of independence.

The Korean people knew little about the heroes of the independence movement for the suppression of information by the Japanese made the populace rely heavily on rumors, legends, and word-of-mouth communication. Thus, although Rhee's legitimacy claim was based on several genuine historical facts (whereas in retrospect it has not even been possible to identify who the "original" Kim Il Sung was, if such an individual existed at all), it was undeniable that many people had heard of a person named Kim Il Sung who could be ranked among the leaders of the resistance struggle. The fact remains that no groups took the half-legendary figure seriously during the period immediately following independence.

Though Syngman Rhee and Kim Il Sung were to be the successful contenders in the struggle for power in the two areas of Korea, each faced several challengers who were to play crucial roles in the post-independence political struggle.

Kim Koo was the most serious challenger to Syngman Rhee for the position of national leader. Born of lower-class background (the nearly untouchable butcher class), Kim Koo attempted to use his origin to his advantage as Rhee did his supposed upper-class background. Adopting the nickname "Paekbŏm" (Butcher-Lawmaker), Kim advocated bringing together the lowest class (the butchers), and the highest class (the lawmakers). There was much that lawmakers could learn from butchers, he suggested.[96]

In 1894, the Tonghak-led peasant rebellion broke out in Korea, with the goal of driving out foreigners and forcing government reform, and Kim Koo headed one of the regional branches of the Tonghak organization, spearheading an attack on the Haeju

local government.[97] Following the rebellion, the Japanese sent
troops to Korea and gained temporary control of the government.
When the Queen proved uncooperative, the Japanese minister to
Korea arranged to have her murdered, and she died by the swords
of Japanese soldiers who invaded the palace in 1895.[98] Incensed
at the Queen's cruel end, Kim Koo sought out her assassin, and,
believing that he had found the man, killed a Japanese in 1896.[99]
Although he was imprisoned, Kim managed to escape and became
known for his never-substantiated but widely reputed claim to
have avenged the national honor by eliminating the Queen's killer.

In 1910, Kim was arrested again in Seoul where he was helping to organize the underground resistance movement, having been
implicated in a plot to assassinate the Japanese governor-general.
Although sentenced to seventeen years in prison, he was later
released in a general amnesty.[100]

During the 1919 uprisings, Kim Koo managed to escape to
China, where he joined the Korean Provisional Government (KPG)
as chief of police.[101] In 1923, he was elevated to home minister,
and in 1927, two years after a dispute which led to an "impeachment" of Rhee (which Rhee never recognized because there was
no provision for impeachment under the Seoul constitution), Kim
became president of the KPG under the Shanghai constitution,
though Rhee continued to claim the title under the constitution
which had been drawn up by the leaders of the 1919 uprising and
adopted in Seoul.[102] Thus Kim Koo claimed to have succeeded
Rhee as president of the KPG.

Kim Koo's activities in China were ineffective until 1932,
when in January, he sent a Korean to Japan with a mission to
assassinate the Japanese emperor. A bomb was thrown at the
emperor's carriage, but it missed.[103] On April 29, 1932, Kim
succeeded in arranging to have bombs thrown at a group of
Japanese military leaders as they addressed a crowd of 100,000
Japanese in Shanghai during a victory celebration. One general
was killed and two seriously wounded.[104] When Kim Koo let it
be known that it was he who had arranged the two bombing
incidents, he became a hero at once to both Koreans and Chinese

who were resentful of the Japanese encroachment in Manchuria and North China; the KPG received de facto recognition and began to receive financial assistance from the Chinese Nationalists.[105]

During World War II the KPG was revitalized with the prospect of a possible alliance with the Allied powers to defeat the Japanese. In 1938, communication between Kim Koo in China and Syngman Rhee in the United States was restored, and although neither admitted the other possessed a legitimate claim to leadership, the objectives of both could be realized only by promoting national independence.

Another set of contenders for leadership within Korea were the *Dong-A Ilbo* (East Asia daily news) gradualists, the most prominent among whom were Kim Sŏng-su, the owner and publisher, Song Chin-u, president, and Chang Tŏk-su, editor. These men, all educated in Japan during the first decade of the occupation (Chang also received a Ph.D. from Columbia University in the United States), had returned to Korea in the 1920's to work for independence from within the country. Song had been an important participant in the planning and organization of the 1919 uprising.[106] Kim Sŏng-su, of upper-class origin and one of the four richest men in Korea by the end of Japanese rule, had decided that independence must be achieved by gradual means—by building up the internal resources of Korea to promote independence. Consequently, he had concentrated on promoting education, nationalist ideology, and independent economic enterprise. He founded the Chung'ang High School in Seoul in 1915, and later became president of the Posong School which was to become Korea University upon independence.[107] In 1920 he created the Seoul Textile Company in accordance with his philosophy of economic self-reliance, and had built up a considerable industrial and agricultural empire by the time of independence. Most importantly, he started the nationalist newspaper, the *Dong-A Ilbo*, in 1920, a paper which remains today the most prestigious and independent news organ in Korea.[108]

The *Dong-A Ilbo* helped to keep alive the nationalist forces of resistance to the Japanese. Song Chin-u, president of the paper, served a prison term from September 1926 to May 1927 as a result of nationalist liberties taken by the paper, and in 1936 he was finally forced to resign from the newspaper as a result of a nationalist incident involving the paper.[109]

Operating within the confines of Japanese rule, the *Dong-A* group had of necessity to adopt a policy of gradualism. Ideas and economics were the resources they sought to use, though their economic growth was limited by the fact that the Japanese controlled the monetary system and dominated the entire economic structure of the society, while the spread of ideas through their news media and educational institutions was strictly limited by censorship and government control. By 1938, the newspaper was forced to close down and the schools had to discontinue Korean instruction when the Japanese decided to ban the use of the Korean language.

Kim Kyu-sik, an activist exile nationalist, first gained national prominence when he attempted to appeal on Korea's behalf at the Paris Peace Conference in 1919.[110] Like Rhee, he had a Ph.D. from Princeton University,[111] and became foreign minister in the KPG. He later left the KPG and joined with another nationalist of more radical bent, Kim Wŏn-bong (who later was minister of labor in North Korea before his purge in the late 1950's) to form a National Revolutionary Party.[112] Kim Kyu-sik returned to the KPG in 1943 to assume the post of vice president.

Yŏ Un-hyŏng spent the years from 1914 to 1930 in China, and in 1918 joined Chang T'ŏk-su, one of the *Dong-A* gradualists, in founding a New Korea Youth Party in Shanghai.[113] He became a member of the Foreign Affairs Committee of the KPG in 1919, and was sent as an emissary to Japan to explain the necessity of Korean independence. In 1921, he joined the Korean Communist Party formed in Shanghai, and attended the First Congress of the Toilers of the Far East in Moscow as a Communist representative, as did Kim Kyu-sik representing the KPG.[114] In 1930, Yŏ was arrested in Shanghai by the Japanese police and taken to prison in Korea. There the Japanese forced out of him a long and detailed account of Korean Communist activities throughout the 1920's.[115]

After his prison release the same year, Yŏ became president of the *Chung'ang Ilbo* (Central daily news), another nationalist paper in Korea, and remained in that position until the paper was forced to close in 1938. In 1944, he organized a secret independence alliance which sought the participation of both the activist and gradualist members of the independence movement.[116] Yŏ was a brilliant and exciting orator, though his ability to carry through on promises was called into question. Attractive in his sporty apparel, with dashing white hair and mustache, he gained the nickname "the Silver Axe"—beautiful, but unable to cut wood.

Not the least among the political contenders in Seoul in 1945 was Pak Hŏn-yŏng, at the age of 45 the youngest of the leading contestants in the South. Pak, a confirmed Communist of long-standing, was to emerge after the Japanese surrender as the leader of the Korean Communists in the South. As early as 1919, he had joined the Korean Communist Youth Alliance in Shanghai and was one of the original members of the Korean Communist Party in Shanghai in 1921. In 1922, he was arrested on a mission to attempt to establish the party within Korea, and served 18 months in prison.[117] In 1925, Pak succeeded, along with sixteen others, in forming the Korean Communist Party in Seoul, where the founding meeting was held in his home on April 18, 1925.[118] Pak became head of the Korean Communist Youth Alliance, and was arrested in December of the same year. Released on grounds of insanity in 1929, he went to Vladivostok in the U.S.S.R.; from there he went on to Moscow to study at Lenin University.[119] In 1931, Pak returned to Shanghai and attempted to revitalize the Communist Party there; he was arrested again in 1933 while attempting to enter Korea, and was imprisoned in Seoul until 1939. After his release, he again began organizing the Communist Party and was quite successful until 1941, when mass arrests of Communists began again. Pak was one of the few to escape, hiding out in the countryside until 1945, at which time he was one of the few Korean Communists not in prison.[120]

Because the major leaders naturally came to the capital city, Seoul, after the Japanese surrender, few contenders were present in Pyongyang, North Korea, to challenge the youthful Kim Il Sung's consolidation. Only two men were to offer him major competition: Cho Man-sik and Kim Tu-bong.

Cho Man-sik was a Christian nationalist, a native of Pyongyang, who played a prominent role in plans for the 1919 uprising, and later was head of the *Chosŏn Ilbo* (Korea daily news) and of the Pyongyang branch of the Shinkanhoë, a nationalist organization in the 1920's.[121] As the best known nationalist in the northern part of Korea, Cho could claim greater legitimacy as a representative of the North than any other leader at the time. The fact that he was a North Korean could have been a drawback to asserting national leadership, but given the division of the country, Cho's prominence in the North made him a logical choice for leader at Pyongyang.

Kim Tu-bong, a famous national literary scholar and author of a Korean-language dictionary in the early twentieth century, and a participant in the 1919 uprising, stood out in North Korea as a central figure in any political contest, despite his South Korean origin. Following the 1919 uprising he published a nationalist newspaper in Shanghai and served as a member of the assembly of the KPG. Kim joined the Korean Communist Party at a later date, and after traveling in Europe to acquaint himself with European revolutionary ideas and Western political thought, went to Yenan in 1940, where the Chinese Communists had their headquarters. He headed a political school there for training Korean Communists,[122] and in 1942 formed a Korean Independence Alliance of Korean Communists in Yenan, which cooperated with the Chinese Communists. In 1945 Kim returned to North Korea, after passing through his native South Korea which was then under American occupation.[123]

The two Koreas which emerged after the withdrawal of Japanese control would have to draw upon these leaders and these resources for their political consolidation. The political culture suggested an extremely competitive and bitter political battle. The acute shortage of internal political resources suggested that external inputs could be very influential. All of the leaders had spent considerable periods of their lives abroad, and the developments which were to take place after 1945 would be strongly influenced by circumstances which had their roots many years before. Americans later dissatisfied with the leadership of the aging Syngman Rhee, for example, might well have observed that Rhee entered the United States in November 1904, just before the United States closed its doors, in 1905, to further Korean immigration. The men, the conditions, and the resources available in 1945 would constitute the base upon which postwar development would be built.

Chapter II

THE STRUGGLE FOR POWER IN SOUTH KOREA, 1945–1948

During the period from 1945 to 1948 in South Korea, an attempt at political consolidation was made by Syngman Rhee, in competition with other political leaders. Dr. Rhee's initial attempts were quite successful in constructing a nation-wide political power base below the 38th parallel, but his goals of immediate independence and isolation of the Communists from participation were contrary to agreements concluded between the United States and the Soviet Union at the Yalta Conference in early 1945, and thus his power base was heavily eroded by American efforts to build an alternative leadership. By 1948, Rhee had become the most powerful leader in South Korea; however, his failing power base was to present serious challenges to the viability of the new government following the American withdrawal.

Although Japan surrendered to the Allies on August 15, 1945, Soviet troops had entered Korea nine days previously, and reached the 38th parallel by August 24; American troops arrived in South Korea almost a month after the surrender, on September 8, to occupy the southern portion of the peninsula. The troops of the two nations remained in Korea for three years until 1948, when they withdrew leaving two separate and antagonistic political systems in their wake. It is generally assumed that the creation of these two systems was strongly affected by the presence of external sources of support from the U.S.S.R. and the United States. To what extent, and how, these external factors influenced the outcome is, however, far from obvious, and the impact of other factors is frequently overlooked.

The sudden liberation of Korea brought an influx of nearly three million repatriates from abroad, seeking to find a home once again in an independent Korea. All of the famous exile leaders returned to enter the contest for political control in Korea, bringing with them their diverse backgrounds, talents, and resources, and their conflicting political ideas, high with expectation and exhilaration at the long-awaited dream of national independence and freedom. The ensuing three years were to become, for most of them, a period of even greater tragedy than the years that had gone before.

The People's Republic Consolidation Attempt

American troops did not arrive in South Korea until September 8, 1945, and Syngman Rhee, who was still in the United States, was unable to gain entry to the country until October 16, two months after the Japanese surrender. In the meantime, South Korea experienced a most unique series of events.

A few days before Japan's surrender, its inevitability had become apparent to the Japanese governor-general's administration in Korea. Hoping to forestall chaos and large-scale reprisals by the Koreans against the Japanese in the interim between the surrender and the arrival of foreign troops, the governor-general took steps to transfer government responsibility to Koreans. Approaching the president of the *Dong-A Ilbo*, Song Chin-u, General Abë requested that he assume authority for maintaining law and order.[1] Song declined, however, for three reasons. First, he felt that government powers should pass directly to the Korean Provisional Government (KPG) then in exile.[2] Second, to cooperate with the Japanese in accepting the reins of government would be tantamount to acknowledging the legitimacy of their control over the preceding forty years and would thus negate the legitimacy of the KPG, which Song considered to have been the only true government authority since 1919, having succeeded that of the emperor who died at that time.[3] Finally, acceptance of the Japanese offer might add fuel to the charges already being made that the gradualists were "collaborators" because they had not, after 1919, advocated open violent resistance to the Japanese.[4]

The governor-general tried for some time to persuade Song and other gradualist leaders to organize the interim governing committee,[5] but when repeated appeals here failed he somewhat reluctantly turned to former Communist Yŏ Un-hyŏng, an "activist" leader. On August 14, 1945, the day before the

surrender, Yŏ accepted the offer. The Japanese turned over to him
the power to maintain law and order, and may also have given him
a subsidy to finance the transfer.[6]

The first task Yŏ undertook was the creation of a core organization—a "Committee for the Establishment of the Korean State."
Yŏ was careful to give this new governing committee the appearance of representing all groups, naming prominent members of
both activist and gradualist groups as members.[7] This committee,
through radio and informal information channels, called on people
of local areas to form local self-governing committees to act in the
interim, and to organize "peace preservation corps" to act in the
role of police, taking over the duties of the Japanese police force
until legitimate organs of government could be constructed to
assume these functions.

On the day of surrender, the Japanese governor-general is
reported to have informed Yŏ that the United States had decided
to occupy only the deep south Pusan-Mokpo area of South Korea,
apparently having been so informed by the Soviet consul-general
in Seoul.[8] Whether or not this was the case, the gradualists' names
were removed from the committee roster on that day, apparently
out of fear that the Russians would refuse to recognize the committee if it included representatives of conservative landowners and
businessmen.[9] The following day, political prisoners—among whom
several thousand had at one time been members of the Korean
Communist Party—were released from jail by the committee. The
Communist Party was refounded in Seoul on August 16, 1945, the
first party to be organized following the Japanese surrender, and
on the following day Pak Hŏn yŏng returned to Seoul from hiding
in the provinces to take over leadership of the party, claiming
Russian instructions to do so.[10] Having authority within the party,
Pak controlled the Communists within Yŏ's committee as well.
On September 3, many of the non-Communist activists were
summarily dismissed from the committee.[11] Yŏ, the chairman of
the committee, had by this time lost control to the Communist
members, as he later admitted.[12] Vice Chairman An Chae-hong,
a well-known non-Communist leader who was not dismissed,

resigned from the committee in protest, and Hŏ Hŏn, a well-known Communist, took his place.[13]

Expanding from the core organization to create local bases of power, committee members fanned out through the provinces encouraging people to join people's committees on the local levels, so that Korea might set up its own form of self-government. The call was certain to have popular appeal, and by August 31, 145 local people's committees had been established.[14] One young man enticed into a people's committee in Seoul, described his experience:

> Right after the surrender, some friends of mine who were Communists came up to me and said that a People's Committee was being set up, and invited me to join. At that time, no one thought there was anything wrong with their being Communists—we were all the same during the Japanese occupation—we were all working for independence. I guess they wanted my name because I had some following among veterans [Koreans who had served in the Japanese Army]. It sounded like a good idea to form the committees, so I went to a couple of the meetings. They got many other people to attend the same way. Then, when they started denouncing landlords and making false charges against prominent people like Kim Sŏng-su, I decided that this was not something I wanted to be associated with, so I stopped going. Then my former "friends" came to me and tried to convince me that I should continue attending. When I refused, they drew a gun on me and told me they would shoot me if I didn't. However, I knew that they would be afraid to shoot me because my friends among the veterans knew who they were and would retaliate, so I told them to go ahead and shoot. After that, they went away and spread rumors about how I was cooperating with landlords and pro-Japanese.[15]

In many local areas, groups of young men who assumed the title of "peace preservation corps," declared their support for the committee in Seoul and disarmed the government-general police force. Able to assert themselves for the first time, many of the newly armed young men became tyrants in the local areas, confiscating Japanese property, retaliating against their former landlords, and frequently abusing the populace in the name of the newly independent governing committee in Seoul.

Acting quickly before the arrival of the American troops, the committee called a conference of the local and provincial people's committee leaders, to meet in Seoul on September 6, and form a government. With planning and control of the conference in the hands of the Communist leaders, a program was pushed through with the 1,000 delegates (mostly non-Communist local leaders) approving the proclamation of a "People's Republic," voting through a proposed Tentative Government Organization Law, approving the recommended slate of fifty-five representatives for a People's Legislative Assembly, and electing Yŏ Un-hyŏng and Hŏ Hŏn chairman and vice chairman, respectively (the posts they already held in the committee), assigning to them the task of appointing a government and cabinet. On the same day, however, Yŏ was attacked by terrorists, and, as he had to be hospitalized, the task of selecting a government fell to the Communist vice chairman, Hŏ Hŏn.[16]

The new People's Republic was formed with an eye to capturing an aura of legitimacy. Syngman Rhee was chosen president, while he was still out of the country and unable to return to Korea, which remained a war zone.[17] Yŏ was appointed to the somewhat irrelevant post of vice president. Hŏ took the position of premier, which put him in effective control of the new "government" within the framework of the new organization. Ministerial posts were divided among the famous figures in the independence movement, about half of them non-Communists, the other half Communists. (The name of Kim Il Sung was not mentioned.) The unpublicized vice ministers, who were to act in the absence of those leaders still abroad, were almost all Communists.[18]

The rapid organization of a government was apparently facilitated by funds made available by the Communist Party, whose economic resources became evident several months later when the U.S. Army captured the party's account books. Some of the sources of Communist financing were reported to be: "illegal" speculation in seized Japanese land,[19] a "Mr. X" who was suspected, but never proved, to be the Soviet consul[20] (who made one quick trip to his embassy in Japan during this period), and funds arriving through agents from north of the 38th parallel.[21] (Since the currency in Japan and North Korea was the same as in South Korea during this period, there was no problem of monetary exchange.) Later these resources were augmented by a counterfeiting operation.[22]

At this point, claiming legitimate control of the "Korean government" by virtue of having received a direct transfer of authority from the Japanese, having been "elected" by the most prominent local leaders (neither the local leaders, nor the government leaders were elected; the latter were selected by the committee under the direction of Hŏ Hŏn), and being headed by the most prominent independence leaders (though absent from the country and unaware of the honor), the Communist Party seemed well on its way to winning the struggle among the contending leadership groups to become the elite which would ultimately determine the institutionalization of a new political system. The beginnings of a nation-wide organizational base had been introduced, a temporary source of financing had been acquired, guns in many areas were in the hands of "peace preservation corps" who supported the People's Republic because it legitimated their power on the local level, and the government promoted itself on the simple idea of independence and self-government, legitimizing its claim by adopting the famous leaders of the independence movement. To those who had known the endemic factionalism and lack of organizational unity of the Korean Communist Party prior to 1945, the apparently well-organized takeover was a matter of utter astonishment. Many concluded, rightly or wrongly, that the plans had emanated from the still-operative Soviet Consulate in Seoul.

Other activist groups were slow to mount resistance to the Communist initiative. The natural tendency of the leaders of other groups had been to cooperate at first with the committee and to compete within it, until they were suddenly expelled by the Communists. Several tried belatedly to organize political parties, but, lacking the funds and governmental trappings of the "People's Republic," they had little success.[23]

The gradualists, however, quickly resisted the new organization. As landholders, and in some cases industrialists, they had no desire to see a Communist-dominated group gain control of the government, which might result in the expropriation of their economic resources. On September 3, following the expulsion of many of the non-Communist members from Yŏ's "preparatory committee," gradualist and non-Communist activist leaders met.[24] On September 6, when the People's Republic was declared, they issued a statement criticizing the "preparatory committee," and called for a "political conference" to oppose it. On September 16, after the American troops had arrived, they formally announced the founding of the Han'guk Minju-dang, or Korean Democratic Party (KDP).[25] Although this new organization's source of financing was almost exclusively gradualists, the members included, at the outset, many well-known activists.[26] The KDP pledged its support to the Korean Provisional Government (KPG) insisting that it had been the only legitimate government of Korea since 1919. Like the People's Republic, the KDP tried to insure its claim to leadership by naming as its leaders Syngman Rhee and Kim Koo, both still in exile.[27] Ultimately, it would be the American and Soviet occupiers who would determine whether the People's Republic, the KPG, or any other group was to become the government of Korea.

The Intrusion of External Forces: Consolidation of the American Military Government

The Korea policy of the United States in 1945 was very poorly coordinated. In part, of course, it can be said that this was the inevitable result of the death of Roosevelt just two months after the Yalta Conference, and the necessity for a new administration to pick up the pieces. The Yalta talks between Stalin and Roosevelt in February 1945 had reached agreement, at the suggestion of

Roosevelt, that Korea be placed under a joint trusteeship of four powers—the United States, the U.S.S.R., Great Britain, and China.[28] Roosevelt had, in fact, suggested that the trusteeship last for as long as twenty to thirty years, and Stalin responded that a shorter period would be preferable. Many branches of the government dealing with Korea policy were uninformed of this decision. As previously noted, Koreans were informed in their own language through Office of War Information broadcasts that they should prepare themselves for independence.[29] As late as December 1945, General Hodge, the American military governor in Korea, claimed to have been taken by surprise when informed of the trusteeship decision.[30] The new administration's reassessment of policy retained the decision on trusteeship.[31] Explaining this to the American Military Government in Korea, the State Department wrote that trusteeship was necessary because it would permit the other powers to counteract Russian plans to take over Korea.[32]

Upon arrival in South Korea in early September 1945, the American forces set up an American Military Government (AMG), refused to recognize either the People's Republic or the KPG, and set about forming an American administration. The first action taken, creating a burst of antagonism on the part of the Korean populace,[33] was an announcement that the Japanese administration would be temporarily retained, an order which had to be quickly rescinded.[34] The Military Government took over the administration and began rapidly replacing the Japanese with Koreans. Most of the Koreans who had been serving in the Japanese bureaucracy were retained and, although a new police force was created, most of the Koreans who had served the Japanese as police were rehired, large numbers as officers of the AMG police force.[35] Backed by the American occupation forces, the new administration and the police force moved into local areas to wrest control from the people's committees and "peace preservation corps" which had sprung up after the Japanese surrender nearly two months before.

During the period prior to the arrival of the American forces in Korea, while the activists and gradualists were gathering, the Koreans who had participated in the former Japanese administratio

kept scrupulously out of political activity, dreading reprisals from
the more nationalist-minded community. When the Americans
began to create a new administration, however, they required personnel capable of keeping the economy functioning, the transportation system operating, and so on, and it was thus natural, and
perhaps inevitable, that large numbers of those who had been trained
in the Japanese administration should be retained.[36] The retention
of the Japanese-trained members of the police force, however, was
a policy which was to have serious implications for Korea for many
years to come. Eighty-five percent of the Korean police trained by
the Japanese found their way into the AMG police force, and when
the occupation ended, more than 50 percent of all the officers of
the South Korean police had previously served Japan.[37]

Although the Japanese-trained members of the bureaucracy
made up the bulk of the new administration, the highest-level
Koreans brought in by the AMG to replace the Japanese were those
who could speak English.[38] This ability meant that these personnel
had either been educated abroad in the United States or Great
Britain, and hence were more than likely of wealthy background,
or had been trained in the Christian mission schools, and hence
were Christians. All three of the groups in the new bureaucracy—
the so-called "collaborators" (that is, those who had served the
Japanese government), the wealthy foreign-educated, and the
Christians—had strong reasons for opposing the Communists.

Assuming the government of Korea in the wake of the Japanese departure, the AMG came into possession of all of the assets
left by the Japanese regime—the centralized banking system, public
utilities, and vast monopolies—as well as the property and resources
abandoned by former Japanese nationals in Korea. When the AMG
turned over these "vested properties" to the Republic of Korea in
1948, they were valued at ¥307,557,867,503.77.[39] Besides frozen
bank accounts and income from the formerly Japanese-owned land
holdings, the vested properties included 2,576 enterprises, among
which, for example, were 43 banks, 136 commercial enterprises,
51 electrical enterprises, 472 food and brewing companies, 322
machine manufacturers, 102 printing companies, 111 contracting

firms, 75 transportation companies (excluding shipping, of which there were five), 74 mining companies, 35 oil companies, and 84 metal enterprises, in addition to the International Telephone Communications Company and other government monopoly operations.[40] The New Korea Company alone, which had previously been the Korean branch of Japan's Oriental Development Company, had holdings in 82 subsidiary companies, encompassing land development, mining, lumber, alcohol manufacturing, woolen manufacturing, livestock, railroads, rubber, chemicals, machine tools, shipbuilding, petroleum, rice storage, aviation, paper manufacturing, salt, aluminum, cotton, and fisheries.[41] The New Korea Company operated under the AMG throughout the American occupation. All of these economic resources were available to the AMG to influence the outcome of a political contest in Korea.

Furthermore, the AMG had a virtual monopoly of the instruments of force within the southern part of the peninsula. The 50,000 American troops disarmed the approximately 50,000 surrendering Japanese, who rapidly departed, and the AMG police force replaced that of the Japanese, moving quickly in an effort to secure control in the countryside.

Although the AMG held a monopoly of most political resources, it was lacking in ideas capable of appealing to the Korean populace, and in a leadership which was even aware of the tremendous political resources at its disposal. What impact these instruments were to have on the outcome of the political contest in South Korea was to be almost completely accidental. The great, awkward American military administration in Korea, however well-meaning, was an enormous, politically insensitive creature, in a populace which had become, through centuries of highly sophisticated political manipulation and intrigue, one of the most politically sensitized of societies. The Korean political contenders, many of them unaware of the extreme insensitivity of American soldiers to the political implications of AMG actions, were soon to be baffled by the politically uncoordinated policies of the new regime which sought to consolidate control.

Syngman Rhee's First Consolidation Attempt

Before Syngman Rhee's arrival in South Korea on October 16, 1945, two political clusters, the People's Republic group and the Korean Democratic Party (supporting the KPG), had developed, with the AMG taking a position as "neutral" between them.[42] Nonetheless, the administration created by the U.S. Army was strongly biased against the People's Republic group, if only by virtue of its own composition.

Syngman Rhee's return home was difficult. Because he was a fiery advocate of immediate independence, he was considered by the State Department to be a liability, and efforts were made to prevent his return to Korea.[43] Rhee had friends in the War Department, however, and they managed to circumvent the State Department (which was supposed to issue his travel papers), and delivered Rhee to Korea aboard General Douglas MacArthur's personal plane.[44] Thus Rhee returned with the appearance, though not the substance, of American support. He was introduced to a welcoming rally in Seoul by General Hodge, the American Military Governor, who gave him a ringing endorsement.[45] After his arrival, Rhee wrote enthusiastically to a friend in the United States that General Hodge had come to meet him in Tokyo, had provided him with a military escort, and welcomed him as an "honored guest" in Korea, even offering to prepare the imperial palace for his stay, an offer Rhee said he had rejected.[46] Though some Americans have since suggested that Rhee's enthusiastic reception in Korea was an outgrowth of this appearance of American support, the fact that he had been named as the leader of the two major political groups long before the Americans arrived on the scene was sufficient evidence that he did not require identification with the American occupation forces to make him appear a legitimate leader.

The Communists had already gained a symbolic advantage in the popular eye by capitalizing on the desire for independence in proclaiming the People's Republic, and an organizational advantage by going out into the provinces to mobilize support before the American armed forces arrived and called a halt to competitive recruitment on behalf of the two "governments." Immediately identifying the Communists as his most powerful opposition, Rhee's plans for consolidation called for a three-pronged strategy to overcome this head start. Writing to a friend in the United States Rhee explained that he planned first to use the KPG as a focus of legitimacy to undermine the People's Republic, second to unify all groups for independence and to isolate the Communists, much as they had done in reverse, and third to pressure the United States into calling for a joint withdrawal of Soviet and American troops before the Communists, with Soviet assistance, could become entrenched in the North.[47]

Rhee's first act, like that of the Communist consolidators before him, was to form a group of all representative political leaders, in the interest of "independence."[48] Even the Communists joined the organization, which was given the title "Central Consultative Committee for the Promotion of Independence" (Tongnip ch'oksŏng chung'ang hyŏp-hoë).[49] Explaining why they must all stand together, Rhee commented that when he had met with General MacArthur in Tokyo: "he told me bluntly that Koreans are not capable of self-government. This is very bad propaganda. We do not want trusteeship . . . we must all unite together . . . to demonstrate to the world that we *are* capable of self-government. The American Military Government is our friend and will help us gain our independence."[50] After a few weeks of such unity-promoting activities, Rhee began his campaign to eliminate the participation of the Communists, much as they had previously sought to oust individuals who might disagree with them over the form of political system to be introduced. Some Communists, Rhee pointed out, were patriots interested in economic theories which might be beneficial for Korea's development, and their cooperation should be welcomed. Others, however, wanted only a Communist government, subordinate to the Soviet Union, and their participation would only create schisms which would "tear the nation asunder."[51]

On November 23, Kim Koo returned from China. The United States had refused to allow him, or others in the KPG, re-entry to

South Korea until they signed papers to the effect that they would enter the country as individuals, not as a government.[52] Kim Koo's return was a signal for the Communists to drop all formal support for Syngman Rhee and shift support to his erstwhile rival, Kim Koo. Withdrawing from Rhee's committee, they announced support for Kim Koo. Rhee also immediately announced support for Kim.[53] Meeting with the famous nationalist, however, Rhee was unable to convince him to cooperate in isolating the Communists. Kim argued that all patriots, regardless of ideology, should be included in the government.[54] Nonetheless, Kim Koo rejected the offer made by the Communists to "merge" the People's Republic with the Korean Provisional Government (on condition that both be given 50 percent representation),[55] insisting that the latter government "expects to be recognized, and it would be better if it were recognized at once."[56]

The Communists turned a full-scale attack on Rhee, using their publicity resources, which were at the time the most widely circulated in the South. Rhee was charged with splitting the unity movement, in an effort to promote his personal ambitions.

From the time Syngman Rhee arrived in Korea, he received the backing of the gradualists, most of whom were landowners and some of whom had industrial or business enterprises, and he could count on financial assistance from many Korean Christian organizations as well. Nonetheless, this money did not seem to match that available to the Communists, for they were able to finance considerably more publicity. Since the Americans held all of the assets left by the Japanese regime, the only remaining source of political financing in Korea was the group of a few wealthy so-called "pro-Japanese" Korean businessmen—those who had set up enterprises in cooperation with the Japanese. All groups shied away from approaching these individuals because they would be a political liability. It was from them, however, that Rhee, a veteran fund-raiser, would seek to secure financing, despite the political risk. On December 16, 1945, under the guise of a meeting to "relieve the food crisis," Dr. Rhee called together the Korean businessmen who had made their fortunes during the Japanese occupation. An "Economic Contributor's Association" was formed at this meeting—

designed, it was announced, to prove to the public that the wealthy men of Korea were patriotic, and to solicit funds for the KPG. Dr. Rhee was named the agent for the KPG and the amount of funds to be collected was set at ¥200,000,000. Promissory notes were made out by many present.[57] It may well have seemed a small price to pay to avoid retaliation from the government, and possibly expropriation, after independence. Syngman Rhee also set up a National Assistance Fund Executive Committee (Poguk kigŭm silhaeng wiwŏnhoë), headed by seventeen prominent Korean businessmen.[58]

At this juncture an external political event was to thrust Rhee into center stage, and to provide him with the necessary political momentum to create an organized political base in South Korea. This was the announcement on December 28, 1945, that an agreement had been reached between representatives of the United States and the Soviet Union, meeting in Moscow, to create a five-year trusteeship for Korea, under the United States, the U.S.S.R., Great Britain, and China.[59]

The announcement of trusteeship brought an immediate angry reaction from the Korean populace. Spread across the front page of every newspaper, it was the same word, in ideographs, as the "protectorate" which the Japanese had established over Korea in 1905.[60] An American information officer on the scene in Korea described the reaction of the Korean people: "As wave after wave of resentment swept the country, dangerous tension began building up in Seoul. On December 29th, crowds of surly Koreans milled the streets. Armed American troops tried to disperse them. Most of the shops were closed. At noon, all Korean translators and interpreters employed by the Military Government held a mass meeting to decide whether or not they would strike . . . the Military Government very shrewdly declared a ten-day holiday for Korean employees."[61] At this point, Song Chin-u, former president of the *Dong-A Ilbo* and prominent gradualist leader, voiced his opinion that the Koreans would have to accept the decision, now that it had been made. He was promptly assassinated, on December

30, 1945, by a misguided patriot. The assassin was a follower of KPG head Kim Koo.[62]

> Tension continued to mount. All Americans were ordered to stay off the streets after eleven in the evening. But it was not until December 31st that the emotional dam broke. Army intelligence had issued warnings of an impending demonstration . . . During the morning of the 31st rumors of coming violence and terrorism were current . . . Thousands upon thousands of people poured into the central part of Seoul. Korean flags flew from every building. The day was bitterly cold, but still the people came—old and young. At two in the afternoon the demonstration started; a great mass of madly cheering people marched past the Capitol gates. The city rang with the "manzai's" (100,000 years for Korea) from a hundred thousand throats. The hills echoed with the plaintive melody of the Korean national song . . . But despite the crowds and tremendous patriotic fervor of the people, there was no violence or disorder . . . Throughout South Korea similar demonstrations were held.[63]

As in 1919, the Koreans demonstrated their desire for independence by nonviolent protest.

The reaction of Kim Koo, however, was his first attempt to carry out a coup d'état against the American Military Government. Giving orders that henceforth the bureaucracy and police were to take orders from him,[64] he was deterred by a rapid intervention of U.S. Army personnel who prevented his radio announcement from being broadcast. Called to task by the American Military Governor, quick thinking by the U.S. General was required to deter the elderly Korean nationalist from committing suicide in his presence to dramatize what he considered to be both a personal and a national insult.[65]

Syngman Rhee neither advocated violent resistance nor accepted the trusteeship decision. The self-respect of Koreans, he announced, would not permit acceptance of anything short of complete independence.[66] Had Rhee joined with Kim Koo in an attempt to resist the authority of the occupation forces, the result would probably have been bloodshed. Had he accepted trusteeship, he would have lost all influence with the nationalist following, and been open to Communist charges that he was an American puppet. Instead, Rhee continued to seek means of putting pressure upon the United States.[67]

The Communist Party, not to be outdone by the nationalist-organized demonstration on December 31, began plans for its own anti-trusteeship demonstration to be held on January 3. The demonstration had been announced, and placards denouncing trusteeship painted, when instructions arrived from North Korea specifying that all loyal Communists should support trusteeship.[68] On January 2, the central committee of the Korean Communist Party announced that it would support the Moscow agreement, and the demonstration turned into a confused affair, with some demonstrating for and some against, while most of the signs were hastily and obviously altered; some with "down with trusteeship" had the "down" crossed out and "up" scrawled in.[69]

The Communist stand apparently took Kim Koo by surprise. Unwilling to believe that the Korean Communists could seriously prefer trusteeship to independence, Kim, like the Communists and Rhee before him, now attempted to form a central organization which could include all political leaders. Kim Koo called an "Emergency Political Conference," inviting both the "left"—that is, supporters of the People's Republic—and the "right"—supporters of the Provisional Government—with the intention of forming a "coalition" as a basis for an independent Korean government.[70] Kim urged all groups to join together so that they would not have to submit to a humiliating trusteeship. The Communists, however, unable to secure a commitment that they would be granted 50 percent representation in the political conference, and unwilling to abandon their endorsement of the trusteeship, walked out of the meeting. They were followed by Yŏ Un-hyŏng's People's Party, and a couple of minor "left-wing" parties, protesting that Kim Koo's following was too "right-wing" because it did not contain the Communist Party. This was the basis for the permanent split between "left" and "right" in South Korea. The relative followings of the two groups in the capital was illustrated on March 1, 1946, the twenty-seventh anniversary of the 1919 uprising, when about 100,000 people showed up for the independence celebration sponsored by the nationalists, while about 15,000 attended that sponsored by the "leftists."[71]

Following the split, Kim Koo and Syngman Rhee joined together in promoting the "anti-trusteeship" movement, expanding on Kim Koo's Political Conference to create an organization entitled, "The National Society for the Rapid Realization of Korean Independence" (Taehan tongnip ch'oksŏng kungmin-hoë). The Communists, with the other groups which had walked out of Kim's conference, formed a "People's Democratic Front" supporting trusteeship.[72] It had been six months since the People's Republic had begun its organizational efforts on the local level, and Syngman Rhee began immediately to expand the new nationalist organization into the provinces. Stumping throughout the peninsula, the 71-year-old Rhee carried one theme to all parts of the country: "We must forget all partisan differences and join together to oppose trusteeship and support national independence." In each area, he left behind a local chapter of the "National Society." Kim Koo, who lacked the capacity for oratory Rhee possessed, made some less extensive tours on behalf of the organization, using the same political line. By April 15, 1946, the Society claimed 1,149 town and village branches, 105 city and district branches, and 9 provincial branches, in addition to the central organization, and it claimed a membership of 1,068,479.[73] It was by far the strongest organization in the area south of the 38th parallel by mid-1946.[74] Meeting in Seoul on June 10, 1946, 1,163 representatives from the local branches elected new officers, and outlined a political program.

Elected temporary speaker of the meeting of the National Society, Yi Shi-yŏng, an aging participant in the Korean Provisional Government, reaching out for the broadest possible membership, declared that this new organization must be a non-partisan national movement, encompassing all political views, and every region of Korea, with the sole purpose of forcing the foreign powers to grant Korean independence.[75] On the following day, Syngman Rhee was elected chairman of the Society, replacing Kim Koo. Addressing the representatives, he declared:

> As I have travelled up and down the peninsula, wherever I went the people turned out in enthusiastic crowds, and welcomed me wholeheartedly. At one place I met an 80 year old man, who had walked for dozens of miles to see me. He grasped my hand and said, "Oh, Dr. Rhee, when, when shall we truly have our independence?" And I answered him, "Whenever all our people unite, then we shall have our independence!" And I say the same thing to you here today. After we have our independence, we can sit down and discuss and hammer out agreements on our differing views as to how best to serve the nation's welfare. But in order to get that independence, we must unite!
> [He added that he would accept the position of Chairman] only if every one of you is willing to stake your life for the cause of independence whenever I give the command, and to die together for the cause . . . (He was interrupted with applause and shouts of "Yes! We will!") Will all those willing to do so please raise your hands? (Everyone raised a hand.) Well, I see that everyone has put up *one* hand, and so I assume that everyone in the room is *half* ready to die . . . (He put up both his hands amidst a roar of laughter; everyone followed suit.) All right! I see that every one of you is fully determined to devote himself to the independence of our country! (Applause. Many of the participants were in tears.) Are you ready to answer when I give the command? (Applause and shouts.)[76]

Syngman Rhee, standing for the long dreamed-of goal of national independence, became a leadership magnet in the tense political atmosphere in South Korea.

The Communist Party was having difficulty competing. Their organization had suffered seriously when they took a stand in favor of trusteeship, and as funds became more readily available to the nationalists from Korean businessmen, landowners, and religious organizations, the Communists could no longer match them. Desperate for financing, they undertook a new enterprise, and in May 1946 an extensive counterfeiting operation, being carried out by the Communists in their headquarters building, was exposed.[77] Both the printers' plates and the paper were authentic, having been stolen from government mints. At the same time, American authorities uncovered positive evidence of the connection between the Communist activities in the South and the northern regime, including orders from the North explicitly outlining activities to be undertaken, ranging from daily publication outlines for the Communist newspapers to forms for filling in espionage reports on American troop locations in the South. Records were also uncovered of frequent trips made by agents back and forth across the parallel, and passes printed in Russian and Korean permitting them to do so.[78]

While the U.S.S.R. had thus apparently been channeling some support to the Communists in the South, the American Military Government had received orders in January 1946 (made more explicit in July of that year) that *no* assistance was to be given to Syngman Rhee or Kim Koo and their organization—but that an alternative leadership of "younger, more liberal leaders" was to be sought.[79] This policy should have elicited no surprise, for Rhee and Kim were operating in direct opposition to the concluded agreement on trusteeship between the United States and the U.S.S.R., on a policy proposal initiated by the United States. A leadership would have to be found which would cooperate with this American policy.

From March to May, 1946, the first Joint Commission meetings between Soviet and American representatives, designed to initiate procedures for establishing a trusteeship government, were held in Seoul. They quickly reached a stalemate. The first stage of negotiations was designed to arrange for consultation with Korean political groups on the nature, form, and program of government to be introduced. The U.S.S.R., however, insisted on the exclusion of anyone from such consultation who had expressed opposition to the trusteeship, on the grounds that anyone opposing trusteeship was hardly in a position to give constructive recommendations. Although this position was quite logical, it meant the exclusion of all political groups in the South but the Communists. The United States refused to yield on this point on the grounds that the nationalists should not be excluded on the basis of anti-trusteeship statements they had made, for this was denying the right of free speech. The Joint Commission meetings closed without having achieved any results, and without provision for another meeting.[80]

Up to this point, the contest between Rhee's nationalist organization and the Communists for consolidation had been restricted to the arena of ideas, organization, and funds. Guns had not been of great importance in the competition. The AMG pointed with pride to the low rate of crime and disorders in April 1946, attributing it to the "efficiency and disciplined organization" of the police.[81] The breakdown of the Joint Commission's efforts at negotiation in May, however, was followed by a growth of violence in the society, as the contest moved into the arena of guns, and South Korea became a scene of chaos and violence in the latter part of 1946.

When the Japanese had transferred authority to the "People's Republic" group, police in many local areas had been disarmed, and "peace preservation corps" had taken over.[82] When the AMG came, however, it had restored the power of the Japanese-trained police, who in turn disarmed the new groups which had previously disarmed the police in anticipation of independence. In many areas, the newly-armed groups had resisted this action of the police, and American armed forces had to assist in returning power to the re-organized police force.[83] The Communists capitalized on the position of the AMG, which was defending the hated police force, and stirred popular resistance against the police. Anti-police riots broke out in Taegu and other South Korean cities in October 1946.[84] The police and the Communists had been antagonists throughout the period of Japanese rule, for the Japanese suppression of the Communist movement in Korea, through the police force, had been

harsh, imprisonment and torture being the common fare for those
who tried to resist the Japanese rule. Fearing that the Communists
might gain control of the new government and then retaliate
against them, the police threw their support to the nationalists.
Needing protection from Communist terrorism, the nationalists
were not in a position to reject this support—in fact, many may
have gone out of their way to assure the police of lenient treatment after independence in order to be guaranteed police protection.

The Korean police force was an important instrument of
control in South Korea, for it possessed voluminous files of information regarding individuals. Membership in the Communist
Party or cooperation with the Japanese was noted in these files,
and the intelligence bureau possessed 700,000 fingerprint records
of individuals who had been involved in crime or "intrigue" under
Japanese rule.[85] These records could become a highly effective
political instrument to the party which could secure access to
them.

That the police were supporting the nationalists was a matter
of considerable concern to the American Military Government:
"It was *our* police force, and yet they were supporting Kim Koo
and Syngman Rhee. All over the country, pictures of Syngman
Rhee kept appearing on the walls of police stations. Obviously,
Rhee was infiltrating the police and trying to take over the
country that way."[86] That Rhee could have infiltrated the police
is questionable, in view of the fact that most of the police were
hired before he returned to Korea, and long before he had built
an organizational base. The police, however, knew that the Communists were threatening them with punishment and possibly
execution, and it was therefore natural that they should support
the groups opposing the Communists. In Taegu alone, fifty-
three policemen were killed by mobs who had been egged on by
the Communist press.[87] Following the outbreak of these riots,
the Communist press was suppressed by the AMG, and warrants
were issued for the arrest of Communist leaders Pak Hŏn-yŏng,
Yi Kang-guk, and Yi Chu-ha.[88]

In opposition to the police, the Communists attracted many unemployed young men into their terrorist "youth groups." This was not difficult, for unemployment in South Korea at the beginning of 1946 was officially numbered at 1,050,937.[89] The nationalists, in turn, formed their own youth groups. The largest and most prominent of these was the "Racial (that is, National) Youth Corps." Headed by Yi Pŏm-sŏk, a former officer of the KPG armed unit in China who had worked for U.S. Army intelligence, this powerful organization was financed as a "non-political" youth group by the AMG.[90] Membership in this group, organized throughout South Korea, reached 404,585 by December 1947. Another youth group formed by the nationalists was the Great Korea Democratic Youth Alliance, whose members were followers of Kim Koo. The most powerful Communist youth group took the name Chosŏn (Korean) Democratic Youth Alliance.

Both sides also created labor union organizations, and between the two poles of the political spectrum gang warfare and terrorism spread on a massive and nation-wide scale.[91] Frustration and growing bitterness over the lack of progress toward independence fed the growing chaos.[92] The Joint Commission meetings closed in May, with no indication that they would reopen, and the United States was making no move to turn over its control to Koreans. Having simply stepped into the shoes of the former ruler, Japan, the AMG could not anticipate indefinite acquiescence by the populace in its rule. While the Communists attacked the police and the constituted authority of the AMG, the nationalists sought to gain control indirectly, both with the ultimate objective of ousting American rule.

A second cause for the upheaval was the growing economic crisis. Inflation had spiraled to such an extent that food cost almost ten times as much as it had the previous year, textiles, fifteen times, fertilizers twenty times, and building materials thirty times as much as they had in August 1945.[93] The composite wholesale price index for October 1946 was 2,025 as compared with 100 in August 1945. This climbed to 7,066 by December 1947.[94] Prices nearly doubled again by the end of 1948.[95] In the meantime, hundreds of thousand

of Koreans were repatriating from abroad, complicating efforts to
establish a stable rule. Communist-organized labor unions, taking
advantage of the pressure the incredible inflation placed on salaried
persons whose wages could not keep pace with the price increases,
instigated strikes, further choking the economy. A strike by railroad workers prevented the shipment of food arriving from the
United States into the cities, making food not only expensive but
scarce.[96] Many government employees demanded payment of
salaries in rice.[97] The Communists also encouraged the farmers to
resist the rice collection undertaken by the AMG to feed the
cities.[98]

The competition between the Communists and the nationalists for control in South Korea had become fully mobilized, and
the southern part of the nation was on the verge of full-scale civil
war. Under instructions from Washington not to support either
side in the contest, but to build up another leadership, the AMG
sought to organize a third group and to promote its political consolidation, hoping to undermine the antagonistic organizations then
at war with one another in South Korea.

The "Coalition Committee" Consolidation Attempt

In accordance with State Department instructions in July
1946, the AMG began construction of a new leadership group—the
"Coalition Committee," designed as a modus vivendi for reopening
negotiation with the Soviet Union.[99] Chosen by the AMG to head
the new coalition committee were Dr. Kim Kyu-sik, formerly vice
president of the KPG and now vice chairman of the National
Society, and Yŏ Un-hyŏng, former vice president of the People's
Republic.[100] Neither of these two men had proved themselves
effective political organizers, although both were well known. Yŏ
had repeatedly sought to prevent the Communists from gaining
control of his organization without success. When his "People's
Party" voted itself into the Communist-dominated South Korean
Workers' Party, for example, he had withdrawn from his own party
and re-formed it with the members who had voted to stay out. The
party was then re-infiltrated and again voted itself into the Workers'

Party. He reorganized at least three times to get out from under Communist control, but it was a losing battle.[101] The two leaders were more useful as leadership symbols than as effective organizers.

The new coalition organization sponsored by the AMG had no local bases of power, shared no consensus on the type of political system to be introduced, and was provided with no source of financing and no guns. Therefore, while it could reduce the strength of other groups by drawing away members, it could not provide an alternative cohesion. Frightened and dismayed by the increasing turmoil, riots, demonstrations, and terrorism, many leaders in Seoul were attracted away from the nationalists.

Realizing that the Koreans could not be kept in the dark indefinitely about their fate, the Military Government took two steps to bolster its public support: first it created a "Korean Interim Legislature," and second it "transferred" authority in the administration to top-level Korean bureaucrats, with their American counterparts assuming the role of "advisers."[102] Members of the new legislature were to number 90, of whom 45 were to be elected and 45 appointed by the American Military Government.[103]

Elections to the Korean Interim Legislature were held in October and November of 1946, and for the first time competition for political office through an election procedure became a reality in South Korea. Countless political organizations put up candidates throughout the southern part of the peninsula, but the election system, relying upon the Japanese laws which enfranchised only taxpayers, contained an inherent bias in favor of nationalists, especially the gradualist landowners in the Korean Democratic Party (KDP), who were cooperating with the nationalists.[104] The actual election results were confusing because many KDP members had chosen to run as independents in areas where the party label would not help them. Of the 45 elected, it was estimated that 15 were members of the KDP, 14 of Dr. Rhee's National Society, 2 of Kim Koo's Independence Party (both the KDP and Kim Koo had run their followers separately, although they were also members of the National Society), and of the remaining 14 who were independents, 12 were said to be sympathetic to the nationalists.[105]

The results were overwhelmingly pro-nationalist; indeed, not a single member of the American-sponsored Coalition Committee was elected, although a number of candidates ran. Since the Committee did not possess electioneering funds or effective local organization, this outcome was hardly surprising.

The Committee contested the election results in several districts, and re-runs were held in six districts, although the outcome was altered in only one—that in which Kim Kyu-sik, vice chairman of the National Society and co-chairman of the Coalition Committee, had sought a seat. He was elected in the second balloting.[106]

The remaining 45 members of the legislature were then appointed by the Military Government from a slate recommended by the Coalition Committee.[107] Several nationalists were so incensed at the appointment of half the assembly by this committee (which had itself been selected by the AMG), that they boycotted the first two weeks of sessions, and when they did come in it was to introduce bills for immediate independence.[108] Indeed, Kim Koo was said to have come to the conclusion that the United States was simply trying to create a puppet government, for it appointed half the membership of the legislature from the recommendations of those who had demonstrated a willingness to cooperate with American policy.

Although the late spring and early summer of 1946 had seen the nationalist organization at peak strength, it was already beginning to disintegrate by fall. Pressed by Kim Koo and the hard-core nationalists to demand immediate independence even at the cost of bloodshed, yet financed by the landed KDP members and Korean businessmen who stood to lose from the outbreak of violence, Rhee found it increasingly difficult to tread the line between nationalist agitation and conciliation with the American rulers. Conciliation became next to impossible when the United States began to support a rival organization which would be more amenable to the U.S. trusteeship policy. Convinced that Communist dominance was by this time a *fait accompli* in the North (see Chapter III), Rhee began as early as mid-1946 to insist that South Korea might have to gain its independence alone, in order to be rid of the American military rule.[109]

The administration was called the "South Korean Interim Government," after the functions of government had been turned over to Korean department heads and the Interim Legislature had been established; nationalist discontent with this government continued to grow. Since department heads could act only in accordance with the advice of their American "advisers" because the AMG still had the power to hire and fire them, and since the legislature was half-appointed by the AMG and could have its laws not only vetoed by the military governor but suspended on his oral order after they had been passed into law, the appellation "Korean" to the new government structure was viewed with cynicism. From the beginning of 1947, nationalist agitation against American rule increased to such an extent that the Korean civil administrator, An Chae-hong, had to be escorted to and from his office by an American military escort to protect him from attack, and members of the "Coalition Committee" were greeted in the streets by jeering youths shouting "traitors! "[110] Yŏ Un-hyŏng, the "left-wing" head of the Coalition Committee, resigned from his position after having been subjected to several terrorist attacks. He later came to the AMG and requested that the Communist Party be outlawed, implying that it was responsible for his injuries, although he refused to make a public statement to that effect.[111]

There are two versions of the nationalist coup d'état attempt led by Kim Koo against the AMG which occurred in March 1947, following the establishment of the Interim Legislature and the transfer of administrative powers. One version, based on American intelligence sources of the AMG, suggests that Syngman Rhee and Kim Koo together outlined a "blackmail" plan, whereby Kim Koo would prepare for a coup, while Rhee went to Washington to plead for independence with Kim's coup offered as a threat.[112] The other, told by an American friend of Rhee who claimed to have the story from Syngman Rhee, is that Kim Koo decided upon the coup and Rhee made him agree to *drop* the plans if Rhee could persuade the American government to grant independence.[113] The latter view appears more probable, for a coup plan which is not kept secret seems a most ineffective threat. It also seems more in line with the long-time conflict between Kim's advocacy of violent "direct-action" policies, and Rhee's insistence on the use of nonviolence and the channels of international diplomacy. In either case, when the coup attempt was made by Kim, mention of which is very briefly made in the records of the AMG, Syngman Rhee was in the United States making a plea for immediate independence.[114] Just prior to Kim's coup effort Rhee announced, apparently on fictitious grounds (the State Department issued a denial), that the United States had agreed to unilateral independence for South Korea.[115] In the meantime, U.S. intelligence intercepted a telegram from Rhee to Kim Koo stating, "Hold the problem of a Korean Provisional Government in abeyance until I return to Korea."[116] The AMG later discovered documents in Kim Koo's possession proclaiming the establishment of the KPG as the legal government, and ordering that American personnel who sought to oppose it should be dealt with severely.[117]

Rhee's statement that the United States had agreed to grant independence was carried in the Korean papers, without the U.S. State Department's denial, and Kim Koo's putsch fizzled. Rhee's announcement was not a complete fabrication, however. On April 12, *The New York Times* published a letter from Secretary of State Marshall to Molotov indicating that because of the failure of the Joint Commission to reach any agreement, the United States would consider establishing the independence of the southern portion of Korea separately from that of the northern portion.[118] While this was apparently a bluff to get the Soviets back to the negotiating table, it could also be interpreted as a victory for Rhee.

Syngman Rhee's own bluff caused considerable embarrassment to the American Military Government in Korea, which was under no orders to grant Korea its independence. Apparently concerned that Rhee's presence in Korea would undermine American policy efforts, the military governor issued orders that he was not to be permitted to return to the country.[119] Rhee, the perpetual political manipulator, secured an invitation from Chiang Kai-shek to visit China, then had the Chinese Nationalists fly him home, making it politically embarrassing for the AMG to refuse his admittance to Korea. He was received home as a returning national hero.

After the failure of Kim Koo's second coup attempt, the nationalists' position declined rapidly, as the United States sought to build up the Coalition Committee. With the reopening of the Joint Commission talks on May 21, 1947 (the Soviets *had* responded to Marshall's bluff), agreement was reached between the United States and the Soviet delegations to exclude from participation only those who would refuse to sign a commitment to support trusteeship, and to abide by the decisions of the Joint Commission, regardless of what positions they might have taken on the issue of trusteeship in the past.[120] Syngman Rhee and Kim Koo, of course, refused to sign, but many former supporters of the nationalists began to reconsider their stand, and to accept the American position, fearing that the United States and the U.S.S.R. would create a new Korean government which would exclude them. The two nationalist leaders were kept under virtual house arrest, and Syngman Rhee, in particular, was isolated. "No one thought Rhee had any chance left. Even his house, which had been lent to him by a Korean businessman, was repossessed, and he had to move to the outskirts of town," reported his press secretary, who also left Rhee in 1947.[121] Chang Taek-sang, chief of police of Seoul City, later wrote that the AMG had called him in and said, "We're trying to promote a government under Kim Kyu-sik, so stay away from Syngman Rhee!"[122] Chang responded, according to a different source, that he would cooperate with the AMG because "Rhee's finished."[123]

Once Syngman Rhee and Kim Koo had been isolated from much of their following by these proceedings, the Soviet representatives to the commission renewed their old intransigence and reverted to the stand of the preceding year that no one who had *ever* opposed trusteeship, despite later agreement to sign the commitment to support it, should be allowed to participate. This, of course, would mean including only Communists. The Joint Commission talks broke down again.[124]

With the collapse of the talks, the somewhat amateurish attempts of the American Military Government to promote the political consolidation of the new "coalition" group ended in failure. Although the AMG had selected two well-known leaders to head the group, neither had the status of Syngman Rhee or Kim Koo, and Yŏ Un-hyŏng had been forced to withdraw from cooperation after repeated terrorist attacks on him. The prestige of the committee rested with Kim Kyu-sik, who was respected among the Korean elite but less well-known at the grass-roots level; furthermore, Kim was not an effective political organizer. Unwilling to commit political resources to the group, the AMG was apparently unaware of the need for local organization, and waited for support on the local level to coalesce voluntarily in support of the committee. The inability of the Coalition Committee to win the election for the Interim Legislature in 1946 had left the AMG leaders somewhat baffled, and many attributed it to dishonest or terroristic tactics on the part of the nationalists, rather than to the obvious fact that the committee simply did not possess the broad organizational and economic support held by the nationalists. American efforts to strengthen the committee by appointing its members to the assembly and by publicly endorsing the committee only further undermined its popular support in local areas, where it came to be viewed as a puppet group of the new American rulers.

The Coalition Committee, whose political ideas had always been necessarily vague because of the intense disagreement among its members, had virtually staked its fate on the outcome of the Joint Commission meetings between the representatives of the United States and the Soviet Union in 1947, for it endorsed the concept of trusteeship and vowed its cooperation with the two powers. The failure of the commission to come to any conclusions left the committee looking somewhat ludicrous for having placed any faith in cooperation between the two antagonistic superpowers.

Although the Coalition Committee had failed to consolidate a political base of its own, it had succeeded in 1947 in heavily undermining much of the organizational base and open support of the nationalists. Politicians concerned with being on the winning side had left the nationalists to support the committee, when it had appeared for a time that it would indeed inherit the reins of power. Fear of "betting on the wrong horse" had induced most businessmen to completely withdraw from funding the nationalists, leaving the coffers of the latter nearly barren. Disharmony between the nationalists and those who had chosen to join the committee had created a permanent enmity between many individuals who had formerly been willing to cooperate in the formation of a Korean government, and left divisions that time would not erase. Many nationalists henceforth disdained members of the committee as opportunists, who had sought American support for their own gain, even at the cost of the independence of the nation, while committee members viewed nationalists as irrational fanatics who were committed to standing by an unrealistic ideal of immediate independence. The unity which had appeared among the nationalist supporters of the National Society in mid-1946 had faded by mid-1947, and bitter antagonisms had been created which would not be forgotten in the years ahead.

Syngman Rhee's Second Consolidation Attempt

Although Syngman Rhee's overt political base had been heavily undermined by mid-1947, the Joint Commission talks brought him a new source of support—the Korean bureaucracy. Successful negotiations between the United States and the Soviet Union could have two results unfavorable to the Korean bureaucrats: it could mean a changeover in the bureaucracy, and thus the loss of their jobs, and it could mean the ascendance of the Communists and their associates who had taken a hard line against the "Japanese collaborators," a term which encompassed the bulk of the bureaucracy. Fear and the need for security drove the bureaucracy into cooperation with the nationalists. The Americans, who because of the language barrier could provide only minimal supervision over the bureaucratic organization, began to suspect nationalist subversion and infiltration in the administration.

As the nationalists' position became progressively worse in 1947, they began to run short of financing. Increasing inflation and terror drew people away from the political arena, and American policy discouraged any hopes that helping the nationalists would be politically beneficial. The bureaucracy's role then came into full play. Though the American Military Government could not be sure where the funds were coming from to finance the nationalist operations, they became suspicious. As the chairman of the National Economic Board, Dr. Wilhelm Anderson, pointed out in a personal interview:

> There were vague indications. For instance, there was a kind of cooperative organization which had many functions— banking, selling things, etc. The United States would give millions of dollars worth of goods to the Korean government— for instance, fertilizer, barley, wheat. We thought it should be sold to the farmers for what it cost. However, pressure kept being put on the military government to sell it for half. Where the pressure came from, I don't know, but it came through the Korean officials. Finally we gave in and sold aid products for half price. However, by the time they got to the farmers, they were double the original price. One could only speculate where the funds went.[125]

The police, too, were suspected of beginning to play a role in funneling funds to the nationalists, according to the American civil administrator, Dr. E.A.J. Johnson:

> The civil service felt that they were underpaid, and they were. Goods were scarce, and thus prices were high. The police combatted this problem in a special way. All over the country, the police would organize "police protective associations." The police would "ask" for contributions from shopkeepers, etc. We found that the real income of the police was higher than other civil servants. And, of course, it was also true that at this time Rhee's picture began appearing in all the police stations. If you put two and two together, you might assume that some of the funds were going to Rhee.[126]

The police, the bureaucracy, the "Racial Youth Corps" and other nationalist youth groups, and the gradualist Korean Democratic Party, remained behind Rhee, providing him with sufficient support to survive.

Before abandoning the idea of a government headed by leaders other than the nationalists, the American Military Government tried once again to form a "centrist" government, as explained by the American civil administrator, Dr. E.A.J. Johnson:

> Our instructions were to try to form a government of the center. We decided to try to offset the rightism of the administration with the leftism of Lyuh Woon Hyung (Yŏ Un-hyŏng). It was finally decided that I would speak to Lyuh about joining the government. It was decided that the meeting must be very quiet and that it wouldn't do for Lyuh to come to the government building to meet me, so we arranged for him to come to meet me at my house. Lyuh was contacted, and he was willing. He agreed to come, and it was decided that the interpreter would be Dr. Chang of the New Korea Company. Lyuh was to come to my house at 4 o'clock. I waited past 4, 4:30 . . . and then finally at 4:35 the interpreter arrived panting and alarmed at my door. His driver had been unable to make it up the hill and he had run up the hill. He looked terrified. And then he told me. Just one block before he reached my house, Lyuh had been shot. That of course ended our attempts at forming a centrist government.[127]

Yŏ Un-hyŏng was assassinated on July 19, 1947, in circumstances reminiscent of the killing of Song Chin-u (the gradualist leader who had said trusteeship would have to be accepted) by a misguided and fanatic patriot. Once again, the assassin was a follower of Kim Koo.[128]

As late as December 1947, just nine months before the United States transferred the reigns of government to Syngman Rhee, publications of the AMG continued to be highly critical

of the aged leader and his followers, and continued to refer to
them as the "extreme right wing," in view of their continued
unwillingness to cooperate with American policy. Rhee continued
to insist on direct elections to determine the future government
of Korea.

The United States, unable to bring order out of the complex
political situation, yet under pressure both from Koreans and
from the American public (who wanted soldiers stationed abroad
to return home), finally decided to submit the Korean problem
to the United Nations. The United Nations decided to send a
temporary commission to Korea, and, upon the recommendations
of this commission, to hold an election in May 1948, in whatever
parts of Korea the election could be observed.[129] The Soviet
Union would not permit a supervised election in the North, so
this meant that it would be held only in South Korea, where
two-thirds of the population resided. The decision for the U.N.-
supervised election in South Korea brought still another realignment of forces in Korea.

Dr. Kim Kyu-sik, one of the leaders of the American-
sponsored coalition, opposed the election on the grounds that
it would mean a permanent division of the country.[130] Kim Koo
objected also, insisting that the U.N. was a foreign organization,
which had no right to intervene in Korea's internal affairs.[131]
Dr. Chang Tŏk-su, who had succeeded the assassinated Song
Chin-u as head of the Korean Democratic Party, came out in
favor of the elections. Shortly thereafter, he was assassinated,
and again the assassins were followers of Kim Koo.[132] Syngman
Rhee nonetheless also endorsed the U.N.-supervised election,
insisting that the only alternative was continued subordination
to the United States, a condition which was unacceptable.

The "separate election" issue marked the final split between
Dr. Rhee and Kim Koo. However, this split had been long in
coming. The two had been rivals throughout the period of the
independence movement, each claiming the title of president of
the KPG, and strongly disapproving of the tactics and activities
of the other. Rhee had always held that Kim's terrorist activities

could only detract from the independence movement, by repulsing other governments and losing the sympathy of other nations.[133] Kim Koo, on the other hand, thought Rhee's insistence on non-violence and appeals to international opinion and the use of the channels of diplomacy demeaning—efforts to seek help from others rather than employing "direct action" against the Japanese. But the event which actually created the final public break between the two was the trial for the assassination of KDP leader Chang Tŏk-su.

After the assassination of Dr. Chang, the third South Korean leader to have been killed for his political views, the AMG decided that it would have to crack down, and the trial of Chang's assassin was transferred to an American military court in the hopes that American legal procedures could bring to light the necessary evidence to reach the persons ultimately responsible.[134] Because the assassins in this case (as well as in the previous cases) were followers of Kim Koo, and they named him as their "inspiration," the old leader was called as a witness in the trial. Although this was standard procedure in an American court, a Korean called as a witness in a murder trial was virtually assumed guilty by association. In desperation, Kim Koo appealed to Dr. Rhee to use his great influence with the Americans so that he would not be called to take the stand.[135] Rhee's "great influence," however, was largely mythical, and Kim Koo was called.[136] At the trial, he had to be kept on the witness stand by court guards, as the aging independence leader shouted defiantly, "I never advocated killing anybody but Japanese! "[137] The results of the trial were inconclusive, but the old nationalist had been publicly disgraced, and permanently embittered against Rhee. Public rumor speculated that Rhee had arranged to have Kim Koo called in order to get rid of him as a rival.[138]

After the trial, Kim Koo joined with Dr. Kim Kyu-sik in calling for opposition to the new elections and for the convening of a meeting with the North Koreans to find a way out of the impasse. The Communists in the North immediately took up the suggestion, and invited Kim Koo, Dr. Kim, and others who opposed the U.N. elections to a "unity meeting" in the North. The meeting was obviously rigged, and the southern politicians became propaganda showpieces for the northern audience.[139] Kim Kyu-sik returned disillusioned, and retired from politics; he was captured and carried away by the North Koreans in the invasion of 1950, and his ultimate fate was never learned. Kim Koo returned, publicly announced that the Communists had promised cooperation, and cited as evidence a promise that the flow of electricity from North to South would not be discontinued.[140] It was cut off the following week.[141]

On May 10, 1948, the U.N.-supervised election for seats in the Korean National Assembly, which was to form an independent government, was held in South Korea, under a new franchise law granting universal suffrage. Approximately 90 percent of the eligible voters had been registered, and 93 percent of these turned out to vote in what was, by and large, a free election.[142] Despite scattered incidents of terrorism, which the nationalists blamed on the Communists and vice versa,[143] the U.N. Commission passed its approval of the election.[144] Probably the most signigicant factor in the election outcome was that most of the population of Korea were unsophisticated rural residents to whom the various political philosophies meant nothing. They voted because they were expected to, and because in voting they were expressing their desire for independence. The best-financed and most organized groups, who were capable of publicizing their candidates, and the individuals most well known in the local areas emerged victorious. It was not surprising that the new assembly was dominated by two groups—the former participants in the provisional government, and the large landowners.

The results might well have been anticipated. With the Communist leadership outlawed, the assassinated Yŏ Un-hyŏng's party of little significance, Kim Koo no longer participating, and most of the members of the American-sponsored coalition committee boycotting the election, the well-financed Korean Democratic Party of the gradualists carried the largest number of seats, although the results were masked by the fact that most of the

KDP members ran as independents. It was estimated that between 70 and 80 of the 198 members elected were associated in some way with the KDP. Members of Rhee's National Society held the second largest bloc of seats, with 55 of the total. The official results, which masked the affiliates of the KDP under the category "independents" were as follows:[145]

National Assembly Election Results, May 10, 1948

Party or Organization	Leader	No. Candidates	No. Elected	Percent Elected
Independents	- - -	417	85	20.3
National Society	Syngman Rhee	235	55	23.4
Korean Democratic Party	Kim Song-su	91	29	31.9
Great Korea Youth Alliance	Kim Koo	87	12	13.8
Racial Youth Corps	Yi Pŏm-sŏk	20	6	30.0
		893	198	

If the effectiveness of an organization is judged by the percentage of the candidates it elects, the gradualist-financed Korean Democratic Party (KDP) and the U.S. Army-financed Racial Youth Corps of Yi Pŏm-sŏk were the most effective. Most of the independents elected were either affiliated with the KDP or were returnees from the provisional government, as were most of those in Kim Koo's Youth Alliance and Yi Pŏm-sŏk's Youth Corps. Other organizations or "parties" had contested the election, but proved unsuccessful. With the backing of the Korean Democratic Party and its independent affiliates, his own National Society, and the Racial Youth Corps, Syngman Rhee was overwhelmingly elected chairman of the new assembly, with the understanding that he would assume the presidency upon independence.

The Bases for Development in South Korea after 1948

Syngman Rhee's ultimate consolidation of political control by 1948 did not come without high cost to the resources which would have to be utilized to construct a new political system after independence. The political arena had opened in 1945, at

the time of liberation, with much excitement, joy, and anticipation, and with an overwhelming outflow of goodwill. Groups
formed rapidly, and in many instances spontaneously, to organize
for independence and provide for the necessities of life. The
answer to four decades of prayer came with the national liberation. All groups appeared ready to endorse, at least outwardly,
the most famous leaders of the independence movement, among
whom the most prominent were Syngman Rhee and Kim Koo.
Few could have imagined the tragedy to follow.

By the middle of 1946, South Korea's political arena
appeared well-organized, even if the Communists (who numbered
7,000 in January 1946) refused to participate after their initial
consolidation was undermined. The nationalists had established
a broad organizational base in the countryside, and secured the
loyalty of individuals of nearly all political persuasions but the
Communists and a few small neo-Marxist groups. Political financing was available to the nationalists, and the national press was
optimistic. By 1948, this organizational base was in disarray,
political financing had gone underground, the society was pervaded by terrorism and violence, and the strongest political
groups were the bureaucracy, the police, and the youth gangs.

By 1948, a zealous Korean police force of 26,386 had been
created, which dominated political life. Although a constabulary
of 97,000 also existed, it was poorly organized, had equipment
for only half that number, and lacked the driving *esprit* of the
police. The police force supported the nationalists and the
nationalist figurehead Syngman Rhee, because it was in the
interest of the police to do so. They were not, however, *controlled* by the nationalists, being a kingdom unto themselves.

Economic resources in 1948 were concentrated in the hands
of the bureaucracy. Not only did the administration control the
"vested properties" which had been left by the Japanese, but it
was also responsible for the distribution of the bulk of all consumer commodities in South Korea through the Financial
Association, an agency of the Korean government.[146] The bureaucracy was also responsible for granting and guaranteeing loans to

all major enterprises in South Korea, a means through which it could penalize those "private" corporations for financial assistance to undesirable organizations and groups. Indeed, the portion of national financial resources available to the government bureaucracy had increased markedly during American rule. In 1947 alone total government cash deposits in banking institutions increased from 35 percent of all deposits to 65 percent of all deposits.[147] Thus the government owned two-thirds of all the cash savings in the country. The political power of the South Korean bureaucracy was augmented accordingly. Syngman Rhee did not control the Korean bureaucracy. Like the police force, bureaucrats chose to support the famous independence leader as an insurance against takeover by the Communists as well as against later retaliation by the more nationalist-minded populace.

Social conditions had also undergone significant changes. The repatriation of hundreds of thousands of returnees had produced rapid urbanization and considerable dislocation. The demand for education, uncorked by the liberation, brought an opening of vast numbers of new schools. The number of primary students in school doubled in two years, while the number of secondary and university students tripled.[148] More than anything else, the economic crisis had permeated every development during the period of American rule. Although much of the transportation and communications systems had been repaired, the Korean economy had a long way to go before it could operate on a level of self-sufficiency, let alone match the role it had played in the Japanese system.

South Korea at the end of the American occupation was in chaos and on the brink of civil war. Song Chin-u, Chang Tŏk-su, and Yŏ Un-hyŏng had been assassinated; Kim Kyu-sik and Kim Koo had retired from politics; Pak Hŏn-yŏng, wanted by the South Korean police, had escaped to North Korea. Inflation had gotten completely out of hand. People were pouring into cities where mobs of unemployed were attracted into "youth corps" of opposing political tendencies. These groups, together with the hated police force, survived in part by extorting "voluntary" contributions from an intimidated populace. Enthusiasm in South Korea had been replaced by fear, bitterness, and antagonisms which would be perpetuated for decades to come. It was on this 1948 political base, rather than that of 1945, that Syngman Rhee would have to try to build a new political system in South Korea.

Chapter III

CONSOLIDATION OF POWER IN NORTH KOREA, 1945–1948

While South Korea experienced a struggle for power during the period from 1945 to 1948, under American Military Government rule, North Korea was undergoing a different pattern of consolidation under the supervision of the occupying Russian forces. By 1948, a more viable political base had been established in the North than in the South, largely because the Russians had followed a single-minded policy in backing up the consolidation of a political regime.[1]

In this crucial initial period, the Russians succeeded in creating an organizational base which supported the system they sought to introduce. Eliminating those whose views were irrevocably antagonistic to those of the Russians on the basic nature of the political system to be introduced, and placing at the helm Kim Il Sung, who appeared to be in fundamental agreement on this issue, the northern regime settled this problem from the outset with the support of the Soviet military stationed there. By 1948 the complete organizational base of the new system had been constructed. Though political competition was to continue, it would be within the framework of a Communist regime.

Soviet troops entered Korea on August 6, 1945, the U.S.S.R. declared war on Japan on August 9, and Japan surrendered on August 15.[2] Soviet troops brought with them perhaps as many as 30,000 Soviet-Koreans (Koreans of Soviet citizenship),[3] about 3,000 of them soldiers in the Soviet Army, as well as Kim Il Sung and his immediate entourage. This latter group of young men had gone from Manchuria into the U.S.S.R., where they had received political training.[4] Kim had apparently been trained in a Russian military academy,[5] and, according to some sources, had distinguished himself by leading a Soviet-Korean unit in defense of Stalingrad.[6] He held the rank of major in the Soviet Army.[7] Kim's loyalty to communism and to the U.S.S.R.,

86

combined with his military skills, may well have seemed a boon to the Soviet Union, which had been training Soviet-Koreans in separate military units for some time, apparently with the thought of using them as a "liberating force" in Korea.[8]

As the leader of such a "liberating force," Kim Il Sung would have become famous throughout Korea—so famous, in fact, as to give him an aura of legitimate leadership far outweighing that of Syngman Rhee, who had pleaded the "Korean cause" at international tribunals for years without achieving any results. Japanese police files in June 1945, in fact, noted intelligence reports that Kim Il Sung was to lead a "liberation force" from the Soviet Union into Korea in August 1945.[9] It may well be that Kim was to give the impression of having brought the Russian troops in as allies to free the country from "imperialism." The sudden capitulation of Japan, however, following the U.S. use of the atomic bomb, gave the liberation force no opportunity to "liberate." Japan surrendered before the Soviet troops and their Korean units had an opportunity to fight the Japanese.

Consolidation, Pre-Kim Phase

When the Russians arrived in Pyongyang, then the largest city as well as the largest provincial capital north of the 38th parallel, they did not set up a military government, but rather welcomed the formation of the "people's committees" which were being formed, as in South Korea, on the suggestion of the preparatory committee in Seoul headed by Yŏ Un-hyŏng who had received the transfer of power from the Japanese governor-general.[10] Although the U.S.S.R. extended no recognition to the short-lived People's Republic in Seoul, it did not deny the legitimacy of its organs at the local level, nor did it make any statements expressing the view that Koreans were incapable of governing themselves. On the contrary, every effort was made to assure the North Koreans that the Soviet troops were present only to guarantee a smooth transfer of power to Koreans, and to prevent any takeover by another foreign power during the period of temporary Korean weakness in this transition. The

Soviet commander reportedly announced on his arrival: "Korean people! Remember that you have future happiness in your own hands. You have attained liberty and independence. Now everything is up to you. The Soviet Army will provide the Korean people with all conditions for the free and creative ventures you are bound to embark on. Koreans must make themselves the creators of their own happiness."[11] At the same time the Japanese transferred power in Seoul, the provincial governor in the northern province of Pyongan-namdo, of which Pyongyang is the capital, turned over his authority to the local people's committee. The head of this committee was a well-known Christian nationalist leader, Cho Man-sik, famous for his participation in the planning of the 1919 resistance.[12] Included in the committee in Pyongyang, as elsewhere, were Communist leaders, for they, too, had participated in the amorphous independence movement. The majority of committee members, however, were not Communists. Of the two vice-chairmen, one, Hyŏn Chun-hyŏk, was a well-known member of the Communist Party of Korea.[13]

The first step which the Russians took was to meet with Cho and his committee and to express their desire to render any needed assistance. Where people's committees had not been established, the Russians promoted them, and assisted them in setting up procedures for rationing and distributing food and other necessities, the most urgent task of administration. Likewise, the "peace preservation corps" units which had been created by the people's committees were assisted by Soviet troops in taking over the maintenance of law and order, while disarming the Japanese-trained police force.[14] The Japanese-trained local bureaucrats were ignored, and the police, fearing retaliation as "collaborators," fled south, large numbers of them to be taken in by the American Military Government police force.[15] As the people's committees secured control both of rationing of goods and maintenance of order, they were able to extend effective control over much of the populace.[16]

After assisting in the establishment of the people's committees throughout North Korea, the Soviet Command called a

meeting of representatives of the five provincial committees on
October 8.[17] At this gathering, a new organ was created, known
as the "Five Provinces Temporary People's Committee" (Imsi
odo inmin wiwŏnhoë), with a membership of thirty—fifteen of
whom were Communists and fifteen "non-Communists" (that is,
any of the large variety of other political convictions).[18] The
Christian-nationalist Cho Man-sik, who had been chairman of the
provincial committee in Pyongan-namdo, became the chairman of
the new top-level committee.[19]

A number of measures were adopted by the new committee.
Local and provincial people's committees were to be standardized,
and the committee prescribed the administrative organization and
set the size and structure of the local committees at each level.
Specific administrative bureaus were to be set up under each
committee, and the local organs were each to be responsible to
the people's committee on the next highest level, pyramiding
from the local districts to the central "Five Provinces Temporary
People's Committee." Also, a procedure for electing members to
the people's committees was determined: villages were to elect a
head by general vote; these heads were to select electors who
would choose the members of the district people's committees.
The district people's committees would elect the county committees, and so on. The franchise was to be given to all citizens
over twenty, except those deprived of the right by the courts.[20]
What was not clarified was who was to nominate the people to
stand for election in the first place at the base of the system.
Elections were not, in fact, held until the following year, when
the Communists had consolidated complete control over political
activity and hence were responsible for the nomination of all
candidates.[21]

While the administrative organization was being constructed,
the Soviet command concentrated its political concern on the
development of the Korean Communist Party. As in the South,
the Communists had begun organization immediately after the
Japanese surrender. The most prominent Communist of Pyongyang
was Hyŏn Chun-hyŏk, one of the vice chairmen of the Pyongan-

namdo provincial people's committee. On August 16, before the Soviet troops arrived in Pyongyang, he began the organization of a provincial branch of the Korean Communist Party, whose headquarters had been established the day before in Seoul, under the leadership of Pak Hŏn-yŏng.[22] Hyŏn, like most of the domestic Communists, was an intellectual and a theorist, and like the rest of Korean intellectuals was more interested in developing his own ideas than in following Soviet instructions. According to his interpretation, the time was not "ripe" in Korea for a "proletarian" revolution (there being no proletariat to speak of), but a "democratic" revolution must come first, and hence it was necessary to work in cooperation with the other nationalists.[23] The Soviet command made several futile attempts to get Hyŏn's cooperation. Finally, on September 28, 1945, he was assassinated by an unknown assailant shortly after leaving Russian headquarters.[24] It was rumored that the assassination had been carried out by a group of Soviet-Koreans who had joined the provincial party branch, prominent among whom was Soviet-educated Kim Yŏng-pŏm, but in fact no charges were ever brought against anyone, and the event remains shrouded in mystery.[25] Although the fact has since been expunged from party records, Kim Yŏng-pŏm became the first chairman of the North Korean Communist Party a few weeks later.

On October 10, 1945, the Soviet command called a meeting of the heads of all the provincial branches of the Communist Party in North Korea to form a "North Korean Branch of the Korean Communist Party."[26] Most of the domestic Communists objected to this move, insisting that it would split the Communist movement into separate northern and southern organizations. O Ki-sŏp, head of the provincial headquarters in Hamgyongnamdo, had to be forcibly abducted to Pyongyang.[27] After the assassinated Hyŏn, O was the best-known Communist in the North, and his arrival in Pyongyang signaled other Communists to make a choice between abandoning the party, fleeing south to join the party in Seoul (which would have meant a loss of their regional bases of power), or attending the meeting. Most chose to attend. At the meeting, Soviet-educated Kim Yŏng-pŏm, sometimes identified as a Soviet-Korean, was selected to chair the party,[28] while Mu Chŏng (Kim Mu-chŏng), recently returned from North China where he had served with Mao Tse-tung and participated in the 1934–1935 Long March of the Chinese Communists, and O Ki-sŏp of the domestic Communists, were named vice chairmen.[29] Although Pak Hŏn yŏng, chairman of the Korean Communist Party with headquarters in Seoul, objected to the creation of a separate North Korean Branch, the KCP in Seoul finally extended recognition to the new "branch" on October 23.[30]

While the Soviet occupiers sponsored the growth and reorganization of the Korean Communist Party, they secured control over it through Soviet-Koreans who joined and overwhelmed the domestic Communists. These Soviet-Koreans retained their membership in the Communist Party of the Soviet Union (CPSU) and remained subject to Soviet party discipline. Indeed, many had left their families home in the Soviet Union. This party, in turn, secured control over the central "people's committee" by virtue of the fact that the Russians, in appointing the committee from representatives in the provincial committees, managed to make sure that 50 percent of the 30 members were Communists. (It will be remembered that the Communists in the South persistently demanded 50 percent representation as a price for any cooperation with another political group.) Consolidation of Communist political control was well on its way within a few short months after the Russian troops had first arrived.

Kim Il Sung's Rise to Power

Kim Il Sung returned from the U.S.S.R. with the Soviet troops in August, but did not make a public appearance until October.[31] Later, he claimed to have sent his men around to encourage the people to form "people's committees."[32] Though he was in Pyongyang in early September 1945, he had gone almost to the 38th parallel by the 15th of that month, perhaps with the original intention of going to Seoul, but had then returned to Pyongyang.[33] At a rally in Pyongyang, called by the Russians in October, he was given great praise by the Soviet commander,

General Christiakov, as a "patriot hero," and Kim Il Sung
declared:

> We sincerely thank the Soviet Army which has fought for
> our freedom and liberation. Japanese imperialism, which had
> oppressed us for thirty-six years, has been smashed by the
> heroic champions of the Soviet Army . . . The Korean
> nation must go forth from this time uniting its forces in the
> construction of a new democratic Korea. No party, faction,
> or individual can complete this task alone. Let all who really
> love their country and freedom join together in complete,
> national, harmonious solidarity to create a democratic,
> autonomous, independent state.[34]

Kim Il Sung brought back with him to Korea an entourage of
his friends from Manchuria. The leadership group included the "Kim
triumvirate": Kim Il Sung, whose name means "Establishing the Sun,"
was to be the symbolic leader; Kim Il, whose name means "Number
One," who had received a degree in politics and economics from the
University of Tashkent, was to be the brains; and Kim Ch'aek, whose
name means "Tactics," was to be the effective organizer and tactician.[35]
The inner circle also included Ch'oë Yŏng-gŏn ("Healthy Dragon"), a
graduate of Yenan Military School. All of these names were fictitious,
having been adopted during the independent movement.[36]

After the creation of the Five Provinces Temporary People's
Committee on October 8, the Communists moved rapidly to consolidate control over the governing organs which had become subordinate to the central people's committee. While the standardization
process had given effective authority over the lower committees
to the central committee, the fact that the Communists made up
one half of the central organ gave them ultimate control. The
reason for this was simple: because the Communists were subject
to a higher authority in the party outside the committee, they
always adopted a unified policy within the committee, whereas
the other members rarely agreed with one another. As the central
committee gradually weeded "collaborators" out of the lower
branches of the government, local Communists moved in to take
their places.

By early November 1945, Cho Man-sik, the national chairman of the central people's committee, became aware of the tide of events, and to counter the Communist strength he organized a nationalist party, the Chosŏn Democratic Party, on November 3, 1945.[37] Although Cho sought primarily to attract other Christian nationalists, the party was joined by many Communists, including Kim Il Sung's companions Kim Ch'aek and Ch'oë Yŏng-gŏn. Ch'oë was elected vice chairman of the party.[38]

On December 18, 1945, Kim Il Sung moved into the post of chairman of the North Korean Communist Party, thereafter no longer called the North Korean "Branch."[39] (Kim Yŏng pŏm, who had been chairman, subsequently died in September 1947, while undergoing what was termed a "premature" operation for cancer). Exactly how Kim Il Sung maneuvered into this position is not clear, though he apparently had the backing of the Soviet-Korean party members, who outnumbered domestic Communists, and some reports indicate that he was helped by having his military unit surround the hall where the central committee was meeting.[40] At the time, Mu Chŏng from Yenan and the domestic Communist O Ki-sŏp retained their posts as vice chairmen. Of the forty-three members of the new central committee, twenty-nine were domestic Communists, and the remainder were Soviet-Koreans or Manchurian-Korean followers of Kim Il Sung.[41]

Following the announcement of the Moscow Agreement on trusteeship (which the Soviets translated "guardianship") in late December, Cho Man-sik, chairman of the Five Provinces Temporary People's Committee, announced his opposition to this decision, as had the nationalists in the South.[42] When the Soviet command was unable to persuade him to change his position, a meeting of the People's Committee was called. It is not known whether the nationalist members were not informed of the meeting or were prevented from attending, but at the meeting on January 4, 1946 (the day after the Communist-sponsored pro-trusteeship demonstration in Seoul), only six of the fifteen nationalist members were present while the fifteen Communists were all in attendance.[43] The result was an endorsement of the Moscow Agreement. Cho submitted his resignation in protest, and when he could not be dissuaded, he was placed under arrest the following day.[44] For at least a year, Cho was known to be under house arrest in Pyongyang, but his ultimate fate was never learned. It was rumored that he was killed before the North Koreans abandoned Pyongyang during the Korean War.

After Cho's arrest, Ch'oë Yŏng-gŏn, Kim Il Sung's companion from Manchurian days, succeeded to the leadership of the nationalist Chosŏn Democratic Party.[45] Most of Cho's nationalist followers then fled to Seoul, where the headquarters of the party was re-established and it became a source of cohesive organization for the Northern refugees. Another political party, the Ch'ŏndokyo Party, whose members were affiliated with the Ch'ŏndokyo religion, met a similar fate, with its leader replaced by one controlled by the Communists.[46]

Following the elimination of the nationalists from power, "representatives" from the provincial and district committees, the political parties (all now under Communist control) and the "social organizations" met to form a new central people's committee. The "social organizations" created by the Soviet-sponsored regime had been expanding rapidly, absorbing much the same elements who were drawn into the "youth corps" groups in the South. By April 1946, two months after the formation of the new committee, membership in the Peasants' League was said to number 800,000, in Workers' Leagues 350,000, in the Democratic Youth League 500,000, and in the Women's League 350,000.[47] The new central people's committee dropped all pretense of compromising with the nationalists. Of its twenty-three members, all but four were known to be members of the Communist Party, and of these four, one was Kim Il Sung's Manchurian-Korean comrade, Ch'oë Yŏng-gŏn, and another was reported to be a second cousin of Kim Il Sung.[48] Kim Il Sung became chairman of this reorganized committee, the post which Cho had previously held, and which was henceforth to be the central focus of political control, under the Soviet command, in North Korea. This new committee, formally inaugurated on February 8, 1946, changed its name from the "Five Provinces Temporary People's Committee" to the "North Korean Interim

People's Committee."[49] On the same day, domestic Communist
O Ki-sŏp was removed from his post as vice chairman of the North
Korean Communist Party, though appointed chief of propaganda
for the new people's committee.[50]

The first Joint Commission talks on Korean trusteeship were
initiated at this time, with the Soviet representatives insisting that
Korean participants in the conference should include only those
who had never expressed opposition to trusteeship.

A significant factor in the strength of the new regime of
Kim Il Sung was its ability to secure the financial assets of the
state, and hence to limit the political participation of "unreliable
elements." Not only was the regime responsible for the rationing
of all food and other necessities, but it also secured control over
all bank deposits and currency. In February 1946, a North Korean
Central Bank was established under direct control of the Soviet
Military Command. All banks came under this central bank except
the "North Korean Farmers' Bank," which operated directly under
the central people's committee.[51]

In the South, shortly after the formation of the People's
Republic in early September 1945, gradualists—both landlords and
those with industrial holdings had quickly formed a privately
financed opposition, although they did not declare themselves
until the arrival of American troops. In the North, on the contrary, no such group had formed; Cho's nationalists were largely
of Christian background, and Korea's Christians were primarily
drawn from the poorer classes. The reasons for the lack of resistance by the landed groups in the North were several: fear of
the Russians, concentration of efforts in Seoul—the primary
reason being that there was no strong element of the landed elite
in the North, which was a mountainous area, devoid of the large
rice plantations of the South.

One of the first acts of the new central committee, nonetheless, was the proclamation on March 5, 1946, of a land reform.[52]
Although landlords of North Korea were not as politically powerful as they were in the South, the landholding pattern was still
highly inequitable.[53] Kim Il Sung reported in 1947 that before

the land reform 6.8 percent of the farmers owned 54 percent of the cultivable land.[54] According to one study, 25.8 percent of the rural population had owned land in North Korea in 1945, while 22.4 percent were part owners and part tenants, 44.9 percent were tenants, 5.4 percent were squatters, and 1.5 percent were farm laborers.[55] Both the lands previously held in tenancy and those previously held by the Japanese were confiscated and redistributed. This eliminated the possibility of an opposing privately-financed political group based on landed interests. Kim Il Sung later said that 44,000 Korean landowners had been completely dispossessed.[56] Others had large amounts confiscated. Statistics on land confiscation during the land reform were given as follows:[57]

Land Confiscated in North Korean Land Reform

Owners	Amount of Land (in Chŏngbo)*
Japanese	100,797
Collaborators	21,718
Landlords owning more than 5 chŏngbo	285,692
Landlords renting all their land	538,067
Landlords renting parts of their land	239,650
Religious organizations	14,401
Total Confiscated	1,000,325

*One chŏngbo equals approximately 2.45 acres.

Redistribution of the land is estimated to have benefited more than 70 percent of the rural population, or about 50 percent of the total population of North Korea, and to have involved more than 50 percent of the cultivable acreage.[58] Because the Korean landlords were not organized, resistance was not great and there was no widespread bloodletting as in mainland China or North Vietnam.[59] In part, this was because confiscation came in stages, the largest landholdings first, then medium-sized landholdings, and so on.[60] Large numbers of former landowners fled south. Redistribution of the land was reported as follows:[61]

Land Redistributed in North Korean Land Reform

Recipients	Number of Families	Amount of Land (in Chŏngbo)
Farm laborers	17,137	22,387
Landless tenants	442,973	603,407
Farmers with little land	260,501	345,974
Landlords moved to new areas	3,911	9,622
	724,522	981,390

Implementation of land reform was carried out by special committees at the village level, of which about 11,500 were formed. Each committee numbered between five and nine members, and was composed of farm laborers, landless tenant farmers, and tenant farmers who owned only a small amount of land. The transfer of land was undertaken by issuing new land certificates, which then had to be registered in the land ledgers of the provincial people's committees, which could thereby oversee and supervise the redistribution.[62] The land, once distributed, could not be subdivided, leased, or sold.

The land reform had two important effects upon the assets of the North Korean regime. First, it eliminated the possibility of funds flowing from a land-based elite to an opposition organization. Second, it made available for taxation the sums which had previously gone to the landlords in rent. In many areas, pre-independence rentals had been as high as 50 or 60 percent of crop yields.[63] Although the new regime set the *legal* tax levels quite low—27 percent on paddy land, 23 percent on dry land, and 10 percent on "fire fields" (low-yield land cleared for one-year cultivation by burning overgrowth)—it is estimated that the new government actually collected as much as 50 percent, and in some cases 60 or 70 percent, in taxes, through the expediency of over-estimating crop yields.[64]

On August 10, 1946, land reform was followed by the nationalization of all industry previously owned by the Japanese

—90 percent of all industrial facilities in North Korea.[65] The political effect of placing these assets in the hands of the regime was overwhelming. No organization or informational system in opposition to the government could be financed, as there were virtually no assets available to channel into other organizations.

The implications of the land reform were far more than simply financial, of course, as the movement was also used as a means to absorb peasants into the Communist Party. The party grew from 6,000 members in December 1945 to 134,000 members in August 1946. Similarly, the Communist-sponsored Peasants' League grew from 800,000 to 1,800,000 between April and July, 1946.[66]

Kim Il Sung was by no means in complete control of politics in North Korea by early 1946, despite his rise to public prominence. Not only did he depend upon the support of the Soviet-Koreans to remain at the head of the party, but he was faced with considerable political resistance. This resistance came not from the nationalists but from two Communist groups—the domestic Communists and a group trained in Yenan, China, where Mao Tse-tung and the Chinese Communists had their headquarters. The latter were commonly referred to as the "Yenan Koreans." The domestic Korean Communists, dissatisfied as they were, had been absorbed into the North Korean Communist Party, but the Yenan Koreans were not prepared to subordinate themselves to either the Soviet-Koreans or the youthful entourage of Kim Il Sung. Led by Kim Tu-bong, a well-known Korean literary scholar and prominent figure in the 1919 uprisings who was twenty-two years Kim Il Sung's senior, this group set out to form its own party independent of Soviet control.[67]

Friction between the trainees from the Soviet Union and those from China had developed very early. In September and October of 1945, Chinese-trained members of the Korean Independence Alliance, which had been formed in Yenan in 1941, tried to return to Korea across the Yalu River, but were halted by the Soviet military.[68] In early November, they were given permission to enter Korea at the border town of Sinŭiju, where the men—about 4,000 of them—were lodged in a local high school building. During the night they were surrounded by the local peace-preservation corps and disarmed. Angrily, they retreated back across the Yalu. Kim Tu-bong and some of his followers later returned by way of South Korea.[69]

The Yenan Korean Communists undertook a broad recruitment policy beginning in March 1946.[70] Establishing a party called the New People's Party, a reincarnation of the Korean Independence Alliance they had built in Yenan, they apparently set out with the goal of overtaking the Soviet-sponsored Communist Party in membership and prestige. The Yenan Koreans may well have been spurred on in their organizational efforts by the accelerated expansion of the North Korean Communist Party as land reform progressed. Because at least two Yenan Korean leaders were renowned scholars prior to their political exile (Kim Tu-bong and Ch'oë Chang-ik), the Korean intelligentsia tended to flock to the Yenan leadership. The Communists were accused of recruiting only "rabble" and "hoodlums"—eager to have a stake in the redistribution of land—from among the peasantry.[71] In turn, it was hinted by the Communists that former "collaborators" were swarming to the New People's Party in order to protect themselves from Communist retaliation.[72] Possibly those with some remaining financial resources did join the NPP, for it was not assisted by the Soviet regime, yet it managed to carry out effective organizational activities.

Whatever the source of support of the New People's Party, the leadership of the Yenan group apparently realized the futility of trying to build an independent base, and in July initial discussions were undertaken with the idea of merging the two parties.[73] At whose initiative these discussions came is not known. Kim Il Sung's insistence that they were at the request of the Yenan group may indicate the opposite, but that is pure speculation.[74] Figuring backward from the Russian figures on the membership of the Communist Party before the merger and the size of the new party afterward, it appears that the Yenan party had become considerably larger than that sponsored by the Soviets.[75] However, no figures are actually available on the size of the Yenan group. Though discussions were initiated in July, serious merger plans did not crystallize until late August, and the opening of the merger conference was held on August 28, less than three weeks after the nationalization of all of North Korea's industrial resources which had been formerly held by either the Japanese or "collaborators." It may well be that the NPP was forced into the merger in part because of the collapse of its financial resources.

A new party emerged from this conference, taking the title "North Korean Workers' Party," and the merger meeting has been retrospectively named the First Congress of the Korean Workers' Party. The chairman of the new party was not Kim Il Sung, but Yenan Korean Kim Tu-bong. Kim Il Sung was relegated to the post of vice chairman, along with a relatively obscure domestic Korean Communist, Chu Yŏng-ha, who had been a young protegé of the prominent domestic Communist O Ki-sŏp. The reason for Kim Il Sung's emergence in second place was described by one observer at the meeting:

> When the meeting came to the procedure of electing the members of the central committee, Pak Pyŏng-so . . . was the first man to take the floor . . . he shouted . . . "It is a matter of course that our heroic national leader, Kim Il Sung, shall be chairman of the North Korean Workers' Party." Delegates from the New People's Party were shocked and alarmed . . . the provincial delegates had been lukewarm to the merger all along, feeling that they were being sold out to the Communists as "captive brides." With this sudden unexpected motion, a dead silence fell over the delegates from the New People's Party.
>
> Senior Colonel Ignatiev, present as a guest . . . sent a slip to the speaker, who immediately called for a recess . . . A conference of the leaders of both parties met during the recess . . . When the meeting was resumed, O Ki-sŏp took the floor and declared that there was no iron rule that the new Chairman must be Kim Il Sung. This was followed by thunderous applause from the delegates of the New People's Party.[76]

Kim Il Sung then stood up and nominated the elder Kim Tu-bong to the number one post.[77]

On accepting the chairmanship of the new party, Kim Tu-bong remarked that the Communist Party could not get along without the members of the New People's Party because of the paucity of intellectuals in the Communist ranks, making it a "mass without a head."[78] In his address, Kim Il Sung responded in equally condescending tones, that to make revolution one must depend on the workers and peasants, but that it was well to have the cooperation of the "intellectuals and petty bourgeoisie" (from the New People's Party).[79] It was rumored that members of the Communist Party were concerned that the influx of such heterogeneous elements as the membership of the New People's Party would make the new party "impure." Nonetheless, it was reported that of the 366,000 members of the new party, 73,000 were workers and 105,000 were of "poor peasant" origin.[80] The party organization at this time was said to be composed of 12,000 cells, and membership represented about 4 percent of the population.[81] The five-member political committee consisted of Kim Tu-bong, Kim Il Sung, and Chu Yŏng-ha, the chairman and vice chairmen, plus Ch'oë Ch'ang-ik of the Yenan group and Hŏ Ka-ŭi, a Soviet-Korean.

Hŏ Ka-ŭi was placed in charge of party organization, giving him power over decisions as to who was to be admitted to the new party. Because the party was expanding rapidly, the power of this post was considerable. With the bureaucracy becoming increasingly the domain of Workers' Party members, Hŏ wielded enviable power in the North Korean regime. A year after the merger, Kim Il Sung reported that cells had been created on all levels, penetrating the provinces, cities, counties, districts, factories, and farms, and that membership had expanded to more than 700,000.[82]

The Communist auxiliary organizations also expanded. By July 1946 membership in the Peasants' Leagues was said to have reached 1,800,000, in the Workers' League 350,000, in the Democratic Youth League 1,000,000, and in the Women's League 600,000.[83] Also, all labor unions had been merged into a single United Labor Union in November 1945, with a membership of

190,000. By May 1947, it was said to have 390,570 members.[84]
Undoubtedly, most of these were nominal and involuntary
members, yet portions could be mobilized for political purposes.

The consolidation of control in North Korea was heavily
dependent on force. Three major sources of weapons existed in
North Korea: those taken over from the Japanese-trained police
by the new peace preservation corps, those in the hands of the
Soviet Army, and those surrendered by the Japanese troops and
turned over to a new North Korean People's Army, trained by the
Soviet forces.[85]

The police force, which was to maintain internal security,
was well developed before the army was trained. Consisting of
both a regular police force, developed from the original peace
preservation corps groups, and the political (that is, secret) police,
this force operated as an effective arm of the government. The
ostensible purpose of the secret police was to root out "collaborators"—those who had in any way given aid or assistance to the
Japanese rulers during the forty-year period of Japanese occupation. Ultimately, the "enemies of the state," over whom the secret
police apparatus was to keep watch, included all persons thought
to be interested in resisting the new government organization:
those who had been purged from government or party positions,
those who had lost land, those who feared losing other forms of
property, and, especially, Christians.[86]

The regular police force was not difficult to staff. The members of the peace preservation corps had been those who first
stepped forward to disarm the colonial police, and thus had an
interest in keeping their new jobs. Many were beneficiaries of the
land reform, and they of course assisted in its implementation;
their greatest fear was a political reversal which would not only
deprive them of their new land, but make them accomplices in
the illegal seizure from the former owners. The secret police had
to be chosen with greater care. Most were chosen from members
of the Communist Party, and all automatically became members
of the North Korean Workers' Party upon being hired. Their
backgrounds were carefully checked.[87] At the head of both

police organizations were a few Soviet-Koreans, as well as some Yenan Koreans with military training.[88]

The police organizations penetrated the countryside, using informants to reach into the roots of the society. Informants for the regular police were paid only on proof of substantial information, whereas regularly-paid informants were assigned by the secret police to each village and factory. With this system of police controls, opposition to the regime could not be easily organized.

The North Korean Army was not formally inaugurated until February 8, 1948, but its organization was actually begun in July 1946, when a Security Staff General Training Station was created. Heading this "General Training Station" as commander-in-chief was Ch'oë Yŏng-gŏn, Kim Il Sung's former Manchurian compatriot, still the leader of the Chosŏn Democratic Party (the post he had assumed on the incarceration of Cho Man-sik).[89] Others in the new army command were Kim Il, the Soviet-educated member of the Kim triumvirate, who became "political commissar" and Mu Chŏng, the experienced military leader of the Yenan group, who was made "artillery commander."[90] A number of training stations were set up throughout North Korea, to recruit and train new officers. By and large, the 3,000 Soviet-Koreans in the Soviet Army were used to staff the training stations, with Yenan Koreans with military experience taking secondary roles.[91]

By 1947, the total force was only about 20,000, but it was well-trained and well-equipped, partly with surrendered Japanese weapons and partly with Soviet weapons.[92] This force was expanded to 60,000 with the formal establishment of the army in February 1948.[93] Soviet advisers and a "political command"—a political and propaganda wing of the army—were within every unit. It is estimated that by 1948 there were 150 (Caucasian) Soviet advisers per division—that is, one per company.[94] Soviet troops were, of course, still in North Korea; the original total of 40,000 was reduced in 1946 to only 10,000, as the North Koreans took over their own policing and military forces.[95]

By August 1946 most political resources were well consolidated behind the Kim Il Sung regime. Dissatisfied with this

limited political base, however, the new government set out on a
second phase of political consolidation.

Consolidation Second Phase: Expansion of the Political Base
Communist consolidation over the North Korean government
did not end with Kim Il Sung's ascent to control over the "North
Korean Interim People's Committee." On the contrary, this was
only the first step in a consolidation of political and administrative
control reaching down to the lowest level of local government.
After the Communists had secured control over the two "opposition" parties—the Chosŏn Democratic Party and Ch'ŏndokyo
Party—the three political parties and four "social organizations"
(created by the regime) were brought together in July 1946,
while retaining their separate identities, into a "New People's
Front." Following the creation of the "North Korean Workers'
Party" in August 1946 by the merger of the Communist and Yenan
groups, and the "South Korean Workers' Party" in Seoul where
Communist and Yenan groups in addition to Yŏ Un-hyŏng's party
had also merged on November 23, 1946, the name was changed to
the "Korean National Democratic Front," to include all remaining
parties in the North and the "Workers'" Party in the South.[96]
This "Front" then claimed to represent all Koreans—North and
South—except the "reactionaries" following Kim Koo and Syngman
Rhee.

The first elections to the people's committees on the provincial, county, and city level were held in November 1946. The
"Korean National Democratic Front" nominated all candidates—
one for each post. The election procedure provided for each voter
to vote for or against the slate of candidates by putting his ballot
in a white box for "yes" and a black box for "no." People who
later fled South described the elections:

> Two days before the election, officials "explained" the
> procedure to us. Some people were threatened. We were
> told that the wells of those who did not vote would be
> poisoned.

Voting began at five o'clock in the morning. We showed
our registration slips to the election official. The numbers of
our slips were placed on our ballots so that it would be easy
to determine how we voted. As we went in to the voting
place, all the officials pointed out the white ballot box and
urged us to place our ballot there. The black and white boxes
were supposedly placed close enough together so that by
stretching both arms one could reach either without being
detected. But, it didn't work that way. The boxes were
placed so far apart that it was obvious which box was used
for the ballot.

Voting stopped officially at midnight and the results were
announced the following morning at nine. We all voted because we were afraid not to . . . Others in the village who
did not vote were taken away at gun point. One old lady did
not get a ballot. Election officials, however, announced a
100 percent vote.[97]

It was officially reported that 4,501,813 persons, or 99.6 percent
of the registered voters voted and 97 percent of these voted for
the proposed slate.[98] The party composition of the new committees
was about 50 percent "no party," with about two-thirds of the
remainder members of the Workers' Party and one-third divided
between the Chosŏn Democratic Party and the Ch'ŏndokyo Party
in a ratio of about 3:2.[99]

In February 1947, elections were held at a lower level for the
village people's committees. Again, candidates were put up by the
"Front," and, in this case, 60 percent were members of the Workers'
Party. It was said that 99.85 percent of the eligible voters voted,
and 80.63 percent approved the slate.[100] Given the rigid system of
controls, the nearly 20 percent who voted "no" represented a
sizable protest.

Also in February 1947, a "Congress of People's Committees"
met to form a "People's Assembly." Representatives to this People's
Assembly included, out of a total of 237, 88 members of the Workers'
Party, 89 of "no party," and 30 each from the Chosŏn Democratic and Ch'ŏndokyo Parties. The average age of the members

was under 40. The assembly met on February 21 and 22, elected Kim Tu-bong chairman, then routinely "approved" all of the actions taken to that date by the "Interim People's Committee." Then a new "People's Committee," no longer called "Interim," was named of twenty-two members, of whom sixteen belonged to the Workers' Party, two each to the Chosŏn Democratic and Ch'ŏndokyo Parties, while two were of "no party."[101] This new People's Committee, like the one before it, was chaired by Kim Il Sung.

The final round of elections for members of the district committees (a division between the village and county), by the familiar procedure came on March 5, 1947; approximately 56 percent of these nominees for district committees were members of the Workers' Party.[102] Thus, the entire round of elections consolidating the hold of the Workers' Party on North Korea was completed before the opening of the second Joint Commission meetings between the United States and the Soviet Union. In the meantime, dissenters generally "voted with their feet;" between October 1945 and April 1948, the official count of refugees to the South from the North numbered 829,886, while many came without passing checkpoints.[103] At the end of 1947, the United Nations Temporary Commission on Korea estimated that there were 1,116,600 North Korean refugees in the South.[104] By 1948, there were more than one and one-half million persons in the South claiming northern origin, and by 1950 the number was estimated at two million.[105] Out of an estimated population in North Korea in 1945 of 9,170,000, this represents more than a 20 percent exodus.[106]

In November 1947, a committee was appointed to draft a constitution. The chairman of the committee was Kim T'aek-yŏng, a Soviet-Korean, and the constitution which emerged was patterned after that of the Soviet Union.[107] The constitution was completed, with "public suggestions," in April 1948, and "adopted" by the People's Assembly on July 9.[108] Under the new constitution, the People's Assembly became the Supreme People's Assembly of the new state, while the "People's Committee" became the "Cabinet." The proclamation of the Democratic People's Republic of Korea in September 1948 was an anti-climax to the step-by-step consolidation of the regime which preceded it.

Although by 1948 the regime itself was firmly entrenched, under the control of the North Korean Workers' Party (NKWP), Kim Il Sung's consolidation of control over the party itself was far from complete. Within the party two factions opposed him—the domestic Korean Communists and the Yenan Koreans. His own position was secured only by the support of his Soviet-trained Manchurian-Korean compatriots, numbering perhaps less than one hundred, and the Soviet-Koreans who possessed joint membership in the NKWP and the CPSU. A large number of members had been inducted into the party from the peasantry, however, and were committed to no faction. To them, the name Kim Il Sung was introduced as that of a legendary hero, whose exploits had led to the eventual downfall of Japan, by bringing in the Soviet Army to drive out the enemy. Many, knowing vaguely of the name Kim Il Sung as that of a guerrilla leader of renown, may have been inclined to accept the story at face value. Furthermore, Kim was the figurehead of the regime which had given them land. He could therefore count on at least passive support from most of the peasant members of the party. It was the middle ranks which were teeming with possible sources of resistance.

Two purges were carried out within the party between 1945 and 1948. The first, carried out immediately after Kim seized control of the Communist Party in December 1945, was directed at the domestic Communists, among whom were some "pro-Japanese and reactionary elements [and] . . . those who violated the political policies of the central headquarters, those local separatists who had liberalistic and sectarian inclinations . . . and those who adhered to leftist opportunism against the political course of the central headquarters."[109] The purge was painless and was carried out simply by issuing membership cards to party members and by-passing those to be purged.

After the combination of the North Korean Communist Party and the New People's Party into the North Korean Workers' Party on August 29, 1946, another purge was carried out affecting

between 40,000 and 60,000 members.[110] Again the method was
the issuance of new membership cards. Both of these purges were
aimed at eliminating troublesome members of the domestic Communist group and their supporters.[111] In the second instance, both
the Kim-Soviet coalition and the Yenan Koreans found it convenient to work together to submerge the domestic Communists, who
were more anarchistic than their disciplined comrades raised in the
ranks of the CPSU and the Chinese Communist Party (CCP). Kim
later explained that the domestic Communists had never learned
how to follow orders.[112] In spite of these purges, the number of
party members increased from 366,000 at the time of the merger in
August 1946 to more than 700,000 in January 1948.[113] By this
time, the number of party cells was said to be 28,000, and party
membership made up about 8 percent of the population.[114]

From March 28 to 30, 1948, the Second Congress of the North
Korean Workers' Party was held in Pyongyang. Of the 999 delegates
to the Congress, 466 were said to be workers, 270 farmers, 234 office
workers, and 29 others. The chairman, Kim Tu-bong, and the vice
chairmen, Kim Il Sung and Chu Yŏng-ha, were retained, but the political committee was expanded to a membership of seven. In addition
to the three just mentioned and to Ch'oë Ch'ang-ik of the Yenan faction and Soviet-Korean party organizer, Hŏ Ka-ŭi, Kim Il Sung's companion Kim Ch'aek was added as was Pak Il-u of the Yenan group. The
make-up of the central committee was also altered somewhat, by the
removal of several domestic Communists.

Although several points of business were raised at the Second
Congress, its primary purpose appears to have been to publicize
the party's displeasure with the domestic Communist leaders,
especially O Ki-sŏp. O had been demoted from his position as
vice chairman of the party in February 1946, but had remained
a party functionary. At the Second Congress Kim Il Sung presented
a report on the party's activities, in which he attacked O Ki-sŏp
and the domestic faction: "Some comrades in the Party remain
factionalists possessed only of personal ambitions. These factional
leaders are like the frog in a small well whose view is limited to a
tiny fraction of the sky, and who have in the past indulged

themselves in regarding themselves as the one and only man, next to none, in a small locality. They have no experience of true Party life. These factional elements are seeking to prolong their outdated factional lives in divided local sects. Among them, O Ki-sŏp is typical."[115] O nonetheless retained his position as a member of the central committee, which had been expanded to a membership of sixty-seven, with twenty alternates.

Except in intra-party relations, the regime did not appeal directly to the Communist cause in its initial consolidation attempt. On the contrary, it sought to give the new government a democratic facade, retaining "opposition" parties which no longer had any independence or political leverage. It did not advocate collectivization of agriculture, or radical Communist social reforms. Kim Il Sung later explained: "If we had shouted about building socialism in the period of construction directly after liberation, who would have accepted it? Even the people would not have been won to our side. If we ask why, it is because the Japanese imperialists had spread the evil propaganda that socialism means sleeping under the same blanket and eating out of the same pot. If we had not taken this into account at that time and raised our socialist slogans we would have frightened the people and they would not have joined us."[116]

The Bases for Development in North Korea after 1948

The period from 1945 to 1948 had altered the bases for development in North Korea considerably. In the North, as in the South, the lack of political organization had initially created a highly fluid political situation, in which famous names stood out prominently as arbiters of political events. The cooperation of Kim Il Sung, Kim Tu-bong, and domestic Communist O Ki-sŏp with the Soviet regime—though the latter two did so with reservations—and the elimination of Cho Man-sik, rendered the U.S.S.R. capable of manipulating political events. The three leaders were willing to cooperate in part because of their ideological affinity with the Soviets, and also because the Russians were willing to give them at least temporary backing with all available political tools at their disposal. These Korean leaders were able to cooperate without a complete collapse of their political influence because the Russians, unlike their American counterparts in the South, did not take a public position against Korean independence, and did not set themselves up as the new rulers of the Korean people. The Russians, although behind the scenes, were more effective in directing events in the North than were the Americans in the South, whose Korean bureaucrats outwardly followed American instructions yet worked to undermine U.S. policy.

Political resources were concentrated almost exclusively in the hands of the central political regime by the end of the three-year period of Russian occupation. The Ministry of Internal Affairs in the new regime controlled the police, who numbered approximately 60,000 (the number the Japanese had to rule *all* Korea), including the regular police (12,000), secret police (3,000), Security Guards (5,000), and Border Constabulary and Railroad Guard Brigade (40,000). In addition, there were 4,000 to 5,000 employees in the central ministry.[117] The North Korean Army consisted of approximately 60,000 troops in 1948, including 10,000 who had been trained in Siberia during the three-year period to operate tanks, aircraft, and modern communications equipment.[118]

Most financial resources had been brought under the control of the regime. While farmers owned the land, the wealthier farmers had been expropriated and hence persons who owned land after the land reform lived at a marginal subsistence level and could not be expected to organize or finance political opposition. These persons were dependent upon the regime for the rationing of foods that were not grown on their land, as well as for consumer goods including clothing or textiles. Most industrial enterprises, as well as utilities, transportation and communication, were placed in the hands of the regime. The few "private enterprises" left, found themselves being gradually squeezed out by the lack of raw materials and the inability to obtain financial credit. Furthermore, their employees were lured away by the state enterprises which paid special rations to the workers.

Most important to the consolidation of financial control was the reorganization of the banking system. While the Central Bank at first came under the Soviet command, it was placed under the People's Committee on October 31, 1946. Old bank workers were dismissed and Workers' Party members replaced them.[119] In December 1947, a currency reform further tightened the economic vise. Deposits were frozen, then redeemed on a scale determined by the regime. Those under 2,000 *won* were redeemed in full, those between 2,000 and 50,000 at a percentage of the holdings, the percentage declining with the increasing balance. Depositors with balances above 50,000 received 13,000 *won* in new currency, plus 10 percent of the balance over 50,000. The purpose as announced by the regime, was to limit the accumulation of private capital.[120]

With 725,000 members, the Workers' Party dominated the political scene by 1948. Minor parties continued to exist in name, but their directorates had been taken over by the Communists, and a series of purges eliminated unreliable individuals from membership.[121] "Auxiliary" organizations had been brought into existence by the regime, and all of the organizations were members of the "Democratic Front" which nominated candidates for office. All of these organizations were financed by the government.

The regime monopolized the circulation of ideas in the society by controlling the press, radio, printing companies, and the educational system. A network of police informants insured against "reactionary" propaganda, and persons whose views were politically suspect were kept under surveillance. Ideas became the special domain of the regime's professional propagandists, in the Ministry of Propaganda, the Workers' Party Press, and other information organs.

Undeniably, the external factors provided by the Soviet Union were most instrumental in bringing about the political consolidation of the Kim Il Sung regime. Having a well-trained group of Koreans loyal to the U.S.S.R., the Soviet command was able to set up a government and party in the Soviet style and initiate a program which was Soviet-oriented. Dealing directly with this small group of Soviet-Koreans, the Soviet Army command could avoid becoming involved in the actual administration of government or party and turn over the operation to Koreans. Nonetheless, they did not rely solely on the loyalty of Kim Il Sung and his followers to keep the government under Russian control.

Most of the key power positions in the new regime were given to the Soviet-Koreans, selected from the communities in the U.S.S.R., who were members of the Communist Party of the Soviet Union (CPSU). These men retained their Soviet citizenship and membership in the Soviet party, and were thus subject to discipline by the Soviet occupiers, their movements watched closely by the Soviet secret police.[122]

Within the government departments, prominent domestic Koreans were given the positions bearing the title "chairman" or "minister," but the second post, to which the real power was inevitably entrusted, was put in the hands of a Soviet-Korean.[123] An estimate of approximately two hundred key Soviet-Koreans in control posts was made by the U.S. Department of State, on the basis of information from captured Soviet documents and interrogations in North Korea during the occupation of Pyongyang by U.S. forces during the Korean War.[124] These key posts were in areas most directly affecting the distribution of political instruments—the Ministry of Internal Affairs, and the Army, the Ministry of Finance and the Central Bank, the organization bureau of the Workers' Party and directorates of some auxiliary organizations, and the editors of the major press organs, head of the party training school, head of the major university. In short, the Korean returnees from the Soviet Union controlled the instruments of force, financing, dissemination of information, and the organizational apparatus of the North Korean regime.

In addition to the Soviet-Koreans, Caucasian Soviet advisers were assigned to every level of government. These advisers were always ready to make suggestions, which were approved by the Soviet-Koreans, and thus forced on the domestic Koreans supposedly heading each organ. Also, the North Koreans were supplied with Soviet technicians and consultants without whom they could not operate, having no previous training in administration or in managerial and technical skills. Both the Army and industry were heavily dependent on Soviet supplies.

The entire operation of the government was coordinated by the Soviet Political Command under General Romanenko. The command was obscurely housed in the Pyongyang Tax Office, with no identifying designation, but all governmental decisions flowed from the Romanenko Command, issued under the name of Kim Il Sung.[125]

Because of a lack of statistics, it is difficult to evaluate the changes in the nonpolitical factors in North Korea during the period of initial consolidation. Educational facilities were expanded and North Korean sources report that 94.3 percent of school-age children were enrolled in schools by 1948.[126] Urbanization also expanded in the North, but since there was a net population loss during the period (approximately 351,000 returnees from abroad; a loss to the South of more than 800,000) the North experienced no acute urban crisis as did the South.

The most significant nonpolitical advances in the three-year period 1945–1948 were in the effective organization and promotion of industrial development. Annual plans for 1947 and 1948 were put into effect, and according to North Korean reports, goals were met in most sectors.[127] Nonetheless, with the exception of the production of electricity and textiles, no sector approached its pre-Liberation output.[128] Despite the obstacles to development created by the severance of the North Korean economy from that of Japan and of the South, North Korean economic development during this period was substantial. The U.S. State Department, analyzing the growth of the North Korean economy before the Korean War, pointed out: "Extraordinary fiscal strength enabled the regime to infuse a dynamic force in the North Korean economy, to provide for conditions of growth through the diversion of an increasing volume of resources to investment purposes."[129]

Although the North Korean economy certainly was faced with many serious problems during the three years of Soviet control, the economic chaos and extremes of inflation experienced by

South Korea (where prices increased to more than 140 times the 1945 levels) were avoided, and the 1948 economy was at least functioning in a coordinated fashion, if still far from fully restored.

During the period from August 15, 1945, until nominal independence on September 9, 1948, there were significant alterations in North Korea. The regime had consolidated a fairly effective political base. Kim Il Sung himself did not have full control over this base, but depended upon the support of Soviet-Koreans who in turn depended on Moscow. The regime was still challenged by domestic Communists and Yenan Korean Communists. The period after 1948 in North Korea, therefore, like that in the South, was to involve a continued struggle for the consolidation of political power.

Chapter IV

ATTEMPTED INTRODUCTION OF THE FIRST REPU
IN SOUTH KOREA, 1948–1960

From August 15, 1948, until his resignation on April 26, 1960, Syngman Rhee sought to establish a political system in South Korea consciously patterned after that of the United States. Although his sincerity in this regard may be, and has been, called into question (especially in view of the patent violations, during his administration, of political procedures considered normal in the United States), it appears evident from the events which occurred during this period that Rhee actually thought himself to be pursuing this objective. On the other hand, members of the Democratic Party sought to introduce a parliamentary form of government, patterned after European systems. The bitter struggle between the two forces ultimately resulted in the collapse of Rhee's efforts, and the rise to power of the Democratic Party in 1960 in the short-lived Second Republic. They in turn yielded to the coup-makers of 1961.

Prior to 1948, Syngman Rhee had consolidated a very limited political base, which itself was poorly constructed, to support the form of system he advocated. Not only did the various groups composing this base support Rhee only for temporary, opportunistic reasons, but they were not so organized as to share his interest in constructing a system patterned after that of the United States. The domination of the society by a powerful bureaucracy, which controlled most of the economy, by a strong police force that had great *esprit de corps* and was virtually uncontrollable from outside its ranks, by youth corps groups which were equally independent and volatile, and by political organizations among which the strongest rested on a land-based elite, augured poorly for the introduction of a genuinely competitive, two-party democracy, which Rhee stated was his ultimate goal. Yet these were the only sources of support available to Syngman Rhee in 1948. His efforts over the next few years would be directed at maintaining these sources of support while creating other, alternative sources, more inclined to support his advocated system, and then using the latter to undermine the former. His efforts were to prove only partially successful, and the final result was failure to establish the system he sought to create, and the collapse of his consolidation efforts. Yet the period provides a dramatic example of an attempt by a masterful political manipulator to establish and consolidate a new political system in a society with very weak developmental bases.

Pre-Korean War Political Disintegration, 1948-1950

Between the granting of independence to the Republic of Korea on August 15, 1948, and the outbreak of the Korean War, on June 25, 1950, the political talents of the new South Korean political leader, Syngman Rhee, who turned 75 in 1950, were taxed to the fullest by efforts to simply maintain a minimum of political support to prevent the new government from collapsing. The coming of political independence was a signal to all sources of political support to scatter in opposing directions, defending their own political interests. The police, the youth groups, the bureaucracy, the various political organizations, and the sources of external (that is, American) support for the new regime had achieved the goal of preventing a Communist takeover, while the internal sources of support, in opposition to the external sources, had managed to realize the goal of an independent government. Having done so, the various groups no longer shared common purposes. Nor did any of them share with Syngman Rhee the desire to pattern a new political system after that of the United States, with the exception of American policy-makers who would influence any continuing American inputs, and who seriously disagreed with Syngman Rhee over the methods of achieving such a system within the context of the Korean political setting. The first political battle between these groups took place even before formal independence, between Rhee and certain of the political organizations in the new Korean National Assembly, over the writing of a constitution.

The most powerful group in the new assembly was the Korean Democratic Party (KDP). Although only 29 of the 198 member assembly[1] were elected under the official KDP label, it was estimated that as many as 80 were actually KDP members, although most had run as independents.[2] The 55 assembly members from Rhee's National Society and the six from the Racial Youth Corps accounted for only 61 sure votes in support of Rhee. Most of the remaining independents, as well as the 12 members of Kim Koo's Great Korea Youth Alliance, had been associated with the Korean Provisional Government (KPG) in China, and were not controlled by either Rhee or the KDP. Hence, there was essentially a three-way alignment within the assembly: 80 votes controlled by the KDP, 61 votes committed to Rhee, and 57 affiliated with the KPG group (or "Kopogo," as it was sometimes called).

When originally formed in 1945, the Korean Democratic Party had been composed of a broad membership base, encompassing both the gradualists and the liberal activists who had been expelled from the preparatory committee, as the Communist Party members had secured control of that organ. The American coalition effort in 1947, however, and the growth of violence and terrorism in the society, had driven out many of the more liberal members, and by 1948 the base of the party was the gradualist *Dong-A Ilbo* group and the absentee landholders and related industrialists who had joined with them to finance the organization and defend their mutual interests. The sponsor of the party, Kim Sŏng-su, was undeniably a man of great sincerity and integrity, and the efforts of the *Dong-A Ilbo* group to foster nationalism and build the internal strength of Korean society through gradualist means during the Japanese occupation had been most admirable. The composition of the KDP by 1948, however, rendered its goals extremely conservative, while the structure of the party was essentially that of a traditional faction group, bound together by familial, regional, economic, and friendship ties. As the strongest faction on the political scene, the KDP fully expected to have an opportunity to monopolize bureaucratic patronage and rule in the fashion that faction groups had done for centuries during the Yi dynasty. In their eyes, Syngman Rhee served as a convenient figurehead, much as had the traditional Yi monarch.

The KDP was not only the strongest group in the assembly, but also the most highly educated, since many of its members came from landlord and business backgrounds and had been able to afford the expense of a university education in Japan. The KDP opposed the introduction of the "presidential" political system suggested by Rhee, endorsing instead a parliamentary system. The reasons for supporting a parliamentary system were quite transparent: seeking the traditionally coveted government bureaucratic positions for themselves, KDP members of the assembly were prepared to support the system which would permit them to ascend from assembly membership to the bureaucracy as cabinet ministers and hence to monopolize the administrative system in traditional fashion, appointing other members of the faction and their retainers to bureaucratic posts. The KDP had a monopoly of lawyers available in Korea who could prepare the draft of a constitution, and for this reason it dominated the assembly's constitutional committee, and drafted a constitution for a parliamentary system. Rhee, displeased with the draft, refused to accept the position of president unless the committee would accept a compromise with his advocated presidential system. The committee yielded, and the constitution was altered in a one-night sitting.[3]

Rhee is quoted by one writer as explaining his role in the process:

There was another question which created a strong division of opinion. This was about the premier and the cabinet. Certain leaders of the Assembly who have high aspirations secretly advocated the idea of the premier being the head of the government. They were about to present a resolution to the Assembly to this effect when I learned of it and met with them. I explained that when England adopted its cabinet system, they had a king who could not be the executive head and whom they could not get rid of. But in Korea we have no king and there is no reason to create a president who would be outside of the government. The moment the Assembly voted against a premier the government would lose stability. Therefore, we should adopt the American system and insure stability at least for the duration of the presidential term of office. Overnight the committee changed its recommendation and decided to keep the premier in name, but to make him an assistant to the president, who will be the real executive head.[4]

The resulting compromise package was so ambiguous as to be unsatisfactory to both the KDP and Rhee. Both sides were under pressure, because the constitution had to be produced before the United States could grant Korea its independence.

In July 1948, shortly before independence, Rhee began the appointment of his cabinet, the first test of the new constitution. Under a parliamentary constitution, Rhee would be obliged to appoint a cabinet dominated by the same forces which dominated the National Assembly; under a presidential system, however, it would be the task of the president to appoint a cabinet committed to carrying out his own advocated policies. In this matter of cabinet appointments, the strength of the president's powers under the new constitution became evident; while the president himself was elected by the assembly, and the prime minister's appointment had to be confirmed by the assembly, the other cabinet appointments did not require legislative confirmation, contrary to the American presidential system.

Because their 80-member group constituted the largest bloc in the 198-member National Assembly, the Korean Democratic Party demanded of Rhee at least half of the ministries, including the post of prime minister.[5] Rhee, however, appointed only one KDP member to the cabinet. He explained in a letter to a friend that he had done so in order to maintain necessary external support, as well as because he felt that the KDP had anti-democratic tendencies. "Friendly outsiders," he explained, had advised that if many KDP "capitalists" were appointed to the cabinet, the Republic of Korea would not be recognized in the United Nations, because many countries would consider it too "right wing;"[6] and without U.N. recognition, the South Korean government could not hope to survive.[7]

The first clash between Rhee and the KDP came with the appointment of the prime minister, since the constitution required that the assembly confirm this appointment. Rhee selected Yi Yun-yŏng, a Christian activist from North Korea, who was vice chairman of the Christian-nationalist Chosŏn Democratic Party (CDP), which had been formed in North Korea under the leadership of Cho Man-sik. After Cho had been imprisoned by the Russians in January 1946, the CDP had moved its headquarters to Seoul, where it came to be a center of organization for northern refugees who fled south. The assembly rejected Rhee's appointment of Reverend Yi. Rhee explained his view of the confrontation over the appointment in a letter to a friend:

Dem. party insisted on Kim Sung Soo [Kim Sŏng-su], Kopogo on Tjo Sowang [Cho So-wang], Shin Iki [Shin Ik-hi] on himself and . . . many on Lee Pumsuk [Yi Pŏm-sŏk] . . . Local Chinese approached Kim Koo to see if he wishes to come in; but he . . . reserves his stand . . . The job of Premier is the beginning of the battle of the political machine. [I] did not want to pull either this way or that, because [I am] opposed to the machinery of N. Korea and of the Democratic Party. The last one is as vicious as it can be because money speaks. In the country the people are thru with them, and hope there will be a change to the other side. Rev. Lee [Yi] of the Chosen Democratic party was considered by many friendly outsiders as the best choice—because he represents the north which would be a help at Paris; he is no capitalist and would meet as little opposition as possible. In the meantime, the Democratic Party and Shin Iki [Shin Ik-hi], Lee Ghun Chun [Yi Chŏng-chon] and Tjo Sowang [Cho So-wang] tied up the Assembly with the plea, if our man is not elected vote against whoever is appointed, never mind who he is. The vote against Rev. Lee represents the two parties voting together because he is not "the party man." They did not unite in this vote, but the fact that Rev. Lee was the choice of neither combined their vote in the negative . . . Kim Sung Soo [Kim Sŏng-su] is the man [I] would really like to have, but his men close to him are bunched up in a "run or ruin" policy which is very much resented by the people in the country.[8]

Following the rejection of Reverend Yi, Rhee named Yi Pŏm-sŏk, head of the Racial Youth Corps, to the position of prime minister, having already selected him to serve as defense minister. Yi secured the necessary KDP backing for his approval by promising that eight members of the cabinet would be selected from the KDP, but Rhee refused to honor Yi's promise.[9] According to Yi, when he went to see Rhee about the appointments, the president indicated that he had already decided upon other persons, and that since it was a presidential system of government, it was not within the scope of the prime minister's concerns to consider cabinet appointments.[10]

Most of Rhee's appointments to the new cabinet were activists associated with the independence movement, and all of them had been educated abroad—four in the United States, two in Europe, two in Japan, one in China, and one in the Soviet Union. All had good educational backgrounds, and their qualifications seemed to fit the posts to which they had been appointed: the foreign minister, Chang T'aek-sang, had studied political science at the University of Edinburgh, Scotland, and had attended the Paris Peace Conference to plead on Korea's behalf in 1919. The minister of justice, Yi In, was a lawyer, educated in Japan, who had provided legal defense for the nationalists during the Japanese occupation, and had served a prison term for nationalist activities. The minister of finance, Kim Do-yun, the only member of the KDP appointed to the cabinet, had received a Ph.D. in economics from American University in Washington, D.C., while the minister of the interior, Yun Chi-yŏng, had an American legal education and was a long-time Rhee supporter. Yi Pŏm-sŏk, the minister of defense and Rhee's compromise choice for prime minister, had graduated from Whampoa Military Academy in China, had been the head of the military unit which had operated under the Korean

Provisional Government, and was now the head of the powerful "Racial Youth Corps." The minister of agriculture, Cho Bong-am, was a graduate of Moscow University, and had been a member of the Communist Party while ardently advocating agrarian reform. An Ho-sang, the minister of education, had graduated from Jena University in Germany, and was a professor of philosophy at Seoul National University, while the social welfare minister, Chŏn Chin-han, a graduate of Waseda University in Japan, had headed the nationalist Taehan Labor Union. The minister of transportation, Min Hi-sik, was a graduate of the University of Nevada, and had served as director of transportation for three years under the American Military Government. The most controversial of Rhee's appointments was that of Miss Louise Yim, head of the Women's Democratic Party, as minister of commerce. American-educated and experienced in fund-raising activities in the United States for the nationalist cause and for Korean educational institutions, Rhee told her that because of this experience she could be helpful in promoting American investment in Korea to help boost the economy.[11] He told a friend that the main reason for appointing her was to set the precedent of having a woman in the first cabinet.[12]

The cabinet appointments were designed in part to consolidate sources of internal support, in part to consolidate sources of external support, and in part to allocate the scarce skilled manpower to government positions. To consolidate internal support, Rhee had appointed the leaders of the Racial Youth Corps, the Taehan Labor Union, and the Women's Democratic Party to the cabinet. The first two of these groups were politically more powerful in the society than any of the "political parties." To consolidate external support, Rhee had appointed Yi Pŏm-sŏk, who had demonstrated both in China and in Korea an ability to secure U.S. Army support and financing. The appointment of a Communist to the agriculture ministry and the attempted appointment of a North Korean nationalist to the prime minister's post were also aimed at international endorsement. The choice of appointees represented an effort to bestow both national and international legitimacy on the new regime: several of the appointees were famous nationalists, while the broad range of educational backgrounds abroad could obviously appeal to international supporters. At the same time, all of the individuals appeared to possess the requisite skills for their posts —at least as fully as any other personnel. Nonetheless, the gradualists' *Dong-A Ilbo* newspaper strongly criticized the appointments as "very poorly qualified," and the U.N. report on the new government repeated this as a general observation of Korean political participants.[13]

The KDP was not the only group dissatisfied with the cabinet appointments. The KPG group in the assembly also protested the absence of representation of their membership. Together, the two groups formed a joint opposition in February 1949, only seven months after independence, taking the name the Democratic Nationalist Party (DNP).[14] Rhee's new opposition encompassed slightly more than two-thirds of the National Assembly—a sufficient number to amend the constitution and make Rhee a figurehead president with no political powers. Before attempting such an amendment, however, the new opposition struck at the president's sources of support in the bureaucracy and the police.

In September 1948, the assembly passed the National Traitors' Law, designed to arrest, try, and punish those charged with collaboration with the Japanese.[15] Because much of Rhee's remaining support came from persons in the bureaucracy and police who could be encompassed in the term "collaborator," this was one means of decimating Rhee's power base. The law also served to identify Rhee with the "collaborators" in the bureaucracy and the police force which he had inherited from the American Military Government. Rhee could neither veto the legislation nor enforce it, for to veto it would be to support "collaborators," and to enforce it would require the cooperation of the bureaucracy and the police, against whom it was aimed. The assembly therefore established its own courts, investigators, prosecutors, and even special police force, to implement the legislation.[16] As the assembly's special committee began to carry out its program of arrests, investigations, trials, and imposition of prison sentences, the police

became increasingly restive, and after several months began to
retaliate by first arresting six national assemblymen (who were
constitutionally immune from arrest), on charges of "communism."[17]
Not long thereafter, they smashed into the headquarters of the
assembly's "special committee" and attacked the "special police."
To resolve the crisis, Rhee issued an executive order under his
constitutional emergency powers, dissolving the assembly's police
force, and the attempt to purge the police and bureaucracy came
to an end on February 16, 1950.[18]

The second step which the opposition took to undermine
Rhee's position was to try to amend the constitution to reinstate
the DNP-advocated parliamentary system. Rhee wanted a separate
executive, they argued, so that he could be a "dictator." Through
its control over the most prestigious newspaper outlets, the DNP
publicized its advocated parliamentary system as "anti-dictatorial."[19]
The government sought to dissuade assemblymen from voting for
the parliamentary amendments, but when the vote approached
with no sign of retreat by the assemblymen, administration de-
fenses were made ready. The home minister ordered the police
force to stand by, to "take action whenever the President issues
the order," and the cabinet instructed the bureaucracy to oppose
the amendments by any means within its power.[20] By executive
order, Rhee merged all existing "youth groups" into one, under
Yi Pŏm-sŏk.[21] Demonstrations against the proposed constitutional
changes were staged, largely at the initiative of Yi Pŏm-sŏk's Youth
Corps. The amendments failed, on March 14, 1950, by the abstention of 66 assemblymen (slightly more than one-third, and five
more than Rhee's usual voting bloc) partly because of the intimidation of Yi's "toughs."[22]

Rhee had come to power with the financial assistance of the
KDP landowners (now in the DNP), but his new position forced
him to dispense with their support. The provisions of the Korean
constitution gave the government a monopoly in many major
industries and in all utilities, but output was small, and all appropriations of the government were the responsibility of the assembly.
DNP members were not eager to provide financial resources for a

bureaucracy which they did not control. They had approved, even advocated, the government's economic monopolies as provided for in the constitution, under the assumption that the bureaucratic economic empire was to come under their own control. Rhee was reluctant to increase taxes in order to augment the government's resources, for in doing so he would increase the resources over which the hostile assembly could extend its supervision.[24] One observer estimated that probably as much as half of the national revenues actually came from the "voluntary" collections which the Youth Corps extracted from the populace, and over which the assembly thus had no control.[25] The police also continued their collection of funds for the "police protective associations," avoiding submitting control over their expenditures to the hostile assembly.

Following the failure of the DNP to undermine his support by purging the police and the bureaucracy or by changing the constitution, Rhee moved to counterattack in an effort to undermine the resources of the DNP. An obvious means of reducing their financial resources would be land reform. Redistribution of landholdings would not only decrease the financial resources of the DNP, but it would also undercut their political bases in local areas, for it was the economic role of the landlords in the provinces which carried with it political persuasion that could be felt at the local level. Landowners, however, controlled the National Assembly, and were unlikely to support a bill whose objective was their own political and financial destruction. In order to secure the objective of undermining their political base, Rhee temporarily ignored the task of destroying their financial resources. The land reform bill which was introduced to the assembly with Rhee's blessing was so financially attractive that the landlords readily voted it through: a good price for the land was guaranteed by the government, to be paid in government bonds which were immediately acceptable in payment for the purchase of the industries formerly owned by the Japanese.[26] Lured by the chance to convert their agricultural holdings into lucrative industrial holdings, landowners joined in support for the bill, not realizing that they were voting away their local bases of control which had enabled them to dominate the assembly in the 1948 election. The land reform bill passed the assembly on February 2, 1950, and was signed by the president.[27]

The collision between Rhee and the DNP was only one of the many challenges to his political base during the period between 1948 and 1950. While the South Korean police force firmly supported the administration (persuaded that either a takeover by the Communists or by the opposition DNP would mean its own purge), the position of the army was less certain. The army, like the police force, had been created by the American Military Government, but unlike the police force, it had not been drawn from a single pre-existing political base, and hence did not possess the unity and *esprit* of the police. Members of the army included not only those previously trained in Japanese military academies, but also returnees from China and Manchuria, as well as many others with no previous military experience. The uncertainty of the army's commitment became evident when, in October 1948, a Communist-instigated rebellion within the army occurred at Yosu, in southern Korea.[28] The police, acting primarily out of fear, were harsh in retaliation not only against the dissident rebels, but also against persons suspected of being sympathetic to the rebel cause. If the rebels were cruel—and reports came in from the villages that landlords, police, and Christians had been tied together and summarily executed[29]—the response of the police matched their zeal. The number of persons arrested ran into the thousands; many were executed. One group treated with little tolerance were the intellectuals, whom the police considered sympathetic to the rebellion, and student committees were ordered established in all schools to report on deviant outlooks of teachers and students.[30] While the harsh police tactics were attributed by some outside observers to the personal predilections of Syngman Rhee, in fact the administration had little means of effective control over either its army or its police force, who turned against each other. The rebellion was at length brought under control by loyal army forces, but guerrillas remained scattered in the countryside.

Another threat to the Rhee government followed close on

the heels of the army rebellion. On June 26, 1949, Kim Koo was assassinated by an army officer, one of his subordinates in the Great Korea Youth Alliance, who gave as his reason, "He was planning to use part of the Korean Army for his own purposes."[31] It was reported that Kim Koo had been planning his third coup attempt. Many people attributed the assassination of Kim Koo to Syngman Rhee, as Kim's most obvious rival. Up to that time Rhee had been extremely cautious in attempting to utilize Kim Koo's claims to legitimacy in the independence movement to strengthen the new government and had even approached him for the post of prime minister. Without a strong organizational base, Kim Koo could not have posed a serious threat to Rhee through the electoral process. Only through a coup d'état could Kim have been successful in unseating Rhee. In commenting upon Kim Koo's death, the President called him a "great patriot," but indicated that Kim had been involved in undesirable activities which the government would not reveal, for it would be unfitting to denigrate a dead national hero. Kim was given a state funeral, which Rhee pointedly did not attend. Kim Koo's assassin was imprisoned, but quietly released and reinstated in the army several years later.[32]

Not only were Rhee's internal political bases disintegrating, but his sources of external support were becoming increasingly uncertain. Very much in need of both economic and military backing from the United States in order to maintain the government and resist initiatives from the North, Rhee became increasingly concerned over the fact that American aid was rapidly being phased out. During the two years of South Korea's independence prior to the Korean War, the United States and the South Korean government were continually at odds over economic policy. Because American policy focused primarily on promoting economic stability, economics was the realm of particular American concern.[33] Before turning its economic assets over to the new Republic of Korea government, the AMG had sought special arrangements to continue its supervision of Korean government expenditures, in view of the fact that South Korea would be receiving U.S. economic assistance. The formula settled upon was that of having a

minister of supply within the Korean government, whose appointment would be made on the recommendation of the United States,
and who would be responsible for all government purchasing and
distribution of goods.[34] Rhee at first refused this arrangement,
but when the United States made it clear that it would not transfer
the government assets to the new Republic of Korea government
until such an agreement had been reached, he gave in. Within a
few months the government had jailed the unwanted minister on
a trumped-up charge of corruption.[35]

Rhee's wish to avoid American financial control had at least
one simple motive: under American supervision, the essential
political expenditures needed to keep the government in power
would be difficult to arrange, for the constitution placed financial
responsibilities under the National Assembly, whose members were
seeking to undercut the power of the administration and to change
the constitutional system. Without American control, the bureaucracy could continue its financial independence by the system
established during the period of the American Military Government.
Under the AMG, the bureaucracy had apparently earned large
profits through the sale of aid goods from the United States, and
then used these funds to finance the efforts of the nationalists to
gain independence.

American policy-makers were highly critical of Rhee's unwillingness to increase taxes as a means of controlling the inflation
which had begun under the AMG period of rule and which continued
to spiral.[36] U.S. observers were generally unaware of, or discounted,
the large scale extralegal taxation entering government coffers
through the Youth Corps and police. American advisers, for instance,
were exasperated with the defense minister, Yi Pŏm-sŏk (who also
headed the Youth Corps), because he displayed a total lack of
"economic know-how" by spending several times more on defense
than the assembly had budgeted.[37] Rhee's stock response to protests by American economic advisers, according to one of them,
was, "You're just economists! You don't understand politics!"[38]
Rice prices continued to increase following the independence of
the ROK, for in the first year the Ministry of Agriculture, under

its former Communist minister, failed to collect more than 30 percent of the government rice quota required to feed the cities.[39] The rising rice prices, combined with news of growing guerrilla activity in the countryside and rumors of a coming northern invasion,[40] produced hoarding behavior which swelled inflation further.

Attributing the increasing inflation to the personal obstinacy of Syngman Rhee in refusing to accept American advice to increase taxes, the U.S. secretary of state, Dean Acheson, wrote a letter in early 1950 rebuking the South Korean president and admonishing Rhee that unless taxes were increased and government expenditures decreased, the United States would have to "re-examine, and perhaps make adjustments in," the aid program to Korea.[41] This communication was also concerned with another aspect of Rhee's battle with the DNP in the assembly; when the latter refused to approve any budget, Rhee threatened to delay assembly elections and keep the assembly in session until a budget was passed. The American secretary of state reprimanded him for this action, insisting that economic and military aid from the United States to South Korea was based on the "existence and growth of democratic institutions in the Republic," and that this would mean holding elections on schedule according to the basic laws of the country.[42] Three days after receiving the note from Secretary Acheson, the home minister announced that elections would be held on May 30.[43]

Economic assistance from the United States was essential to the consolidation of the new government, as it permitted the government to maintain the salaries and essential expenses of government organs. Yet in January 1950, the Korean aid bill was defeated in the U.S. Congress,[44] and economic aid which had dropped from $179,593,000 in 1948 to $116,509,000 in 1949, plummeted to $58,706,000—half that of the previous year—in 1950.[45]

Rhee and the United States had a more serious disagreement over the question of American military assistance and a defense commitment to South Korea. American troops were withdrawn from Korea after the ROK was granted its independence, leaving a constabulary force of 97,000 which became the Korean army, with equipment for about half that number. When Rhee asked whether the United States would assist in South Korea's defense, he was told that the United States wanted only to assist economic recovery and insure internal stability.[46] Requests for heavy military equipment were not answered. Finally, in January 1950, U.S. Secretary of State Dean Acheson defined the American defense perimeter with an obvious omission of South Korea.[47]

By the time the Korean War began, the political bases of the Rhee government were in an advanced state of disintegration. Although Syngman Rhee had begun his first term with support from the gradualists and former members of the KPG, they had united against him within a few months of the inauguration of the new government. Rhee had secured the support of such organizations as the Youth Corps, the Taehan Labor Union, and the Women's Democratic Party, by appointing their heads to the cabinet, but it was not long before the cabinet itself had begun to fall apart. The social affairs minister, head of the Taehan Labor Union, resigned in December 1948, protesting the arrest of a youth group leader in his home.[48] He demanded that the home minister assume responsibility and resign as well. The home minister, a loyal Rhee supporter who had not succeeded in establishing control over the police, was not constitutionally required to accept responsibility. Nonetheless, the assembly quickly passed a resolution backing the demand of the social affairs minister and calling for the home minister's resignation. The home minister resigned, followed by the foreign minister, who had headed the Seoul police under the American Military Government.[49] Soon thereafter, the agriculture minister accepted responsibility for the failure to collect the grain harvest, and he resigned.[50] The defense minister, pressed to accept the responsibility for the rebellion in the army, over which he had not as yet established full control, submitted his resignation.[51] The minister of transportation was charged by the assembly with responsibility for the sinking of a Korean ship which had been in poor condition, and the minister of commerce was accused of misuse of funds,[52] and they resigned. Although the assembly did not have the constitutional power to force the resignation of cabinet ministers, the traditional requirement that government officials save "face" pressed the ministers to resign after the accusations against them were publicized in the gradualist-controlled press.

As political pressures overturned the cabinet one-by-one, Rhee's coalition rapidly fell apart. Outside of the Democratic Nationalist Party—the new opposition—few people of the level of talent or renown of the first cabinet remained who had not been publicly discredited during the AMG period. Individuals of lesser capabilities and relatively unknown backgrounds moved into the cabinet posts, giving greater credence to the DNP insistence that Rhee was not using the "best talent available" (that is, themselves). The United States joined those abandoning the sinking ship when, in January 1950, the Congress rejected the bill for economic assistance to Korea (some Congressmen argued against "pouring money down the Korean rat hole"), and the secretary of state clearly implied that the United States did not intend to defend the Republic of Korea. North Korea invaded the South on June 25, 1950.

The United States had helped the Rhee government to remain in power, but also made demands upon the government in exchange for such support. If these demands had been carried out, they would have undercut Korea's internal resources and furthered its dependence upon the United States. In general, U.S. demands were for increased legal taxation (as opposed to the extralegal taxation through the police and the Youth Corps), which would have augmented the power of Rhee's assembly opposition; decreased government expenditures, which would have reduced the resources to the bureaucracy, Rhee's most important source of political support; accession to assembly demands (for example, in the scheduling of the election), thus yielding to Rhee's assembly opposition; reduction of defense expenditures, which would have reduced his already uncertain army support; and reduction of the arbitrary power of the police, which Rhee did not effectively control, and whose opposition he could not afford and still remain in power. In short, the United States, though unaware of the implications of its demands, sought to make the price of its external support the destruction of Rhee's internal bases of support. Rhee refused to accede to these demands, and American support was in the process of being phased out, when the outbreak of the Korean War reversed the process of disintegration of the government of the Republic of Korea.

When the Korean War broke out, the South Korean political system, under the leadership of Syngman Rhee, was in an advanced state of political disintegration, its initially weak political bases nearing internal collapse. It was North Korea's decision to unite the country by force under a Communist system which renewed the sources of support to the new government and permitted a new and much more effective consolidation of political power under Syngman Rhee.

Wartime and Postwar Reconsolidation, 1950-1956

Syngman Rhee was, above all else, a student of international politics. From his early twenties, when he had protested against the employment of Russian advisers by the Korean court as an impingement on national sovereignty, through his years of appeals to international tribunals and to international opinion in support of Korean independence, his primary efforts had been directed toward the international arena. Even while consolidating his base at home after 1945, Syngman Rhee had continued to concentrate his attention on international legitimation of and support for the new Republic of Korea. He had fully endorsed and welcomed the U.N.-sponsored elections in South Korea, even though it led to a split with Kim Koo, whose support was needed to boost domestic legitimation. He had then sought to form a cabinet which would help secure U.N. recognition and international support, though it meant sacrificing an important source of his internal support—the Korean Democratic Party. The high value he placed on such international endorsement was an important gamble on the vicissitudes of international politics which few inside Korea could understand. Having secured international endorsement of his regime through

U.N. recognition, he proved to have anticipated events with some accuracy when the Korean War broke out.

The United States had built its postwar policy on two pillars —support for the United Nations and containment of Soviet-sponsored communism. The North Korean attack in June 1950 was a direct challenge to both, for Syngman Rhee had succeeded in tying the survival of his government to both essentials of American foreign policy. The United States could not afford to allow the U.N.-endorsed Republic of Korea to collapse without seeing both of the basic policy guidelines, one or the other of which was supported by a broad political spectrum in the United States, become meaningless. Inputs from the United States immediately returned to back up the reconsolidation of the South Korean political system, ultimately allowing Rhee to build a new political base. Rhee's efforts during the period from mid-1950 to 1956 almost succeeded in permitting his regime to consolidate a base for the system he advocated.

Perhaps the most important factor in renewing the strength of the Rhee government during the war was the growth of the Korean army. Rhee had little control over the recruitment and expansion of the army, which, like the bureaucracy and police force on which he had come to rely, was constructed by Americans.[53] Under United Nations command, the army was even less "his" than the other organs of government; however, as with the bureaucracy and police before it, Rhee found a way to secure effective control over the army, under the surface of overt American command. Syngman Rhee at first requested that the United States take the Youth Corps, which had grown to an estimated membership of 1,250,000,[54] into the army, knowing that this large and disciplined group would be loyal to his government. However, it was precisely because of this political loyalty to Rhee's government that the United States refused the request. President Truman later explained: "The ROK government had consistently urged that it be given weapons for its various youth groups. I had indicated to the Joint Chiefs of Staff that I would not agree to our arming what amounted to political units."[55] The United States considered it essential that the armed forces *not* be politically subordinate to Rhee.

Rhee did manage to control the high-level officers, however, by encouraging the leaders of the different factions in the army to compete for the major positions, so that they could secure appointments for their retainers. Quite naturally, the groups in the army, like the groups in the National Assembly, had formed into competing political factions. Since most of the officers were of North Korean origin, the factions in the army divided largely between those from northwest Korea, and those from the northeast. Part of the attraction of the chief of staff position was the ability to control vast sums of money coming in in the form of American military assistance. American surveillance could never effectively control the leakage to the factions, for supplies could be sold on the black market to line the pockets of the factions.[56] To retain the loyalty of the army, the government was intentionally lax in prosecuting offenders.[57] An army investigative agency, directly under the office of the president, was created to keep a check on the top officers, whose corrupt activities were overlooked until they either got out of hand, to the extent that they might damage the war effort, or until the officer showed signs of wavering in his support for Rhee. Then, the head of the investigative agency, Kim Chang-yŏng, who reported directly to Rhee, would move in and secure the removal of the officer, for enough evidence would have been accumulated of the officer's corrupt practices to bring about his dismissal.[58] Besides this system of control, Rhee maintained a charismatic influence over the rank and file of the army. General Van Fleet commented that Rhee was "worth his weight in diamonds" in his ability to inspire the men to fight.[59]

The army gave Rhee both a new organizational base of support, and a new source of funds. Rhee's generosity in permitting corruption among his officers was in proportion to their willingness to channel some of the diverted military aid money to his efforts at political organization.[60] For the first time, Rhee had a large source of political financing independent of the wealthy

DNP gradualists. The political collections from the populace by the Youth Corps and police, which had not only made them unpopular, but which had rendered them independent of Rhee's control, could be dispensed with. At length, in 1953, with the army serving as a strong counterbalance to the police, the president made a public announcement condemning the police for making unauthorized collections from the populace.[61] This action could not have been taken had the president not been able to check the actions of the police by consolidating control over the local levels of government. Such a consolidation was possible during the war because the new source of funds from the army permitted him to create a political party capable of consolidating control at the local level.

The second elections to the National Assembly were held on May 30, 1950, before the outbreak of the war. These elections returned fewer members of the DNP, as well as fewer members of Rhee's National Society, than the first assembly, both organizations having declined during two years of political disintegration.[62] A large majority of the new assemblymen were independents, though once again many of them were landowners associated with the DNP, as the land reform had not yet been implemented. Both Rhee and the DNP set out to win the support of genuinely unaffiliated members. In order to secure the backing of members of the assembly, Rhee began the construction of a new political party, financed by the diverted army funds. The party was given the name "Liberal Party" (Chayudang), in an effort to distinguish it from the conservative DNP, dominated as it still was by a relatively wealthy, tradition-oriented elite. By early 1952, ninety-three members of the National Assembly had been persuaded to join the Liberal Party.[63] Outside of the assembly, an organizational base was formed by combining Yi Pŏm-sŏk's Youth Corps with the remnants of Rhee's National Society and its affiliated organizations. Other political aspirants joined the party, as did some former DNP members who found the DNP dominated by wealthier interests with which they could not hope to compete for control.[64] To Rhee's dismay, however, the new members of the Liberal

Party in the National Assembly refused, almost to a man, to endorse his advocated form of government. Instead, they insisted on a parliamentary government in which they would be able to assure their own appointment to cabinet posts. The members of the Liberal Party outside the assembly, on the other hand, were willing to follow the instructions of the party leadership. The result was the split of the party into two "factions," the "inside party" (wŏnae chayudang) and the "outside party" (wŏnoë chayudang), competing for hegemony in traditional fashion. The outer faction was dominated by the Youth Corps element under the leadership of Yi Pŏm-sŏk.

In February 1952, nation-wide elections were held in South Korea to establish, for the first time, elected local governments, creating local political assemblies. Yi Pŏm-sŏk, the head of the Youth Corps, which was now a part of the Liberal Party, was appointed to the post of home minister before the elections, giving him authority over the national police force.[65] Both factions of the Liberal Party, as well as the DNP and some minority organizations, put up candidates, but by this time land reform had been carried out weakening the DNP's hold on the countryside, and the "outer" Liberal Party, nationally organized and indirectly financed from government sources, easily won control throughout most of the countryside. For the first time since the initial consolidation of his National Society in 1946, which had largely disintegrated in 1947 under AMG opposition, Rhee had a strong organized base of political support at the local level.[66] The Youth Corps element of the Liberal Party was able to carry the election not only because of its strong organization, and its even more important government funding, but also because of the support of the local police, who acted as communicators in publicizing the party, as well as hampering the electioneering of opposing groups. With a nation-wide system of telegraphic communication, and nation-wide organization, the police were easily able to inform the populace that the president wished them to vote for the Liberal Party candidates.[67] In most areas, the reported endorsement of candidates by Syngman Rhee was an important factor in carrying the Liberal Party to victory.

Although the president had finally managed to create a political party with local roots, he still had no control over the National Assembly, which remained hostile. This was a critical situation, for according to the constitution Rhee's first term of office was to expire in 1952, and the assembly was to elect the new president. It was clear that he would not be their choice, for he was the only obstacle preventing their securing control over the vast patronage system of the bureaucracy. With this in mind, Rhee began to prepare to introduce an amendment to the constitution which would permit the populace at large to elect the president.

The constitution could be amended, according to the 1948 political compromise, embedded in Article 98 of the constitution, only by a two-thirds vote of the National Assembly. On November 30, 1951, therefore, the president sent his amendment for popular election of the president to the assembly. As everyone expected, it came back on January 18, 1952, with a resounding defeat: 143 against to 19 in favor, with one abstention.[68] In response, the assembly reintroduced its own amendments for a parliamentary system, and the vote on these amendments fell just short of receiving the necessary two-thirds majority.[69]

In May 1952, the president re-introduced his amendments, with a number of concessions to the parliamentary advocates included. On this occasion, he brought all of his political cards into play. The Liberal Party, in virtual control of local governments throughout the countryside, began stirring up popular support for Rhee's amendments. Petitions of support for the "right of the people" to elect their own president began pouring in from the local assemblies all over the country.[70] Popular demonstrations, apparently organized by the Youth Corps, were stirred up in Pusan, the temporary wartime capital, surrounding the building where the National Assembly was meeting, and demanding that it grant to the people the right to select the president.[71] The bureaucracy assisted by making sure that shops and schools were closed to allow for the demonstrations. The police arrested several assemblymen, ignoring their immunity, charging that they had accepted bribes from the Communists.[72] As the demonstrations

began to get out of order, the army used the excuse to declare
martial law in Pusan, and, in an obvious attempt at intimidation,
forty-seven assemblymen on a bus were "detained" by the army for
refusing to show their identifications.[73] At length, on the order of
Home Minister Yi Pŏm-sŏk, the Youth Corps chief, the police
rounded up the uncooperative assemblymen—many of whom had
to be scouted out of hiding places—and herded them to the
assembly, where they were held until they obligingly voted through
the president's amendments.[74] These amendments were passed,
however, with the inclusion of Rhee's concessions to the DNP.
The assembly was given the power to approve or reject all cabinet
appointments, the position of prime minister was retained (Rhee
had wanted to eliminate it), and the president was obliged, under
the new amendments, to accept the suggestions of the prime
minister in making cabinet appointments.[75]

The events of 1952, leading to the amendment to permit
Rhee to be elected by popular vote, were received with bitterness
both in Korea and internationally because of the heavy-handed use
of the Korean police force by the Youth Corps leader and home
minister, Yi Pŏm-sŏk. By and large both Korean and foreign observers shared the illusion that Rhee fully controlled the actions
of his subordinates, an illusion actively promoted by those beneath
him who wished thereby to legitimize their actions. Yet one fact
that must be taken into consideration in evaluating the role of Yi
Pŏm-sŏk during this period, however, is that it was he who had
built and controlled the powerful Youth Corps, and Rhee was
dependent upon him for support, rather than vice-versa, for Rhee
himself did not have direct control over his political base. It was
in the interest of Yi Pŏm-sŏk, as much as of Syngman Rhee, to
secure the passage of the constitutional amendments, for it was
the aim of the Youth Corps leader to gain the vice presidential
nomination of the party he controlled, and hence to insure his own
election riding on the coattails of the national leader. This would
make him the annointed successor in the event that the 77-year
old leader should die before the next election in 1956.[76]

Having succeeded in securing the amendment permitting a

popular-vote election of the president, Rhee was easily returned to office for a second term, carrying 74.6 percent of the popular vote.[77] The DNP did not even attempt to run a candidate against him, aware that it would be a waste of its political funds. His only serious challenger was his first minister of agriculture, Cho Bong-am, who received 797,504 votes, as against 5,238,769 for Syngman Rhee.[78] The big surprise of the election, however, was the vice presidential contest. The Liberal Party, still dominated by the Youth Corps, was largely controlled by Yi Pŏm-sŏk, and while it nominated Rhee for president, Yi was given the vice presidential nomination.[79] Apparently concerned over Yi's independent power base, and embarrassed by the international uproar which followed Yi's use of the police to secure passage of the constitutional amendments, Rhee refused to endorse him. Rhee instead removed Yi from the post of home minister, and began to disassociate himself from the youth group leader. A week before the election, Rhee chose to endorse an unannounced candidate, Reverend Hahm Tae-yŏng, a North Korean Christian minister older than Rhee himself, who had played an important role in organizing the 1919 uprising.[80] In choosing one older than himself, Rhee was clearly avoiding choosing a successor. With the endorsement of Syngman Rhee, Reverend Hahm was elected, receiving 2,943,813 votes out of 7,133,297 cast.[81] Yi Pŏm-sŏk received 1,815,692.[82]

A foreign correspondent in Korea, observing the elections, aptly explained the power that Rhee exerted over the electorate:

> Without speeches, without campaigning and without acknowledging the party that nominated him, President Syngman Rhee swept South Korea this week in its first Presidential election by direct popular vote.
>
> When the final returns are in the iron-fisted leader is expected to have about 70 percent of the secret ballots and while there seems to be good reason for believing that the police did some last-minute proselytizing, observers who watched the voting are generally convinced that the secret ballot was preserved.

. . . The most important fact for South Korean voters is that even today, seven years after this country obtained its freedom from the Japanese, only one name and one face is known in every bamboo backyard and paddy clearing— Syngman Rhee's.

The South Koreans have taken orders for centuries and when they go down into town and pick up word that a particular candidate is the "proper" man to get their vote they file obedient ballots. In this election it has been charged, and with good reason apparently, that the police—acting upon directions from the Home Minister . . . spread the word that Ham Tai Yong, a 78 year old unknown and unambitious candidate for vice president was the best man for the job. He got it.

One neat trick adopted to get word across to South Korean voters on the "right" selection is for the polling official, acting upon suggestions of the police, to put his finger on the name of the preferred candidate as he slips the ballot across the table. Most of the voters catch on and obey.

This does not mean police pressure in the Western sense, but rather police guidance and direction on "authority." The tremendous turnout of voters is another good indication of how respected authority works.

No one was surprised at the enormous vote given to President Rhee—"That is the way it must be"—and if no one knew the new vice president it made no difference. Nobody knows who is "the government" anyhow, except, of course, for President Syngman Rhee.[83]

Rhee's political machine was now operating effectively. Working through a secret ballot, however, it could not have done so had the voters at the local levels had serious reservations about the "rightness" of that "authority" to which they bowed. The presidency of Syngman Rhee rendered the system legitimate.

Following his re-election, Rhee's political efforts turned toward the assembly elections of 1954, when for the first time the Liberal Party would contest for seats in the National Assembly. His first task was the elimination of Yi Pŏm-sŏk's power within the party. This was done by first outlawing "youth groups" by presidential decree, hence eliminating the existence of the Youth Corps independent of the party. Then Rhee personally intervened to stack the central committee at the second national convention of the party in May 1953. The central committee, in turn, voted Yi out of his position as vice chairman of the party, condemning him and his followers for being "divisive activists."[84] Once Yi Pŏm-sŏk was eliminated from power within the party, Rhee maneuvered his personal friend Yi Ki-pung into the secondary leadership position.[85] Yi, an American-educated accountant and financial manager, could be trusted to handle the political funds being channeled into the party from the army and to allocate them according to political need. This dependability, combined with his unswerving loyalty to Rhee, made him indispensable to the president's goals, and to the operation of the nation-wide political party system.[86] The Liberal Party then experienced a weeding out as the followers of Yi Pŏm-sŏk were gradually removed from significant party posts between August 1952 and April 1954.[87]

The aim of the Liberal Party in the 1954 elections was to capture a two-thirds majority of the assembly, making possible new amendments to the constitution which would abolish all vestiges of the parliamentary system. The DNP, with a more effective press with which to influence the cities, but with political funds derived almost entirely from the private resources of its members, could not match the Liberal Party's funds, or its police-communications network in the countryside. The Liberal Party carried the assembly elections by a margin just short of two-thirds majority.[88] Within a few days, enough independents were gathered into the Liberal fold to give it the required two-thirds majority, and the president's constitutional amendments were introduced.[89]

Rhee's amendments included the abolition of the position of prime minister and the substitution of a "secretary of state," as well as the abolition of all other elements of a parliamentary system embodied in the original constitution. They also provided for a revision of the economic clauses of the constitution, turning many of the government monopolies over to "free enterprise."

But the most publicized amendment was a provision that the first president, and only the first president, was not limited to two terms of office.[90] The amendments passed the assembly, but not without considerable controversy, for they received only 135 of the 203 votes, whereas an exact two-thirds majority required 135.3 votes. The speaker, assuming that two-thirds required 136 votes, at first declared the amendments defeated, and only at the next session did he reverse this decision, declaring that by rounding off to the nearest whole number only 135 votes were needed for passage, and therefore the amendments had carried.[91] Thus by 1954, Syngman Rhee had at length succeeded in consolidating his political position to the extent that the system of government he advocated could be embodied in a constitution.

Rhee's consolidation was, however, far from complete. His system of control over the army was ad hoc and vulnerable, while the source of financial inputs was temporary—American military aid could be expected to be sharply reduced at the close of the war. The Liberal Party organization was new and as yet far from well established. And the ideas that Rhee supported were far from widely understood and accepted.

Although Syngman Rhee had succeeded in pressing through the amendments to the constitution which would help to create the system he endorsed, opposition to this form of system remained strong. In 1955 members of Rhee's own party in the National Assembly became disillusioned when they found that they could not force the president to appoint them and their followers to the coveted bureaucratic positions. Several of them, angered by this discovery, abandoned the Liberal Party and merged with the DNP to form a new opposition party, the Democratic Party (Minjudang).[92] Although Rhee expressed pleasure that the formation of this new opposition would guarantee a two-party system, which he advocated, he was aware that the platform of the new party called for the establishment of a parliamentary political system.[93] Should the opposition succeed in gaining power, it would mean the collapse of Rhee's efforts to introduce a presidential system. The test of Rhee's strength against his new opposition came in the presidential–vice presidential elections of 1956.

In 1956, Syngman Rhee was 81 years of age. He ran for election to the presidency for a third term, endorsing as his vice president, Yi Ki-pung, the administrator of his Liberal Party, and hence annointing him as successor. Should Rhee die in office during his third term, an event generally expected, he would be succeeded by his vice president. If the vice president were the head of the Liberal Party, he could be counted on to continue to support the system Rhee had sought to introduce. If Rhee's vice presidential nominee were not elected, and the candidate of the Democratic Party should emerge as Rhee's probable successor, the result would be a total failure of Rhee's consolidation efforts up to that point. At Rhee's death, the Democratic Party would introduce its long-advocated parliamentary system, enabling it to parcel out bureaucratic patronage to faction members in traditional fashion. Syngman Rhee did everything possible to pass on his own mantle of legitimacy to the soft-spoken Yi Ki-pung, a member of the same Yi family as Rhee of the succeeding clan generation. Traditionally, had Rhee been monarch, Yi would have been an eligible successor by virtue of the family relationship. Rhee confirmed the tie by adopting Yi's son as his own.[94]

Rhee had failed to introduce one important provision of the American system, namely, the joint election of president and vice president from the same ticket. This failure proved fatal to his consolidation efforts. The newly-formed Democratic Party, now composed of the "old faction" members who had formerly constituted the DNP, and the "new faction" members who had recently joined the party, nominated as its candidates "old faction" member Shin Ik-hi for the presidency, and "new faction" member Chang Myŏn for the vice presidency. Shin Ik-hi (whose English name was Patrick Henry Shinicky) had been associated with the Korean Provisional Government in China, while Chang Myŏn (whose English name was John M. Chang), had been Syngman Rhee's first ambassador to the United States, and before that had been a member of an anti-Rhee group in the United States. When Shin suddenly died of a stroke at the height of the campaign, the vice presidential race became the focus of attention. Without a major opponent, Syngman Rhee won re-election to a third term, but the Democratic Party's vice presidential candidate, Chang Myŏn, a soft-spoken American-educated Catholic, defeated Rhee's annointed successor Yi Ki-pung by 4,012,654 votes to 3,805,502.[95]

Of all the opposition leaders Chang Myŏn was probably the most deeply disliked by Syngman Rhee. In 1952, during the controversy over Rhee's first round of amendments to permit the election of the president by direct popular vote, members of Rhee's opposition, outflanked by the president's maneuvering, sought support against Rhee from the U.S. Embassy.[96] The United States considered the request to intervene against Rhee, but turned it down on the grounds that it would be unwise to overturn the government during the war.[97] It is unclear what individuals made the approach to American authorities, but implications were that it was Chang Myŏn. For one thing, Chang, who had been ambassador to Washington, had been brought home by Rhee, in a compromise maneuver, to assume the post of prime minister—a gesture of conciliation to his opposition. In that position, Chang was destined to benefit most if Rhee failed to be re-elected and the assembly members then successfully introduced their parliamentary system, making the prime minister the head of government. Furthermore, Chang suddenly resigned and disappeared from public view, and the Rhee administration charged a number of assemblymen with involvement in a so-called "Communist conspiracy plot." Among those so charged were Chang's secretary and "one other person" whom the administration declined to name (perhaps Chang himself?), and Rhee claimed that these two persons were being shielded by the American ambassador.[98] Although the evidence is inconclusive, the implications were that it *was* Chang who had sought American intervention against Rhee, and that Rhee euphemistically termed it a "Communist conspiracy plot" because he could not charge the United States with intervention in Korea's internal affairs during the middle of the Korean War. Following the

1952 "political turmoil" as it was later called, Syngman Rhee was implacably hostile to Chang Myŏn, and while the precise cause was never pinpointed it was broadly accepted that the hostility was traceable to the events of 1952.[99] Rhee later told a friend that he could not countenance Chang because he was convinced that Chang would make Korea into a puppet of the United States.[100] It was the same Chang Myŏn who was elected to the post of vice president on the Democratic Party ballot in 1956—the apparent successor to the South Korean presidency.

An important factor in the election of Chang was the change in political behavior in the cities. This change was affected by rapid changes in urbanization and education, as well as by the expansion of communication within the cities and the great disruption of rural life caused by the Korean War. By 1955, 43.2 percent of the population were living in cities of over 20,000, as compared with only 27.5 percent in 1949.[101] The percentage of the population in cities over 50,000 and over 100,000 had increased from 18.3 percent and 14.7 percent to 34.5 percent and 28.8 percent, respectively.[102] Although the number of children in primary school had not increased markedly, the number in secondary school had more than tripled from 227,400 in 1947 to 733,185 in 1956 and students in higher education rose from 10,300 to 90,104 over the same period.[103] Furthermore, increases in the circulation of daily newspapers, primarily within urban areas, had been marked—from 381,300 in 1946 to 1,980,000 in 1955, reflecting the growth of urban areas as well as the expansion of education.[104]

The effects of mushrooming urbanization, expansion of education, and the growth of the urban press were quite clear in the 1956 elections. It was the very strong polling of Chang Myŏn in the cities which enabled him to decisively defeat Rhee's candidate, Yi Ki-pung.[105]

The resources of political tools in South Korea had quite clearly changed by 1956. The Youth Corps had been eliminated, and administrative control was being consolidated over the police. A very large army of 700,000 men[106] had been created, with reasonably effective control exercised by Syngman Rhee, despite the direct subordination of the army to American command under the U.N. forces. American aid had increased markedly during and following the Korean War, and these resources were channeled into the creation of a new political party destined to serve as an organizational source of support for the Rhee government. Rhee's opposition was still a traditional combination of elite faction groups, and observers referred to the system as a "one-and-a-half party system," reflecting the superficial organizational structure of the opposition DP, without a grass-roots organizational base.[107] At the same time, the very political ideas which Rhee had sought to introduce to support his new system were beginning to undermine his political consolidation, for so long as he was advocating "democracy" he was obviously subject to the charge that his efforts at political consolidation were not "democratic."

Additionally, South Korea was facing economic difficulties. The economy had suffered considerably during the war, with the gross national product (GNP) dropping 15.1 percent in 1950, and another 6.1 percent in 1951. Recovery began in 1952, with an 8 percent growth and was spurred on in 1953, with the end of the war, by a 25.7 percent increase. Yet the GNP growth rate after this period again began to decline; the rate was 5.2 percent in 1954, 4.0 percent in 1955, and 0.3 percent in 1956.[108] Inflation continued to be a serious problem. Prices had risen 33.3 percent in 1948 and 62.5 percent in 1949; during the war they shot up fantastically, 184.6 percent in 1950, 213.5 percent in 1951, and 101.7 percent in 1952. Inflation continued to plague the economy even with the close of the war, with prices increasing 26.4 percent, 51.0 percent, 42.9 percent, and 37.8 percent, respectively, over the next four years.[109] The greatest impact of these economic problems fell on the urban populace.

External inputs continued to be of major importance in South Korea, and as in the prewar period operated both to assist and to undermine the government's consolidation efforts. Only the American support of the Korean armed forces and the inflow of American military aid rescued the Rhee government from the disintegration spiral it had entered in the prewar period. Though the United

States and Rhee continued at odds over the distribution of financial resources, the abundance of American inputs enabled Rhee to secure control over enough funds to assist his consolidation. In fact, American aid rose rapidly throughout the period, from only $58,706,000 in 1950 to $106,542,000 in 1951, $161,327,000 in 1952, $194,170,000 in 1953, $153,925,000 in 1954, $236,707,000 in 1955, and $326,705,000 in 1956.[110] The input of American armed forces during the war, a total of 5,720,000 men (June 25, 1950-July 27, 1953), was essential to the survival of the regime.[111] Their presence allowed the Republic of Korea to maintain its existence independent of the Soviet-sponsored regime in the North.

The most damaging input from the United States, in terms of Rhee's consolidation attempts, was that of ideas. Paradoxically, while Rhee saw himself seeking to build a political base which would support a system patterned after the United States, his efforts brought a considerable amount of American criticism. Because the ideas which Rhee used were borrowed from American textbooks, he was particularly vulnerable to American criticism that the system he was seeking to introduce was undemocratic. The opposition took advantage of any American criticism of the government policies, by reprinting U.S. press attacks in its own newspapers. To a newspaper-reading urban populace, such criticism made it appear that Rhee's advocacy of a system patterned after the United States was simply a façade behind which he sought to operate a police state. Yi Pŏm-sŏk's use of the police force to press through the constitutional amendments in 1952, to permit popular election of the president, had aroused justifiable concern in the United States, leading to open criticism of Syngman Rhee by the president of the United States, who wrote expressing "shock."[112] Indeed, American disapproval of the actions of the Rhee government in 1952 had been so severe that the Korean Office of Information cut off Voice of America broadcasts into South Korea.[113]

Rhee was unable to reconcile ideologically the necessity of building a political base to support his advocated system, which also meant undermining the political bases of those who would oppose that system, with the operation of politics within the already established, ongoing political system of the United States. In the United States the "establishment" which supported the system was already sufficiently powerful to prevent the development of political bases which would support strong opposition to the system itself. Relying solely on American political theory, Rhee was unable to find any ideological justification for the actions of his regime. This ultimately led to the destruction of his consolidation efforts.

The Decline and Fall of the Rhee Government, 1956-1960

If the defeat of Rhee's annointed successor in the 1956 elections seemed to spell the doom of the consolidation efforts of Syngman Rhee, it did not discourage the octogenarian leader. In part, this was due to the stubborn personality of a man who had dedicated his entire life to a goal virtually everyone had considered an unrealistic dream. Rhee had reached the age of seventy in 1945, forty years after Korea had lost its independence, still believing in the possibility of genuine independence for Korea if the game of international politics were played with sufficient skill. Suddenly, he had seen that opportunity within his grasp during the period following the second world war. Now, Rhee was not prepared to admit or to accept the defeat of his political consolidation. Convinced that the reintroduction in Korea of a system which encouraged the full play of Korean factional bitterness would bring a repeat of the tragic end of the Yi dynasty, which he had witnessed in his youth, Rhee was determined to continue his efforts at consolidation during the period from 1956 to 1960. When he ran for a fourth term of office in 1960, in a second attempt to transfer his political mantle to Yi Ki-pung, he believed he had succeeded in consolidating his advocated political system. The 85-year old leader, by then increasingly senile, was unable to comprehend the sudden collapse of the political system he had built in Korea.

By 1956, the 81-year old Syngman Rhee had become increasingly a prisoner of his advancing age. Unable to be as active and mobile as he had been in his seventies, when he had stumped the Korean peninsula to build his first political base, the National Society, Rhee came increasingly to depend on information supplied to him by his subordinates. Out of these circumstances grew what came to be known as the "human curtain" surrounding the aging man, gradually removing him from the sources of information which would permit him to respond effectively to domestic developments.[114]

The conviction that a "human curtain" existed around the president became widespread in his last years in office, and was frequently referred to in the press as early as 1956. When a reporter questioned Rhee about it, Rhee retorted that it was opposition propaganda.[115] However, most reporters soon came to take it for granted. One journalist explained: "Before a press conference with the President, we had to submit a list of questions to his secretaries. Then we could only ask the questions which they had approved. One time a reporter asked one of the questions which had been scratched off the list. Later he was arrested on some charge and fired from the newspaper." [116]

As the Liberal Party began to develop vested interests in remaining in power, it devised means of protecting itself from presidential scrutiny. By 1958, it was obvious among informed persons that the president, 83 years old, was not aware of much of what was happening in the country. At a press conference in 1958, the *Dong-A Ilbo* newspaper reported that the president's office contained only copies of newspapers which supported the Liberal Party. No opposition, or even "neutral," newspapers were apparent. The president chided the opposition newspapers, saying that he heard that they were making "false reports," and added that if they wanted to increase their circulation to large volumes —say 100,000 or more—they would have to be more accurate in their reporting. At the time, the *Dong-A Ilbo* and the *Kyunghyang Shinmun*, the leading newspapers in the country, both of which were opposition papers, had circulations of 200,000 and 150,000 respectively. Journalists saw this as an illustration of the president's lack of information on the circumstances of the times.[117]

In the last few years of his administration, Rhee turned most of the work of government over to his subordinates, commenting that, "It is no longer necessary for me to oversee the details of the activities in each of the executive departments."[118] He expressed both pleasure and concern over the progress of the political system he had established, remaining convinced that the basic structure of the system was sound and that a change to a parliamentary form of system would be highly detrimental to Korea:

> The Constitution is the fundamental law of the land and as such has a high degree of permanence. Amendments should not be undertaken lightly, and in no event without sound reasons involving the welfare or security of the nation. Our system of government is largely based upon that of the United States. It is, in other words, the presidential system . . . At the outset of our self-governing, democratic experience, we experimented with a mixture of the presidential and cabinet systems. The experiment was interesting and worthwhile in the sense that we learned from it. What we learned is that the combination did not work too well. The presidential system has certain advantages, the cabinet system others, and both have liabilities. But it does not seem politically practical to integrate them.
>
> It seems to me that in the Korean situation of today, the presidential system is best suited to our governmental require-ments. In an old, long-established cabinet system such as that of Great Britain, governments may change rarely and in an orderly manner. But there seems to be a tendency toward instability among the cabinet systems of countries with less political experience. Even France, which scarcely can be accused of not having had a long democratic experience, has been compelled to depart from many of the elements of the pure cabinet system. I would be opposed to any Korean govern mental changes that would tend toward instability.[119]

Rhee expressed satisfaction with the emergence of a two-party system in South Korea, noting that:

Most political scientists are agreed that a two-party system
is democratically more effective than multi-party politics
. . . Multi-party systems sound very democratic in theory,
but do not seem to work out that way. The political situation
tends to become so chaotic that the voters have no real choice,
and legislation is impeded by the necessity for uneasy coali-
tions and the certainty of frequent changes in government . . .
the two-party system appears to be firmly established and
that is a tribute to the sagacity of Korean political understanding.[120]

Yet, because the opposition party was seeking to change the form
of the political system, rather than working within the framework
of a "loyal opposition," Rhee became concerned that the two
parties did not "complement" each other. "If the existing parties
fail to complement each other," he reportedly said in April 1958,
"we may have to form a new party."[121] Also, he noted with dissatisfaction developments within his own Liberal Party: "We are
informed that there is an extremist faction in the Liberal Party.
Their way of thinking is in contradiction to the principles of
democracy, and they tend to justify any undemocratic means or
methods, including the oppression of freedom, in the name of the
national interest."[122]

Political consolidation in 1956 was far from complete. While
the government had secured the backing of the armed forces and
maintained the support of the police, and had built an organizational
base in the Liberal Party as well as maintaining support of the bureaucracy, it had secured no permanent source of funds to support
the system. Diversions of United States military aid to the party
could only be temporary. Rhee set out to convert to a permanent
source of financing after the Korean War. The conversion involved
a two-step process. First, the inputs had to be transferred from
military aid to economic aid sources, for with the withdrawal of
many of the American troops the efficiency of the armed forces
could no longer afford to be threatened by economic corruption.
Furthermore, such military aid resources were obviously temporary.

Second, these aid resources would have to be used to build a permanent source of economic support in anticipation of the eventual termination of these externally-supplied funds.

The system of financing which developed in the post-Korean War period grew out of the U.S. economic aid program. Bids for commodities financed by American aid became restricted by government licensing practices to industries which would provide kickbacks to the Liberal Party, or to industries over which the LP had a controlling interest. By 1960, Yi Ki-pung, controller of the party, was estimated to have large interests in twenty-nine projects, and the party was believed to have a substantial interest in at least 50 percent·of all of the private projects receiving American aid.[123] The constitutional amendments Rhee had introduced in 1954, shifting government monopolies into the realm of free enterprise, helped in the construction of the Liberal Party financial empire. The kickback system became complex and extensive, pervading the entire economy. For example, in the 1956 presidential elections it was said that the Commerce Bank was pressured by the LP to loan 17 billion *hwan* to twelve industries which in turn handed the money to the Liberal Party for campaign funds. The same system was employed again in the 1958 assembly elections. Later the bank president was rewarded by becoming a member of the cabinet.[124] Seven of the companies which were said to have participated in the arrangements were as follows: [125]

Name of Company	Amount of loan	Contribution to party
T'aechang Textile	Hw 100 million	Hw 100 million
Chong'ang Commercial	670 "	50 "
Kumsŏng Textile	200 "	100 "
Sudo Film	200 "	100 "
Tongnip Commercial	700 "	120 "
Tongyang Cement	154 "	50 "
Chosŏn Textile	150 "	150 "

Another important element in the new financing system was the undervaluation of the official U.S. dollar-*hwan* exchange rate.

Because the dollar was undervalued, those firms which could secure the precious licenses permitting them to deal in matters involving foreign exchange could make a large profit by purchasing foreign goods at far below true market cost and selling them at a tremendous profit. The firms were quite willing to provide regular kickbacks to the Liberal Party in exchange for the licensing privilege.[126] This system, of course, undermined the efficiency of the economy, much as the earlier system had undermined the efficiency of the army. It did, however, provide the necessary financing for the now long-extended efforts at political consolidation.

As the system of financing was converted from military to economic aid inputs, the government began to close out the previous financing system. The president's army investigative committee, which had been intentionally lax during the war in supervising corruption in the army in order to secure funds for the party, began to tighten its control and clamp down on high-level military corruption. This followed the precedent established when the regime had transferred from police-financing to military financing and had begun to close out police collections from the populace. Promotion in the army came to be determined more and more by the approval of the president's investigative committee, which chose now to advance military personnel who had *not* been involved in flagrant corruption. Attempts were made to undermine the strength of the factions in the army by transferring military personnel around the country so that members of the same faction were separated.[127] Men who had previously been obliging in funneling funds into the Liberal Party found their careers caught short in some dead end, while those who had not been involved began to move up. The practice of appointing faction leaders to the position of chief of staff was brought to an end.[128] Neither in the earlier case of the police, nor in the present case of the military, was the government able to fully eliminate the pre-existing system of corruption, but it was evident that the system was being brought increasingly under government control.

The second stage of economic consolidation was more complex. While the conversion from military aid to economic aid inputs from the United States was essential, economic aid inputs could be no more permanent to back up the political system than were the military aid inputs. Since it was necessary to build a permanent source of funds, it was essential that the Liberal Party enterprises become more than a conduit for party funds; they would have to become independently economically viable and the economy they supported would have to become self-sufficient. If American aid should be withdrawn before a base of economic self-sufficiency were built, the system would collapse from the lack of internal financial resources. Indeed, the Korean economy did finally begin to move into a period of growth, reaching 7 and 8 percent GNP growth rates in 1957 and 1958, with inflation declining sharply over the same period.[129] This trend reversed quickly, however, in response to sharp cuts in U.S. aid in 1959 and 1960, following serious political disagreements with the Rhee government.

The fall of the Liberal Party regime could be said to have begun in 1955, when the Democratic Party opposition was formed including several defectors from the Liberal Party, or in 1956, when Chang Myŏn was elected vice president. Indeed, it would be impossible to pinpoint the origin of the "fall," for the regime had never fully succeeded in "rising" to the point of full consolidation.

When the Democratic Party had been founded in 1945, it rested financially on the landlord "class." Even when joined by a "new faction," the old blue-bloods maintained their hegemony over the party because it was they who brought in the necessary funds. Compared with Korea's *nouveau riche* Liberal Party plutocrats created by the new system of political financing, however, the resources of the Democratic Party now seemed paltry. Whereas the landowners had been induced to transfer their financial holdings from land to industry by the land reform provisions, the government's control over licensing, foreign exchange, and loan resources assured that the DP-supporters did not have a competitive position vis-a-vis the Liberal Party entrepreneurs. However, the election of Vice President Chang provided new inputs to the Democratic Party enabling it to contest Liberal Party control. Fearing that the president might die in office before 1960 and be succeeded by Chang, the Liberal Party enterprises began to channel covert funds to the Democratic Party as "insurance" in the event of a DP rise to power.[130] The very financial base that Rhee was building to support his system was also funneling inputs into the opposition which sought to alter the basic structure of that system.

Resentment in the army began to increase the tendency of military leaders to feel alienated from the Liberal Party government. Those who felt their factions being undermined by the new con- solidation of control over the army began to chafe, while those newly rising in the hierarchy still nursed resentments against the officers who had been involved in the old system of corruption. They disapproved of the fact that corrupt officers were not openly discredited and removed from army posts.[131] In 1958, a member of one of the factions feeling the squeeze from the army's investi- gative committee retaliated by assassinating Kim Chang-yŏng, the committee's head.[132] National Assembly investigations which fol- lowed uncovered a good deal of the system of corruption within the army, laying the blame upon the Liberal Party, and giving the Democratic Party ample ammunition to support its charges of corruption in the Rhee government.

As corruption in government was becoming a growing politi- cal issue, so, too, was the role of the police. By the mid-1950's, the Liberal Party had successfully consolidated its control over the national police. Once the Liberal Party had gained ascendancy in the assembly through the 1954 elections, the role of the police as communicators became quite apparent. After their election to the assembly, therefore, the Liberal Party assemblymen were quite conscious of the role the police in their districts had played in assuring their election, and were concerned that police friendly to them should remain in their posts. The Home Ministry was put under pressure to grant a form of "Senatorial courtesy" to the assemblymen who wished to oversee the appointment and removal of the police chiefs in their districts. The police chiefs from districts in which Liberals were defeated were replaced.[133] The police had initially been effective simply because they provided an effective means of *communication* to the population. This new system placed them under pressure to take positive action to assure the vote for the Liberal Party. Under this form of pressure, the police began undertaking efforts to coerce pro-government votes. The effort proved to be self-defeating.

Local elections in 1956 showed the extent to which the Liberal Party had consolidated its hold on the countryside. Opposition newspapers charged that so many opposition candidates had been forced by local police to cancel their registrations that 17 percent of the Liberals ran completely unopposed.[134] In these elections, the Liberal Party carried 74 percent of the vote, independents 23 percent, and opposition DP candidates only 2 percent.[135] The Liberal Party was unable to control the elections in the cities, however, and in Seoul the DP won 40 of the 47 seats on the municipal council, while only one Liberal was elected.[136]

The more the police became involved in the elections, the more critical became Korea's rapidly-expanding press. Although often irresponsible and sensationalist in its reporting, Korean journalism was quick to note and criticize the powers of the police. While those surrounding Rhee could prevent critical press reports from reaching the president, they could not stop his reading American newspapers, a habit he had continued from his residence in the United States, and the American press occasionally picked up stories from the Korean press. Due to fear of publicity in the American press, the police were highly restrained in attempts to clamp down on the big-city newspapers.

Of Korea's five biggest newspapers, three were "pro-opposition," and two "neutral." The two with the greatest circulation were the *Dong-A Ilbo*, with a circulation of 200,000, and the *Kyunghyang Shinmun*, with a circulation of 150,000, and both supported the opposition. The *Dong-A Ilbo*, Korea's oldest and most prestigious paper, founded by the gradualists in the 1920's, was the mouthpiece of the "old faction" DP, whereas the *Kyunghyang Shinmun*, then owned by a Catholic group, made no secret of its support for the Catholic vice president, Chang, of the "new faction" DP. Thus, while the police were partisan toward the Liberal Party, and controlled the countryside, the press was

equally partisan toward the Democratic Party, and held sway over
the cities. Recognizing this, a compromise election bill was passed
with the support of both parties before the 1958 elections to the
National Assembly, providing that the police would not intervene
in the elections in exchange for which the press was not to engage
in any partisan reporting of the campaign.[137] Neither the police
nor the press were pleased with the restrictions, and it was impossible to hold either to the commitment. The Korean press appealed
to international opinion and journalists' associations to pressure
the government to withdraw restrictions on political reporting as
contrary to "freedom of the press," and the police simply ignored
the law, thereby making it unenforceable.

As newspaper circulation and education expanded, the effectiveness of police efforts, even in the countryside, diminished. Education in Korea had grown phenomenally since the time of independence. A population survey of 1962 showed that the number of college
graduates in the country had increased from 22,064 in 1944 to
284,417, the number of middle and high school graduates had increased from 199,642 to 1,876,822 and the number of primary
school graduates had increased from 1,637,042 to 5,542,265.[138]
The number of illiterates had declined from 19,642,795 in 1944 to
1,833,146.[139] Students in school in 1960 numbered 4,429,900, as
compared with 1,461,000 in 1945.[140] Newspaper circulation had
reached nearly 2,000,000 in 1956, with 600 daily newspapers registered in South Korea in 1960.[141]

The original influence of the police rested on their role as the
communicators representing the wishes of respected authority. During the 1950's, however, the political awareness of the populace had
mushroomed. When the Liberal Party pressures on the police began
to require more positive means than "advice," to assure victory at the
polls, the police shifted to acts of intimidation, which weakened rather
than strengthened their influence over the outcome of the elections.

An important part of the new system of voter intimidation
was an organizational system, under the Home Ministry, known as
the *kungminban*, or "neighborhood people's association." Ostensibly, the neighborhood associations, to which all citizens were

required to belong, were designed to improve communications between the people and the government, and to identify Communist infiltrators.[142] However, they could well be used to identify and intimidate supporters of the opposition.

In 1958, elections to the National Assembly were again held and the Liberal Party set out to capture two-thirds of the seats in the assembly and introduce one more constitutional amendment— the joint-ticket election of president and vice president—to insure the succession from Syngman Rhee to Yi Ki-pung. It was when the LP *failed* to return a two-thirds majority of LP assemblymen to the assembly in 1958 that excessive abuses of LP power became commonplace, as the ruling party began to take drastic steps to insure the succession by some other means. Expelling opposition assemblymen from the assembly by force, Liberal Party assemblymen voted through a series of controversial bills which were ostensibly aimed at Communist infiltration, but which could be used to foster their own consolidation of power vis-à-vis the Democratic Party. One of these measures, the National Security Law, contained much-criticized press clauses, and another abolished the elective local offices, making the posts appointive instead.[143] Both moves could be interpreted as having been designed to help ensure the success of the Liberal Party in the upcoming presidential elections of 1960, in which Rhee was once again to try to pull LP leader Yi Ki-pung into the position of vice president, and successor, on his coattails.

American opinion became increasingly uneasy over developments in the Republic of Korea. The Rhee government seemed unwilling to respond to American advice to reduce the flagrant violations of the democratic code. Furthermore, American observers were aware of the corruption involved in the Rhee government's use of aid funds, though unaware of the underlying political causes of the diversions of funds. Rhee was unwilling to yield to pressure to decrease the size of the armed forces, following the withdrawal of Chinese forces from North Korea, or to alter the exchange rate to a more "realistic" level, to correspond to the market value, which American economists believed would be more stabilizing

for the Korean economy. These two sources of support—the army
and the exchange-rate profiteering—were still essential to the
stability of the regime. Conditions seemed to call for the United
States to take a stand vis-à-vis the developments in South Korea.
The *New York Times* noted in January, 1959:

> The U.S. Ambassador, Walter C. Dowling, left here today
> for Washington for consultation with State Department
> officials on South Korea's mounting political troubles. He
> was called home by the Department Wednesday. Observers
> believe reappraisal of relations between the United States and
> South Korea is bound to follow in the light of the reaction
> here and abroad to the new South Korean security law. The
> political Opposition and the press have vehemently charged
> the new law menaced freedom of the press and basic human
> rights. U.S. officials here have made no secret of their grave
> concern over public reaction should the anti-espionage and
> antisubversion law be used to silence press criticism of the
> Government and curtail the Opposition's political activities
> in the name of anti-Communist policy.[144]

The following day, a report of the crisis continued: "American
experts here say frankly that it 'looks like' Dr. Rhee's party is
attempting by these means to perpetuate its role. U.S. official
representatives are deeply concerned with the probable impression
abroad. 'We hate to see the ROK sacrifice the high standard of
democracy it has achieved,' one American said. 'This is not helping our common cause.'"[145] President Eisenhower underlined the
degree of concern in the American government by writing a letter
to Syngman Rhee expressing opposition to the developments in
Korea.[146] The role of the United States in Korea was seen as more
than sufficient cause for the United States to place the Korean
government under pressure.[147]

When the *Kyunghyang Shinmun* newspaper became the first
(and only one) to be closed down under the new security law, for
implying the need for violent revolution in Korea, the U.S.
ambassador issued a public statement criticizing the action:

"Suppression of the press is not a remedy for press errors," he reportedly said.[148] (Yet the American military government in Korea during 1945 to 1948 had set the precedent, by closing the Communist newspapers for advocating violence.) When both public and private criticism of the Rhee government, as well as critical economic advisory reports, failed to alter the policy of the South Korean government, the United States began to cut its economic aid, and made a unilateral change in the exchange rate.

In 1958, economic assistance was reduced from $382,893,000 in the previous year to $321,272,000. It fell sharply in 1959 to $222,204,000, nearly a $100,000,000 cut.[149] Immediately, the Korean economy went into decline. The economy had seen an 8.7 percent GNP growth rate in 1957. With the cut in U.S. aid, it declined to 7.0 percent in 1958 and then plunged to 5.2 percent in 1959.[150] Inflation, which had at last been brought under control, returned.[151] The price index had *decreased* by 0.6 percent in 1957 and by 2.6 percent in 1958. After the United States changed the exchange rate from $1:hw500 to $1:hw650, and reduced aid, the price index rose 10.3 percent.[152] Compared with the war period, this rise was minor, but it was enough of a reversal to cause alarm to the urban populace which had come to rely on greater economic stability. Per capita income also dropped slightly; having risen from $80.5 in 1956 to $84.3 in 1957 and $85.0 in 1958, it dropped back to $84.3 in 1959.[153] Most significant, perhaps, was the decline in the number of jobs in industry and commerce which had depended on inputs of U.S. aid. Industrial employees dropped from 212,090 in 1956 to 194,503 in 1959, and those employed in commerce declined from 495,462 to 402,639 over the same period.[154] The Liberal Party enterprises, as yet unable to sustain themselves without American aid inputs, became extremely uneasy. More covert funds flowed into the Democratic Party coffers.

As American pressures increased, Syngman Rhee became all the more adamant in resisting them. Less and less in touch with reality, he became increasingly convinced that American pressures were part of the continuing American opposition to him which he had first experienced under the American Military Government.

The election of Chang Myŏn as vice president in 1956 had upset and angered Rhee, partly because it was so difficult to comprehend. The Democratic Party had neither the resources nor the organization of the Liberal Party. Chang was no better known in the country than was Yi Ki-pung, and Rhee's endorsement of the latter seemed to give him a decided advantage. Yet despite this, Chang had won. What Rhee did not understand was that political circumstances in South Korea had changed in the post-Korean War period. The uprooting of old patterns of life in the countryside and the booming expansion of Korea's urban areas had led to considerable unrest and increasing dissatisfaction with existing conditions. The phenomenal growth of the Korean press, almost entirely critical of the government, was having an increasing impact, particularly in the urban areas. The Korean electorate was becoming more dissatisfied. Not yet prepared to reject the national leader, its dissatisfaction was reflected in its transfer of blame to the ruling faction—now the Liberal Party. Yi Ki-pung, as controller of the party, became the target of the growing unrest. The result had been the election in 1956 of the opposition candidate Chang Myŏn, primarily because he was the alternative. To the aging Syngman Rhee, however, confined to limited quarters and limited activities, the election of Chang seemed rational only if attributed to covert support of Chang by the United States.

Rhee never openly stated this apparently unfounded assumption, but implied it on several occasions.[155] Rhee's suspicions were not entirely irrational—the United States had openly opposed Rhee before 1948, supporting the "coalition committee," and had since been extremely critical of him. His conflicts with American policymakers were numerous throughout his political tenure. Furthermore, Rhee nursed forty years of slights by the U.S. government in his efforts to secure recognition for the Korean Provisional Government. He was quite prepared to believe that the United States would prefer to see him replaced by the soft-spoken, American-educated former Korean ambassador to Washington, Chang Myŏn, who quite readily echoed much of the American criticism of the Rhee government.

Syngman Rhee's subordinates played on Rhee's suspicion of covert American support of the opposition. When the opposition held a protest demonstration in 1956, for example, whose avowed intention was to "March to Kyungmudae (the presidential residence)" and give Rhee the "real facts" of Korean politics which they claimed were being withheld from him by his subordinates, the police force stopped them in front of the American Embassy, which happened to be on the way to the presidential residence. The president was then informed that the opposition had been protesting in front of the American Embassy in an effort to secure U.S. intervention against Rhee.[156] The police arrested several of the assemblymen involved in the demonstrations, but avoided taking in those who were personal acquaintances of the president even though some of them demanded to be arrested.[157] Rhee issued a statement to the effect that it was very undignified of the assemblymen to appeal to the United States for support.[158]

The collapse of the Rhee government came swiftly. In 1960, the Liberal Party leader Yi Ki-pung, again Rhee's vice presidential candidate, had been ill for some time, and was in fact virtually an invalid.[159] At the outset of the presidential campaign, the opposition's presidential candidate, Cho Pyŏng-ok (Chough Byong Ok) died while undergoing stomach surgery in Walter Reed Army Hospital in Washington, D.C.[160] Rhee would run unopposed for a fourth term.[161] Chang Myŏn was again the vice presidential candidate of the Democratic Party. This time, almost everyone assumed that the 85-year old president would not survive through his fourth four-year term of office (though, in fact, he lived five more years), and the vice presidency became the focus of the political contest. All factors seemed to point to Chang's re-election. Not only had he won by a substantial margin in the preceding election, but now he was opposed by an invalid incapable of campaigning. When it was announced that Yi, instead of Chang, had won the election by an overwhelming majority of 8,221,000 to 1,844,000 votes, election rigging was obvious.[162]

In fact, the press had for some time been charging that the election was going to be rigged. In February, photographs had appeared in newspapers which were identified as pictures of police attempting to prevent the registration of the candidacy of DP vice presidential candidate Chang, and of news photographers being beaten for attempting to photograph the scene.[163] The national chief of police intelligence was identifiable in the pictures. In March, the press openly reported the DP's charge that the election was going to be "a fraud" and photographs identified as pictures of "forged ballots" appeared.[164] On the day of the election, protest demonstrations took place in several cities.

The discovery of the mauled body of a student, killed during protests over election irregularities in the city of Masan, finally sparked the "revolution." Nation-wide student protests developed as the press spread the story throughout Korea's cities.[165] When students in Seoul marched upon the president's residence with the intention of protesting the election rigging, they were fired upon by police, and almost 100 were killed.[166] The United States was quicker than the students themselves to charge the aged president with responsibility for the tragedy, and to demand his resignation. As *The New York Times* pointed out: "The resignation of President Syngman Rhee was regarded by officials in Washington as a necessary step in ending the political crisis in South Korea. It followed by a day of renewed U.S. warning that he would end the turmoil in his country only by quitting office and calling for new elections."[167] The only internal demand for Rhee's resignation had been made by a group of university professors, marching in sympathy with the students, and it was made on April 25, in the afternoon of the day before Rhee submitted his resignation.[168] The American demand, however, had been backed up by the Korean army chief of staff, Song Yo-chan, who was released from the U.N. command to maintain order under martial law in Seoul.[169]

Neither the students, surveyed after the uprising, nor the army chief of staff, General Song Yo-chan, writing of the events of the uprising, indicated a serious desire to unseat President Rhee. General Song wrote that when he confronted the president with the seriousness of the situation, Rhee at first did not believe him, and queried, "Why is it that what you say is at variance with what my ministers tell me?" The general responded that if the president did not believe him, he could call in outside observers.[170] "Most painful to me," Song wrote, "was that the President was forced to resign. However, as chief of martial law, I could see no means to preserve the President's position. I still believe that it is an eternal truth that he was a great patriot. Personally, I respect Dr. Rhee, but history has turned him down, has scorned him, and has lost its trust in him. I, who saw the march of events, am sick inside about it."[171]

A study undertaken among students in one of the major universities in Seoul after the uprising—at a time when it was no longer popular to voice support for Rhee—was enlightening about the students' aims in participating. According to the questionnaires tabulated among both participants and nonparticipants in the demonstrations, the major reasons for the uprising were seen, in order of importance from most to least significant, as: (1) corruption in government, (2) election riggings, (3) economic depression, (4) Rhee in power too long, (5) police attacking Korea University students, (6) support of the vice president (Chang Myŏn), and (7) no specific reason.[172] In response to a question of persons most disliked by the students, the order of response was: (1) Lee Ki-poong (Yi Ki-pung), (2) Liberal Party leadership, (3) police, flatterers, social and political favor-seekers in general, (4) profiteers, irregular financial contributors for profit, (5) Syngman Rhee, and (6) government bureaucrats.[173] In neither response was the president seen as a major target of the uprising; on the contrary, while 84.5 percent of respondents indicated that they were opposing the Liberal Party, only 11.3 percent of the respondents indicated opposition to Syngman Rhee.[174] It was clear that Syngman Rhee himself had not been a primary target of the student uprisings. Nor had the students been "for" the Democratic Party opposition.

Citizens of the city of Seoul watched in tearful silence or wept openly as the former president left his twelve-year residence to return to a final political exile in the United States. That Rhee would soon have left the scene was inevitable; that he left in disgrace meant the collapse of the symbolism of legitimate succession from the independence movement to the South Korean political system.

Two days after Rhee's resignation the Liberal Party vice presidential candidate, Yi Ki-pung, and his wife and sons, including Rhee's adopted son, were shot, reportedly in a family suicide pact. With Rhee's withdrawal, the Liberal Party, no longer attached to his personal aura of legitimacy, collapsed. Knowing that the continued rule of Rhee and the Liberal Party would have meant the withdrawal of U.S. aid, without which they could not operate, the Liberal Party enterprises had quickly deserted the party. The police force, afraid of popular retaliation, partly disintegrated, many of its members quickly donning civilian clothing and disappearing into the crowded cities. Within months, the constitution had been amended to a parliamentary system and the government fell by default into the hands of the Democratic Party.

The attempt to consolidate a base of support for the South Korean political system under Syngman Rhee had been extended over a very prolonged period—far too prolonged to be productive of beneficial results. The perpetual political manipulations of a corrupt system, which had been endemic during the last centuries of the Yi dynasty, had been reintroduced. The army and bureaucracy did not collapse in 1960, but the Liberal Party and the police did disintegrate, while the Liberal Party's embryonic financial empire remained in limbo, awaiting the policy of the Democratic Party's Second Republic. With the collapse of the Liberal Party, the Democratic Party was left to introduce its advocated parliamentary system and to attempt to build a base of support that would sustain such a system in Korea.

Chapter V

RECONSOLIDATION AND ESTABLISHMENT OF A "SOCIALIST" POLITICAL SYSTEM IN NORTH KOREA, 1948-1961

While the government of Syngman Rhee failed to consolidate its power base in South Korea during the period from 1948 to 1960, the North Korean regime under Kim Il Sung succeeded in its consolidation during this period, and appeared to be on its way toward institutionalizing a Communist (or, in its terminology, "socialist") system of government. The question which one must ask is why one succeeded while the other failed. During the initial period of consolidation external factors favored Kim Il Sung; during this later period, however, Kim found himself unable to complete his consolidation without coming into conflict with the Soviet Union—much as the Rhee government had ultimately faced opposition from the United States. Kim's own internal position had become strong enough by the time of the confrontation, however, to resist Soviet pressures, and thus Kim was able to consolidate despite external factors which opposed him—using the opposition of these external factors, to prove the nationalist "purity" of the regime and hence improve his claim to legitimacy.

Pre-Korean War Build-up, 1948-1950

The Republic of Korea in the south came into existence on August 15, 1948, and the regime in the north followed suit by proclaiming the establishment of the Democratic People's Republic of Korea (DPRK) on September 9, 1948. The Supreme People's Assembly (SPA) of North Korea was holding its first session, from September 2-11, 1948, at the time the new constitution was promulgated on September 3, and the creation of the new state was announced on September 9. This new SPA, which replaced the assembly elected in 1947, was composed of 572 members, of whom 212 were said to represent the North, and 360 the South, on the basis of a ratio of representatives to population of 1:50,000.[1]

166

Elections to the South Korean seats were said to have been held "indirectly" with 77.8 percent of 8,681,745 eligible South Korean voters voting "secretly" for 1,002 electors, who then met in North Korea from August 22-24 to elect the 360 deputies to the assembly.[2] This reported number of South Korean voters hardly seems credible as it was even larger than the number who participated in the open legal election in the South.[3]

Deputies from the North were elected "directly" in an election held on August 25, in which it was said that 98.49 percent of the voters voted for the single slate of candidates.[4] Membership in the new Supreme People's Assembly was distributed among the political parties as follows:[5]

Party or organization	Number of deputies
Korean Workers' Party	102
Chosŏn Democratic Party	35
Ch'ŏndokyo Young Friends Party	35
Working People's Party	20
Democratic Independence Party	20
People's Republican Party	20
Other Organizations	171
Independents	114
	572

Kim Tu-bong was re-elected chairman of the Supreme People's Assembly, and the SPA authorized Kim Il Sung to form a cabinet. Kim Il Sung himself became premier, while three deputy premiers were chosen: Pak Hŏn-yŏng, former head of the Korean Communist Party in Seoul, who had come north in 1948; Hong Myŏng-hŭi, another South Korean who had been chairman of the Democratic Independence Party in Seoul (and had once been managing editor of the Dong-A Ilbo newspaper), who also came north in 1948;[6] and Kim Il Sung's comrade, Kim Ch'aek, a North Korean who had been a member of the Chosŏn Democratic Party which had been founded by the Christian-nationalist Cho Man-sik, but who had emerged at the Second Congress of the KWP in March 1948 as a member of its Political Committee. Of the sixteen ministers in the new cabinet, eight were from South Korea and eight from North Korea.[7]

Kim Il Sung's regime seemed as eager to establish its appearance of national legitimacy as Rhee had been in the creation of his first cabinet in the South. (The North Korean Assembly was not empowered to reject the Southern ministers, however, as the Southern Assembly had rejected Rhee's North Korean nominee for prime minister). As with Rhee's cabinet, one female member was included: Hŏ Chong-suk, the daughter of Hŏ Hŏn (who had been the vice chairman of the preparatory committee which had received the transfer of power from the Japanese in Seoul, and had become prime minister under the short-lived "People's Republic").[8] Ten of the new ministers were domestic Communists (seven of these from South Korea), two were from Yenan, and four (including Kim Il Sung) were members of Kim's Manchurian-Korean entourage. No Soviet-Koreans were included in the cabinet. The Supreme People's Assembly recessed on September 11, after a nine-day session.

Following the proclamation of the new state, the DPRK formally requested the withdrawal of Soviet troops, of whom 10,000 were still in North Korea; they were promptly removed—but many of the Soviet-Koreans who had been trained in the Soviet army remained behind as a command nucleus in the new North Korean army, much as many Soviet-Koreans remained as vice ministers in the new administration. The Caucasian Soviet advisers to the army remained behind as well.

The Supreme People's Assembly met again in January 1949, and approved a recommendation that elections to the People's Committees be held once again.[9] Since many of the domestic Communists in the party had been purged at the Second Congress (March 1948), it was perhaps necessary to reconsolidate the party's control over the local levels of government. Elections were held to the committees at the level of the provinces and special cities,[10] cities, counties (kun) and districts (kuyŏk), on March 3, 1949. Elections to the sub-district (myŏn) and village (li) level were not held at this time, but were postponed until later in the year. At the provincial level, 689 persons were said to have been elected, with 460 at the city level, 4,561 at the county level, and 143 at the district level.[11] The total number of deputies to these committees was almost double the number of deputies elected to the same committees in the elections of 1946 and 1947.[12]

Before these elections, another step in the consolidation of power at the local level was taken when new land certificates were issued in late 1948. Those persons who did not sympathize with the Workers' Party—as evidenced by previous votes against the party slate—had their certificates withdrawn and reissued to others on the grounds that the first recipients were "traitors to the Korean people."[13]

Another major party reorganization took place in June 1949, when the South Korean Workers' Party members who had come north were brought into the party by a new merger, following which the party dropped the appellation "North" from its title and was called the "Korean Workers' Party."[14] In the political juggling which took place with this new merger, Kim Il Sung was finally promoted to the position of chairman of the party, replacing Kim Tu-bong who had acquired that post at the time of the merger of the North Korean Communist Party and the New People's Party in August 1946. Pak Hŏn-yŏng, the South Korean Communist leader, was made vice chairman, along with Hŏ Ka-ŭi, the party organizer from the Soviet Union. Another Soviet-Korean, Kim Yŏl, moved in to take Hŏ Ka-ŭi's place as director of the organization bureau of the party. Both Kim Tu-bong, of the Yenan faction, who had been the chairman, and Chu Yŏng-ha of the domestic faction, who had been a vice chairman, receded into the background, as the strength of their factions was checked by the South Korean influx. Kim Tu-bong was relegated to spending the rest of his active career in the prominent but powerless post of chairman of the Presidium of the Supreme People's Assembly;[15] Chu was sent off to the post of ambassador to the U.S.S.R., a sinecure position since communication between the two countries was conducted through the Soviet representatives in Korea.[16]

The admission of Pak and his followers to the party in the North was important for two reasons. First, it was essential to obtain the cooperation of the South Korean party through which the Northern regime would have to work in consolidating control over the South. Second, the Soviets needed another faction to insure their controls, for it was always possible that Kim Il Sung and his entourage (who had been trained in the Chinese Communist Party) and the Yenan Korean group might join forces to resist Soviet controls. This seemed especially possible in mid-1949, as the Communists in China prepared to move into control of the Chinese mainland, and as a number of Koreans who had been fighting with the Chinese forces prepared to return to Korea.

Pak Hŏn-yŏng was a clear threat to Kim Il Sung, in view of the tremendous prestige he derived from having been one of the original founders of the Korean Communist Party; he continued to exert considerable influence over Koreans in the party who had not gone abroad during the period of Japanese rule. Furthermore, Pak had shown unswerving obedience to Soviet instructions during the period of his activities in the South.

According to Kim Il Sung's later charges, the South Korean followers of Pak Hŏn-yŏng were given a greater role in the party than he and his entourage would have liked—and the person responsible was the Soviet-Korean Hŏ Ka-ŭi.[17] Although Hŏ had moved up from the post of party organizer to that of vice chairman, he had been replaced by Soviet-Korean Kim Yŏl who worked closely under him, and who also continued to hold membership in the Communist Party of the Soviet Union (CPSU).[18]

The admission of South Korean domestic Communists into the party brought in many traditional behavior patterns which Kim had hoped to eliminate in the earlier purges of the northern domestic faction. Whereas the exiled Communists who had come up through the ranks of the Chinese and Soviet Communist Parties had learned to submit to party discipline or be purged, to the domestic Communists, such discipline was unknown because they had never been able to consolidate an effective party under Japanese rule. Kim had bitterly criticized the factional behavior of the North Korean domestic faction at the Second Party Congress, on March 28, 1948, claiming that: "some people in the Party who had no experience of the fundamentals of discipline which call for submission to the Party organization and the higher organs, came out against the formation of the North Korean Organizing Committee . . . They were still held captive by the old factional habits and . . . sought to tear the Party apart into local groups . . . to

continue living a musty life of factional activity, each commanding
his own local sphere of influence."[19] Pak Hŏn-yŏng in the South, of
course, had been one who opposed the establishment of a separate
North Korean organ. The purges of the northern domestic Communists
had solved the problem, Kim Il Sung said, by bringing these groups
under control and providing new leadership.[20] However, by taking
South Korean domestic Communists into the party, such factional
behavior was reintroduced. "Pak Hŏn-yŏng and his clique . . . found
their way into North Korea and made an attempt to disorganize
the Party . . . They strove not for the interests of the Party and the
revolution, but for their personal position."[21]

Following this new party reorganization, elections were held
again, this time to the lowest levels of government—to the village
(*li*) People's Committees on November 24 and 25, and to the sub-
district (*myŏn*) People's Committees on December 3, 1949. This
time it was reported that 98.9 percent of the electorate voted for
the deputies to the *myŏn*, or sub-districts, whereas the voting in
the preceding election in March 1947 had been reported as 99.98
percent. At the village level, however, the percentage of "yes" votes
was said to have increased from 80.63 percent in the village elections
of February 1947 to 95.99 percent in the elections of November
1949.[22] These elections, unlike those at the higher level, were not
used to expand the number of participants in the governing process.
While the number of village deputies increased from 53,314 to
56,113, the number of sub-district deputies decreased slightly from
13,444 to 13,354.[23]

While political consolidation was continuing, the "socialization"
of the economy was turning most of the society's financial resources
over to the government. By 1949, 90.7 percent of all industrial
production was said to be in the public sector, as opposed to 72.4
percent in 1946.[24] Private trade was said to have declined over the
same period from 96.5 percent of all trade to 43.5 percent.[25] As
the consolidation of the party over the government progressed,
these resources became available to the party. With no serious
challenge to its sources of financing, the party had neither to seek
devious means to accumulate money for political purposes such
as the financing of the local elections (as did the regime in the

South), nor to put aside a large portion of resources for use in persuading the populace not to support a wealthy opposition in an open election campaign. The Soviet Union did not protest the earmarking of funds for political purposes, and a ministry of propaganda became a formal organ of the government, receiving normal budget appropriations from the regime. As it was in the interest of the party to expand its financial resources, it was also in the regime's interest to increase the total production of the system, in order to increase its ability to control the populace and to expand and equip the armed forces—needed in sustaining and expanding its realm of control.

In 1947 and 1948, economic planning had begun under one-year plans, and in 1949 a two-year plan was introduced in which the economic resources of the regime began to be fully mobilized, with Soviet technical advisers in each industry.[26] Apparently, the North Korean government was required to pay the salaries of these technical advisers, while the Soviet Union provided economic assistance in the form of a 212 million rubles loan.[27] (It has been estimated that total Soviet assistance to North Korea, including both loans and grants, from the beginning of 1946 to the end of 1950, amounted to $546,000,000.[28] This compares with $684,609,000 in grants to the South from the United States over the same period; the South, of course, had more than twice the population of the North.)[29]

The most important steps taken in 1948 and 1949 were preparations for military mobilization. The prestige of army officers was built up to a new high, and favorable rations were given to the army.[30] Although Kim Il Sung announced the formation of the Korean People's Army on February 8, 1948, recruitment and training had been going on for some time, and the officers' training school had produced its first class of graduates on October 26, 1947.[31] About 10,000 men had been sent to Siberia for advanced training in the operation of tanks, planes, and other weapons of modern warfare.[32] In 1947, between 50,000 and 100,000 Koreans, mostly from Manchuria, but some from the peninsula itself, had been inducted into the Chinese Communist Army, following a military

agreement between the Chinese and the North Koreans.[33] Following
the victory on the Chinese mainland, these Koreans were brought
back to North Korea and reintegrated into the North Korean Army
in July 1949 and April 1950. In April and May of 1950, tanks and
heavy guns were supplied to the North Korean Army by the Soviet
Union. Having consolidated its position in the North, the new
government was prepared to move South.

There has been a good deal of dispute about the origins of
the Korean War; both Korean governments attribute the initial
attack to the other.[34] While not dismissing the possibility of a
small South Korean foray across the border—especially in view of
the fact that North Korean troops had made such forays repeatedly,
notably a large-scale attack on May 3, 1949, in the Kaesong area[35] —
a number of factors must be kept in mind. First of all, the South
Korean political system was rapidly disintegrating and on the verge
of collapse. Its army was severely underequipped and poorly
disciplined, and had not been effectively brought under government
control. Indeed, it had already gone into open rebellion once against
the government. The Northern government, on the other hand, was
well consolidated, its army well-disciplined and equipped. Most of
its officers had either been trained in the Soviet Army as a
"liberating force" for Korea—and then been deprived of the chance
to fight by the precipitate Japanese surrender—or had recently been
reintegrated into the Korean army after having served in the
victorious Communist campaign to take over China. Furthermore,
the United States had stated categorically that Korea was not
within its "defense perimeter."[36] Certainly the Rhee government
exhibited most of the weaknesses that the Chiang Kai-shek government had exhibited in China, before the Chinese Communists
defeated the Nationalists in 1949. To accuse the North Koreans of
being unwilling to take the same risks as the Chinese Communists
before them, in view of their similar ideological commitments,
would be tantamount to charging them with cowardice. Kim Il Sung
had declared that he reserved the right to exercise the use of force
in reunifying the peninsula in a letter to U.N. Secretary-General
Trygvie Lie in 1949.[37]

The Soviet system of controls had continued up through the beginning of the Korean War, with Soviet Koreans in the controlling positions throughout the party, government, and army. North Korean industry depended heavily on Soviet technical personnel, while the army depended upon day-to-day supplies and equipment from the U.S.S.R.; both the economic and military reliance upon the Soviet Union gave the U.S.S.R. powerful levers of control. Given the Soviet system of controls over the North Korean government and army, through both personnel and supplies such as gasoline (rationed on a short-term basis) for military vehicles, it would have been impossible for any initiative to have been taken without the endorsement of the Soviet command in Pyongyang.

The People's Republic of China (PRC), on the other hand, played almost no role at all in North Korea prior to the Korean War, in part because the Communists did not secure control in China until October 1949, just nine months before the outbreak of the Korean War, and were then busy consolidating their own position at home. Relations between North Korea and the Chinese Communists during this period were strained. Although Korean members of the CPSU automatically became members of the Korean Worker's Party, retaining their Soviet citizenship and membership in the mother party, members of the Chinese Communist Party (CCP) had to relinquish their membership in that organization and undergo an investigation before acquiring KWP membership. Even so, not all Korean members of the CCP who returned home were granted admission to the Korean party.[38] No formal diplomatic relations were established between North Korea and the PRC until after the outbreak of the War.

During the period prior to the Korean War, the government continued its efforts to promote the appearance of a nationalist coalition under a facade of democracy. In the meantime, Russian cultural influence became increasingly significant, as Russian textbooks were imported into Korea and Russian studies were introduced into the school curriculums. Several years later, Kim Il Sung was to denounce this Russianization, saying:

Once I visited a People's Army vacation hostel, where I saw a picture of the Siberian steppe on the wall. That landscape of the steppe probably pleases the Russians. But the Korean people prefer the beautiful scenes of their own country . . . One day this summer when I dropped in at a local Democratic Propaganda Hall, I saw diagrams of the Soviet Union's Five Year Plan . . . but no diagrams illustrating our Three Year Plan . . . I noticed in a primary school that all the portraits were of foreigners, such as Mayakovsky, Pushkin, etc., but there were none of Koreans. If we educate our children in this way, how can we expect them to have national pride? . . . In compiling school textbooks, too, materials are foreign ones.[39]

As Russian culture was penetrating the northern part of the peninsula, efforts were being made to eliminate vestiges of Chinese culture. In June 1949, the use of Chinese characters was abolished, all newspapers and texts henceforth to be published in the Korean phonetic alphabet. The alphabet had been created by King Sejong five hundred years before, but had not achieved widespread usage because of the Yi dynasty's deference to Sinitic culture. (A mixed use of the phonetic alphabet and Chinese characters continues in the South). This change meant that, unlike their predecessors, the young North Korean generation would be unable to read Chinese. On the other hand, the Russian language was introduced as a required part of the curriculum.

While Soviet control was evident in the governmental apparatus and Soviet culture was increasingly penetrating the peninsula, efforts were being made to integrate North Korea into the Soviet economy.[40] A large portion of the production of minerals, metals, and chemicals was destined for export to the Soviet Union.[41] At this stage, the North Korean system seemed to be moving so rapidly into the Soviet orbit that to some observers it appeared to be progressing toward the status of a province within the Soviet Union.

Although nonpolitical factors were expanding rapidly, neither the degree of urbanization nor the educational expansion matched that of the South, where the liberation from Japan had released long-repressed pressures for improved conditions, and where long-time expatriates flowed in to swell the urban centers, the schools, and the ranks of the unemployed. On the other hand, economic developments provided a striking contrast to the disintegrating economy of the South. The 1949-1950 Two Year Plan put a heavy emphasis on industrial investment. More manpower was required for industry, and various incentives were used to draw people from the rural areas into the urban labor force. These were not sufficient, however, and soon such practices as industrial conscription and compulsory labor (farmers working in industry during off-season) were inaugurated. As one North Korean source explained, "[I]t could hardly be expected that labour power would flow of itself into factories and mines."[42] By 1949, the percentage of population in agriculture had dropped from the 1946 level of 74.1 percent of the work force to 69.3 percent, whereas the industrial labor force grew from 12.5 percent to 19 percent. Office workers increased from 6.2 percent to 7 percent, while businessmen and entrepreneurs decreased from 3.3. percent and 0.2 percent respectively, to 1.7 percent and 0.1 percent.[43] The decision to unify the country through military action soon caused resources and manpower to be redirected to the military build-up, and war began in June 1950.

Wartime and Postwar Reconsolidation, 1950-1956

If the war altered the course of events in the internal politics of South Korea, it had an even more significant effect on North Korea: it destroyed the Soviet system of controls. Ironically, the same input of external factors—the United States military involvement—that built up the strength of the southern system from its prewar disintegrative spiral, also created the internal dissension in the North that led to the successful North Korean effort to break the stranglehold of Soviet controls through a realignment of the political factions as a result of the events of the war.

On June 26, 1950, the day after the outbreak of the war, a military committee was formed to take over the functions of government during the war. This committee was composed of seven men, four of whom were members of Kim Il Sung's Manchurian-

Korean entourage. The seven men were: Kim Il Sung (Manchurian faction), Pak Hŏn-yŏng (domestic South Korean), Hong Myŏng-hŭi (domestic South Korean), Kim Ch'aek (Manchurian faction), Ch'oë Yŏng-gŏn (Manchurian faction), Pak Il-u (Yenan faction), and Chŏng Chun-t'aek (Manchurian faction).[44] A few days later a decree placed all organs of state in areas of war operations under the Military Committee. In each of these areas a military committee was to be created, consisting of a chairman, the people's committee chairman for the area, a representative from the military, and a representative of the ministry of internal affairs.[45]

The North Korean drive south nearly reached the tip of the peninsula before United Nations troops (primarily American) arrived to assist the South Korean government. By October, the North Korean armed forces had been driven back across the 38th parallel and back up toward the Yalu River which provides part of the border between China and Korea. Negotiations were opened by the U.S.S.R. to bring the Chinese into the fighting, and as a result of three-way talks between North Korea, the Soviet Union, and China, the "Chinese People's Volunteers" joined the battle in support of the North Koreans on October 25.[46]

By the time the Chinese moved into Korea, the Korean Workers' Party was in a state of virtual collapse. As the U.N. forces progressed north, the North Korean government retreated from Pyongyang up to the Chinese border. Party members began destroying their identification cards in expectation of defeat and possible capture. Kim Il Sung later said that of the 600,000 party members remaining in October 1950 (it is not clear what had become of the other 150,000 who made up the 750,000-member party at the time of the Second Congress in March 1948), 450,000 had "lost" or destroyed their membership cards.[47]

On December 4, 1950, in a village near the Chinese border known as P'yoyo-li, the party's third plenary meeting of the Central Committee was held, for the purpose of assessing the war situation. In many cases, the military had fallen apart and scattered in the retreat; the party was in disarray; and many of the factories and other economic facilities had been destroyed. Refugees were flowing south. It has been said that at this time Major General Rebezev, Kim Il Sung's political adviser, suggested that blame for the defeat be apportioned.[48] Kim Il Sung gave a speech listing the defects in the war effort. He then addressed himself to the problems within the army: "Among the military commanders there is abundant evidence that a number of them have shown cowardice, and instead of saving their units have concentrated on egoism and their own individual lives. For example, such division commanders include Kim Hang-chŏng and Ch'oë Kwang, and these persons have already been removed from their posts."[49] As for the party, Kim observed: "Through this war it has been clearly revealed who is a true party member and who is false. Not all of our party members who entered the party under the circumstances of peaceful and calm conditions have proved true members of the frontiers of workers and peasants. The war caught and exposed ruthlessly the impure, the cowardly, and the opposing elements of the party membership. [W]e must strengthen our party after cleaning out these elements from the party structure."[50]

The most important development at the meeting, however, was the purging of three of the major party leaders: Mu Chŏng, the military leader of the Yenan faction and the commander of the Second Army Corps, who had fought with the Chinese Communists and participated in the Long March with Mao Tsetung; Kim Il, one of Kim Il Sung's comrades and the vice minister of defense; and Kim Yŏl, the Soviet-Korean commander of the rear areas and the powerful party organizer, were dismissed from their posts in the army. Kim Yŏl was charged with "obstructing supplies." Upon Kim Yŏl's removal from the post of party organizer, Hŏ Ka-ŭi resumed that post, so that he remained in direct command of the party's admission policy. Kim Il was charged with "defeatist tendencies." A defector later reported that Kim Il had complained about the Soviet unwillingness to supply more planes, which had rendered North Korea defenseless against American bombing.[51] The most serious accusation—that of treason—was reserved for Mu Chŏng, the Yenan-Korean leader; he was accused of refusing to defend Pyongyang and barbarous treatment of the Korean people.[52]

"When we were in the process of retreating," Kim Il Sung declared: "Mu Chŏng used the state of confusion as a pretext to carry out his feudal method of executing troops without due process of law. Acting like a king in a lawless country, he carried out his barbarous atrocities."[53]

Although Kim Il and Kim Yŏl were shortly thereafter reinstated in the party, Mu Chŏng was stripped of military rank and imprisoned.[54] Upon the insistence of the Chinese, he was later turned over to them and given asylum in the People's Republic of China, where he reportedly died of an illness in 1951.[55] This purge served several purposes. It eliminated the most important leader of the Yenan faction in the army, but by including Kim Il, of Kim Il Sung's entourage, and Kim Yŏl, a Soviet-Korean, along with Mu Chŏng, it did not appear to be placing the blame for the defeat solely on the Yenan faction. Primarily, it served the purpose of shifting the onus of defeat from Kim Il Sung and the Soviet Union, while maintaining the fiction that it was the South that had initiated the war, and it prevented the Yenan faction from being able to team up with the Chinese to claim that they had "saved" the nation. This was the last high-level purge to be influenced by the Soviet system of control.

Kim Il's "defeatism" was symptomatic of the general resentment among North Koreans over the Soviet Union's unwillingness to supply more positive, open support for the war effort. In January 1951, Kim Ch'aek, Kim Il Sung's long-time friend and the "number two man" in the Kim Il Sung faction, was killed in an American bombing raid.[56] Soviet-Korean Hŏ Ka-ŭi moved into the vacated post of deputy premier in November. By mid-1951, the war was stalemated at the 38th parallel, where it had begun. North Korea was devastated, its population decimated. Virtually everything was destroyed—homes, factories, roads, harbors, bridges, railroads. What had North Korea gained? What had it lost? Where lay the fault? On June 23, 1951, the Soviet delegate to the United Nations, Yakov A. Malik, called for an armistice conference.[57] The first meeting took place on July 10. It was now clear that the Soviet Union had no intention of seeing the war through to its objective of unification. For what, then, had been all the sacrifice? The South Korean Communists saw clearly that their goal was unattainable, and many of them chose to defect to South Korea. Resentment toward the Soviet Union became widespread among North Koreans.

Between December 1950 and September 1951, disciplinary action had been undertaken against those party members who had "lost" their membership cards, and it was later reported that 300,000 received disciplinary treatment.[58] In September 1951, Kim Il Sung appealed to the organization committee, headed by Hŏ Ka-ŭi, to cease punishing party members and to undertake a broad recruitment policy, in order to replenish party ranks. According to the party rules, a new member was required to be over twenty years of age, and had to have recommendations from two party members, both of whom must have been members for one year or longer, and one of whom must have known the candidate for more than one year, and both must be willing to act as his "sponsor" and accept responsibility for his actions as a party member.[59] Kim Il Sung argued that these regulations should not be rigidly adhered to during the war, in view of the dire need to reconstruct the party; however, Hŏ was apparently unresponsive. Kim Il Sung later reported that although the disciplinary action was discontinued, no broad recruitment policy was undertaken. At the fourth plenary meeting of the central committee of the party in November 1951, Kim Il Sung criticized Hŏ, charging him with being bureaucratic and formalistic, and refusing to admit members of the peasant class to the party.[60] Following this criticism, party recruitment became more open, and about 450,000 new members were recruited by the end of the war. Of these, about half were unable to read and write.[61]

The criticism of Hŏ did serve a purpose in addition to affecting party admissions policies. It served to focus the resentment of the various groups within the party toward the Soviet system of controls. Hŏ, whom Kim Il Sung later scornfully nicknamed the "Party *Paksa* [Ph.D.]" was the most important link in the Soviet-Korean chain of control. Reportedly, Hŏ had taken great pride in his Soviet citizenship, and bragged about being an "original Bolshevik."[62] As resentment turned toward the Russians, it inevitably centered on Hŏ. Other Soviet-Koreans, sensing the bitter atmosphere, began disassociating themselves from him. The criticism of Hŏ's admissions policies was also an indirect criticism of Soviet party policy which denied the importance of peasant participation, and was couched in terms which reflected the policies of Mao Tse-tung. The presence of Chinese forces in the peninsula may well have given Kim the sense of security he needed to attack the Soviet controls. However, despite the criticism of Hŏ, he was not dismissed from the party at the time, and in fact was elevated to the post of vice prime minister.[63]

In an attempt to regain effective control over local levels of government, whose administrative organs had collapsed during the U.N. offensive, sub-district (*myŏn*) level committees were abolished in December 1952, and the number of village administrative units were reduced from 10,120 to 3,659, all of which continued to operate under the military affairs committee.[64]

In March 1953, mass arrests of members of the South Korean faction of the party were begun, as it became evident that the country would not be reunified. About one-third of the major party positions in the North had been allocated to the South Koreans, but it was later reported that they were disappointed with this limited role in the party, considering themselves to be the "mainstream" of the original Korean Communist Party. Two of the most important leaders of the South Korean faction, Pak Hŏn-yŏng and Yi Sŭng-yŏp, were given the death sentence, along with eight others, following a trial for allegedly having planned a coup d'état to install Pak Hŏn-yŏng as prime minister, with Chu Yŏng-ha and Chang Si-u (both members of the North Korean domestic Communist faction) as vice prime ministers.[65] Although it was the Soviet-Korean Hŏ Ka-ŭi who had enabled the South Korean faction to consolidate strength in the party, the allegations were that the Americans, not the Russians, had put them up to this "American imperialist plot," much as Rhee in the South had accused those who had appealed to the United States to intervene of being involved in a "Communist conspiracy plot." It was charged that Yi Sŭng-yŏp had started building up the strength of the Southern faction when he had been appointed chief of the South Korean operations liaison section of the party in August 1951, when following traditional factional patterns, Yi had appointed only members of the South Korean faction to his section.[66] Besides those sentenced to death, several South Korean faction members were sentenced to 12 to 15 years in prison, and about 5,000 were purged from the party, most of them sent to work in the coal mines.[67] Although Pak Hŏn-yŏng was imprisoned at this time, he was not executed until 1955, with his trial and execution made public only after the death sentence had been carried out.[68]

On July 27, 1953, an armistice agreement was concluded, and immediately thereafter Kim Il Sung moved in to secure the removal of party organizer Hŏ Ka-ŭi, taking advantage of the anti-Soviet atmosphere. At an emergency session of the central committee called by Kim Il Sung in August 1953, Hŏ was charged with being a sympathizer with the South Korean faction and a national traitor.[69] Hŏ, surprised by the unanimous opposition he faced, requested a few days to prepare a statement in his defense. Upon returning home, he committed suicide.[70] Also purged at this time were the ambassadors to both Russia and China, Chu Yŏng-ha and Kwŏn O-chik, both of the North Korean domestic faction —giving rise to some speculation that they may have sought external intervention against the Kim Il Sung leadership, in view of the traditional tendency to seek foreign support. Kim Yŏl, the Soviet-Korean who had worked closely with Hŏ as a member of the CPSU, remained in the party until the following year, when he too was purged. Hŏ Ka-ŭi was replaced as party organizer by one of Kim Il Sung's Manchurian-Korean comrades, Pak Kŭm-ch'ŏl.[71]

The North Korean economy was in ruins with the end of the war. Industrial facilities had suffered almost complete destruction. In 1953 North Korea produced one million kilowatts of electricity as compared with nearly six million in 1949, 3,610 metric tons of steel ingots as compared with 144,403 metric tons in 1949, and 700,000 tons of coal as compared with four million tons before the war.[72] It was estimated that industrial production was only 36 percent of the prewar level. Thousands of homes had been destroyed; it was estimated that 28 million square meters of dwellings were demolished during the war.[73] Furthermore, agricultural lands were ruined, irrigation facilities destroyed, and many farmers had either fled the country or been killed. The population of North Korea had decreased by one million, or more than 10 percent, and most of the losses, both in the fighting and in the refugees who fled south, were young men.[74]

In 1954, a "Three Year Plan" for reconstructing the economy was introduced, supported by foreign aid from the Soviet Union and China, with token amounts from Eastern Europe. While some economic assistance came from the Soviet Union, that given by China was even greater, though it was ultimately spread over a longer time period. It has been estimated that during this Three Year Plan period, foreign aid made up as much as 60 percent of the North Korean budget.[75] The head of the economic planning committee, responsible for carrying out the Three Year Plan, was Pak Ch'ang-ok, a prominent Soviet-Korean. The plan provided for 49.6 percent of economic investment (virtually all expenditures, including those for education and culture, are termed "investment") to be channelled into industry, of which 81.1 percent was for heavy industry, to reconstruct a productive economic base for the country.[76]

In 1953, the government began the collectivization of agriculture, a task placed in the hands of Kim Il, who had been reinstated since being criticized for "defeatism" in 1950. In 1954 the collectivization program began on a full scale; it was endorsed by the plenary meeting of the party's central committee in November 1954, at which time 21.5 percent of the farmers had already been organized into collectives.[77] Within one year, 49 percent of the farmers had been collectivized.[78] By 1956, the number was 80.9 percent.[79] Kim Il Sung later reported that this collectivization had been opposed by the Soviet Union. In a speech in 1965 Kim noted that: "Foreign revisionists [a term then in vogue for the Soviet leadership]—big power chauvinists and their followers in Korea tried to discredit our Party's policy on agricultural cooperation. They alleged that the cooperative transformation of agriculture in our country was proceeding too quickly. They were . . . ignorant of the actual situation in our country and did not try to understand it."[80] Yet the policy was undoubtedly endorsed by China for the Chinese were carrying out a parallel policy of collectivization. The fact that Chinese troops were in Korea throughout this time was probably a very influential factor in allowing Kim Il Sung to pursue a course which was opposed by the Soviet Union.[81]

At the time that the collectivization was being carried out, party ranks were being swelled with new peasant members. Membership grew from about 750,000 at the end of the war,[82] to 1,164,945 by January 1, 1956.[83] Kim Il Sung later said that more than half of the party members in 1956 had been recruited after the beginning of the war.[84] Most of these members had been admitted after Soviet-Korean Hŏ Ka-ŭi had lost control over recruitment policies, following his 1951 criticism, and about half of them were brought in after Manchurian-Korean Pak Kŭm-ch'ŏl had taken over the organization post in 1953. The collectivization of agriculture had meant a reorganization of the local bases of power and party ranks were swelled with members from the peasantry. By April 1956, 56.8 percent of the party members were poor peasants and 3.7 percent "middle peasants."[85]

Taking advantage of the traditional desire for bureaucratic posts, the regime assisted its consolidation by channelling many of the peasants directly into the bureaucracy, and during the three-year period between December 1953 and September 1956, the number of "office workers" rose from 8.5 percent of the labor force to 13.6 percent.[86] Since 98 percent of the economy was classified "socialist" (that is, government owned) as of 1956, these office workers were bureaucratic employees of the regime.[87]

The initial period of consolidation of the North Korean regime, before 1948, had been accomplished while the Soviet army was stationed in North Korea. The reconsolidation following the Korean War, was carried out in the presence of the Chinese Communist troops, who remained until 1958. Joint Chinese and Korean

command over the Chinese People's Volunteers and the North
Korean People's Army persisted even following the war, though
unlike the U.N. command in the South, the Chinese did not have
effective control over the army of their Korean ally. Immediately
following the armistice, Kim Il Sung had managed to remove the
commander-in-chief of the army, Pang Ho-san, and the deputy
commander of the joint Chinese-Korean command, Pak Il-u, both
prominent Yenan Koreans, from their command positions, although
both retained their positions in the party. In December 1955,
however, Pak Il-u was purged for factionalist activities. In criticizing
Pak, Kim Il Sung said:

> He thinks that he is the representative of the people who
> came from China and says we are not appointing those who
> came from China as leaders of the government. He says that
> those who came from the U.S.S.R. and from China have
> different styles of life. He is seeking to organize around him
> the comrades who have weak class consciousness. Pak Il u
> thinks that no one knows about his recruiting efforts. However,
> he is greatly mistaken. So as to achieve his scheme, Pak Il-u,
> like Pak Hŏn-yŏng, Yi Sŭng-yŏp, Hŏ Ka-ŭi and O Ki-sŏp, is
> trying to lead others into his group. He is always looking
> around for those who have unsound feelings of discontent
> and dissatisfaction.[88]

As in the South, factionalism had pervaded the army, as well
as the party, during the war—in the Northern case dividing along
the lines of Soviet-Koreans versus Yenan Koreans. Kim Il Sung later
said:

> During the war, inside the army, Hŏ Ka-ŭi, Kim Chae-uk,
> and Pak Il-u were perpetually criticizing each other over the
> method of achieving political tasks. Those who came from
> the Soviet Union would say that we should use the Soviet
> method, and those who came from China would say that we
> should use the Chinese method. The one would say that the
> Soviet style was best, and the other would say that the Chinese

style was best. What a worthless argument! In order to eat
rice, does it matter whether you eat it with your right hand
or with your left, with a spoon or with chopsticks, so long
as it gets into your mouth? Was there any necessity to select
a method in the midst of the war? The objective was to
achieve victory in the war by strengthening our People's
Army through the carrying out of political tasks, regardless
of the method employed. But Hŏ Ka-ŭi and Pak Il-u continued
criticizing each other in this worthless way, and all they
succeeded in doing was in weakening the effectiveness of the
party.[89]

Along with Kim Il Sung's consolidation of control within the
party and the army, the political line of the regime shifted from
one of "building the bases of democracy" to "building the bases
of socialism." Kim Il Sung began increasingly to emphasize Korean
nationalism, a political force which had previously been played
down by the Soviet-controlled regime. In 1955, Kim insisted: "We
are not engaged in the revolution of another country but in our
Korean revolution . . . Only when the people are educated in the
history of our people's struggle and its traditions can their national
pride be promoted and the masses of the people be aroused to the
revolutionary struggle."[90] He criticized slavish copying of foreign
political methods.[91]

Using the new peasant organizational base of party membership
brought in during the war and post-war period, Kim Il Sung was
able to establish himself in a position of great strength at the Third
Party Congress, which was held April 23-29, 1956. Kim Il Sung
was re-elected party chairman. Of the five vice chairmen, two,
Ch'oë Yŏng-gŏn and Pak Kŭm-ch'ŏl, were members of Kim's
Manchurian-Korean entourage, two, Pak Chŏng-ae and Yi Chong-ok
were domestic Communists, and one, Kim Ch'ang-man, was a
Yenan man. More importantly, of the eleven-member political
committee of the central committee, seven were drawn from Kim
Il Sung's group, while of the remaining four, one, Pak Chŏng-ae
(the widow of Kim Yŏng-pŏm), was a Soviet-educated domestic
Communist, one, Kim Ch'ang-man, was a Yenan Korean, one,

Nam Il, has generally been identified as a Soviet-Korean (although he completed high school in Manchuria before going to study at Tashkent Teacher's College in the U.S.S.R.), and one, Chŏng Il-yong, was a new face, with no identifiable pre-1945 affiliation. In the more prominent but less powerful presidium (standing committee) of the party central committee, also numbering eleven members, six were members of Kim's group, two were of the Yenan group (Kim Tu-bong and Ch'oë Ch'ang-ik), one was domestic (Pak Chŏng-ae), one Soviet-Korean (Nam Il), and one new face (Chŏng Il-yong). Although the three token members from the domestic, Soviet, and new groups were the same in both organs, the token Yenan member of the political committee was not selected from the two most prominent Yenan Koreans who were placed in the presidium. Kim Il Sung was clearly seeking to limit the participation of other factions in his consolidation of control over the party.

The organization committee of the party was re-formed. Of its seven members, three were members of Kim Il Sung's group, to which were added the same three token members of the domestic, Yenan, and new groups as were included in the political committee. No Soviet-Korean was named to this committee. Heading the committee, its seventh member was Han Sang-tu, a domestic Communist elevated from the Hamgyong-pukdo provincial party organization by Kim Il Sung. According to one source, Han had replaced Kim Il Sung's associate Pak Kŭm-ch'ŏl in this post the preceding December, the same month that the execution of the veteran domestic Communist leader, Pak Hŏn-yŏng, had finally been announced.[92]

By 1956, Kim Il Sung clearly seemed to have consolidated control over the party, and the party over the society. External economic and military assistance from both the Soviet Union and China had enhanced his consolidation. The degree of political control in the society seemed evident from the government's ability to restructure the agricultural system, as well as its general capacity to direct social change. While the upheaval of war had swelled the cities of the South so that by 1955 its population was 43 percent urban, in the North the population was still only

29 percent urban in 1956.[93] The total percentage of students in school (from primary level through college) in both areas had increased at a similar rate, but the North with less than half the population of the South had less than one-fourth the number of students in colleges and universities.[94] On the other hand, only 56.6 percent of the North Korean labor force was still employed in agriculture in 1956, while 78 percent of the South Korean labor force was still agricultural. More significantly, the percentage of the working population involved in industry and mining in the North was 27.3 percent, as compared with a miniscule 2.6 percent in the South in 1956.[95] The nonpolitical factors that created the instability which had fomented the frustration in the South, when a "protest vote" had installed Rhee's nemesis Chang Myŏn as his vice president and heir-apparent, were absent in the North. When Kim Il Sung's opponents finally joined together to challenge his consolidation, it was his grass roots party support that would be effectively mobilized against them.

External and Internal Challenge and the Consolidation of the Bases of a "Socialist System," 1956-1961

Assuming that Kim Il Sung was serious in seeking to achieve the "Marxist-Leninist" system he advocated, much as we have assumed that Rhee was serious in his struggle to create what he thought was an "American-style" democratic system in the South, it is clear that the bases of Kim's system were still incomplete as of 1956. By the time of the Fourth Party Congress in 1961, however, Kim was to claim to have consolidated the foundation for the system: the economy had been totally "socialized," and was rapidly industrializing, the party purged of dissident factions, and control solidified over the army. The working class had been enlarged and was assuming an increasingly greater role in the party, and the party was actively utilizing ideological as well as institutional tools to resocialize the population in an effort to eliminate "factionalism," "bureaucratism," and "flunkeyism," among other inherited behavioral ills. Like Rhee in the South, however, whose effort to consolidate new political bases to support his advocated system ultimately met with American opposition, Kim was unable to consolidate the bases of his advocated system without coming into serious conflict with the Soviet Union—the nation which had served as the ideological guidepost for the system he wanted to build.

Though the Stalinist leadership of the U.S.S.R. had well understood the task of political consolidation, it was succeeded by a new breed of leadership who inherited an already established political system, and who, like their American counterparts seeking to influence the system in the South, no longer perceived the need for building new social bases to support the new political system. For the new leaders in the Soviet Union, the revolution was over, the system established, and the time had come to make the system work through institutionalized, routinized functioning—to "normalize" the system so that its now-established foundations would achieve legitimacy among the population. Even more confident about their expertise on "Marxism-Leninism" than the Americans were about theirs on "democracy," the new Soviet leadership met Kim Il Sung in a bitter head-on clash. Just as the ideas Rhee had sought to use to support his consolidation had been turned against him by his political opponents and the external power from which he had sought support, so too were the ideas of "Marxism-Leninism" turned against Kim Il Sung by his opponents and the Soviet leadership. In Kim's case, however, his position was already sufficiently consolidated to resist the challenge; in doing so he was able to endow his regime for the first time with a claim to nationalist legitimacy.

The Soviet challenge to the Kim Il Sung leadership was initiated at the Third Party Congress in 1956, by one of the U.S.S.R.'s rising new leaders, Leonid I. Brezhnev, who had been sent to represent the Soviet Union. Reflecting the break with Soviet controls that had come in the wartime and postwar period, while the Soviets had been preoccupied with the internal political struggle following Stalin's death, the new North Korean economic plans had been drawn up without consultation with, and approval from, the Soviet Union; Soviet-Korean Pak Ch'ang-ok had been removed as head of the economic planning commission on January 4, 1956, three months before the Congress. Brezhnev's speech, though friendly in tone, made it clear that the Soviet Union disapproved of North Korea's new economic plans, and considered them unrealistic: "As we see from the report, the Party and Government are contemplating a stupendous plan for the development in the near future of the economy and culture of the country . . . In carrying out the future Five Year Plan for the development of the national economy . . . you will probably meet with no few difficulties. However, your Congress will draw up resolutions which will make it possible to overcome more quickly and easily these difficulties."[96] (The Chinese delegate, in contrast, said that he was "confident" the plan would be carried out "without fail.") Brezhnev suggested that the plan should include more emphasis on agriculture and on the improvement of living standards.[97]

Soviet criticism of the Five Year Plan was less important than another part of Brezhnev's speech, calling for "collective leadership" which seemed to attack Kim Il Sung's consolidation of control over the party:

> The Twentieth Congress has pointed out with great satisfaction the special significance of the work done recently by the Central Committee of the Communist Party of the Soviet Union to restore the all-important Leninist principle, the principle of collective leadership.
>
> The principle of collective leadership—this is the only correct way of improving the Party leadership from top to bottom . . .
>
> The [North Korean Third] Congress will help to fully establish in the Party organizations from top to bottom the Leninist principle of collective leadership, the enforcement of which lends a powerful force to each Marxist Party and keeps it from making mistakes related to the cult of personality.[98]

Indicating that the Korean Workers' Party "will" establish collective leadership, Brezhnev was obviously implying that such collective leadership was absent in North Korea.

The North Korean leadership did not openly publish its retort to this Brezhnev statement which clearly illustrated the reaction of Kim Il Sung's entourage, until 1963:

> Certain people describe the party congress of a particular country as the opening of a "new stage" in the international communist movement, and proclaim the policies and decision of that particular party to be a "joint program of the international communist movement" and try to impose it upon other fraternal parties.
> Decisions or measures of a party are only obligatory within that party; they cannot be binding on the activities of other parties. It is totally impermissible to try to force the "anti-personality cult" campaign upon other parties, and then behind this smokescreen to interfere in the internal affairs of brother parties and countries, and to even scheme to overthrow the party leadership of other countries.[99]

At the time of Brezhnev's speech, members of the Korean Workers' Party who opposed Kim Il Sung's consolidation of control over the party were encouraged by the prospect of Soviet support. The remaining Soviet-Koreans, led by Pak Ch'ang-ok, the Soviet-Korean who had been ousted from the economic planning commission, joined the Yenan Koreans, led by Ch'oë Ch'ang-ik. Ch'oë, who along with Kim Tu-bong had been among the most prominent leaders of the Yenan group, had been removed from the policy-making political committee of the party at the Congress, although he remained a member of both the central committee and its presidium. Together, the two groups planned an attack upon Kim Il Sung's leadership.

Soon after the Third Party Congress, Kim Il Sung set off for Eastern Europe and the Soviet Union in an effort to secure economic aid to assist the Five Year Plan. Since he had not conformed with the Soviet insistence that the plan be changed, he found his reception cool. East Germany had already made a commitment in 1955 for a loan of $15 million. It offered no further assistance—nor did Czechoslovakia, Poland, or Hungary. Rumania came through with a commitment to loan North Korea $6.25 million and Bulgaria offered a loan of $7.5 million. Albania and Mongolia, as strained

for economic resources as North Korea, offered some commodity
assistance as a token of support. No assistance was requested at that
time from China, which had given North Korea a grant of $200
million in 1953 (as compared with $250 million from the Soviet
Union at the same time). Kim's last stop was the U.S.S.R., where
he learned that for the full five-year-plan period he was to receive
only $75 million in grants and $42.5 million in loans.[100] Kim Il
Sung's visit to the Soviet Union was cut short by urgent news that
trouble was brewing at home.

In Kim's absence, members of the Soviet and Yenan factions
had begun a campaign in the press and other propaganda organs
against the development of a "cult of personality" and in favor
of "collective leadership," gaining considerable support among
the factions whose positions had been diminished during the rise
of Kim Il Sung. According to South Korean intelligence reports,
a complex plan had been worked out to criticize Kim Il Sung at
the central committee's plenary meeting upon his return, to
isolate him by the joint action of the various factions, to mobilize
resistance among the workers, and finally to carry out a coup
with the assistance of faction members in the army and the
Pyongyang police.[101] These reports also indicate that the Soviet
ambassador in Pyongyang was consulted, and that the Korean
ambassador to the U.S.S.R., a Yenan Korean, kept the Soviet
leadership informed. Regardless of the truth or falsity of these
reports, Kim Il Sung blamed the Soviet Union for the crisis.
He later said:

> The attack of the opportunists on our Party became most
> glaring between 1956 and 1957. At that time the handful
> of anti-Party factionalists and die-hard dogmatists lurking
> within our Party challenged the Party, in conspiracy with
> one another on the basis of revisionism and *with the backing
> of outside forces.* They not only calumniated the lines and
> policies of our Party, but also plotted together to subvert
> the leadership of the Party.
> The modern revisionists . . . opposed the socialist revolution
> in our country prattling that it was as yet premature; they

opposed our Party's line of socialist industrialization, the line of construction of an independent national economy in particular; and they *even brought economic pressure to bear upon us* inflicting tremendous losses upon our socialist construction.[102]

The crisis broke in North Korea at an emergency session of the central committee on August 30, 1956. At the meeting, a member of the Yenan faction introduced the criticism of Kim Il Sung, but upon being shouted down a vote was taken as to whether he should be permitted to continue the attack. Kim Il Sung had stacked the committee well—the attack was voted down.

During the next two years, Soviet and Yenan Koreans were weeded out of the Party hierarchy. Among the high level Soviet-Koreans purged between 1956 and 1958 were: Pak Ch'ang-ok, deputy premier, Kim Sŭng-hwa, minister of construction, Ki Sŏk-pok, vice minister of culture and propaganda, Chŏng Chun, vice minister of culture and propaganda, Pak Sa-hyŏn, commander of the Pyongyang Reconstruction Corps, Chang Ha il, editor-in-chief of *Minchu Chosŏn*, Ch'oë Chong-hak, political committee chief of national defense, Hŏ Sŏng-t'aek, minister of coal industry, Pak Ŭi-wan, minister of railroads, Hŏ Ik, principal of the Central Party School, and Hŏ Pin, ambassador to Poland.

Prominent Yenan Koreans purged included: Ch'oë Ch'ang-ik, deputy premier, Yun Kong-hŭm, minister of commerce, Yi P'il-kyu, formerly vice minister of home affairs, Han Mu, director of the National Library, Yi Sang-cho, ambassador to the U.S.S.R., Yang Kye, bureau chief of the cabinet secretariat, Yi Kwŏn-mu, commander in chief of the North Korean People's Army, Kim Ung, vice minister of defense, Kim Ul-kyu, vice minister of defense and chief of staff of the army, Chang P'yŏng-san, division commander of the North Korean People's Army, Pang Ho-san, division commander of the North Korean People's Army, Kim Wŏn-bong, minister of labor, An Han, vice minister of culture and propaganda, An Sin-ho, vice chairman of the Central Women's Alliance, Cho Yŏng, chairman of the Yanggang-do Provincial Party Committee, Yi Yu-min, member of the judicial committee of the Supreme People's Assembly, Ch'oë

Ch'ŏl-hwan, chief of propaganda of the secretariat of the central committee.

A few members of the domestic faction were purged during the same period. Five thousand lower-ranking party members were also said to have been removed.

Kim Il Sung's consolidation of control over the party was matched by the party's further consolidation of control over the society. On November 20, 1956, the first local government elections since 1949 were held. Before the war elections to the higher level committees had been held first and then, as the higher levels consolidated control, elections to the lower level committees were held. Elections to the village committees, numbering 54,279 members, were held first. Seven days later, on November 27, 9,346 members were elected to the district committees (the sub-districts had been abolished during the war, and a constitutional amendment in 1954 had made this abolition permanent), and 1,009 members to the provincial committees.[103]

In August 1957, elections were held to the Supreme People's Assembly for the first time since 1948. It was announced that 99.92 percent of the electorate voted for the proposed slate.[104] No "representation" of the South was included in the Second Assembly, and the pretense of coalition with other parties was rapidly fading. Whereas the Ch'ŏndokyo and Chosŏn Democratic parties had been represented by 35 members each in the preceding assembly, their number was reduced to 11 each in the new assembly. The Working People's Party, the Democratic Independence Party, and the People's Republican Party had each been represented by 20 members in the preceding assembly. Now their membership was 3, 1, and 3, respectively. Two new groups were represented in the new assembly: the "Establishing the People" Association, with 1 member, and the Buddhist Alliance, with 2. The biggest change, however, was in the deputies from "other organizations" and "independents," who had numbered 171 and 114, respectively, in the First Assembly. Their number had now dropped to 5 deputies from other organizations, and no independents. The pretense that the assembly performed some function seemed to be wearing thin, too. While the assembly in 1948 had "deliberated" for a full week, the first session of this assembly met for only three days. The new cabinet endorsed by the assembly was made up largely of members from Kim Il Sung's group, although a few members of other groups who were not to be purged until the following year were included, as well as a few who would not be purged at this time because they cooperated with Kim by turning in fellow faction-members who had plotted the anti-Kim movement.

By 1958, agricultural collectivization had been completed, and by 1959 only 45.7 percent of the labor force was employed in agriculture, as compared with 56.6 percent in 1956, and 66.4 percent in 1953, when collectivization had begun.[105] The peasants withdrawn from the farmland had first been channelled into the bureaucracy, thus creating a large portion of the population dependent upon the continued existence of the regime. The bureaucracy was able to absorb such a large number of people because it was placed in charge of the entire operation of the economy—industry, mining, trade, transportation, communications, the press, publications, propaganda, cultural activities, and the management of the agricultural cooperatives. Thus the regime was able to draw on the traditional desire for bureaucratic posts to support its consolidation of power. By 1958 not only was the size of the party enormous—nearly 12 percent of the population— but the bureaucracy represented perhaps more than 20 percent of the adult population.[106]

The phenomenally large bureaucracy taxed the resources of the regime heavily. In 1958-1959, this was remedied with the introduction of the "Ch'ŏllima (Flying Horse) Movement," similar to China's "Great Leap Forward." The bureaucrats were reportedly herded to a mass rally to initiate the movement and "volunteered" to transfer 50 percent of their number into the industrial labor force.[107]

The traditional pressure for admission to the bureaucracy had been allowed to follow its natural course. The government had lost much of its support among the farmers, which had been derived initially from the popular land reform, when they had been forced into collectives. In place of the support of the peasantry, however, the regime had substituted the support of an enormous party and bureaucracy. The decline in the absolute number of farmers, channelled first into the bureaucracy and from there into industry, and the control through the new collective farm administration, minimized peasant opposition to a level capable of being offset by the support supplied by the bureaucracy and party. By 1958, with the state being the only employer, few could afford to resist the existing political system.

Because of the clash with the Soviet Union, Soviet aid had declined sharply, as the U.S.S.R. continued to pressure Kim's regime to shift its economic and internal political policies. Kim, however, was determined to persist. "If our Party had listened to their views we would not have reached today's level of industrial development in fifty years," Kim retorted in 1959.[108] The lower the level of aid from the outside, the greater was the need to consolidate control over all local sources of funds—hence the great speed with which "socialization" (that is, nationalization and collectivization) of the economy was carried out.

In September 1958, the North Koreans received a loan of $52.5 million from China, just one month after the completion of North Korea's collectivization movement.[109] It was also in September 1958, that the North Koreans adopted a resolution at a plenary session of the central committee, to institute the "Ch'ŏllima Movement."[110] In October, the lowest administrative units were reorganized and merged with the collective farm management, and collective farms were merged into larger units so that their number was reduced from 13,309 to 3,843. This seemed a clear emulation of the Chinese policy adopted in April 1958.[111] On October 26, 1958, Chinese troops, which had remained in the peninsula since October 25, 1950, were finally withdrawn.

"Ch'ŏllima" literally means a "thousand-*li* horse," *li* being a Korean unit for measuring distance. The term was drawn from an ancient legend (originally Chinese) about a horse who could travel a thousand *li* in a single day. As the Ch'ŏllima Movement went into effect, workers were provided with incentives to produce, including awards and public praise. At first, individual "model workers" were awarded Ch'ŏllima awards for top production; however, when this tended to produce antagonism among the workers (often model workers found themselves ostracized because other workers accused them of forcing everyone to work harder), teams of workers were formed and "model brigades" were given Ch'ŏllima awards. Awards were given in sufficient numbers to form a class of "Ch'ŏllima Workers" who were granted special privileges.

The forced competition between workers and the increase in the industrial labor force brought a large jump in production in many sectors. However, the quality of many products was very poor, as the government repeatedly complained. The Ch'ŏllima Movement ended in throwing the economy completely out of balance. Pressure for overproduction in one sector required over-production in another to supply it. Increasing disproportions brought mounting frustrations and rivalries among the various ministries in charge of production, because no sector could rely on any other for definite knowledge of what would be supplied and when.[112] In 1959, balance between the sectors broke down. Raw materials could not be supplied fast enough to keep up with the unplanned demand. Expansion of heavy industry had to be cut back while concentrated efforts were put into the mining industry.

Perhaps one beneficial result of the short-lived emulation of Chinese policies was the pressure it placed on the Soviet Union to renew its support of North Korea. In 1959, the U.S.S.R. agreed to an additional loan of $125 million to assist the growth of the North Korean economy.[113] North Korea had achieved its objectives without yielding to Soviet pressures.

In addition to expanding his organizational support, Kim Il Sung had extended his control within the army. The party was slow to purge Yenan-trained officers in the armed forces, perhaps for fear of antagonizing members of the Chinese forces while they were still in North Korea. In 1958, however, it was reported that the government discovered a coup plan developed by Lt. Gen. Chang

P'yŏng-san, a prominent Yenan-trained division commander, to be carried out on May Day of that year.[114] Whether Chang had anticipated Chinese assistance is not known; the discovery was followed by a purge of Chang and the remaining prominent Yenan officers in the North Korean army. A thorough reorganization of the army followed the Chinese withdrawal. Party cells, which had not completely penetrated the army, were now established at all levels, and "cultural" (that is, party) officials within the army were henceforth required to approve all promotions.

For the first time, the fact that the ideology of the system had an external source began to be a disadvantage, especially because it was during this time that the U.S.S.R. and the P.R.C. began developing conflicting views over the interpretation of this ideology. A regime with its own unique idea system may be free to utilize ideological tools in response to its own internal needs, but where the idea system has external sources, external interpretations can have an impact upon internal politics, as was clearly displayed in the crisis created by the "de-Stalinization movement" in the U.S.S.R., which led to the crisis and purges of the 1956-1958 period in North Korea.

In response to this very serious problem, Kim Il Sung introduced the concept *"chu-ch'e"* (in their English publications the North Koreans spell this word *Jooche* or *Juche*), which he explained as follows: "By 'Jooche' we mean that in carrying out revolution and construction we should creatively apply the general truth of Marxism-Leninism to the specific realities of our own country, and precisely and fully take into account our own historical and actual situation, our own capacity and the traditions, requirements and the level of the consciousness of our own people."[115] Kim Il Sung evidently was unaware that he was almost rephrasing a quotation from Syngman Rhee's political treatise of 1904 when Rhee had said that "all political systems depend upon the level of the people in that country. If, without looking at the level of the people, we simply look at the political system of other nations, we cannot apply them to oriental society . . . We must consider the basic customs, systems, values, and attitudes of our people, and develop a system which reconciles the old and the new, so that development can progress smoothly."[116] While not identical in content (Rhee was talking about applying "Western democracy" to Korea, and Kim about applying "Marxism-Leninism"), the two statements were remarkably similar in emphasizing the "level" of the people, and the unique Korean historical background and customs which required an adaptation of the foreign political system to the conditions of Korea.

Kim Il Sung went on to say that *"chu-ch'e"* meant not only ideological self-reliance as a nation, but the ability to think independently as an individual: "If one loses *chu-ch'e* and falls into flunkeyism, his faculty of independent thinking is paralyzed, with the result that he will not only be unable to display any initiative but in the end, even will become unable to distinguish right from wrong and follow others blindly and will be inclined to depend on only others for everything, losing faith in his own strength."[117] Kim's idea of individual *"chu-ch'e"* strongly resembled something Rhee had written in his book, *The Spirit of Independence,* in 1904: "First we must free the people from the bonds of simply following the dictates of custom and authority, and guide them to reach their *own* conclusions as to what is right and what is wrong. This alone is true freedom."[118] Unlike the ideas of Rhee, which never became required reading in the South and which were known to few, the ideas of Kim Il Sung were soon to be utilized as political tools of the Northern regime, as they became required reading at party meetings, in schools, and in the meetings of economic and "social" organizations in North Korea.

In 1959, another round of local elections was held, to the district and village levels, and the slate was reportedly approved by 99.99 percent of the voters.[119] By 1961, when the Fourth Party Congress of the Korean Worker's Party met from September 11 to 18, full consolidation of the bases of the system was evident. Membership in the party totaled 1,311,563, or 12.2 percent of the population, organized in 65,000 cells. Control over the economy had been fully consolidated, and 38.3 percent of the labor force was emplyed in industry, with 44.4 percent remaining in agriculture, as of 1960. This contrasted with 8.8 percent in industry and 59.7 percent in agriculture in the South in 1962. Furthermore, 13.7 percent of the labor force were employed by the regime as "office workers." The urbanization of the North and South was now virtually the same: 40.6 percent of the population lived in urban areas in the North, 40.8 percent in the South. Not only had North Korea caught up with the South in urbanization, but its university students now numbered 97,000 as compared with 97,800 in the South, while its population was still less than one-half that of the South. North Korea was now willing to mobilize its population, having consolidated political control, and the traditional demand for upward mobility through education was met as one means of mobilizing support for the regime.

Kim Il Sung was clearly unchallengeable by the time of the Fourth Party Congress. Elected chairman once again, four of his vice chairmen were selected from his Manchurian-Korean entourage, while the fifth, Kim Ch'ang-man from Yenan, was reported to have cooperated in the purge of his fellow Yenan comrades. Of the seventeen members of the party's political committee, nine were from Kim's entourage and of the remaining, one, Kim Ch'ang-man, had been identified as Yenan, while one, Nam Il, had been identified with the Soviet group. Of the other six, three were domestic Communists (one of them, Mme. Pak Chŏng-ae, the Soviet-educated widow of Kim Yŏng-pŏm, being fluent in Russian, had accompanied Kim Il Sung on his 1956 tour of Eastern Europe and the U.S.S.R.), and the other three were totally new faces, not having previously been identified with any faction. Of the 12 candidate members to the new political committee, seven were Kim's old comrades (one was Kim's younger brother, Kim Yong Ju), one was domestic, one Yenan, and three were new faces. Kim was accurate in depicting the challenge from the factions as having been brought to an end. He placed his comrade Pak Kum-ch'ŏl back in the post of director of party organization, which he had held during 1953-1956.[120]

By 1961, Kim Il Sung's system was clearly consolidated. The next task would be to use the institutional and ideological instruments of the regime to resocialize the population into channelling political behavior through the new political system, hence "normalizing" the system, and to seek to legitimize the new system by building an aura of legitimacy about its leader, with the goal of transferring this legitimacy to the new institutions of the system.

Chapter VI

ATTEMPTED INTRODUCTION OF THE SECOND
REPUBLIC IN SOUTH KOREA, 1960-1961

The Second Republic, which came into being after the fall of
the Rhee government, lasted but a brief time, yet an examination
of the developments during that period is essential to an understanding
both of the events that came before and of the developments that
have come since this chapter in Korean history. To some, this period
represents the high water mark of Korean democracy—the golden
age to which the nation must ultimately return. To many Koreans,
however, it is a period they would prefer be forgotten—a period
which illustrated dramatically those aspects of Korean political
behavior inherited from the traditional era which most need
alteration before an effective developmental system may be
constructed.

The Korean student revolution of 1960 introduced a new era
in Korean politics, but an era quite different from that anticipated
by the build-up of hopes that came with the outbreak of the revolt.
For nearly a year, the new regime sought to operate without undertaking effective political consolidation, partly because of a lack of
political acumen, but partly out of a positive conviction that the
normal processes of a democratic system preclude the process of
consolidation. It was not long before the predictable occurred:
the most powerful organization and source of guns, the armed
forces, quickly moved into the political vacuum, and overthrew
the short-lived Second Republic.

The Interim Regime
The collapse of the Rhee government did not immediately
lead to chaos. Although the Liberal Party and the police disintegrated
as effective organizational systems, the bureaucracy, the army, the
economic enterprises, and of course the opposition party, remained
intact. Students, reacting responsibly to their new-found voice in

public affairs, helped to direct traffic and maintain order, then returned to their schools while an interim government laid the groundwork for the promulgation of a new constitution and the holding of new elections. Although there seemed to be some danger of anarchic conditions erupting, relative calm was maintained. Rhee himself had turned the administration over to a well-known Korean politician of some stature, Hŏ Chŏng, a former acting prime minister and former mayor of Seoul, providing for a relatively smooth transition. The populace generally took a "wait and see" attitude, while the interim government, acting in cooperation with the assembly, oversaw the major work of the period, the changing of the constitution. It also purged the civil service of those officials most blatantly involved in the abuses of the preceding regime.

Assembly membership during the interim government did not change, although 105 of the 138 assemblymen who had been members of the Liberal Party broke with the party and became independents within a little over a month after Rhee's resignation.[1] The party that Rhee had assembled as an organizational base for his system of government disintegrated and vanished as a force in Korean politics. At the same time that most of the Liberals rejected their former party affiliation, Democratic Party members were smugly confident that history had now proven the inappropriateness of a presidential system of government, and met no serious opposition in their efforts to introduce a parliamentary system.[2] By June 15, 1960, just six weeks after Rhee's fall, a new constitution had been created.[3] Though termed "amendments" to the old constitution, in effect the changes introduced the form of constitution originally advocated by the Korean Democratic Party in 1948: a parliamentary, cabinet-responsible system, headed by a prime minister, with a figurehead president.[4] The amendments were adopted by a vote of 208 to 3.

The new constitution provided that the president would be elected by the assembly, and the "prime minister and a majority of the state council [cabinet] members shall be chosen from among members of the National Assembly."[5] All obstacles to the shift of assembly members into high bureaucratic posts, with the accompanying expanse of patronage, appeared to have been finally eliminated.

Since the primary objective for entering politics continued to be the traditional goal of securing high bureaucratic appointment and patronage, this new constitution insured that the assembly was to become, not a forum for the consideration of legislation, but— explicitly, now, as it had previously been implicitly—a forum for acting out the struggle for bureaucratic power. The new constitution provided for several means of paralyzing the executive in the contest for patronage and appointments. Not only were members of the executive branch to be drawn from the assembly, but the assembly itself was to select the president and then approve the appointment of the prime minister. In order to secure the approval of a majority of the assembly members, in the context of Korean politics, the prime minister would be obliged to promise patronage within the administration in exchange for each vote. Since patronage to the assemblyman generally meant his own appointment to the cabinet, majority consent would be impossible to obtain unless the prime minister could promise a rapid rotation of the cabinet to ensure that all were rewarded. With 223 members of the House of Representatives (lower house) and 58 members of the House of Councilors (upper house), a phenomenal number of cabinet posts would need to be promised in order to obtain majority support. Furthermore, the House of Representatives now had the power to vote "no confidence" in the cabinet—insurance that the disappointed assemblymen could vote down the government if their expected cabinet appointments did not come through on schedule. The implications for the new constitution within the Korean milieu may sound exaggerated, but given the traditional behavior patterns, the results which followed were not unpredictable.

Non-Consolidation of the Second Republic

New elections to the National Assembly were held on July 29, 1960, resulting in an overwhelming election of Democratic Party members. In the vacuum left by the collapse of the Liberal Party, this result was not unanticipated, despite the sudden emergence of

several dozen minor parties following the student revolt. Both
houses of the new assembly were controlled by the Democrats—
175 of 233 seats in the lower house and 31 of 58 seats in the upper
house. The remaining assembly members included, in the House of
Representatives, 46 independents, 4 Popular Socialists, 2 Liberals,
1 Korean Socialist, and a number of splinter group members; in
the House of Councilors, 20 independents, 4 Liberals, 1 Popular
Socialist, 1 Korean Socialist, and 1 member of the National League
of Progressives.[6] The election itself was observed by ten teams
from the U.N. Commission for the Unification and Rehabilitation
of Korea, which pronounced the elections to have been free,
orderly, and fair, after taking into account malpractices in 13
districts in which the elections were consequently repeated.[7]

Election statistics were misleading in two ways: they
under-represented the strength of the Democrats since the
"independents" were available to the Democratic Party upon the
opening of the assembly, and, in fact many of the independents
immediately joined the DP; and they overrepresented the unity
of the party. As soon as the Democrats secured control of the
assembly, they followed traditional patterns in splitting into
factions—in this case the "Old Faction," which had been the
Democratic Nationalist Party prior to 1955, and the "New Faction,"
whose members had joined with the DNP in the merger of 1955
which had created the Democratic Party. The Old Faction, or
former DNP, had been formed in 1949 of the Korean Democratic
Party (KDP), founded in 1945 by the traditionally-oriented
former landowners, and the Korean Provisional Government
group (KPG) from China. The New Faction, on the other hand,
when it had joined the party in 1955, was made up of former
independents and Liberals, largely with bureaucratic backgrounds,
and others disappointed in the Rhee government's distribution of
appointments. An important element among this New Faction
were members of a pre-Liberation group known as the Hŭngsadan
(Rising fighter corps) composed primarily of northern Koreans
from the Pyongyang area, many of whom had spent some years
in the United States. Chang Myŏn, the New Faction leader who

had lost the vice presidency in the rigged election of 1960, was a member of this group.

The first task of the Democratic Party upon its assumption of leadership in the new Second Republic was the organization of an administration. This was no small task, for while the DP had been united in opposing Rhee, in an effort to secure power for its own members, and on the idea of a parliamentary government as a model for Korea, it was united on little else. Yun Po-sŏn, leader of the Old Faction, was elected on August 12 to the ceremonial post of president with little dispute, but his appointment of the prime minister, who under the new constitution would be executive head of government, became a matter of serious controversy. His first nomination, on August 16, was of Kim To-yŏn, another member of the Old Faction. This appointment was rejected by the assembly by a margin of three votes. Yun then nominated Chang Myŏn, head of the New Faction and former vice president, who was accepted by the assembly on August 19 by a margin of only two votes.[8]

As this duo, Yun and Chang, constituted the leadership of the Second Republic, it is important to examine their sources of political legitimacy and their experience in handling the tools of politics. Yun, educated at the University of Edinburgh, Scotland, was 63 in 1960. During 1948-1949, he had served as the appointed mayor of Seoul, and in 1949-1950 was Rhee's minister of commerce and industry. Proudly identifying himself as a *"yangban"* of the old land-owning class, it was apparently on this ground that he claimed legitimacy.

Dr. Chang, a Catholic of North Korean origin, had been Rhee's first ambassador to Washington, and was prime minister just prior to the "political turmoil" of 1952. At that time, the opposition had sought American intervention against Rhee. It was also Chang who had defeated Rhee's vice presidential choice in 1956, causing Rhee to run again in 1960 in an effort to reverse the outcome. It was Chang who had been "defeated" for the vice presidency, obviously by fraudulent means, in the rigged elections of 1960. Chang was also a member of the Hŭngsadan, a group of

Koreans who had provided strong opposition to Rhee during the preindependence period.[9] Having thus represented opposition to Rhee's "dictatorship" on several occasions, Chang could claim legitimacy on the basis of having stood against the same tyranny the "Student Revolution" had been moved to overthrow. The difficulty with this source, however, was that students participating in the movement had *not* done so with the thought either of supporting Chang or of overthrowing Rhee.[10]

The new government immediately faced a problem of a breakdown in its base of political organization. Upon Chang's election to the post of prime minister, seventy of the Old Faction assembly members resolved to depart from the party.[11] Chang did not help matters at all when he then immediately named a cabinet of New Faction members, adding only one Old Faction member and two independents.[12] The Old Faction members, who had at one time constituted the Democratic Nationalist Party, found themselves in precisely the same position as they had been following their election of Syngman Rhee to the presidency in 1948, when he had then named only one of their number to the cabinet. Just as they had then turned bitterly upon Rhee, they now prepared to bolt the Democratic Party in disgust. The threat of these members to leave the party led to a "compromise" in which Chang brought five Old Faction members into the cabinet and agreed to share the committee appointments in the assembly, but this move did not assuage the embittered Old Faction members.[13] Kim To-yŏn, resentful at having been defeated for the post of prime minister by the concerted voting of the New Faction members, led most of his following out of the party to form the "New Democratic Party" (NDP) on October 18.[14] Ironically, the "New" Democratic Party, consisting of the "Old Faction" of the Democratic Party was essentially the direct descendant of the "Korean Democratic Party" originally founded in 1945, whereas the "Democratic Party," now consisting of the "New Faction," was made up of the heterogeneous group that had joined with the Democratic Nationalist Party to form the Democratic Party in 1955. A factor in the split was the resentment

of the Old Faction members over the New Faction's "takeover"
of the party, which, in their view, they had originally founded and
which they had led throughout the long years when it was the
opposition.

The Old Faction was not the only part of the party to challenge
Chang Myŏn's leadership. A so-called "young group" within the
New Faction, resentful of the "old group" of Chang Myŏn and those
he appointed to the cabinet, formed its own "New Breeze Society"
(Shinpunghoë) in an effort to promote its strength vis-à-vis the
newly-formed leadership.[15] Chang, therefore, did not have majority
support within the assembly, as the groups split into factions in
traditional Yi Dynasty fashion over the issue of bureaucratic posts.
As had happened to Rhee before him, Chang found himself faced
with a hostile majority in the assembly.

Efforts to introduce a political program under these circumstances were doomed to legislative paralysis. Though the Democratic
Party had initially held an 80 percent majority in the two houses
of the assembly, the cabinet went through three complete changes
during the next nine months, following its initial formation on
August 23, with reshuffles occurring on September 12, 1960,
January 20, 1961, and May 3, 1961.[16] The comments of Rhee on
the incompatibility of a parliamentary system with the traditional
behavior patterns of Koreans seemed to echo ironically. Observers
who had noted with dismay that the turnover in cabinet positions
under the Rhee government had been quite frequent, resulting in a
seven-month average tenure, were confounded by the record of the
Democratic Party government, with its average of two months
tenure for a cabinet minister.

While faced with a rapid disintegration of its organizational
base, the Democratic Party was unable to secure other effective
political tools. Its sole ideological core had rested on opposition
to the Rhee "dictatorship" and support for a parliamentary system.
Rhee had been overthrown and the parliamentary system introduced
beyond that there was little to hold them together. In fact, according
to an American Embassy official in Korea at the time, the members
of the assembly had to be personally bribed to pass the government

budget at the end of 1960.[17] As one observer pointed out, the group was divided between a majority oriented toward power-exploitation goals, regretful and resentful over the power denied them in the preceding administration, and a minority concerned with developmental goals.[18] Though they claimed to be more "democratic"—that is, more "liberal" than the Rhee government, in fact more than 40 percent of the assembly members of the Democratic Party were the sons of former landlords, and nearly one-fourth of them had served in the Japanese civil service.[19] The lack of ideological focus was one of the fatal shortcomings of the Democratic regime.

The ideological vagueness of the DP was vividly illustrated by the policy-orientation of the new regime, which sought to remain in power by responding only to public pressures, rather than formulating independent programs. The initial goal of the administration's "Economic Development First" policy was in line with general popular demands as evidenced by a public opinion survey conducted by the cabinet secretariat in November 1960, in which more than 70 percent of respondents expressed the opinion that economic problems of the nation were the most urgent area for governmental concern.[20] Yet the perpetual factional disputes within the assembly prohibited the formulation of effective policies in this direction.

The total subordination of policy to "public opinion" became in its extreme, mob rule.[21] Not only did mobs move in to rule in the streets, but even invaded and took over the National Assembly. So hesitant was the new regime to take any action which might be interpreted as "dictatorial," that its police powers almost completely atrophied. During the ten months of the Democratic Party administration, an estimated 2,000 street demonstrations occurred, involving about one million persons.[22] The military junta which came in with the 1961 coup estimated this to mean an average of 7.3 demonstrations *per day* during the Second Republic, with an average of 3,876 individuals demonstrating in the streets of Seoul each day of the period of DP rule. Provided with no organized channels of expression, the people took to the streets.[23] Chang

Myŏn explained the philosophy of the Democratic Party government in dealing with the chaotic situation after he had been overthrown:

> While the Democratic Party was engaged in the bloody struggle against the Liberal Party, the thing that the party promised to the people was the absolute guarantee of freedom and removal of tyranny. Thus, we reaffirmed freedom when we came to power . . .
>
> Even though the society was deep in chaos because of the daily occurrence of demonstrations, the Democratic Party government could not violate its own pledge of freedom that it had made before coming to power . . .
>
> In short, the credo of the Democratic Party government was, "Let them for once enjoy the unlimited freedom that they have been longing for."[24]

The worst example of mob rule was the takeover of the assembly by students and other individuals incensed by the light sentences passed by the courts on some members of the Rhee government. These groups demanded the passage of *ex post facto* laws, imposing greater penalties upon individuals involved in irregular activities prior to the student revolution.[25] Not only did the government not rebuke or seek to oust the intruders, but it apologized to the mob for government laxity in dealing with the former members of the Liberal Party government, and agreed to pass the laws demanded. In November, an amendment to the constitution, passed by the National Assembly, empowered it to formulate *ex post facto* laws affecting those involved in the government prior to April 26, 1960 (the date of Rhee's resignation), and in December a law was passed "restricting the civil rights" of those individuals who held a broad range of positions at the time of the 1960 elections.[26] Only six members of the House of Representatives voted against the law, which, in effect, offered *ex post facto* revenge upon their former political opponents, in the name of democracy.[27]

Several other developments grew out of the ideology of "freedom" created by the Democratic Party regime. The press,

which had been limited in size by licensing measures under the
Rhee government, though reasonably free—as evidenced by its
strong criticism of Rhee throughout the period—now mushroomed.
Nearly three times as many periodicals and newspapers were being
published in early 1961 as in early 1960, employing 160,000
reporters.[28] The number of newspapers and journals increased from
about 600 to about 1,500 during the year of DP rule. Many of
these new "papers" prospered on the business of blackmail—
charging politicians and others for material, spurious or not, that
they *didn't* print—or sold their licenses to others for exhorbitant
profit.[29] "Freedom of the press" was the catchword which protected
journalistic license much as "freedom of assembly" kept the traffic
blocked downtown.

The new-found "freedom" threw Korea's intellectuals and
students into an acute identity crisis. Syngman Rhee, once
visualized as a fiery national hero, both dynamic and learned, who
had worked for Korea's independence and held South Korea
together in the tragedy of war, was now remembered only in his
years of senility as a man who clung unheroically to political
power which was exercised in his name by a corrupt party hierarchy
and a repressive police force. The fact that an opposition which
continually maligned him, and a free press which strongly opposed
him, had persisted throughout Rhee's administration, did not deter
people from characterizing his government as an unmitigated
dictatorship. The ineptness of the Democratic Party rule which
followed the Rhee government compounded the malaise of the
intelligentsia, who, having exalted in the success of the "Student
Revolution" did not know where to turn. "Democracy is not suited
to Korea," became almost a hackneyed phrase.[30]

Intellectuals were not the only ones to demonstrate their
disaffection with the Chang government. By-elections in Seoul in
December 1960 brought out only 38.2 percent of the vote, whereas
previous elections, even in the more apathetic urban centers, had
always involved at least 70 percent participation.[31] A cabinet-
sponsored poll taken in eight of Korea's universities, surveying
3,000 persons, found that only 3.7 percent supported the Chang

government, while 51.5 percent indicated that they would "wait and see."[32] Clearly the chaos, confusion, and economic stagnation of the period were not what the populace had sought through the 1960 revolution. Concerned over government inability to introduce effective economic policies, and disgusted with what appeared to be an increasing subservience to outside pressures, the students began to find the northern regime increasingly attractive. Students started a campaign which aimed to collect one million signatures in favor of reunification. They then threatened the government that unless it undertook immediate measures leading to reunification, they would "march to Panmunjom" and open negotiations with North Korea themselves.[33] When the government did not respond, Seoul National University students, who had formed a "National Unification League," issued a statement on May 4, 1961, that they would meet North Korean students in Panmunjom on May 20.[34] The South Korean government was overthrown by an army coup on May 16.

Problems of organization and ideology were overshadowed by the pressing need for political funds. Having witnessed the influence of the threat of withdrawal of U.S. aid on the collapse of the Rhee government, the new government's first concern was to secure American backing by being highly solicitous of American interests and advice. The United States had been unsuccessfully pressuring the Rhee government to change the exchange rate between the *hwan* and the dollar, and to permit American supervision of aid expenditures. Though Rhee had resisted these efforts, the new government quickly acquiesced to the American demands, the *hwan* being devalued from $1:hw 650 to $1:hw 1000 in January and $1:hw 1300 in February of 1961.[35] The results were disastrous. When the exchange rate changed, the cost of imports on which the economy depended doubled, producing panic and spiraling inflation.[36] Prices, which had been stable in December 1960, rose 15 percent during the first two months of 1961, after the exchange rate change, and showed no signs of levelling off. Industrial product depending heavily on imports, dropped drastically during the same period—in some sectors by as much as 24 percent in a single month.

But a far more important factor was that the portion of American aid in the national budget jumped, due to the exchange rate change and an increase in aid after Rhee's resignation, so that it now constituted 52 percent of the national budget. At the same time, the government concluded an agreement with the United States to permit "without restriction" continuous observation and review by the United States of all aid programs and related records.[37] The result was that the United States was given the authority to supervise more than half of the expenditures of the Korean government. It appeared to many political participants that the Korean economy would be virtually completely controlled by the United States. Dissident assemblymen demanded to know if the American ambassador should henceforth be addressed as "Governor-General."[38]

With the United States "observing and reviewing" all aid appropriations and expenditures, kickbacks could no longer be made to the political parties from the aid dollar recipients—who, using the undervalued dollars, had channelled back the difference in black market value of the dollar to the ruling Liberal Party under the preceding regime. One important alternative to which the new governing party now turned was the importation of Japanese goods: the "game" would now operate with Japanese yen. Granting licenses to import goods previously prohibited because they were non-essential luxury items, the government lifted restrictions on trade with Japan, and the luxury goods began flowing in. Because these goods brought high profits to those who could obtain licenses, kickbacks to the governing party was a prime motive for the sudden lifting of the ban on these commodities.[39]

While imports from Japan climbed to new proportions, domestic production, already stunned by the doubling of the cost of imports on which it depended, continued its decline. The economic growth rate, which had dropped from 8.7 percent in 1957 to 5.2 percent in 1959 as American aid fell, plunged further in 1960 to 2.1 percent—less than the population increase of 2.7 percent during the same period—while unemployment, already high, rose to 23.7 percent.[40] Prices jumped 38 percent in the year of DP rule, while production capacity declined 9.8 percent.[41] While Rhee's system of political funding was a "drag" on economic growth, the new system seems to have been seriously deleterious.

Not all economic problems could be traced to the exchange rate change or the increase of luxury imports from Japan, of course. Equally important was the government's inability, because of factionalist paralysis in the assembly, to undertake any effective economic program. With less than a two-month average tenure for a cabinet minister, officials had no time to become familiar with the operation of the governmental departments, much less initiate new programs. In the spring a serious famine threatened the countryside, as a general food shortage developed. The number of food-short farm families requiring government relief assistance in March totaled 217,456, or a total of 1,153,398 individuals, and the ministry of agriculture predicted it would rise to 1,312,322 farm *families* by the end of May.[42] While the agricultural crisis was due to a drought, a condition beyond the control of the ruling party, many felt that the government's delay in undertaking a needed public works program, promised but never implemented, exacerbated the crisis.

Government enterprises were openly parceled out as patronage appointments, from which political funds were derived. In one year, the government ran up a deficit in the eight government-owned industries totaling Hw 45,500,000,000 ($70 million).[43] Another source of funds was bribery from businessmen to evade taxes. It was later reported that, "One group of thirteen businessmen alone have publicly admitted to evading the *hwan* equivalent of more than $33,449,924 in income taxes . . . through massive bribery of public officials."[44] Since the Democratic Party had not regularized control over its fund inputs, it is unclear whether these sums went into party coffers or into the personal pockets of the individual officials. According to the reported statement of one chief of staff of the army during this period, the prime minister had requested that he divert Hw 1.7 billion to the Chang government, and he was dismissed from the position when he refused.[45] Reported the money used to bribe the members of the National Assembly to pass the national budget came from military appropriations.

The most serious failure of the Second Republic was, obviously, its inability to consolidate control over the sources of guns. To those who have sought to defend the shortcomings of the Second Republic on the grounds that the army did not "give it a chance" to overcome its problems, it must be pointed out that one of the fundamental, and most important tasks of a government is to exert control over its own instruments of force.

While the Democratic Party government undertook a purge of the national police, removing 2,213 men, including 81 chiefs of police, the police force itself was unable to regain control in the society. It not only failed to halt violent demonstrations, including public arson, but the crime rate rose markedly.[46] A total of 140,000 crimes were said to have been committed during the five months from August 1960 to February 1961.[47]

Perhaps because of its "democratic" orientation, the Chang regime failed to make any serious efforts to woo the armed forces. While ten percent of Rhee's cabinet officers had been drawn from the military,[48] the Chang government, despite the rapid turnover of personnel, did not give any cabinet-level appointments to military men. The minister of defense, who under the interim government had been an army general, was replaced by a civilian. Not only did the government undercut the position of chief of staff of the army, by placing it under unsympathetic civilian surveillance, but the post of chief of staff itself was rotated four times during the ten months of DP rule. The prime minister seemed to be playing naively with the old factional makeup of the armed forces—a factionalism which had been being brought increasingly under control as more professionally trained soldiers had begun moving up the ranks. Because senior officers had been drawn heavily from North Korean refugees during the early days of the army's formation, factionalism during the Rhee years was said to divide along the lines of northeasterners versus northwesterners, with southerners being generally nonaligned because of weakness in the high ranks. Chang Myŏn was vocally criticized by his opponents in the assembly, therefore, for his final chief of staff appointment—that of General Chang To-yŏng (Chang Do Young) because General

Chang was from the same region (northwest) of northern Korea as was Prime Minister Chang.[49] Though there may have been no grounds for assertions that he was playing regional favoritism, the appointment did raise the issue of factions once again. This was unfortunate, as there had been no factional appointment to the post for two years.

Military grievances began to accumulate—some in response to government actions, others developing out of increasing pressures and problems within the armed forces.[50] Among the latter were serious difficulties growing out of the early method of formation of the armed forces.

Grievances within the army were two-fold: resentment over rank and promotions, and continuing dissatisfaction over the past political involvement of senior officers. The problems of rank and promotion were serious and derived from the fact that the army itself had been built virtually overnight, from a non-existent force in 1945, to 100,000 men in 1950, and 700,000 by 1955. An army must have officers, and when the armed forces are created in a hurry, officers likewise must be created rapidly. The first class of officers in training received only six weeks of preparation before they were sent into the field; training then increased to three months, six months, and finally to one year. It was not until the Korean War was in progress that the four-year military academy came into exister Yet, for the purposes of regularity, seniority in the service had to take precedence over extent of training in the area of promotions and rank—leading to the result that the higher ranking officers, consequently, were the least trained. In actuality, this situation was mitigated by the fact that the bulk of the first six "classes" of officers who went through officer training—those taken in during the period of the American Military Government—were drawn from men with previous experience in the Japanese army. This common background of the senior officers, however, did not serve to unite them vis-à-vis the junior officers. On the contrary, a vertical division had formed in the armed forces on a regional basis. This division was further complicated by the horizontal rank division among those trained in the Japanese army, on the basis of the extent and quality of their education there, and the previous rank they had attained. Since the class of training within the Korean army was the major basis for rank and promotion, previous Japanese ranks were sometimes reversed within the Korean army. Furthermore, the traditional criteria of age-rank, common throughout the society, was often confused in the army during the first few years because two people of the same age may have entered the officer training classes three or six months apart, or a younger individual may have entered ahead of one older than himself. These problems were generally nonexistent at the junior level, where training had become regularized and recruits of the same age, without previous training, entered and completed the four-year academy together. But among the senior officers recruited under the period of American rule, the confusing hierarchy created by conflicting systems of seniority caused many grievances and much feeling of rank insecurity.

These rank insecurities and antagonisms existing among senior officers were added to the fact that junior officers collectively felt serious grievances against their senior officers. These grievances had many causes. In the first place, the senior officers had moved up the ranks of the army very fast, with the initial expansion of the army. For instance, of the little over 100 officers graduating from the First Class, 42 had become Brigadier Generals within five years, and 69 had reached that rank within eight years.[51] Once the first few classes had reached the top ranks, however, and the army had reached maximum size, there was little room left for upward mobility of the junior officers. Senior officers were still relatively young, and several years were to go by before they would reach retirement age. Yet the junior officers were only a few years younger than their seniors, and had received a longer period of training. It was members of the Eighth Class who ultimately planned the coup which overthrew the Second Republic. Of their 1,801 members, trained just four years after the First Class, only 140 had reached the rank of colonel 12 years after graduation.[52] Grievances against senior officers were exacerbated by the fact that junior officers were aware of the corruption existing during the Rhee regime, and resented the accumulation of wealth by their superiors. Furthermore, the junior officers had carried the major part of the battle experience during the Korean War, and had suffered most from the results of the corruption which had benefited their superiors—often having to make do in battles with the enemy with a serious lack of equipment because supplies had been sold to line the pockets of the senior officers and the coffers of the Liberal Party.

The Student Revolution had led to a general expectation among junior officers that large numbers of senior officers, involved in the Rhee period of corruption, would be purged.[53] When a purge did not follow, the junior officers reached their boiling point.

Several aspects of the policies of the DP government were resented by the armed forces. Troop reductions in 1957 and 1958 had reduced the size of the armed forces from 700,000 to 600,000, which had further reduced promotional opportunities. When the Chang government campaigned on a program to reduce the size of the armed forces to 400,000, therefore, concern among junior officers was quickly aroused. Even when this promise was reduced after Chang became prime minister to a reduction of 100,000 instead of 200,000 men, it still represented a serious threat to the officers. Much of the pressure for reduction in size was seen by the military as coming from the United States.[54] Furthermore, the army was upset by the unwillingness of the government to defend the integrity of the military when sharp attacks were launched upon it by members of the National Assembly. The army chief of staff was humiliated by assembly interrogators, who proceded with impunity to charge the armed forces with collaboration with the Rhee regime, and, unwisely, to tar the entire institution with the brush of corruption. Perhaps the most serious mistake of the DP regime, however, was its promise to purge the armed forces, and then its failure to follow through on the promise. The purge promise brought profound anxiety to senior officers, while the failure to carry it out alienated those junior officers whose hopes and expectations had been raised by the initial commitment. The vacillation of the Chang Myŏn government over the issue of purges in the armed forces was largely due to pressures from the American officers in Korea who warned that such a purge would "endanger the command structure" of the armed forces.[55]

The promise of purges in the armed forces had led a number of junior officers to take steps which they would otherwise never have dared, seeking to bring to light evidence of misconduct on the part of their senior officers. Thus a group of members of the army's Eighth Class, encouraged by the appearance of sympathy in the government, presented a series of demands to the army chief of staff.[56] The group met with a severe reprimand, but to avoid the revelations which would undoubtedly come out in a court-martial trial, the junior officers were permitted to "voluntarily" resign. The instigator of this move among the junior officers, Lt. Col. Kim Jong Pil (Kim Chŏng-p'il), was thus provided with the free time and mobility he would need to coordinate plans for a coup d'etat. Another challenge came within the marine corps, from Brig. Gen. Kim Tong-ha (who later mobilized the bulk of the troops to capture Seoul) who sought to expose evidence detrimental to his superiors, and was also forced to resign. These grievances, then, were far from minor in leading to the coup d'etat.

Other army grievances against the Chang government were secondary. The soldiers were immensely concerned over the student movements seeking unification with North Korea, and coming largely from rural backgrounds were also upset over the government's inability to overcome the serious famine conditions in the country-side. The two main participants in organizing the coup, Lt. Col. Kim and his uncle by marriage, Major Gen. Park Chung Hee (Pak Chŏng-hŭi), had both worked with army intelligence and were familiar with the developments in North Korea, information un-available to most people in the society. They had become especially impressed and concerned with North Korea's rapid economic development which so overshadowed that of the South.

Finally, considerable resentment existed over the government's willingness to "kowtow" to American pressures, both in the realm of economics and in military policies. Although a great many soldiers had been trained in the United States or had worked directly with the American forces, the group involved directly in the coup included those who had had perhaps the least contact with Americans, and consequently resented the advantages others had received. The very fact that the highest-ranking officers in the armed forces were generally also those whose English was most fluent was perhaps reflected in the fact that those who led the coup had an unusual lack of proficiency in the English language.

Although trouble had been evident for some time, Rhee had kept the army firmly under control, keeping careful tabs on all schisms which existed, and was perhaps more closely informed about the army than about any other part of the political arena. For the members of the Democratic Party, however, sources of information about the armed forces were practically non-existent. Since the military had collaborated with the Liberal Party, and since civilian politicians had been prone to consider military personnel "beneath" their social status (a carry-over of traditional attitudes toward the military), information about conditions in the armed forces was lacking to members of the DP government.

Indeed, Democratic Party members and members of the military were inhabitants of vastly different worlds, with virtually no overlap. In social origin, educational background, regional ties, age, ideological outlook, and professional orientation, the two groups could not be farther apart, given the general basis of homogeneity within the Korean culture. By and large, members of the Democratic Party had their roots in the traditional Korean upper class: 41 percent of the DP members who served at cabinet level were sons of landlords.[57] They continued to be influenced by the traditional bureaucracy-as-power orientation. Ideologically, they were conservative, in a laissez-faire sense often identified with earlier forms of liberalism in the West. The strongest regional base for the Democratic Party was the deep southwest, where the original Korean Democratic Party had had its firmest roots. In age, DP leaders were generally in their fifties, with the major leaders nearer sixty, and with party promotions still heavily determined by traditio concepts of seniority by age. Fully 58 percent of the major participa in the DP government had been educated outside of Korea.[58]

Officers in the armed forces, by contrast, were generally of rural, often peasant, origin (71 percent of those who participated in the military government came from rural areas), with their major area of regional origin in North Korea. Most had been educated within Korea, and were in their thirties and forties. They had been trained with an orientation toward efficiency, and failed to understand the inefficiencies created by haggling politicians, while serious problems went unsolved. There were, thus, virtually no ties or mutual concerns existing between the DP government and the officers of the armed forces. Once the soldiers determined to move, no conflicting loyalties existed to deter their action.

The Democratic Party regime had failed to consolidate an effective political base. Organizationally, the party was split in multiple directions over the issue of the possession of bureaucratic power. That this split assisted the coup makers was evident not only because the president, Yun Po-sŏn, head of the Old Faction, welcomed the military intervention as a means of ousting the New Faction from control, but because it was later revealed that he had in fact been consulted and consented to the coup.[59] (He later changed his mind when he learned that Old Faction politicians were to be excluded from power as well).

Ideologically, the Democratic Party regime drew a blank. Though there was no public enthusiasm for the coup, neither was there any outcry defending the DP regime, which had drawn no avid supporters among the politically articulate. Financially, the Democratic Party government was a fiasco. The Rhee regime had been ousted partly because of economic grievances; the DP left the country in worse straits than it had found it, yet it had secured no regularized source of political funding. Finally, the DP government had not only been unable to maintain internal order, but it had actively alienated the armed forces, the most powerful and cohesive organization in the country, and of course, the major instrument of force.

The Democratic Party government in southern Korea had been an example, par excellence, of traditional Korean political behavior given free rein. The scramble for power which occupied the major political participants left many Koreans dejected and disillusioned about the possibility of ever achieving an effective modern government in the country. Many Koreans interpreted this experience as an indictment of themselves, which led to an outpouring of expressions of national shame and self-condemnation.[60] As one writer, observing intellectual attitudes in the post-coup era noted, there is a "nagging doubt [fear] in the Korean mind that there is a fatal flaw in the Korean national character that incapacitates the nation in [its] endeavor to construct an essentially modern and democratic way of life."[61] Surveys conducted following the period of Democratic Party rule showed a general consensus that Koreans were not "ready" for a democratic system of government.[62] The groups surveyed (students, professors, and journalists) did not reject democracy, but rather indicated that they felt that Koreans were not "yet" capable of living up to its requirements. Asked what aspect of social behavior or social policy should be emphasized most in order to achieve democracy, by far the greatest number of intellectuals surveyed in one very thorough and extensive study responded, "Responsibility."[63]

The era of Democratic Party rule was especially illustrative of traditional behavior in large part because the individual participants themselves were drawn from backgrounds most heavily influenced by Korean tradition. The religious affiliations claimed by the leading members, for example, illustrate the heavier impact of tradition on this regime than on either its predecessor or its successor. In a study of the social backgrounds of the participants of the three regimes, 22 percent of those surveyed in the Democratic regime claimed to be Confucianists, as compared with 18 percent in the Liberal Party government and only 9 percent in the succeeding military government. Furthermore, the lower-class religions, Protestantism and Buddhism, were underrepresented in the Democratic Party government as compared with the other regimes. Among Liberals, 39 percent had claimed to be Protestant and 16 percent Buddhist (a total of 55 percent), and among members of the military government, 28 percent claimed to be Protestant and 19 percent Buddhist (a total of 47 percent).

Among the Democrats, on the other hand, only 20 percent claimed
to be Protestant and 7 percent Buddhist (a total of 27 percent).[64]
The Democrats were also more likely than their predecessors or
successors in the government to be of landlord background, 41
percent of them being sons of landlords as opposed to 37 percent
of the Liberals and 26 percent of members of the military government.[65] If the family backgrounds of the participants in the three
governments were to be put on a scale of modernization, we would
find that 44 percent of the participants of the military government
were born in the "modernized" sectors of the society (i.e., were
sons of professionals, businessmen, shopkeepers, bureaucrats,
clerical workers, or laborers), and 38 percent of participants in the
Liberal Party government came from such backgrounds, as opposed
to only 25 percent of the participants in the DP government.[66]
This seems to bear out the thesis that the Democrats were influenced
by a more traditional orientation than the participants in the
governments which came before and after the Second Republic.

Unfavorable internal, external, and nonpolitical factors,
combined with the lack of a consolidation-oriented leadership,
and the inability of the Democratic Party to cohere on ideas, to
maintain an effective organization, to secure a regular source of
political funding, or, most importantly, to assert any control
over the instruments of force in the society, doomed the Second
Republic to failure. A longer period in power would only have led
the society to greater extremes of political disintegration. The
political disintegration of the Second Republic was interrupted
when on May 16, 1961, the army seized control through a military
coup; the DP government fell in the face of the bloodless coup
with hardly a whimper.

Chapter VII

MILITARY RULE AND THE THIRD REPUBLIC
IN SOUTH KOREA, 1961–1971

The military group which came to power in South Korea through
the coup d'etat of May 16, 1961, moved swiftly in an effort to
consolidate political power bases during the initial two-year period
of military rule. Indeed, the new regime was the prototype of a
consolidating regime acting deliberately to secure control over
political resources. Once again, the most serious challenge to the
consolidation effort came from external sources, and much of the
initial program had to be modified to adapt to the political
ideologies of the United States. The military's political regime
consolidated control through its initial period of rule far more
effectively than had its predecessors, but still did not succeed in
building a permanent base of support. By 1972, the initial party
organization built during the military regime had been truncated,
and the system once again reverted to a top-heavy set of elite
organizations without effective political penetration, riding astride
a volatile mobilized society, maintaining somewhat precarious
control through measures little designed to augment its bases of
support. Financial sources became as irregular as they had been
under the Rhee system, and the initial "revolutionary" ideological
impetus evaporated. When the government set out on a renewed
consolidation effort based on a new state of emergency in 1971,
many claimed to see a parallel with the counterproductive extremist
measures of the final years of the Rhee regime.

Initial Consolidation Phase: The Military Government, 1961–1963
During the period from May 1961 to January 1963, while
the country remained under military rule, the coup-makers sought
to create a new organizational base for the Korean political system,
to acquire a source of financing for this organizational system, to
consolidate and keep control over the instruments of force, and to

introduce a "revolutionary" new outlook in the society. The very first challenge they were to meet was from external sources.

The army was under U.N. (U.S.) command, and in moving against the government, the armed forces were also carrying out a mutiny against their American commanding officers. In order to avoid resistance within their own forces, the coup-makers had forced the chief of staff, Lieutenant General Chang To-yŏng, at gun-point, to participate in the coup. Chang's involvement also served to diminish the possibilities for American resistance.

The chief of staff had learned in advance of the unauthorized movement of Korean forces, and before being forced into involvement, had phoned Prime Minister Chang Myŏn, warning him that a coup movement appeared in progress and suggesting that he escape to safety. The prime minister fled immediately to the American Embassy compound.[1] The guards at the compound gates phoned for permission to admit the prime minister, but the long delay in receiving a reply finally induced Chang to go elsewhere, and he went into hiding in a Catholic convent.[2] The Chang government itself offered no resistance whatsoever to the coup, making American efforts to oppose it very difficult. Only about fifty MPs, noting the unauthorized crossing of the Han River bridge by military troops before dawn on May 16, 1961, challenged the move to occupy Seoul. A brief round of gunfire, resulting in the wounding of a few MPs, ended all resistance. Within a few hours, the army was in control of Seoul.

The move by the military forces apparently caught U.S. officials by surprise.[3] The first challenge to the coup came from American officials in Korea, dismayed by the military action. While the Chang government had been politically inept, it had been "democratic," and hence had caused no embarrassment to the United States as had Rhee's government before it. Indeed, virtually every piece of American advice had been accepted and followed. The repressive police force had disappeared. Controls on the press and on assembly had been lifted. The exchange rate had been changed to a more realistic level. And the government had given the United States carte blanche to supervise the use to which all

U.S. aid—now 52 percent of the total Korean budget—was put. The government was even prepared to reduce the size of the armed forces, in accordance with American requests, and it yielded to American military commanders in relinquishing its previously-made promise to purge the higher-level officers in the armed forces who had been involved in the corruption of the Rhee period. No government in Seoul could have proved more amenable to American policy.

Although the Chang government itself took no steps to counter the army coup, the United States officials in Korea reacted quickly. General Carter B. Magruder, Chief of U.N. Command, demanded that the chiefs of the Korean armed forces "use their authority and influence to see that control is immediately turned back to the lawful government authorities and that order is restored to the armed forces."[4] Marshall Green, the U.S. chargé d'affaires in Seoul, declared that the United States was still supporting the "constitutional Government of the Republic of Korea as elected by the people last July and as constituted last August with the election of a Prime Minister."[5] The comments by the American officials were sent to the Seoul newspapers and the Voice of the United Nations Command, a radio broadcasting system controlled by the Americans. While the newspapers could not print the information because they had been placed under censorship by the military forces in Seoul, where martial law had been declared, the Voice of the U.N. Command did broadcast the statements.[6] The American Embassy made a desperate effort to discover the whereabouts of Prime Minister Chang, to receive endorsement for a move against the coup-makers, but he could not be found.

U.S. officials then turned to President Yun. Yun Po-sŏn had already had a visit from Major General Park Chung Hee, and had agreed not to oppose the coup, explaining that he had thought a military coup inevitable in view of the ineptitude of the Chang government.[7] Yun had agreed to Major General Park's request to write personal letters to the army commanders to urge them to avoid any bloodshed.[8] The president was therefore unwilling to yield to the request made by Minister Green and General Magruder that anti-coup forces be mobilized to retake Seoul.

General Magruder returned to headquarters determined to take action on his own initiative, calling an emergency staff meeting where he outlined a plan to mobilize the Korean First Army Corps and the First U.S. Corps.[9] The commander of the Korean First Corps, however, faced mutiny within his own command when he tried to mobilize forces, and found that it was impossible to carry out the American officer's strategy. A few hours later a statement was issued in his name supporting the coup.[10] Although the Chang government's representative in Washington requested that the U.S. forces intervene unilaterally, the initiation of fighting between U.S. and South Korean forces was not a policy alternative to be considered seriously.

The new military regime, still ostensibly led by Lieutenant General Chang To-yŏng, set up a Military Revolutionary Committee, and proclaimed martial law. It issued six pledges as the basis of its policy; including promises to adhere to the policy of anti-communism, to observe the U.N. Charter, to eliminate corruption, to build a self-sufficient economy, to promote unification and then "to turn over the reins of power to new and conscientious politicians and return to our original duties."[11]

Two days after the coup, on May 18, former Prime Minister Chang ventured forth from hiding, obviously shaken. He called a meeting of the cabinet, at which he endorsed the declaration of martial law, after which all cabinet members submitted their resignations. Following this, the Military Revolutionary Committee changed its title to the Supreme Council for National Reconstruction (SCNR). On the same day, General Yi Han-lim, commander of the First Army, who had attempted to mobilize forces against the coup, was arrested. Most of Korea's highest-ranking military men were appointed to the SCNR, in an effort to consolidate control within the armed forces and avoid any threat of a counter-coup. Dr. Yu Chin-o, president of Korea University, who had drafted the initial version of the 1948 constitution (before Rhee's alterations), and had drawn up the 1960 "amendments" which constituted the constitution of the Second Republic, was called in to find a means of legalizing the coup.[12]

With President Yun Po-sŏn still remaining as executive head of government, no problem of international recognition arose. However, the junta was especially concerned over the lack of positive response from the United States, as Washington made no comment on the actions of the U.S. military and diplomatic officials who had declared their opposition to the coup. Lieutenant General Chang To-yŏng decided to write to President Kennedy to explain the reasons for the coup and its objectives. In his letter, Chang referred to the deteriorating situation within the country, listed the six pledges of the Revolutionary Committee, and concluded by saying that "Upon completion of our mission we will hand over the control of the Government to clean and conscientious civilians and to return to our proper duties of the military."[13]

On the day after the resignation of the Chang cabinet and the establishment of the SCNR, a statement was issued by the State Department, saying:

> It has been our purpose in Korea to help the Korean people achieve, through democratic processes, stability, order, constitutional government and the rule of law as the essential basis for sound economic growth and improvement in the welfare of the people as well as for defense of the country against any possible communist threat.
> This continues to be our purpose.
> We are encouraged by the strong intent of the military leaders in Korea to return the government to civilian hands.[14]

The lack of enthusiasm for the military coup was fully evident.

No direct response to General Chang's letter came, but a week after it was sent Minister Green issued an acknowledgement of the letter to President Kennedy, with a statement directed not to the SCNR chairman but to the new Korean foreign minister, stating that the American government "notes with satisfaction the expression of intention to return the Government to civilian control."[15]

The coup d'etat had brought new leadership into the national arena, to supplant that of the First and Second Republics.[16] Although several officers at first served as "front men" it soon

became obvious that the leading force was Major General Park
Chung Hee and his nephew-in-law, Lieutenant Colonel Kim Jong Pil,
along with the latter's classmates of the Eighth Class of the Korean
Military Academy. The Eighth Class, trained just before the Korean
War, had carried the brunt of battle in the Korean War, and it
included those most uncomfortable over the blocked promotional
system within the army. Kim himself, 35 years old in 1961, one
of the few college trained officers of rank (he had studied two years
in the teachers' college of Seoul National University before entering
military training) had become head of the North Korean Section
of the Army Intelligence Bureau in 1952.[17] With access to the
personnel files of the highest ranking Korean officers, Kim Jong Pil
was able to evaluate the background of these men and determine
who would be reliable participants in the coup and post-coup
government. Initial recruitment and planning of the coup had in
fact begun long before the Student Revolution, as the Rhee regime
had begun to deteriorate.[18] A preliminary plan scheduled the coup
for May 1960, when then Chief of Staff Song Yo-chan was to leave
the country on a visit to the United States. These plans were
aborted by the Student Revolution.[19]

Although Kim Jong Pil was clearly the organizer and instigator
of the coup, the cooperation of a higher ranking officer had been
needed, and the willingness of his uncle-by-marriage to join forces
with the younger coup-makers was essential to the success of the
movement. It was the older Park Chung Hee who was soon to
eclipse Kim, and emerge as the strong man of Korean politics while
Kim's own power base seemed to have dwindled. In the early stages,
even while Kim was the real force behind the revolution, Park
emerged as the leadership symbol of the new movement.

Park Chung Hee seemed the antithesis of the ideal leadership
symbol. Of diminutive stature and lacking in physical charm, rarely
known to smile, the new leader was an enigma to Koreans. Even
when he emerged from behind the scenes as the leader, popular
speculation kept up the inquiry as to who *really* was the new leader,
perhaps expecting some dynamic figure to ultimately burst forth
from behind the dour facade. Perhaps for this reason the colorful

Kim Jong Pil became for a time an important focus of attention.

Not only was Park without personal attractiveness, but he had no traceable claim to leadership legitimacy. His background involved training by the Japanese in a military academy in Manchuria from 1940 to 1942, and participation in the Japanese Kwantung army in Manchuria during 1943 through 1945.[20] In 1946, he became an officer in the Republic of Korea Army, after having been trained at the Officers Candidate School in its Second Class.[21] In the same year, his older brother was killed as a participant in the Communist-instigated mob violence in Taegu.[22] In 1948, Park himself was arrested for participation in the Communist-led Yosu rebellion, and sentenced to death.[23] (Park later explained that he had been implicated because of the involvement of his deceased brother's friends.) His sentence was commuted to life imprisonment shortly thereafter, however, and he was reinstated in the army in 1950, with the outbreak of the war. Park's rise through the ranks was slower than that of most of his comrades, perhaps because the Rhee government had been unwilling to place full confidence in him. It may also have been because, as a South Korean, Park did not belong to either of the prominent officer factions. If these factors adversely affected his career opportunities, they did give him the chance to emerge as one of the few high-ranking officers who had been uninvolved in the factionalism and army corruption during the First Republic.

The first task of the new government, once a challenge from the prior government and from the United States had been averted, was to secure firm control over the military. This was done by absorbing all of the important officers who would cooperate into the SCNR, and then eliminating one-by-one those who were considered untrustworthy. The SCNR was originally composed of thirty-two members, including the chiefs of all branches of the armed forces. General Chang To-yŏng was named chairman of the Supreme Council on May 19. On the 20th, a cabinet was established with General Chang as prime minister and defense minister, in addition to the positions he already held as chief of staff of the army and chairman of the SCNR.[24] By early June, the junta had consolidated control over the top levels of the army, having arrested three generals who refused to cooperate.

Then came the move against Chang To-yŏng. On June 6, he "released" the posts of chief of staff of the army and minister of defense, while remaining chairman of the Revolutionary Council and prime minister. General Song Yo-chan, who had pressured Rhee to resign, was named minister of defense.[25] On July 3, Chang To-yŏng "resigned" from the posts of prime minister and chairman of the SCNR.[26] General Song Yo-chan became prime minister and Park Chung Hee became chairman of the SCNR. (It was not long until General Song, too, would leave the SCNR). On July 8, Chang was arrested for an "anti-revolutionary plot," and was sentenced to death on January 10, 1962.[27] (He was subsequently pardoned and went into exile in the United States.)

Having consolidated its control over the top ranks, the junta began a purge of the armed forces in July, and 2,000 officers were retired, forty of them generals, eliminating those who were disaffected with the coup-makers.[28] The junior officers who benefited through the promotions engendered by the purge were indebted to the new regime.

Efforts to legitimize the new regime were relatively weak. The junta announced that it would promote a "new generation" of leaders, but only three civilians were appointed to the cabinet. By and large, the new government was determined to legitimize itself through its actions rather than through symbolism. One of its first acts was a decree (SCNR #6) dissolving all political and social organizations with the exception of those engaged in charitable relief, academic, and religious activities.[29] Fifteen political parties and 238 other organizations were thus eliminated. The press was also placed under strict censorship, and, under Decree #11, which set standards for publication of periodicals (for example, the publisher must own its own printing facilities), 1,170 newspapers and periodicals were forced to close down.[30] As if this were not enough to remove sources of opposition to the new regime, leaders of the Chang Myŏn government were placed under arrest.

On June 6, the SCNR promulgated a new law, the "Law

Regarding Extraordinary Measures for National Reconstruction,"
turning over all government power to the SCNR. Under the new
law, the SCNR was established as a temporary governing organ, to
act "pending the establishment of a government following the
composition of the National Assembly by means of a general
election to be held after the completion of the tasks of the military
revolution of May 16."[31] While the previous constitution was not
formally suspended, the new law provided that "provisions of the
Constitution which may conflict with the Law Regarding Extraordinary Measures for National Reconstruction shall be governed
by this law."[32] Commenting on the new powers of the SCNR,
The New York Times observed that "The junta assumed all
dictatorial powers that not even Rhee had enjoyed."[33]

The new government moved swiftly to illustrate its determination
to "clean up" Korean politics and restore order. On May 22, it was
announced that 4,200 hoodlums, who had terrorized urban areas
during the Second Republic, had been arrested, as well as 2,100
suspected Communist sympathizers.[34] The hoodlums were paraded
through the streets, wearing signs saying, "I was a Hoodlum," to
demonstrate the effectiveness of the new government in clearing
out crime and corruption, and then were sent to serve in a public
works program. By the end of the first few weeks, 13,300 persons
had been arrested.[35] The puritanical approach of the junta group
was sometimes extreme. Denouncing the high living of urban elites,
rice to restaurants was rationed, movies were placed under censorship
to eliminate "immoral influences" and imported luxury items such
as lipsticks and other nonessentials of the bourgeoisie, were seized
and set ablaze in a gigantic bonfire. A total of 440 procurers were
arrested, and 4,411 prostitutes were removed from their place of
business and sent to their homes.[36] Coffee shops, tea rooms, bars,
and dance halls were closed down. Evidencing their rural inclinations,
the military junta decreed the abolition of all usurious debts on the
part of farmers and fishermen, and guaranteed government repayment
of those debts which were within legal interest rates.[37] It was
announced that fifty-one "illicit fortune makers" had been apprehended
and 5,752,543,368 *won* recovered from them by the government.[38]

A purge of the civil service was undertaken, with 41,000 members of the bureaucracy dismissed on the grounds that they had secured their jobs through nepotism, favoritism, or bribery.[39]

Public reaction to these drastic measures was generally favorable. The initiative and élan of the new leadership was admired, and there was general agreement that such sweeping measures were "necessary" to clear away the chaos and corruption of the preceding period. Even the conservative *Dong-A Ilbo* newspaper, with a circulation of 300,000 in 1961 (then, as now, the most influential daily paper), came out in favor of the military revolution on May 28.[40] Although the newspaper was clearly under censorship, it was under no obligation to take a positive stand in favor of the military regime. The highly influential *Sassanggye* intellectual journal, which has suffered government persecution under each succeeding Korean government because of its outspoken character, also congratulated the military government for "Making the citizens respect the law, reinvigorating the sagging morale, banishing hoodlums, punishing illegal fortune makers, and relieving the debt-ridden farmers and fishermen from privation." The journal acknowledged the immense difficulty in undertaking political, social, and moral reforms "in an environment so inimical to reform due to hundreds of years of imbedded social evils, mephitic habits, and primitive poverty . . ."[41] Even Yu Chin-o, president of Korea University and author of the first two Korean constitutions, later the head of the opposition party, described the military coup as "historically inevitable."[42]

Though the junta had earned grudging support from the Korean populace through its zealous efforts at reform, these same measures only served to further alienate official American observers, who were not reluctant to show their disapproval. The newly-arrived American ambassador on July 4 very pointedly praised President Yun Po-sŏn, the only remaining figure of the old regime, calling him the "symbol of the new hopes and aspirations of the Korean people."[43] More important than such indirect criticism, however, was the economic clout the United States possessed. Providing more than 50 percent of the national budget, and 72.4 percent of the defense budget,[44] the United States held a powerful instrument for pressuring the military regime into reversing the policies it had initiated. When the Korean government began in July to discuss economic assistance possibilities with the United States, Washington stipulated two conditions: (1) the release of arrested political leaders, and (2) a specific public commitment to restore the government to civilian control.[45] On August 12, General Park announced that the government would be returned to civilian control in the summer of 1963, and he ordered the release of thousands of prisoners, dropping all charges against former members of the Chang government.[46] When General Park later met with President Kennedy in Washington in November, the U.S. president promised "all possible economic aid," expressing his satisfaction with the pledge "to restore civilian government at the earliest possible date."[47]

With an externally-imposed deadline for completing their consolidation efforts, the new military leadership set about creating a political base at breakneck speed. Park Chung Hee explained in August 1961 that the purpose of the period of military rule was to establish "the foundation for new democratic institutions," to create "a true democratic political order," and to establish "a firm foundation for democratic prosperity of the nation."

The first step in its organizational efforts, was the creation on June 10, 1961 (by Decree #619) of the Korean Central Intelligence Agency [Han'guk chung'ang chŏngbopu] or CIA, headed by Kim Jong Pil. The new agency was designed, unlike its American counterpart, "to supervise and coordinate both international and domestic intelligence activities and criminal investigation by all government intelligence agencies, including that of the military."[48] Originally built on the base of a 3,000-man contingent from the existing Army Counter-Intelligence Corps (which had been Kim Jong Pil's home base within the army), the new CIA was to expand to 370,000 employees by 1964, the most cohesive organization within South Korean society.[49] With its intricate network of informants and agents, it seemed to parallel the secret police instrumentalities of the North.

The first task of the new agency was the screening of all high-ranking government employees. Of 41,000 screened, 1,863 were found to have been involved in past "misdeeds" (corruption) or "anti-revolutionary" activities (anti-military government, or pro-Communist).[50] The new CIA also served to seek out and identify potential countercoup elements. By the end of the first two years, thirteen such "anti-revolutionary" or countercoup attempts had reportedly been discovered. One by one, many of the higher officers who had been absorbed into the SCNR were removed as counter-revolutionaries. By February 1963, only six of the original thirty-two members of the SCNR remained, while others more receptive to the goals of the coupmakers had moved in to take the places of those removed. One effect of the removals was to eliminate virtually all of the high-level officers of North Korean background from participation.[51]

While continuing to consolidate control within the armed forces, the junta initiated a seven-point "moral regeneration" program: to encourage austerity, inspire diligence, promote a creative and productive life, teach respect for national customs, improve the national morality, and improve individual physical fitness.[52] An organization to carry out the People's Movement for National Reconstruction (PMNR) was created, headquartered in Seoul, and Dr. Yu Chin-o, the president of Korea University, was named as its head. The junta appointed the leaders of the most important civic organizations, prominent journalists and publishers, educators, entertainers, and religious leaders, to leadership positions in the movement, and everyone was requested to become a member "voluntarily."[53] Units were to be established in every city, town, and village, and it was hoped that one member of each family would attend meetings. By 1963, the organization was said to have 3.9 million members.[54] Yu Chin-o resigned as head of the organization after only three months, noting that it was a "totalitarian system."[55] Like most organizations initiated in Korean society, unable to secure permanent funding and support, the PMNR ultimately evaporated, but not without first producing some leaders who could be recruited into a new political party. Other "nonpolitical" organizations created and financed by the junta government included the Korean Youth Association, Korean Women's Association, 4-H Clubs, and the Soil Improvement Society.

The organization of the Democratic Republican Party [Minju konghwa-dang], or DRP, was initiated by Kim Jong Pil in the summer of 1962 (while it was still ostensibly illegal to carry out political activities), using the organizational base of the CIA, which was itself funded by a government budget. The objective of the CIA operation was to create a nation-wide skeleton of the party organization, to provide a political base for Park's election campaign in 1963 and the emergence of "new leadership" who would be "honest and conscientious civilians" into the national political arena. Young journalists, professors, and some younger government officials were given indoctrination and instructions on organizational techniques at a special training center.[56] In fact, however, many members of this "new generation" were drawn from the junior officer corps, largely from Kim Jong Pil's Eighth Class, and were prepared to resign from the armed services to operate the party. In the CIA, the party-building operation became known as "Operation V," that is, "Operation Victory."

The new DRP party organization, based on the principle of democratic-centralism, bore striking similarities to the Communist party of the North.[57] The plan of the party was a highly centralized organizational structure, with a disciplined party membership, and a single command from the headquarters to the provincial, city, and district branches. A powerful secretariat structure was envisaged to control party affairs including personnel management and finances of the party from the center to the district level. The theoretical governing body was to be a national convention, which would elect the party central committee, which in turn would elect the central standing committee. Policy would be made by a party council which would nominate all important officers. This party council, to be made up of fifteen persons, was initially envisaged as the controlling body of the party; since the plan was to subordinate government activities to party policy, this council was in effect designed to be the center of national power. The party secretariat, implementing party policy, was to have 1,300 permanent-salaried staff members at all levels. The cost of operation of the secretariat alone was estimated at $700,000 per month.[58] Kim Jong Pil envisaged this system of centralized party control as an effective means of eliminating factionalism and maintaining a unity of purpose.

One prominent member of the junta, General Kim Chae-ch'un, who succeeded Kim Jong Pil as director of the CIA, later charged that the party had not only been patterned after that of the North, but that Kim Jong Pil actually had direct North Korean assistance and advice. General Kim's story was reconstructed by Kim Kyŏng-rae, then political editor and later managing editor of the *Kyunghyang Shinmun* daily newspaper in Seoul, in an article in the intellectual journal *Sassanggye* in 1963.[59] According to General Kim, the North Korean vice minister of foreign trade, Hwang T'ae-sŏng, who had been a close friend of Park Chung Hee's brother (who had been killed in the Communist-led riots in Taegu in 1946), came to Seoul in August 1961, met Park's widowed sister-in-law, who introduced him to Kim Jong Pil, and then explained to the CIA director the organization of the North Korean Workers' Party, upon which the DRP was fashioned. Park Chung Hee later admitted, upon being questioned at a press conference, that Hwang had come to Seoul, but stated that he had been apprehended and executed.[60] Regardless of the truth of the story, it was clear that the two Korean ruling parties were closely parallel in organizational structure.

The new party would face two difficult problems in competing in a political election campaign. One problem was the lack of national reputation of the "new generation" leaders who would have to compete with well-known national political figures. A second problem was that to run such a party organization and to carry out an expensive election campaign, funds in large amounts would be needed.

On March 16, 1962, one solution to the first problem was offered by the passage of the Political Activities Purification Act (PAPA), which placed 4,374 former politicians under a political ban for the next six years.[61] Among those blacklisted were the most prominent leaders of the Liberal Party, the Democratic Party, the New Democratic Party, and the minor socialist and progressive parties, former high government officials, "illicit fortune makers," and student activists who had been involved in the "March to Panmunjom" movement, as well as the former military leaders who had been ousted from the SCNR, and newspapermen who had been critical of the junta. The law barred any kind of political activity for the six-year period, including candidacy for political office, political campaigning, political speech-making, party activities, etc. This law was aimed at keeping the "old politicians" out of political competition long enough for the "new generation" to consolidate its political base, publicize the names of its individual members to the voters, and prove itself to the public through effective political work. The first Five Year Economic Plan would have been completed by the end of the six year period, through which it was hoped much economic improvement would be evident to the population. Also, before six years were over, two national elections would have been held (assuming that the four-year term of office was to be retained under the new system, as was ultimately provided in the new constitution), giving the new party ample time to learn how to operate within the electoral process.

President Yun Po-sŏn, who had remained in office despite the arrest of the leaders of the Chang government the preceding summer, was exempted from the political blacklist. Upon learning that most of his "Old Faction" colleagues were to be excluded from political participation, however, Yun resigned from the presidency in protest on March 22, 1962.[62] Since the junta had passed a law making the chairman of SCNR, its vice chairman, and the head of the cabinet jointly responsible for the duties of the president, "Whenever the President is in default or unable to perform his duties for any reason . . . ,"[63] the resignation of the president created no crisis. More serious, was the incipient split within the coup forces which the political ban initiated or furthered.

From the beginning, there was evidence of friction between the "young Turks" of Kim Jong Pil's Eighth Class (the young colonels' group) and the more senior officers involved in the SCNR. Kim envisaged a quite radical change in the entire political structure of Korea, a "revolution" which would reshape the society and character of the people. Indeed, his goals were as sweeping as those of the leadership of the North, though with an avowedly different aim: to make the people capable of living within the framework of a modern democratic, egalitarian society. The goals of the older military leaders were much more limited: to eliminate the conditions of chaos and corruption, and then turn the system back to the political leaders.

Not all of Kim Jong Pil's more radical ideas were well received by the older leaders who controlled the SCNR, despite the fact that most of the initial policies and élan came from the programs recommended by the young colonels' (Eighth Class) group. The administration of the political ban was an example of the policy conflict. While the initiative clearly came from the Kim Jong Pil group, the law was to be administered by the SCNR. A provision in the law stipulated that a screening committee would be appointed to hear the appeals of those who had been blacklisted, and clearance would be given to those who could demonstrate that they had been uninvolved in corrupt practices, or who could show mitigating circumstances such as action under duress, subsequent repentance, contributions to the military revolution, and so forth. The committee was headed by an older officer, and only one of its seven members was associated with the Eighth Class. Of 2,958 persons who applied for clearance, 1,336 were cleared by May 30, 1962.[64] Considerable pressure on the SCNR finally induced Park Chung Hee to use his special powers under the law to remove the ban from additional persons, so that by February 1963 only 268 politicians were still banned from political participation.[65]

In June 1962, the junta took the first step in consolidating control over financing by declaring a currency reform, involving the freezing of bank deposits of which only sums below certain amounts would be released, the remainder confiscated by the junta as "illegal hoarding."[66] This step was identical with that taken by the North Korean regime in 1946, in its efforts to secure control over financial resources and reduce possible resources to opponents of the regime. The objective of both regimes leaned more toward removing resources available to opponents than to the actual accumulation of the "hoarded" funds. One of the stated objectives of the Five Year Plan the junta had promulgated was "the reform and abolition of vicious social and economic circles."[67] The move was attributed to the instigation of Kim Jong Pil. Politically-motivated, the currency reform had no economic justification; indeed, the economic losses due to the uncertainty it engendered were said to have been greater than the funds accumulated. American economic advisers were baffled by the new policy, and annoyed at the junta for undertaking the "economic reform" without seeking expert economic advice. Within eleven days, the freeze had to be relaxed and by July the junta abandoned the policy entirely.

Another political economic technique, economically disadvantageous but affecting the political balance, was the expansion of currency in circulation. Since the government could affect the distribution of economic resources after it came to power, it could create a new economic balance by putting more resources in the hands of its supporters by simply distributing newly printed currency to them. Although the total value of funds in existence would remain unchanged due to the inflationary pressure created by the currency expansion, the value of the funds in the hands of opponents would be reduced while the value of the funds in the hands of supporters would be increased, shifting the political balance. Such "economic" policy cannot be evaluated purely in terms of economic goals, since positive inflationary policies are often contrary to effective economic development policies. The rationale must be seen rather in the political motivations. Between 1961 and 1963, the total money in circulation increased 70.2 percent.[69]

During the period of military rule, four major scandals occurred, all connected with the operations of the CIA involving financial activities. It was widely believed that these activities were undertaken in order to secure political funds for the DRP.[70] These scandals included: the importation by the CIA of 1,642 Datsun automobiles from Japan, duty-free (the normal duty on

automobiles was 110 percent) and their resale, at twice the import
price, under the name "Saenara" (the New Country) automobiles;
the importation of 880 pinball machines from Japan, duty-free; the
manipulation of the Korean stock market; and the construction of
the Walker Hill Resort. The last-named effort created quite a stir in
the United States, as it was aimed at attracting money from American
GIs. Since the bars and gambling casinos, dance halls, and other
entertainment spots had been closed down, there was nothing left
to attract GIs on leave to spend their money in Korea; most chose
to spend their time in Japan, even before these establishments had
been closed. The idea of the Walker Hill was to permit GIs to spend
their dollars on such activities in Korea, while isolating the Korean
population from such "degenerate" influences. Koreans were not
to be permitted to visit the new resort, except as the guests of
Americans. Profits from the operation would go into the party coffers.
When the news hit the American press, the U.S. army declared the
new resort "off-limits" and as a result it was a financial fiasco.[71]

Another alleged source of funds for the party, which might
explain the extensive resources of the DRP in 1963, involved a
secret agreement between Kim Jong Pil and Japanese Foreign
Minister Ohira, concluded in November 1962, just a little over a
month before the ban on political activities was to be lifted, and
just before the initiation of the first Five Year Plan. The existence
of the secret agreement was later made public but it was never
proved that money had been advanced by the Japanese to Kim
Jong Pil at that time.

For years, South Korea and Japan had carried on intermittent
and unsuccessful negotiations for a normalization of relations.
Several points of disagreement existed, but one of the major
disputes between the two sides had been the Korean demand for
reparations for the Japanese exploitation of the peninsula and
the "pain and suffering" of the Korean people during forty years
of Japanese rule. The Japanese had refused to consider reparations,
claiming that their period of rule had been of immeasurable benefit
to the Korean people, and had counterclaimed for reparations for
property seized from the Japanese at the time of liberation. At one

time Japan actually stated that she was entitled to payment for
85 percent of all Korean property on the grounds that Koreans
had illegally expropriated it from Japanese owners (an argument
which seemed clearly to contradict the argument that Japanese
rule was beneficial to Korea).[72] Although Japan later dropped its
claims for property payments, Korea had remained adamant,
especially since Japan was willing to discuss reparations with
the Philippines, a country which had been occupied by Japan for
only four years. Syngman Rhee had been demanding $2 billion;
Chang Myŏn had reduced the request to $1.25 billion. On
November 12, 1962, Kim Jong Pil made a secret agreement with
Japanese Foreign Minister Ohira Masayoshi, unknown to the
Korean public, outlining a basis for agreement to restore relations
between the two countries. The agreement stipulated that Korea
would settle for a $300 million grant from Japan, a $200 million
loan as "economic aid," $100 million in commercial credits, and
an unspecified amount in Japanese goods and services, to be paid
to Korea over a ten year period.[73]

Later, National Assemblyman Kim Chun-yŏn, a former
minister of justice (and one of only two of the First Republic's
cabinet ministers who had never been implicated in involvement
in corrupt activities, and hence was never placed under the
political ban) charged that Kim Jong Pil had received $130 million
from the Japanese as advance payment to finance the Five Year
Plan, and an additional $20 million on the side to finance party
activities.[74] This, he said, explained the timing and the secrecy of
the agreement. Assemblyman Kim Chun-yŏn, who had been a law
school classmate of the former Japanese Prime Minister Kishi
(the brother of then Prime Minister Sato) at Tokyo Imperial
University, claimed to have received reliable information on the
deal from sources in Japan. The elderly former justice minister
filed suit against Kim Jong Pil for violation of security laws which
prohibit receiving money for political activities from foreign sources.
Unable to subpoena his sources of information in Japan, however, Kim
Chun-yŏn not only lost his case, but was subsequently prosecuted for
"falsification," and sentenced to a year and a half in prison.[75]

The new leaders had a vision of the kind of Korea they would like to see: economically and technologically modernized, with living standards on a level to compare favorably with the Western world, yet rejecting the "degenerate" aspects of Western society which they had conceived through their GI-influenced world view. They wanted a Korea proudly independent and respecting its own basic traditional values, yet rejecting the behavior patterns that had led Korea into decline and collapse under the Yi dynasty. The group sought to utilize these ideas as a means of securing support. Three books were published under Park Chung Hee's name during the first three years of military rule: *Chidojado* [The ways of a leader], *Uri minjŏkŭi nagalki* [Our nation's path], and *Kukka-wa hyŏngmyŏng-kwa na* [The country, the revolution, and I]. These books, among other things, called for a regeneration of the Korean character and the elimination of such dysfunctional characteristics as factionalism, bureaucratism, and "flunkeyism."

In anticipation of the prospective return to "civilian rule," the government began the preparation of a new constitution, through a committee set up on July 11, 1962. The constitution was drafted by the committee, which consisted of nine members of the SCNR and twenty-one civilian advisers, and with the advice of Harvard University Professor Rupert Emerson. Unlike the Rhee government, the military junta did not find it necessary to compromise with an opposition which desired a different form of system. The new constitution provided for a strong presidential system, with the president elected by direct popular vote. The president was empowered to appoint the prime minister (the post of vice president was abolished) as well as all of the cabinet members without legislative advice and consent, although the constitution did have a procedure for no-confidence votes against individual members. The new constitution also prohibited assembly membership by independents, requiring party nomination to run for national office.[76] It provided that an assemblyman who resigned from his party or whose party was dissolved would lose office automatically, although he could retain membership as an independent if the party expelled him against his will. The Supreme Court was given the power to dissolve a political party.

The provisions of the constitution were seen as having been designed to promote strong executive rule and a strong party system, and they were clearly unpalatable to the members of the former Democratic Party. In December 1962, while political activities were still prohibited, the constitution was submitted to a vote by national referendum. Martial law was lifted on December 5, and the vote was held on December 17, 1962. Of 12,412,798 registered voters, 10,585,998 voted and 8,339,333, or 78.8 percent of the voters, approved the new constitution.[77] Even in Seoul, where the opposition had almost always won by large margins, the constitution was endorsed by 74.6 percent of the voters. The military leaders took this as a vote of confidence in their rule.[78] Others pointed out that it might well be an expression of the degree of aspiration for a return to civilian rule as soon as possible.[79]

Not only did the military government unilaterally provide a new constitution, but in December it also drew up and promulgated a stringent Political Party Law, severely restricting party activities. The law prohibited almost all voluntary political activities of the type which make political parties effective channels for open public participation. Only registered members of a party could campaign for the party; parties were prohibited from soliciting or accepting any donations for campaign expenses, except from their own registered members; door-to-door canvassing for votes was outlawed, as was the use of public address systems to solicit votes.[80] Further, large categories of persons were prohibited from joining parties: students, educators, employees of public or semi-public corporations, public officials, members of the armed forces. The law has even been interpreted to exclude from participation leaders of organized interest groups, for example, labor leaders. The election laws gave a clear edge to a governing party, because the government could issue or deny permits for rallies, and it owned and operated most of the radio facilities, which were among the few remaining legal means of communicating with the public. The prohibition of voluntary popular participation in political activities meant that almost all political communication would have to be paid. Since no funds could be donated to a party except by its own registered members, no party could be effective unless it had many wealthy members, or unless it could secure secret, illegal donations—something a ruling party could do, but which an opposition party would find immensely difficult.

By the end of 1962, the junta's position looked fairly secure, and General Park announced on December 27 that those members of the Supreme Council who wished to do so might retire from the military and run in the 1963 elections. Park declared that he himself would retire from military service to be a candidate for public office.[81] On New Year's Day 1963, the government lifted the ban on political activities in preparation for the coming elections. On January 5, a preliminary meeting of the government's Democratic Republican Party was held to plan its formal inauguration, and on January 18, Kim Jong Pil was appointed chairman of the preparatory committee, for the formal inauguration of the party to be held on February 2.[82]

Opposition parties scurried to re-form. Not surprisingly, "Old Faction" and "New Faction" members of the former Democratic Party retained the bitterness that had divided them in the Second Republic, and formed two separate parties. Former President Yun Po-sŏn emerged as the head of a party called the Civil Rule Party (CRP), formed on January 3.[83] Initially members from both of the former Democratic Party faction groups joined the party, but as soon as it became apparent that the Old Faction was dominant, New Faction members withdrew to reconstruct the Democratic Party (DP) on January 17.[84] Since their leader, Chang Myŏn, was still blacklisted, however, they had no prominent national leader to offer as a presidential candidate, and many members chose to join a third opposition group, the New Rule Party (NRP), formed by Hŏ Chŏng, who had been acting president during the interim government between the First and Second Republics.[85]

Factionalist feuding among the "old politicians" encouraged the new DRP leadership, as it was seen as an illustration of the "outmoded factionalist behavior of the old generation," and tended to support the junta's argument that a "new generation" of young revolutionaries was needed. This argument was shattered when a bitter factionalist feud broke out within the DRP itself and nearly destroyed the party.

Although the DRP was primarily the preserve of the "new generation" young colonels of the junta, in January it was joined by senior members of the SCNR, who were dismayed to find the organizational structure already built, with a power base strongly supporting Kim Jong Pil. Clearly, they would play a minimal role in the make-up of the new political system. Marine General Kim Tong-ha, who had mobilized the troops to take Seoul in the coup of May 1961, resigned from the party in protest on January 21, before its formal inauguration, charging that the "democratic-centralist" structure of the party was similar to a Communist system and was a threat to democracy. Furthermore, he said, the party's bureaucratic structure would entail such heavy expenditures that political corruption would be inevitable.[86] General Song Yo-ch'an, who had been defense minister, foreign minister, and prime minister of the military government at various times during the preceding year and a half, refused to join the party at all, saying that the junta leaders should be true to their pledges to turn the government over to civilian leadership and stay out of politics.[87] Other senior members of the SCNR joined in the criticism.[88] As a factional dispute between the military leaders themselves erupted, clearly motivated by the struggle for control over the new party, charges and countercharges between the two groups brought out into the open the "Four Scandals" by which Kim Jong Pil had allegedly financed the new party, as well as the existence of the secret Kim-Ohira agreement. Clearly the "new leadership" had not purged its own ranks of either factionalism or corruption.

Both groups began to put pressure on Park Chung Hee; the young revolutionaries encouraged him to extend military rule for a longer period so that they could effectively consolidate the ranks of the party and eliminate the factionalist old generation leaders who were challenging the party leadership, and emerge as a united revolutionary group to lead the nation. The older leaders, on the other hand, urged him to shift policy and build a "pan-national" party which would absorb all political elements, not

simply the young colonels' clique. Both assured him that under the
existing conditions of intraparty strife, it would be impossible for
him to win the presidential election. As the power struggle progressed,
the different military factions even began mobilizing armed units
in preparation for a possible violent confrontation.[89] At length,
fearing the possibility of open conflict, General Park announced on
February 18 that he would not participate in a future government.
Sadly, Park explained: "As the man responsible for this revolution,
during the past few days I have been compelled to consider this
grave political situation. I have reached the conclusion that to restore
civilian government now, without any change in the body politic,
and to terminate the military government without any guarantee
of the continuation of the revolutionary ideology, is to forfeit the
significance and the value of the May 16 revolution, and to retreat
to the point prior to May 16."[90] Nonetheless Park implied that he
had no choice but to step down and agreed to do so if civilian
leaders would take pledges not to take reprisals against the military
leadership, to permit other former military leaders who resigned
from the armed forces to participate in political activities if they
so desired, to preserve the new constitution, and to cooperate in
reaching a Korean-Japanese agreement.[91]

The civilian leaders readily agreed to Park's terms and the
United States quickly greeted Park's announcement with a warm
endorsement. On the following day the Department of State
announced that Park's decision not to run for the presidency would
provide a basis for a "smooth transition to civilian government
through the democratic processes in an atmosphere of national
unity and stability.[92] Kim Jong Pil, dejected and disillusioned, left
the country for his first political exile on February 25.

On February 27, a solemn ceremony was held to administer
the pledges the civilian politicians had agreed to take. General Park,
on the verge of tears, leading the oath-taking ceremony, proclaimed
that the military revolution had failed. Clearly, no "new generation"
of leadership had emerged, and Park was preparing to transfer
power back to the same "old politicians" from whom it had been
seized.

For nearly three weeks the junta leader brooded over the decision he had made, as members of the young colonels' group tried every means at hand to persuade him to reverse his decision and carry on the revolution, rather than abandon Korea to the fate of "chaos and corruption" from which he had rescued it. Where was his patriotism? Would he let the country fall victim to the decaying forces that had led to its collapse under the Yi dynasty? Or would he carry on the revolution and contribute to the rebuilding of the nation? On March 15, the young officers staged a demonstration in front of the Council building demanding an extension of military rule. At last the general yielded to the persuasive appeals, and on March 16 announced that military rule would be extended an additional four years, if the people would endorse such a move in a national referendum.[93]

The United States was startled and dismayed by this turn of events. Ambassador Berger and other American officials in Seoul immediately began a series of prolonged talks with General Park in an effort to persuade him to reverse his decision.[94] On March 25, after studying the situation, the State Department issued a statement: "The military junta's efforts to continue military rule for four more years has created a difficult situation in Korea. We believe that prolongation of military rule could constitute a threat to stable and effective government, and we understand that this whole matter is being reexamined by the Korean government. We hope that the junta and the major political groups in Korea can work out together a procedure for transition to civil government that will be acceptable to the nation as a whole."[95] In the meantime, President Kennedy sent a more strongly worded protest to the junta leader stressing that the United States opposed the perpetuation of an unconstitutional government,[96] and it was announced that a request for $25 million in economic aid to assist the Five Year Plan was being denied by the United States, "to underscore its determination to bring constitutional government to Korea."[97] Rumors were openly reported that the United States was preparing to phase out all economic aid to Korea.[98]

Some opposition leaders appealed to the United States to

intervene directly.[99] Just at this point, it became apparent that the country was facing a spring rice crisis, and Korea turned to the United States for urgently needed emergency food relief. Observers generally concluded that the negotiations for food were being used by the United States to force the government to reverse its decision and hold elections.[100] With the success of the Five Year Plan in jeopardy, and a spring famine threatening, Park yielded to American demands.

This time, however, Park was determined to stay in the race, convinced by arguments that only by carrying out radical economic programs, could Korea build a self-sufficient economy and escape from the powerful influence of external pressures.

As the junta-sponsored DRP prepared to face the electorate in 1963, it had a mixed record to run on. Although it had introduced economic planning at the beginning of 1962, the results of this planning were yet to appear. The increased currency circulation had driven inflation up, and consumer prices had risen 32 percent during the period of junta rule, the price of rice 64 percent.[101] Average wages had risen only 19 percent.[102] Per capita income declined slightly from $87.71 in 1961 to $85.25 in 1962,[103] while the cost of food and beverages rose 55.7 percent and clothing 10.7 percent.[104] Unemployment, which had been officially 8.4 percent in 1962, rose to an official 8.6 percent in 1963.[105] To the urban consumer and urban worker, these factors were more immediately observable and vital than the fact that during 1962 the planned rate of growth of secondary industry (mining, manufacturing, and construction) had been 11.1 percent, but had actually reached 14.4 percent, and in 1963 while the plan had called for 8.7 percent growth, the results had reached 13.3 percent.[106] No amount of published statistics would convince the urban citizen that he was better off than he had been until the effects were evident in his family budget.

In the meantime, the scandals and disputes coming forth from the military leadership indicated that the "new" leadership was no more immune to the "old evils" than the old. Given the choice of two undesirable leadership groups, voters expressed considerable cynicism. The opposition-oriented *Dong-A Ilbo,* interviewing citizens in Seoul, the biggest opposition stronghold, found little enthusiasm for the "old politicians." Less than a month before the election, the paper found typical reactions to be, "They failed to learn the lesson of their degradation over the past two years and are still involved in factional infighting," "It is very doubtful that they will win," "I doubt their qualification to organize a successful opposition."[107] Yet the "new politicians" fostered no greater enthusiasm. Recognizing that the Democratic Republican Party as it existed could not carry him to victory, and urged by senior members of the junta to avoid the "anti-democratic" party his nephew-in-law had built, Park first promoted the creation of another political party, and then ordered the two to merge. In March 1963, with General Park's blessing, the Liberal Democratic Party (LDP) was organized by former General Kim Chae-ch'un, who had become director of the CIA when Kim Jong Pil had left the post to head the DRP. (General Kim was the man who accused Kim Jong Pil of following North Korean advice in forming the DRP). This party absorbed senior members of the military group and others, including many former politicians. Park then ordered the merger of the two parties, but merger negotiations were unsuccessful because the LDP insisted on the total dissolution of Kim Jong Pil's secretariat organization.[108] Nonetheless, a large number of LDP members followed Park's instructions and joined the DRP.

One result of this move was the reabsorption into the DRP of the leadership of Syngman Rhee's old Liberal Party, whose members possessed the experience and public familiarity necessary to carry out and win an election campaign. Clearly, the "revolution" Kim Jong Pil had envisioned was dead.

In April 1963, following Kim Jong Pil's departure into exile, changes were made in the structure of the Democratic Republican Party (DRP) he had created. The permanent secretariat staff— all strong Kim supporters—was reduced from 1,300 to 600, as many of the members brought in from the older military group and "old politicians" pressed for the elimination of control over the party by the supporters of Kim Jong Pil. Kim's group became known as the "mainstream faction," as opposed to the new group who were now called the "nonmainstream faction." Although the original plan of the party, drawn up by Kim Jong Pil, was for "new faces" to be the backbone of the new party, the party found itself increasingly challenged from within by the new "nonmainstream faction" of "old faces." In writing the official history of the party four years later, the writers (themselves clearly "mainstreamers") pointed out that many of the party's own nominees for the National Assembly were "totally unacceptable to the original ideology of the party."[109]

While absorbing another leadership group at the top, the DRP set out to expand its organization at the local level. With the assistance of the former heads of the local branches of the People's Movement for National Reconstruction (PMNR) organization, as well as local officials (locally chosen) of city blocks (*tong*) and villages (*li*), party membership was reported to have expanded from 154,982 on March 5, 1963, to 706,611 on August 30, and 1,586,000 by presidential election day, October 15.[110]

The remaining members of the LDP who failed to join the DRP, angry that Park had decided to utilize the organization still dominated by his nephew-in-law's supporters as a political base, rather than using the LDP, maintained their party and emerged as another opposition party to challenge Park's leadership. In August, General Song Yo-ch'an, who had become an outspoken critic of the junta's decision to enter politics, wrote an open letter to General Park criticizing his decision to seek the presidency. Three days later, General Song was arrested by the CIA on the charge of having executed a subordinate officer during the Korean War (more than ten years previously) and of having ordered troops to fire on students during the Student Revolution of 1960.[111] (Since the U.N. Command had not permitted the Korean troops any live ammunition during the 1960 uprisings, the latter charge was patently ridiculous). After his arrest, the LDP proceeded to nominate General Song as its candidate for the presidency.

The government did not announce the date of the presidential elections until August 15, 1963. Parties which complied with the Political Party Law were given until September 15 to register the names of their nominees for the presidency, and the 30-day period from September 15 to the October 15 election day was set aside for campaigning. The Civil Rule Party of Yun Po-sŏn, the New Rule Party of Hŏ Chŏng, and the People's Friends Party which had been founded by Yi Pŏm-sŏk (the leader of the Youth Corps during the American Military Government and early Rhee periods) began negotiations for a merger into a united opposition, under the name of the Party of the People [Kungmin-ŭi-dang], or POP. However, since they could not agree on a single presidential candidate (each party was in favor of its own leader), the negotiations broke down. By September 15, seven presidential candidates had been registered for the forthcoming elections: Park Chung Hee of the Democratic Republican Party, who resigned from the army on August 30 in order to accept the party's nomination on August 31; Yun Po-sŏn, former president of the Second Republic, of the Civil Rule Party; Hŏ Chŏng, former acting president of the Interim Government, of the Party of the People; General Song Yo-ch'an, former chief of martial law following the Student Revolution, of the Liberal Democratic Party, who conducted his campaign from his prison cell; O Chae-yŏng of the Autumn Wind Society; Pyŏn Yŏng-t'ae, Syngman Rhee's former foreign minister, of the People's Justice Party; and Chang Yi-sŏk of the Newly Emerging Party. On October 2, former Acting President Hŏ Chŏng withdrew from the race in favor of former President Yun Po-sŏn. On October 8, just a week before the election, General Song followed suit, and the race became largely a contest between General Park and former President Yun Po-sŏn. The results of the October 15 election were as follows:[112]

Candidate	Party	Percent of Total Votes	Percent of Valid Votes
Park Chung Hee	Democratic Republican	42.61	46.65
Yun Po-sŏn	Civil Rule	41.19	45.10
O Chae-yŏng	Autumn Wind Society	3.70	4.05
Pyŏn Yŏng-t'ae	People's Justice	2.03	2.22

Candidate	Party	Percent of Total Votes	Percent of Valid Votes
Chang Yi-sŏk	Newly Emerging	1.80	1.98
Invalid votes	(Withdrawn candidates)	8.67	– 0 –
		100.00	100.00

Of more than 11 million votes cast, General Park had received only 4,702,642, or 42.61 percent of the total votes (46.65 percent of the valid votes), hardly a clear popular mandate. Yun Po-sŏn received only 156,028 votes fewer than Park. Had Hŏ and Song withdrawn from the race in favor of Yun sooner, or had any of the other candidates chosen not to run, Park would not have won.

That the opposition came so close to winning the election, despite their lack of organization and unity, was remarkable, especially since they were extremely short of political funds. It was soon revealed that the well-financed DRP had apparently received funds from still more dubious sources. In 1963, the DRP was accused of receiving $9.6 million in commission fees for arranging the importation into Korea of $2.5 billion worth of capital and goods supposedly belonging to Korean residents in Japan (Koreans in Japan, most of whom are quite poor, are often used as "fronts" for Japanese investment in Korea in order to avoid anti-Japanese reactions on the part of Koreans). The opposition parties also accused the DRP of receiving $38 million in the so-called "Three Flours Scandal" in which a few Korean industrialists (primarily those who had been associated with the Rhee Liberal Party financial establishment) were permitted to make illegal profits through the sugar, flour, and cement industries, by making a pay-off to the pro-junta party.[113]

The DRP itself pointed out that one of the factors in its success in the 1963 elections was "the timely and efficient distribution of campaign funds."[114] Officially reported expenses for the presidential election (which must be assumed to be considerably below actual expenditures) appeared to be correlated with the success of the presidential candidates. Out of a total 110 million *won* reportedly spent by the seven presidential candidates, Park's campaign spent 76.9 percent of the total, second place candidate

Yun expended 17.3 percent of the funds, Hŏ, who withdrew in favor of Yun, spent 3.5 percent, O Chae-yŏng, in third place, expended 1.3 percent of the total funds, Pyŏn Yŏng-t'ae in fourth place, spent 0.5 percent, General Song expended 0.4 percent before he withdrew, and last place candidate Chang Yi-sŏk expended only 0.1 percent of the total.[115]

Not only did Park's party have a considerable advantage in funding, but reportedly a number of "nonpolitical" organizations were utilized to appeal to the voters on Park's behalf, prior to the time when campaigning was officially permitted. Among these organizations, the 300,000-member "May Comrades' Society," of which Park was president (a group of Park's supporters largely led by his military buddies), sent speakers on tours around the country making "non-political" lectures during the summer of 1963, explaining the achievements of the military government.[116] Other organizations or associations accused of participating in the campaign in favor of Park, in violation of the election laws which prohibited campaigning by non-members of the party itself, included a new plethora of militant "youth corps" groups, some led by the same "hoodlums" who had been arrested at the outset of military government: The Patriotic Corps, the United Youth Corps, and the Korean Youth Society. Campaign assistance was also received from the New People's Society, as well as the newly organized 4-H Clubs, the Korean Women's Association, the Soil Improvement Societies , and other government-financed organizations.

Despite the serious disputes over the activities of the DRP during the campaign, there was a general consensus that the voting itself involved few irregularities, and for the first time in Korean history, the defeated candidate, former President Yun, sent a message of congratulations to the winner, President-elect Park.

The breakdown of votes between the two leading candidates was revealing: Park carried the five southernmost provinces, while Yun carried the four northern provinces. The breakdown of rural-urban votes showed that Park carried 50.8 percent of the rural votes, while Yun carried 57.1 percent of the urban votes.[117]

In November, elections to the National Assembly were held. Although the DRP received only 32.4 percent of the vote, it won 110 of the 175 seats, due to the splintering of the opposition into eleven different parties, with an average of six candidates competing in each district.[118] Although the personalities and programs of the candidates had some influence in the presidential election, the overwhelming role of funds in the assembly election was evident from the close correlation between the percentage of total election funds expended by each party, and the percentage of the total vote received. Of the five parties which succeeded in capturing seats in the assembly, the percentage of total expenditures and percentage of total votes were reported as follows:[119]

Party	No. of Seats	% of total Expenditures	% of total Votes
Democratic-Republican	110	38.2	32.4
Civil Rule	41	15.1	19.3
Democratic	13	13.8	13.2
Party of the People	2	12.8	8.6
Liberal Democratic	9	9.1	7.6
Others	0	11.0	19.0
	175	100.0	100.0

One notable fact in the election was that in every district in which a former Liberal Party leader ran under the DRP label, he won.

The victory of the DRP in the 1963 elections was more than a victory of party, despite the clearly weak mandate given the new government. All of the opposition parties had agreed on one issue in the campaign besides opposition to Park: they had all promised to scrap the new constitution and provide the nation with a "democratic" parliamentary system. Though the opposition parties together carried a majority of the vote, this could not be interpreted as an expression of preference for a parliamentary system. A government-sponsored survey of voting behavior conducted by the Second Republic in 1960 had indicated that 72.7 percent of voters voted for the "personality of the candidate," whereas only 14.7 percent responded that they voted for the party or party platform.[120] Now, with the elections

behind it, the new government of the Third Republic had four
years to attempt to reconsolidate its position in the society.

*Consolidation Phase II: Riding the Tiger with External Inputs,
1963-1967*

When the new military-turned-civilian political group had
prepared to face the national elections of 1963, it was anyone's
guess what the outcome would be. By 1967, the probabilities
of a return to power through elections was more certain, even
though by that time the government faced a united opposition,
as it had not in the 1963 campaigns. Ironically, the most important
factors in bolstering the new ruling group now came from external
sources. As with the Korean War before it, the Vietnam War
brought an influx of resources to the newly structured political
system, and the conclusion of a normalization treaty with Japan—
with the strong support of the United States against determined
internal Korean opposition—made trade with and "aid" from
that prosperous neighbor available to bolster the increasingly
secure new regime.

During the four years of President Park's first term of office,
the government encountered one of the most serious internal
crises of the contemporary period. The crisis was centered
around two government policies: the conclusion of a treaty with
Japan, and the dispatch of Korean troops to fight in Vietnam.
The Korea-Japan treaty crisis far overwhelmed the Vietnam issue,
although the alignment on the two issues was similar. The two
issues polarized South Korean society into bitter antagonisms
and left many angry and frustrated over the futility of dissent.
One writer estimates that 3.5 million persons took part in the
debate, discussions, demonstrations, and protest over the treaty
issue—the most active political participation modern Korea had
witnessed.[121] Like the anti-trusteeship movement of 1946, once
again the bulk of the internal movement was aligned against the
external factors. On the one hand, the students, intellectuals,
press, opposition parties, and religious organizations, were
mobilized against the government. On the other side stood the

government and government-sponsored organizations and Korean business groups, with the firm support of the United States. By the end of the four-year term in 1967, the issues were largely dead, and the government had emerged with a temporarily stronger— albeit externally bolstered—base of support.

The Korea-Japan treaty issue was repeatedly misinterpreted abroad as a reflection of an irrational or emotional Korean reaction to the Japanese because of the bitter experiences of Japanese rule.[122] In fact, the majority of Korean people regularly expressed the opinion that relations between Korea and Japan should be normalized. A public opinion survey conducted by the government ministry of information in November 1964 reported that 99.1 percent of Koreans expressed approval of an eventual normalization of relations with Japan.[123] Another poll conducted by the *Dong-A Ilbo* in December 1964 found that 45 percent were in favor of normalization at that time, 28 percent were opposed, and 27 percent were undecided.[124] The primary issue throughout the political crisis in Korea was not opposition to Japan, but opposition to the Korean government, which it was feared would use financial resources from Japan to further consolidate its internal control, and in so doing would create an economic dependence on Japan in order to stay in power.[125]

The government desperately needed financial resources from Japan to carry out its Five Year Plan, to set up a system of indirect funding for the party, and to replace U.S. aid which was rapidly being phased out. When Syngman Rhee came to power in 1948, despite U.S. efforts to promote alternative leadership, U.S. assistance had been hastily withdrawn. Now that Park Chung Hee had succeeded in perpetuating his rule, again in opposition to U.S. policy, the United States was similarly eager to withdraw. Unlike the preceding period, however, it was now apparent that this must be done without unsettling the existing political balance in East Asia. The promotion of Korean-Japanese rapprochement could help the United States attain its goal of stability in the Far East while reducing its expenditure in Korea. If Japan could be persuaded to give economic aid to Korea, it could diminish Korean reliance on U.S. aid. Furthermore, an opening of economic relations between Korea and Japan would provide another market for Korean goods, and make Japanese capital investment available for Korea—both of which could help the growth of the Korean economy to a point where it might ultimately be able to exist without foreign aid.

That the United States was pressing hard for an early rapprochement between Japan and Korea was abundantly evident. Each successive American ambassador to Korea emphasized the necessity of a rapid reconciliation. Ambassador Walter P. McConaughy in 1961 said in his departing statement that he hoped the relations would be normalized, "at an early date." [126] U.S. Ambassador to Japan, Edwin O. Reischauer, arriving in Tokyo a few days later expressed his "deep concern" for an early agreement. [127] Ambassador Samuel D. Berger, who replaced McConaughy in Korea, repeatedly emphasized the need for normalization. [128] Ambassador Winthrop G. Brown, upon replacing Ambassador Berger, declared that "My task is going to be to try to cement friendly relations between the two countries [Japan and Korea] further." [129] David Bell, head of the U.S. Agency for International Development (AID) noted in early 1964 that U.S. grant-aid to Korea could be phased out over the next three to five years because of growing self-sufficiency and "another economic aid source." [130] In October 1964, U.S. Assistant Secretary of State for Far Eastern Affairs, William P. Bundy, pointed out that "normalization of relations between Korea and Japan would be an important contribution to the cause of peace in Asia." [131] As these statements were being made, U.S. grant-aid to South Korea was declining rapidly: from $165 million in 1962, to $119 million in 1963, $88 million in 1964, and $71 million in 1965, when the agreement with Japan was finally concluded. [132] (By contrast, grant-aid to the Second Republic in 1960 had been $225 million.)

Realizing the weakness of his mandate in the election, and his overwhelming defeat in Seoul, the cultural and intellectual center of the nation (Park had won only 30.2 percent of the valid votes in Seoul as opposed to 65.1 percent for Yun Po-sŏn), Park Chung

Hee at first approached the opposition parties with a gesture of conciliation, asking for proposals of "sound alternative policies."[133] The government sought to bolster a spirit of cooperation with the opposition—for example, by giving a vice speaker's post to an opposition member in the National Assembly; but Park's opponents were unprepared for cooperation. Having been arrested, maligned, belittled, and held up to public ridicule as the "evil remnants of rotten and outmoded Yi dynasty behavior," by the military regime, the opposition members were clearly unwilling now to sit down amicably with the new regime and work out an approach to the solution of a problem (Korea-Japan rapprochement) which would vastly augment the financial resources of the ruling group.

Kim Jong Pil had returned from his temporary exile abroad in October 1963 in time to resume his chairmanship of the DRP and run for election to the National Assembly in November. Almost immediately, the new government sent Kim to Japan to work out the final arrangements for signing a treaty. Kim, having already negotiated the preliminary arrangements in secret during the military government period, soon announced that a final agreement would be concluded by March and a treaty signed by May. However, the partisan and semi-secret negotiations had aroused considerable suspicion and concern in the public at home. Kim Jong Pil did not help matters by professing that he didn't care if he was called a second Yi Wan-yŏng.[134] (Yi Wan-yŏng was the infamous prime minister of Korea who had secretly signed the treaty annexing Korea to Japan, and who is to Koreans the most reviled of national traitors.)

On March 6, all of the opposition parties joined together in a "Pan-National Struggle Committee to Oppose Humiliating Diplomacy."[135] Many leaders of various fields, who generally did not participate in political activities, joined this opposition group, and carried out speaking campaigns around the country in mid-March, attracting large crowds. On March 23, Kim Jong Pil announced in Tokyo that a treaty would be signed in early May. The following day, 80,000 students poured forth in South Korea's major cities to protest, and the demonstrations continued for five days, despite the use of military forces in an effort to restore order. The students were strongly supported by the Korean press. Finally, on March 28, Kim Jong Pil was recalled from Tokyo, and student protests came to a temporary halt.[136]

Although the Korean government publicly promised not to arrange any dealings with the Japanese prior to conclusion of the treaty, the Japanese government announced that it had already arranged for $100 million in commercial loans to Korean enterprises.[13]
In May the Korean government announced its intention of renewing the negotiations. By the end of May, the students were out in the streets again.

On June 3, 15,000 students attempted to storm major government buildings, including the presidential residence, demanding the resignation of President Park. Overpowering the police, they were driven back only by combat troops, called in by the government. The government then declared martial law, prohibited assembly, placed newspapers under severe censorship, closed down the schools, and arrested leaders of the student movement and outspoken journalists (168 students, 7 reporters, and 173 others).[138] On June 5, Kim Jong Pil resigned again from the party chairmanship and went into his second exile—this time to a summer seminar at Harvard University.[139]

During the period of martial law, the government rammed through the National Assembly a new law on "press ethics" designed to quiet journalistic commentary opposing government policy, and attempted to pass a law restricting student activities, failing only because of a determined filibuster by the opposition parties.[140] One condition for lifting the martial law was an agreement by the opposition not to block the passage of the press ethics law.

When martial law was finally lifted on July 29, after nearly two months, the government and the press were at war. Newspaper and magazine publishers formed struggle committees and passed resolutions to boycott all propagandistic statements of the government, beginning with the president's August 15 liberation day speech. The government fought back by cancelling all of its advertising, ordering businesses receiving government assistance or government contracts to do likewise, ordering all government employees to boycott the opposition papers *Kyunghyang Shinmun, Choson Ilbo,* and *Dong-A Ilbo,* urging banks to suspend the credits of these papers, and cancelling special privileges of the press. The International Press Institute issued a protest against the new law.[141] Finally, the conflict was eased by an agreement to suspend the law in exchange for an agreement from the press to exercise "voluntary self-regulation."

Continued American support of the government's position on treaty relations with Japan created an incipient feeling of anti-Americanism among Korean students and intelligentsia, who felt that the United States was only concerned about Japan's interest in the negotiations. Statements by Americans supporting normalization and condemning the student protests angered the Korean intelligentsia, and on one occasion students marched in protest carrying a sign reading, "Yankee, Keep Silent!"[142]

As 1965 dawned, the anti-treaty movement was renewed with increased vigor. By June, the streets and campuses were filled daily with protesting students, demonstrations occurring in every major city in South Korea. In the midst of the crisis, all of the opposition groups merged into a single opposition party, the People's Party, on June 14. On June 21, the government closed the thirteen universities and fifty-eight high schools which were the major centers of protest, for an early summer holiday, and on June 22 the treaty was signed, while all of the major opposition leaders were on a hunger strike.[143]

Pending ratification, the protests continued. On July 1, seventy-seven Christian leaders issued a statement of protest against the treaty and "prayers for the nation" were held in Christian churches throughout the country.[144] On July 12, professors from 18 colleges and universities appealed to the assembly not to ratify the treaty. On the 14th, as violence broke out in the assembly between opposition and ruling parties, the item was placed on the agenda.

Aware that they did not have enough votes to block passage of the treaty, opposition members tried to find means of killing the bill through filibusters, and other delaying tactics in the committee, hoping to postpone consideration until the students returned to school for the fall session. At 11:10 p.m. on the night of August 11, the ruling party suddenly managed to pass the treaty out of the committee in a one-minute blitz which became known in Korea as "the snatch." Opposition party members submitted their resignations to the National Assembly in protest. The speaker, however, rejected their resignations and on August 14, the one-party National Assembly passed the ratification by the vote of all 110 DRP members and one independent.[145] While they were in complete control, the one-party assembly went on to pass, on August 18, an authorization for the government to dispatch 20,000 troops to Vietnam, by a vote of 101 for, 1 against, and 2 abstentions.[146] Protest continued until August 26 when Seoul was placed under "garrison law" (similar to martial law, but without press censorship and other administrative controls), two universities were closed down, and the government forced universities to expel student protest leaders and professors who had participated in the anti-treaty movement.

The *Dong-A Ilbo* editorialized on the day the treaty was to be concluded: "A great and grave turning point, which will tragically affect us and our offspring is about to be effectuated. It is indeed a national tragedy that the normalization agreements, the contents of which are unsatisfactory to almost every citizen, are to be formally signed while the opposition wages extreme struggle, the doors of schools are closed down, and hunger strikes and demonstrations occur among the students."[147] On signing the treaty, President Park remarked that widespread opposition to its conclusion was based on an erroneous and harmful belief that Koreans were so inherently weak that they could not avoid being subjugated by Japan.[148] What Park refused to recognize was that the students and intellectuals were not expressing a lack of confidence in their own strength, vis-à-vis Japan, but in that of the Korean leadership.

In March 1966, the government voted to send 20,000 additional Korean troops to Vietnam, in the face of a determined, but ineffectual, opposition. Once again, the opposition came primarily because of the awareness that money coming in from the Vietnam venture would bolster the government's position, rather than because of a general opposition to the policy measure itself. On March 7, 1966, U.S. Ambassador to Korea Winthrop G. Brown announced fourteen points which were the basis for the U.S. concessions to Korea in exchange for the commitment of the additional troops.[149] Among the inducements were: the total cost of sending the additional troops to Vietnam would be met by the U.S. government; the seventeen army divisions and one marine division of the Korean armed forces would be brought up to date with modern equipment; the United States would equip three additional reserve divisions in Korea to replace the troops being sent to Vietnam; the Military Assistance Program (MAP) to Korea would cease to purchase American goods and replace them with purchases of Korean goods paid for by American dollars; as far as practical, in accordance with Korean production capacity, skills, and ability to meet production schedules and prices, the United States would purchase supplies and services for the Korean troops in Korea; as far as practical, materials and services in connection with AID relief, construction, rehabilitation, and the like, in Vietnam would be purchased in Korea; assistance would be rendered so that Korean contractors would be given every opportunity to participate in the Vietnam reconstruction, and Korean technicians and workers would be employed in Vietnam where qualified and available, providing the South Vietnamese government gave approval; the United States would provide additional AID funds and military assistance to Korea, additional technical assistance and training to Koreans in the promotion of exports, additional loans to Korea to promote Korean exports to South Vietnam and Southeast Asia and for other developmental projects; the United States would improve anti-infiltration measures in South Korea; increased production of ammunition and materiel in Korea would be promoted; communications facilities to maintain continuous contact between Seoul and the forces in Vietnam would be provided at the expense of the U.S. government.[150]

The Japan-Korea Treaty and the commitment of troops to

Vietnam were to provide important new resources to the Park government, both directly and indirectly. The new financial resources would provide funds not only for the carrying out of the government's economic plans, but new resources for political funding as well. During the period from 1965 to 1967, in addition to the claims payments from Japan ($12.08 million in grants and $14.07 in loans in 1966, the first year of payment, $37 million in grants and $25 million in loans in 1967),[151] the treaty agreement with Japan opened the way to commercial loans from that country. During 1966 and 1967, South Korea received a total of $108.5 million in private loans from Japan.[152] Since private loans required government approval and repayment guarantees, the Korean party receiving foreign loans was required to pay a percentage (popularly believed to be 10-15 percent and sometimes as much as 20 percent of the loan amount) in payoffs to obtain the necessary government guarantees.[153] The system, of course, applied to foreign loans from other nations as well. The decision to send troops to Vietnam in 1965 and 1966 bolstered confidence abroad in the American willingness to defend South Korea, and helped to induce commercial loans from other nations. During 1966 and 1967, South Korea received $19.9 million in commercial loans from the United States, $53.1 million from West Germany, $30.9 million from Italy and France, $2.5 million from Great Britain, and $41.2 million from other nations, making a total of $256.1 million in private commercial loans during those two years alone.[154] Assuming a kickback-ratio as low as 10 percent, this would mean political fund resources of $25.6 million from this source.

The increase in external resources was not limited to private commercial loans. Public loans to South Korea (including those from the United States) during 1965-1967 totalled $309 million. There was also $34 million in direct foreign investment in Korea.[155] Earnings from Vietnam during 1966 and 1967 amounted to $203.6 million.[156]

The abundance of funds flowing in from abroad served purposes far broader than the funding of the party, of course. Increased resources for governmental agencies permitted the regime to expand its political controls in the society in numerous indirect ways. The most apparent extension of political control was through the vast expansion of the activities of the Korean Central Intelligence Agency (CIA), during this phase headed by Kim Hyŏng-uk, a classmate (Eighth Class) of Kim Jong Pil. CIA agents began appearing everywhere: on the campuses, on newspaper staffs, overhearing conversations in every bar and tea room. CIA funds entered every activity. The cost of running for a student-body office on campuses skyrocketed with the entrance of the CIA into the fray. Funds instead of guns became the new means of controlling dissent. Instead of locking up troublesome student leaders, they were sent abroad on scholarships. By the time of the 1967 elections, the government's pervasive control of the society through indirect means was well known. Conversations on sensitive subjects became noticeably hushed, and the glance over the shoulder began to take on the characteristic of a national nervous tic.

Another means of indirect control was the new role of banking and credit in the society. Key enterprises were offered highly favorable bank loans and credits up to the point that they acquired an uncomfortable debt-ratio. The banks then became a means of enforcing adherence to government policy by persons associated with the dependent enterprises. Most key newspapers fell into the credit trap. In 1966 the *Kyunghyang Shinmun* published an article advocating national unification, and banks suddenly called in their loans and cancelled the newspaper's credits. It was forced into bankruptcy and sale.[157] Overt government repression was no longer necessary. Journalists nostalgically recalled the relative freedom of the press during the administration of Syngman Rhee.[158] The broad dissent of 1964-1965 was no longer tolerated.

While funds were utilized as a means of controlling political dissent, the new resources were also used positively to carry out the goals of economic development. Two forms of political funding which had acted as a drag on the economy were now discontinued: the kickbacks from import licensing, which had depended on a restrictive import policy, were discontinued so that the import system could be put on a more rational basis, and 80-90 percent of essential import commodities were placed on an automatic-approval list. The domestic banking-kickback system was also discontinued. Through this system, the banks had lent money at low-interest to favored enterprises, which in turn had lent out the funds at higher rates, kicking back a percentage of the profits to the party. This depended on a low-interest restricted credit system. After closing out this system, the banks converted to a high-interest system which induced a vast increase in private savings, increasing internal resources for economic investment.[159] Just as Rhee had converted the system from military aid funding to economic aid funding, the government was able to close out old systems of funding only because a new system was now available.

As the new system of funding developed, the organizational base of the system began to shift perceptibly. Though the DRP had at the outset been independently financed, the new system required that the inputs be channelled in by appointees of the executive. Political funding was placed in the hands of those immediately responsible to the president, making the party an appendage of the executive, rather than vice-versa, as Kim Jong Pil had originally intended. The power of the young colonels' group within the party began to wane, and soon many were calling the old "mainstream faction" the "new nonmainstream," whereas the old "nonmainstream," was soon being referred to as the "new mainstream." The factional struggle within the party became increasingly acute. At the same time, the power of the cabinet and the bureaucracy began to overshadow the once-important functions of the party.

As the old nonmainstream faction increased its importance in the party, it continued making demands for changes in the make-up of the party which would reduce the power of the old mainstream faction. Kim Sŏng-kŏn of the old nonmainstream faction was put in charge of the party finance committee. The original power of the secretariat organization was eroded as the members of the National Assembly began insisting upon the power to control the local party organizations. At length, the power to appoint local party officials was given to the members of the assembly, with the local officials in turn given responsibility to select the local party workers. The party thus became restructured into a collection of personal factions around National Assembly members, as Korean political parties had been since independence.

The DRP began planning for the 1967 elections in October 1965.[160] Kim Jong Pil resumed the chairmanship of the party in December of that year. By the middle of 1966, 1.2 million members had been organized into so-called "key" and "cell" organizations, down to the village level, and large sums of money were reportedly being expended. A new headquarters building was opened in Seoul by the DRP to train party workers. Throughout 1966, opposition parties repeatedly charged harassment of their activities, obstruction of their rallies, political infiltration of social and economic organizations, electronic eavesdropping, and the partisan use of the local officials to support DRP programs.

The opposition was still divided. Former President Yun had formed a New Korea Party [Shinhan-dang], or NKP, and by August 19, 1966, the party was reported to have a membership of 300,000 members.[161] The People's Party which was chaired by Madame Pak Sun-ch'ŏn (widow of Chang Tŏk-su, the KDP leader assassinated in 1948) claimed a membership of 520,000.[162] On October 20, the People's Party nominated Dr. Yu Chin-o, the widely respected former president of Korea University, as their presidential candidate. The Democrats appealed to Yun Po-sŏn to stay out of the race in order to unify the opposition. Yun, however, determined to have a last try at the presidency, said that the idea of presenting a single candidate was "practically impracticable," and refused to withdraw.[163] By November 1966, eight parties had registered to compete in the 1967 elections. In the atmosphere of suspicion that had been created by the extensive expansion of CIA activities, many opposition groups began to suspect one another of being financed by the government in order to split the opposition. Uniting the parties became even more difficult as each group feared an inadvertent absorption of pro-government elements who would disrupt the party internally, or who would support DRP policies once elected to public office.

On February 2, 1967, the DRP once again nominated President Park as its presidential candidate. Six days later, the two major opposition parties, Yun's NKP and Yu's People's Party, finally reached agreement on a merger on the basis of Yu's agreement to step aside in favor of Yun Po-sŏn. In exchange for this concession Yu became chairman of the new party, which took the name of New Democratic Party [Shinmin-dang]; the two factions of the former Democratic Party were finally reunited into a single party. Later in the campaign, Sŏ Min-ho, the nominee of the Democratic Socialist Party, withdrew in favor of Yun, making the election once again primarily a two-man race between Park and Yun.

Conditions in 1967 were markedly different from those of 1963. The funds which had flowed into Korea from external sources had not only been channelled into political expenditures, but into the Five Year Plan as well. South Korea's first Five Year Plan had been completed in 1966 with remarkable success. The expected annual GNP growth rate under the plan had been 7.1 percent; the average annual GNP growth rate actually achieved was 8.3 percent. Industrial production had risen from 18 percent of GNP in 1960 to 28 percent in 1967.[164] The value of exports had increased from $54.8 million in 1962 to $320.2 million in 1967. Per capita income had increased from $83.60 in 1962 to $123.50 in 1967. Much of the increase in income was in nonfarm areas, where income had almost doubled. The number of persons employed in industry rose from 390,000 in 1962 to 1,307,000 in 1967.[165] Although the percentage of Koreans in urban areas had risen from 40.8 percent of the population in 1960 to 49 percent in 1966, the urban centers could no longer be viewed as solid pro-opposition areas.[166] Monthly income of both agricultural and industrial workers had risen faster during 1965-1967 than consumer prices.[167] The grain harvest of 1966 had been the best in Korean history, up from 5,423,000 metric tons in 1962, to 7,568,000 metric tons in 1966.[168] Fertilizers available to farmers had increased 2.3 times over 1960 amounts and pesticides available were 4.5 times the amounts in 1960.[169]

In short, the government was succeeding in bringing about rapid economic development, one of the major ingredients of popular demand, and appeared to be on its way to achieving a certain degree of legitimacy through performance. Even intellectuals, surveyed in a major study of 1,515 professors and journalists in late 1966, indicated that they believed that individual freedom would have to be sacrificed somewhat to achieve economic development, and placed economic development of the nation as the highest priority national goal.[170]

Of course, the government was not beyond manipulating its role in economic development for electoral purposes. The second Five Year Plan was published in the summer of 1966, and widely distributed and publicized for a year before the 1967 elections, calling attention to the fact that it was the DRP government which had drawn up and carried out the economic "miracle" of the first plan, and that its re-election was necessary to the successful carrying out of the second plan. In 1966, new mayors were appointed to the three major cities with instructions to undertake broadscale "show" projects to modernize the cities, in many cases tearing down and rebuilding less for the needs of efficiency than for the psychological impact to be achieved by the "modern" results. Even among the more sophisticated observers who could see through the political motivations, the sudden conversion of the cities into showplaces of the twentieth century could not but awaken a burst of national pride.

To ensure the continuation of support from its essential power bases in the bureaucracy and military, the government announced in 1966 the first of a three-part wage increase designed to raise the salaries of public employees 100 percent.[171] The government had also succeeded in putting a large number of new employees on the government payroll: between 1961 and 1967, the total number of civilian government employees (excluding police and firemen) increased from 235,456 to 355,931. The number of police and firemen increased over the same period from 29,477 to 40,384.

On May 11, 1967, the presidential elections were held. Although it was the lowest turnout for a presidential election in South

Korea's history (83.6 percent of the electorate, or 11,646,621 out of 13,953,093),[172] the results this time were far more decisive than the election of 1963. President Park won 51.4 percent of the total valid votes, as opposed to only 41 percent for Yun Po-sŏn, and 8 percent for other candidates.[173] Voting patterns had also changed. Whereas in 1963, Park had won the southern provinces and lost the northern ones, in 1967, he won those along the east coast and lost those along the west coast. Speculation was that the southwest, which had supported Park in 1963, was resentful of the government's heavy investment programs in the southeast, especially Park's home area of Kyongsang-do. Most marked, though, was Park's showing in the urban areas, where he carried 50.4 percent of the total vote, as opposed to only 37.7 percent in 1963, while also carrying 52.2 percent of the rural vote, as compared with 50.8 percent of the total in 1963. In Seoul, predictably, Park lost, but he made a much better showing than he had in 1963: 46 percent against Yun's 49 percent, as compared with 30.2 percent versus 65.1 percent in 1963. The DRP had expended 66.5 percent of the total reported campaign expenses, while the NDP had expended 29.4 percent.[174]

On June 8, 1967, elections were held to the National Assembly. Although eleven parties put up candidates for election, the results showed that Korea had become a strictly two-party system once again. Only one member from a third party was elected. The DRP won 129 of the seats (102 on the district basis, and 27 of the 44 proportionally-distributed seats), the NDP won 45 (28 on the district basis and 17 proportional seats), and the Mass Party (MP) won one district with no proportional seats.[175]

Widespread irregularities in the assembly voting, as contrasted with the presidential election, were reported. The fact that the NDP carried only three constituencies outside of the major cities was especially suspect. Reports of ballot-stuffing, vote-buying, intimidation, and other dishonest practices came from many areas.[176] Many suspected that the DRP had intentionally arranged the outcome so that it would hold a two-thirds majority in the assembly, in order to amend the constitution to permit a third term for President Park. Shortly after the elections, student demonstrations broke out in Seoul and provincial cities, but the government cut them off by immediately closing down many universities and high schools. Park yielded to pressures to some extent, by ordering one DRP member to turn over his seat to his NDP opponent and having six DRP members expelled from the party for voting irregularities in their districts (although they retained their seats in the assembly as independents). However, the government clearly was not going to permit its membership in the assembly to be reduced below the two-thirds margin. Insisting on new elections, the NDP leadership caucused and voted to boycott the National Assembly, knowing that its demand was unlikely to be met.

The role of funds in the National Assembly elections was quite apparent, although reported expenses clearly did not reflect the actual expenditures which were much greater. The breakdown of expenses and votes in the election was as follows: [177]

Party	Seats Won	% of total Expenditures	% of Votes
Democratic-Republican	129	45.8	50.6
New Democratic	45	27.2	32.7
All Others	1	27.0	16.7
	175	100.0	100.0

By 1967, the Park government had achieved a more solid consolidation of power than the Rhee government had before it. Its control over a now professional military establishment seemed firm. Its organizational control over the society was clear—although this rested primarily upon manipulation and control from above, without effective organizational penetration of the society. Clearly the government had acquired ample resources of funds to influence and control political activity. Ideas now seemed somewhat irrelevant to the whole process. So long as Korea was developing, what need had it for ideological niceties which might conflict with practical policies? If anything, economic development itself had become the ideology of the day. Arguments over "class struggle" or "freedom of the press" which had engaged intellectual circles in by-gone days were replaced by discussions of optimum resource allocation, investment structure, GNP growth rates, and so forth. Some optimistic observers saw the new political system on its way to achieving not only effective political consolidation, but political legitimacy as well, through the dynamic success of its economic performance.[178]

Phase III: Political Erosion, 1967-1971

By 1967, the Third Republic in South Korea appeared to have achieved a fairly effective consolidation of control over the society. Yet, if one looked beneath the surface, it was clear that the system had failed to establish firm bases of support. While the military seemed securely under the control of the leadership, six years had passed since the military coup, and the more professionally-trained military leaders who had completed the full four-year training program of the Korean Military Academy (which neither the senior officers nor the "young colonels" of 1961 had experienced) were moving up the ranks of the military establishment. The regime had secured abundant sources of funding, but as with the governments before it, most of its funding still depended on external sources. Organizationally, controls from the top seemed effective, but the party system had been truncated and no effective channels of political participation or communication upward existed for the population at large. Ideologically the regime drew a blank. The ideals of the "revolution" had clearly been discarded: corruption, irregularities, factionalism, and political opportunism were as prevalent as they had been under previous governments. Without effective institutions to alter behavior, the characteristics of the past had re-emerged. Legitimacy through performance was an admirable aim, but what would happen if performance failed to live up to par? Gradual erosion of the bases of support was apparent by the end of the second term in 1971, when a sharp reversal in external factors once again threatened the stability of the system. A shortage of funds forced a reversion to reliance on force once more, as the government declared a state of national emergency at the end of 1971.

The 1967 elections buoyed the DRP with the appearance of public support, which was evident despite election irregularities. The inability of the opposition to mobilize broad support against the election irregularities seemed evidence of the weakness of the sources of challenge within the society. Though the newly-elected NDP members continued to boycott the assembly for six months, the DRP barely took notice of the challenge. Finally, at the end of November 1967, the NDP agreed to return to the assembly in exchange for a promise from the DRP to establish a committee to investigate the election irregularities and to amend the election laws, promises which ultimately came to nought. Even after the NDP's return to the assembly, the DRP viewed the opposition as only a nuisance element, and went on to pass the budget for 1968 after a three minute debate.[179]

Of more critical importance to the DRP was the factional struggle within the party, which now became the arena for acting out the battle for succession. Since Park was required by the constitution to step aside in 1971, contention between factions for the choice of a successor soon reached a boiling point. On May 24, 1968, Assemblyman Kim Yong-tae was expelled from the DRP for his activities in recruiting support for Kim Jong Pil as Park Chung Hee's successor. Assemblyman Kim was charged by the party's disciplinary committee with recruiting about 900 former secretariat members in this endeavor, under the cover of an organization called the "Korean People's Welfare Research Institute," which he was supposedly using as a base for planning the strategy for Kim Jong Pil's takeover of the party.[180] The expelled assemblyman was charged with factionalist activity, "creating a party within the party" as well as with disobeying the orders of President Park to avoid competition for the succession until 1970. The institute had prepared a strategy paper for opposing any constitutional amendment allowing Park to seek a third term.[181] On May 30, Kim Jong Pil, in angry protest, resigned from the chairmanship of the party as well as from his membership, thereby losing his seat in the National Assembly. The nonmainstream faction was clearly in control.

By 1969 it had become obvious that it would be impossible to promote a successor to President Park without splitting the party wide open. Mainstream faction members would not support any individual other than Kim Jong Pil, while nonmainstream members (who now had the upper hand in the party) would adamantly oppose Kim. A split in the party would be disastrous: two opposing candidates in the 1971 elections from a divided DRP could easily lead to victory for the opposition. And with all of the "corruption" involved in political financing for the DRP, the NDP could turn around and prosecute the DRP leadership in retaliation for their own treatment at the hands of the military regime. The cost of a fall from power was too great to risk. Although promotion of a successor other than Kim Jong Pil would split the party, the re-election of Park Chung Hee to a third term, although opposed by Kim's supporters, would at least postpone the choice and possibly avoid a split. An amendment to the constitution would be necessary.

In January 1969, the DRP announced its intention to seek a constitutional amendment permitting a third term for President Park. The opposition NDP immediately declared that it would oppose the amendment. The assembly's minority floor leader, Kim Young Sam, stated that his party would "fight to the death" to block it, and the opposition once again formed a "Pan-National Struggle Committee" to mobilize popular support for its position.[182] Despite denials from the president that he sought re-election, the power-play within the DRP seemed to overshadow all other developments. In April 1969, Kim Jong Pil's supporters in the assembly, determined to show that the government still depended upon their support, revolted against the party leadership and joined with the opposition to pass a no-confidence vote against Minister of Education Kwŏn O-pyŏng, by a vote of 89 to 57 with 3 abstentions, the first no-confidence vote carried against a member of the administration since the inauguration of the Third Republic. In retaliation the five DRP members who had led the revolt were ousted from the party.[183] Having expelled several of its own members during intraparty factional strife, the DRP no longer held the two thirds majority needed to pass the constitutional amendment although its expelled members remained in the assembly as independents. The DRP set about repairing its bridges and by August had finally persuaded 119 DRP or former DRP members to sign a petition to support the amendment. Supporters of Kim Jong Pil were induced to sign in return for a five-point agreement including the dismissal of some powerful government officials, such as the President's Chief Secretary Lee Hu Rak (Yi Hu-rak).[184] Since 117 votes were needed for passage, three members of the opposition were also induced to sign, as a guarantee against possible last-minute defections among the DRP members. The methods used to induce the three opposition signatures were not disclosed, but the three spent the next few weeks vacationing in luxury hotels and playing golf in Tokyo.

Once again, it was clear that parliamentary opposition would be fruitless, and the conflict over the amendment moved into the streets. Students began staging violent demonstrations in mid-June. Five thousand clashed with police on the third of July and again on the following day, with 259 persons reported injured on those two days. The Korean press, however, failed to report the demonstrations. On July 7, President Park announced that he wouldn't oppose the amendment and on July 25 he not only gave it his firm backing but threatened to immediately resign if the amendment did not carry in the national referendum (required following the passage of the amendment referendum bill in the national assembly), on the grounds that he would consider its nonpassage as a vote of no-confidence in the government.[185] The NDP tried to introduce an impeachment motion against the president for his threatened resignation, but failed to gain much support, especially in view of the fact that Park had flown off to San Francisco to meet with President Nixon.[186]

In an effort to block the voting on the amendment bill, the NDP members occupied the rostrum of the National Assembly building, around which they built a barricade, to prevent any voting taking place on the bill, while 3,000 students outside staged a protest. On Friday, September 12, Speaker Rhee Hyo-sang recessed the National Assembly, scheduling the next meeting for the following Monday,

September 15. On Sunday morning, September 14, however, at
2:30 a.m., during curfew hours (Seoul has had a 12:00 midnight
to 4:00 a.m. curfew since the Korean War), while the opposition
held a sleep-in on the rostrum of the assembly building, the 122
assemblymen who had signed the petition surreptitiously entered
a back service entrance in the assembly's annex building, where the
speaker called the meeting to order in the committee room, and in
two minutes the DRP passed the constitutional amendment by a
vote of 122-0.[187]

Despite charges that the secret voting had been illegal, and
student demonstrations which were quickly quashed, the amendment
was submitted to a national referendum on October 17, in which
77.1 percent of the eligible voters went to the polls, and 65.1 percent
of them, or about 50 percent of all eligible voters, reportedly voted
in favor of the amendment. Predictably, the amendment did not
carry in the city of Seoul, where 40 percent of the voters stayed
away from the polls, and 53 percent of those who voted opposed
the amendment.[188] Once again, funds contributed to the outcome
of the vote. It was reported that local government party officials
openly passed out money and bread to villagers in the rural areas,
and it was estimated that the government expended about $15 million
in support of the amendment, as opposed to about $1.5 million
spent by the opposition. It was also reported that the DRP spent
$600,000 for awards to 8,471 local party officials following the
referendum, the amount paid to each official varying by the
percentage of pro-government votes received in his district.[189] The
large sums of money available for such political expenditures could
perhaps be traceable in part to the great influx of foreign loans:
during 1968 and 1969 South Korea borrowed a total of $886.4
million, $677.3 million of it in commercial loans.[190]

In addition to providing for three consecutive terms for the
president, the new amendments eliminated the possibility of future
crisis created by opposition resignations to bring the membership
to below the minimum legal number by eliminating the minimum.
Another provision raised from 30 to 50 the minimum number of
assemblymen needed to support the initiation of an impeachment

proceeding against the president. The amendment also provided that members of the National Assembly could concurrently hold other public or private offices, thus yielding to pressure from DRP assemblymen who wanted the opportunity to hold cabinet or other posts without losing their membership in the assembly.

A factor in the referendum vote continued to be the economic situation: 1969 was the highest growth year in South Korea's history, its GNP expanding 15.9 percent. Because 1968 had been a drought year with a relatively poor harvest, the introduction of the constitutional amendment bill in the assembly had been delayed until it was obvious that 1969 was to be a peak crop year, and the referendum followed the best harvest in recent history: a total of 7,737,000 metric tons of grains. This bumper crop, combined with the fact that almost one-half million persons had left the farms due to the droughts of the preceding year, meant an unprecedented increase in the income of the farm population. Income per farm household increased 21 percent in 1969 over 1968.[191] Officially recorded unemployment also declined to 4.8 percent in 1969.[192] The year 1969 had the lowest rate of inflation of consumer prices since 1962: 9.2 percent as compared with 11.1 percent the previous year. Per capita income had risen from $143.4 in 1967 to $198.0 in 1969.[193] "Legitimacy through performance" was still a workable policy.

During the next two years, however, the situation was to change considerably. By the end of 1969, South Korea had acquired foreign loans totalling $1.9 billion; by the end of 1970, the total was $3,000,294,000.[194] In 1971, $648.6 million more was borrowed. Many of these loans had been approved without studies of the projects to be undertaken. Commercial banks abroad had consented to lend the money on the basis of the Korean government's guarantee of repayment, being unwilling and unable to undertake independent feasibility studies. By the end of 1969, the structure was beginning to fall through; by August the government had been forced to assume control of, auction, or refinance under new management thirty enterprises which had failed to meet foreign loan repayments; almost three times as many more were being threatened with bankruptcy.[195] It was suggested that these businesses were facing collapse because they had been built on an unsound base: more than 95 percent of the total capital invested in them was derived from loans.[196] Seoul banks, which had guaranteed repayment on the loans and had been forced to assume payment, were running up large deficits.[197] By 1971 the number of enterprises which had taken out foreign loans and had gone into bankruptcy was more than two hundred. Most of the unsound enterprises were related to commercial loans from Japan; it was reported that 85 percent of all enterprises which had borrowed private funds from Japan had filed a declaration of bankruptcy by 1971, leading to speculation that the businesses had actually been designed only as conduits for Japanese funds.[198] The government-owned Korean banks were obligated to repay the loans to the Japanese from their own resources. At the insistence of the International Monetary Fund (IMF), South Korea placed a ceiling on loans from commercial sources in 1971, and was forced to cancel 61 loans already approved for that year, totalling more than $250 million.[199]

After the peak economic year of 1969, loan funds began to decline. Following the IMF ceiling on commercial loans in 1971, even those seeking loans with government approval found foreign banks reluctant to commit further funds. Although the IMF had set the ceiling at $468 million in commercial loans, only $345.2 million was received in 1971.[200]

As the external resources for political funding declined, the government was forced to rely more upon its internal sources, but these, too, became less plentiful. The primary internal means for acquiring political funds was through the tax system. This operated through the legislation of high tax rates, and the application of lower actual rates through unrealistically low assessments. Payoffs were given in exchange for favorable assessment rates.[201] But the system worked only if there was sufficient surplus in profits to pay both the tax and the political payoff with a comfortable margin A slowdown in the economy would mean both lower tax revenue and lower payoffs. During 1970 and 1971, the economy, while continuing to grow at a rapid rate, was growing more slowly than

in 1969. Although the GNP growth rate had reached 15.9 percent
in 1969, it slowed down to 8.9 percent in 1970 and 10.2 percent
in 1971. This would hardly appear to be an economic crisis, but it
did create a great strain on political funding because profits were
reduced by the slower rate of growth. At the same time, to achieve
its economic plans in the face of falling external resources, the
government was being forced to increase the amount of taxes
collected. Taxes collected rose from 31 billion *won* in 1969 to
39.8 billion *won* in 1970, and 50.1 billion *won* in 1971, rising from
10.8 percent of GNP in 1966 to 15.5 percent in 1971.[202]

While the government's political funds were being squeezed,
leaks in the system began to appear, and the funds wound up
increasingly in the pockets of individuals instead of in the expense
funds of the party and other political and semi-political organizations.
In May 1970, the Health and Social Affairs Ministry issued a report
that the inequitable distribution of income was creating a serious
social problem.[203] Most troublesome was the conspicuous consumption of the new elite, who began building luxurious homes and
riding through Seoul in expensive imported Cadillacs and Mercedes-
Benz (a *used* Mercedes sold for as much as $35,000 in Korea).

In a critique on the new elite, the young poet Kim Chi-ha wrote
a piece entitled "Five Thieves" (*O chŏk*) in the intellectual journal
Sassanggye in May 1970, criticizing military generals, high
bureaucrats, millionaire industrialists, cabinet members and national
assemblymen, as being the "five thieves" of Korea.[204] The opposition
NDP, seeing this as a lively political issue, reprinted the poem in its
news organ, "Democratic Front" (*Minju chŏnsŏn*). The government
immediately seized all copies of the edition, arrested the poet, the
editor of the political journal, and the editor and staff writer of
Sassanggye.[205] The group was prosecuted on the grounds that the
poem was intended to "stir up class struggle," and was therefore
in violation of the Anti-Communist Law. The area where the luxury
homes of government officials and others had been built became
popularly known as "Five Thieves' Village," and soon any street
peddler or taxi driver could direct the visitor to that area of Seoul
without any further description.

In the same issue of *Sassanggye* [Ideology] as the notorious poem, a collection of articles by an increasingly skeptical intelligentsia appeared, questioning the "ideology" of economic development, and raising serious queries as to just where the country was headed. The articles bore such titles as, "We Cannot Live by Economic Development Alone," "Tracing the Undertaking of a Great Task Without a Philosophical Foundation," and "Out-of-Kilter Economic Development Model."[206] The consensus of the articles was that some ideological or philosophical underpinnings for social development were essential.

The government became more and more defensive as the 1971 elections approached. One-by-one, external sources of funds began a sharp downturn. In June 1970, the United States announced that it intended to withdraw troops from Korea, and one-third of the American troops stationed in Korea were withdrawn by June 1971. Since the stationing of American troops in Korea was estimated to have contributed perhaps as much as $250 million annually to the Korean economy, this loss of revenue was to be sorely felt. In 1971, U.S. economic aid was terminated, as had been planned and expected in Korean economic planning; in 1971, PL480 food assistance was terminated—a move which had *not* been anticipated in Korean planning. Food assistance had been very important to the Korean economy: PL480 grants had been as high as $74.8 million in 1969. In 1970, they totalled $61.7, and in 1971, the final year, $33.7 million.[207] Facing a serious food shortage in 1971, South Korea had to purchase $297,302,000 in food grains from the United States.[208] Furthermore, the Vietnam War was drawing to a close and income from Vietnam had taken a sharp downturn. The number of Korean civilian employees in Vietnam dropped from 25,120 in 1968, when $38 million had been sent back to Korea from this source alone, to only 4,598 in 1971. In 1971, Korean troops began to return from Vietnam, reducing available military remittances from that source as well.[209] On top of this, an import quota was placed on Korean textiles (South Korea's most important export product) by the United States in October 1971. Exports to the United States fell by 15 percent in the final quarter of 1971. The government estimated that Korea would suffer a loss of $840 million of export income due to the textile quotas during the period of the third Five Year Plan.

The economic impact of many of these factors was not to take effect until the end of 1971 and the beginning of 1972: Korean troops did not start their exit from Vietnam until December 1971; U.S. troop withdrawals (of one-third of the forces in Korea) were completed in mid-1971; IMF loan ceilings were not agreed upon until late 1971; import quotas did not come into being until October 1971. Thus, the problems of economic retrenchment were largely postponed until after the 1971 presidential and assembly elections, held in April and May. The timing of the election was clearly influenced by the hope of avoiding any adverse effect a poor harvest might have: floods and droughts which result in poor harvests generally come in July and August when Korea normally receives about 40 percent of its yearly rainfall.[210] As it happened, the 1971 harvest did fall below the output of 1970, which had itself been less than the peak harvest of 1969.

The DRP was to face an unexpectedly vigorous challenge in the 1971 elections. Although factional disputes had kept the DRP preoccupied with its internal affairs, a minor revolt in the NDP brought new leadership to the top. Kim Young Sam, the young minority floor leader of the NDP who had led the fight against the constitutional amendment, and had been subject to a terrorist attack in mid-1969 (which he blamed on the CIA), resigned from his post in November 1969 and announced his intention to seek the party nomination for the presidency in 1971, anticipating the resignation of ailing party chief Dr. Yu Chin-o. Kim, who would be 44 in 1971, declared that it was time for the NDP to turn over leadership to the "40-year generation," to present a reinvigorated image to the public. Two other young party leaders, Kim Dae Jung (45 in 1971) and Lee Chul-seung (48 in 1971), soon followed suit. It was an unprecedented move to break the seniority system within the party which had in the past condemned the opposition to nominating men of advancing age (with the result that its nominees in 1956 and 1960 had both died in the heat of the campaign). In January 1970 the NDP held its annual convention and, following the resignation of Dr. Yu on grounds of health, elected Vice Chairman Yu Chin-san (no relation) to the post of party chairman. When the new chairman (66 in 1971) tried to press his own bid for the presidential nomination, however, he found the reception cool. The nomination would clearly be a three-way fight between the "40-year generation" leaders.

In September 1970, the NDP held its national convention. In an effort to avoid a factional clash between majority faction candidate Kim Young Sam and minority faction candidate Kim Dae Jung, which might embitter their members and divide the party in the upcoming elections, party chairman Yu, himself of the majority faction, offered to endorse a candidate if the two Kims and splinter faction leader Lee Chul-seung would agree to accept his choice. Kim Young Sam agreed, as did Lee, who felt it his best chance to be accepted as a compromise choice, and both put the agreement in writing. Kim Dae Jung refused, and Yu subsequently announced his choice of Kim Young Sam. At the convention, Kim Young Sam had a clear plurality of votes on the first ballot, but Lee, upset over the action of the party chairman, advised his followers to switch their votes to Kim Dae Jung, and the minority faction candidate received the nomination on the second ballot. Kim Young Sam, determined that the "new politics" should prevail, asked his followers to support the minority faction nominee, and himself took to the campaign trail on behalf of the party's candidate.

Kim Dae Jung proved an attractive campaigner, and by mid-campaign had the government running scared. As Kim's campaign reached a dramatic climax with a rally in Seoul which drew nearly half a million people, Park announced in unequivocal terms that this would be his final bid for office.[211] When the votes were counted Park had won again with a reported 51.2 percent of the total vote as against Kim's reported 43.6 percent. Of the total valid votes, the percentages were 53.2 and 45.3 percent.[212] Election irregularities were again charged, including open intimidation of voters in rural areas.[213] The large increase in Park's rural vote was especially suspect. Although he had won 50.8 percent of the rural vote in

1963 and 52.2 percent in 1967, he was reported to have carried 58.0 percent in 1971.[214] This seemed odd since the rural areas were facing an economic slump—the government's own statistics showed that 1.5 million persons, or ten percent of the total farming population, had left their farms in the two-year period from 1968 to 1970, and it was generally conceded that the abandonment of farms was due to poor farm conditions. Cultivated land had dropped by 200,000 *chongbo*, or 490,000 acres, over the same two-year period.[215] NDP candidate Kim carried the urban population by 51.5 percent. In Seoul (which had reached a population of 5.5 million and had a larger electorate than any single province), he received 58 percent of the vote, to Park's 39 percent. One factor in the outcome was the regional distribution of the vote. In the 1967 elections, the southwest had swung sharply against Park, some felt out of resentment for the heavy government investment in Park's home region, the southeast. Kim, a southwesterner himself, apparently intensified the trend. Kim reportedly carried the southwestern Cholla provinces by 58 percent of the vote (58.8 percent in Cholla-pukdo and 58.4 percent in Cholla-namdo) while Park carried the southeastern Kyongsang provinces with a phenomenal 68.6 percent in Kyongsang-pukdo and 70.8 percent in his native Kyongsang-namdo.[216] Since Cholla-do (the southwest) seemed certain to go for the opposition regardless of the regional origin of the candidate, on the basis of the 1967 trend, it is interesting to speculate what the outcome would have been had the candidate been Kim Young Sam, himself from Kyongsang-do (the southeast), who would undoubtedly have cut into Park's margins in that region. In fact, the NDP carried the city of Pusan in the later assembly elections, though it lost the city to Park in the presidential election.

With considerable popular resentment over reported irregularities evident following the presidential elections, stern orders of caution were sent out to party workers preceding the National Assembly elections in late May.[217] In contrast to the presidential elections, most observers felt that the assembly elections were relatively "clean." One factor may have been a fear of widespread resistance if the activities of the presidential election were repeated; but another factor was clearly the fact that Kim Jong Pil had returned to the post of acting party chairman (Park Chung Hee was nominally chairman). To solidify his party support, Park Chung Hee had induced Kim to return to the post in March. No party leader could have been more eager than Kim to insure that the DRP did *not* come near to two-thirds control of the assembly which would have enabled the party to pass another constitutional amendment to extend the president's term. On the other hand, the party would need a simple majority to remain in control of legislation. With 204 seats in the new assembly, 136 would constitute a two-thirds majority, and 103 a simple majority. When the results were in, the DRP had captured 113 seats (86 by districts and 27 by proportional seats), and the NDP 89 seats (65 by districts and 24 by proportional seats).

Following the election, Park Chung Hee appointed Kim Jong Pil to the post of prime minister, and several of Kim's associates to the cabinet, leaving the party organization in the hands of the new prime minister's opponents. By October, the factional battle for succession within the DRP broke open, as the old nonmainstream group joined with the opposition to carry a vote of no-confidence against Home Minister O Chi-sŏng, one of Kim Jong Pil's Eighth Class comrades.[218] Two of the instigators of the move, Kim Sŏng-kŏn, chairman of the central committee and former finance committee chairman, and Kil Chae-ho, policy committee chairman, were expelled from the party and forced to resign their assembly seats.

To some observers, the relatively close outcome of the election meant the hope of a possible peaceful change of power four years hence. For others, however, the developments of 1969–71 were evidence of a serious erosion of the power bases on which the system as a whole rested. As the military groups from Vietnam began the return home in December 1971, many feared that the Vietnam veterans might share common grievances and become a threat to the government.[219] As tax burdens increased, internal resources for political funding were becoming scarce. While external sources declined, internal groups had begun demanding a greater piece of the pie. In 1971, riots involving 30,000 persons broke out in a public housing development in Seoul. Labor unions, whose membership had grown from 23,000 in October 1963 to 493,000 in August 1971, began urgent demands for higher wages, at the same time that the IMF warned that wages must be kept within levels of rising productivity. In June, the Office of Labor reported that average earnings were 20,767 *won* per month, while the Economic Planning Board reported that average household expenditures for wage earners were 33,680 *won* per month.[220] Labor unions demanded representation in the National Assembly and began organizing "political education" committees for their members.[221] In the fall, student protest movements broke out against military training in the schools and political corruption, and by October the military and police had moved onto the campuses. About 200 student leaders were expelled from schools and 6,000 "disciplined."

Political and economic crises converged: ceilings on loans, the return of troops, student demonstrations, labor trouble, a cut-off of U.S. aid and food assistance, the flow of farmers into cities, the withdrawal of U.S. troops, the intra-party parliamentary revolt, textile quotas, Nixon's visit to China, and rumors of impending northern invasion. On December 6, 1971, President Park Chung Hee declared a state of national emergency.

From 1961 to 1971, a third experiment in nation-building had been taking place in South Korea. After being forced to reject its original "revolutionary" goals, the regime had sought "legitimacy through performance." With economic development as its primary goal and justification, it had achieved a considerable degree of support, as long as things were going well, even with heavy restrictions on personal freedom. The Third Republic, like the First Republic, achieved an ad hoc consolidation of power, shifting from reliance on guns to reliance on funds, opening sophisticated new means of control. Its organizational base, however, rather than growing and becoming regularized within the society, became truncated by factional strife; by 1971 relatively small elite factions were once again struggling for power in Yi Dynasty fashion while a volatile mobilized society was kept under precarious control. The economy had grown remarkably: 1971's GNP was ten times that of 1962. GNP per capita had grown from $94.90 in 1962 to $252.90 in 1971.[222] On the other hand, South Korea was $3.6 billion in debt. Even with the optimistic levels of growth anticipated for the third Five Year Plan, which were made unrealistic by the economic developments of 1971—for example, textile quotas, IMF ceilings, and revaluation of the Japanese *yen* (increasing the cost of imports from Japan)—South Korea would be required to pay 30 percent of its total export income on loan repayments. With economic and political pressures closing in, the "ideology" of economic development no longer seemed to provide a direction for national policy. Where to go from here? At the close of 1971, as the government shifted back to an increasing reliance on the instruments of force, the question remained unanswered.

Chapter VIII

INSTITUTIONALIZING THE NEW SYSTEM IN NORTH KOREA, 1961-1971: REFORMATION OF ELITES, RESOCIALIZATION OF THE MASSES, AND THE SEARCH FOR LEGITIMACY

Having consolidated the bases of the system in North Korea by 1961, the tasks for the regime in the period which followed would be to maintain and strengthen the organizational system, to resocialize the populace to accept and work through the system by means of a "cultural revolution," and to prepare for succession within the system by drawing new elites up through the new political process. These tasks would be complicated by the continuing involvement of external influences, forcing the regime to drive forcefully toward a condition of "self-reliance," in order to exclude dysfunctional external factors. They would also be complicated by the absence of a genuine source of legitimacy through the existing leadership, spurring the regime to exaggerate and falsify the background of the leader—and even to seek to trace his legitimacy through his family genealogy, as Rhee had done in the South. But most of all, the total process would continue to be threatened by the existence of an alternative system in the South, for the most powerful source of legitimacy and most potent source of ideology would continue to be Korean nationalism. If the regime should prove incapable of providing a means to unite the Korean people, alternatives for bringing about such unification might be found appealing, and might undermine the support for the existing system, much as the same appeal had undermined Soviet controls when the U.S.S.R. proved unwilling to supply the degree of support necessary to achieve national unification during the Korean War. Thus, a program for national unification would of necessity be an essential aspect of the campaign to institutionalize the new system.

Institutionalization, Phase I: Reforming the Elites and Remoulding the Populace through "Cultural Revolution"

In 1961 Kim Il Sung pointed to two essential tasks to be carried out. The first was to improve the functioning of the state organs, and the second was the promotion of a cultural revolution among the populace. Both tasks had already been begun.

An important part of the process of improving the functioning of these organs would be a reformation of the behavior patterns of the elites designated to carry out the functions of the state:

> Of importance for the consolidation of state organs is the enhancement of the level of leadership of the functionaries and the improvement of their style of work.
>
> With a view to doing away with the state of affairs that the level of leadership of the functionaries lagged behind the economic development, we have intensified the training and education of the cadres, and at the same time further strengthened the guidance of and assistance to lower organs by the higher. Along with this, we have incessantly waged an energetic struggle against bureaucratism, for the establishment of the popular method of work in the state bodies of all levels. Today, in all these organs, such a bureaucratic and armchair method of work that the functionaries simply sit down at their tables and stick to complicated statistics and issue piles of orders, has been remedied in the main; and there now prevails among the cadres the way of work of going down to lower bodies, factories and enterprises to see on the spot how matters stand, and to give effective assistance to the functionaries of lower bodies.[1]

Of the cultural revolution, Kim said: "Comrades, the cultural revolution is an important component part of socialist construction. During the period under review we have scored tremendous results in the improvement of public education, the enhancement of the cultural and technical level of the working people and the development of national culture and the arts."[2]

Kim Il Sung first sought to bring about a change in the work patterns of party leaders when he spoke to the training course for party organizers on February 26, 1959, in an address entitled, "On the Method of Party Work."[3] To change the society, he pointed out, they must first change themselves. The first duty of the party organizations was to educate and reform party members. The party's duty, then would be to reshape the masses, especially through the "peripheral organizations" of the party—such as the Democratic Youth League, the General Federation of Trade Unions and the Women's Union. The greatest difficulty standing in the way of the party's transformation of the behavior patterns of the population was their own traditional "bureaucratic" style of work: "I have pondered over the reason why our Party work should ever have been conducted in such a way . . . [A]t the time of the formation of our Party, there were few people who knew how to educate Party members and perform Party work by revolutionary methods, whereas there were many who practiced bureaucracy. This led many people to believe that Party work was something that should be conducted only by a sort of administrative method and by issuing orders. This has never, from the first, been the correct method of Party work."[4] Referring to the traditional attitudes toward the role and significance of bureaucratic positions, Kim Il Sung argued that these attitudes could not be permitted to persist among Party leaders: "You should not try to boost your prestige with the help of a big desk and an armchair. No red tape is needed for our Party work. . . . If certain persons do not come to see you, you go and see them first. What is wrong with that? There is nothing wrong with it even if you visit them ten times, or even a hundred times. . . "[5]

In February 1960, Kim Il Sung took his own advice and went down to the Kangso County organization, and from there to the Chongsan-li (village) organization and its component work teams to examine the local problems and set an example of the "method of party work" in resolving the problems of the area. His report on his fifteen-day stay in Kangso County later became a text on proper party method, known as the "Ch'ongsan-li method." The major problem, Kim pointed out, was the lack of knowledge and educational capacities of the local cadres. "A large number of specialists and technicians with higher learning are required if we are to run successfully such modern industry and large-scale co-operative farming as we have today. But we are in great want of such cadres. And it takes four or five years for one to finish the college course . . . we cannot sit and wait, for four or five years, for specialists and technicians to gush forth in streams . . . Therefore, in order to break through the immediate bottleneck, we must establish a work system whereby the centre helps the province, the province in its turn helps the county, and the county helps the *li*. In particular, it is necessary radically to improve the method of the county's guidance to the *li*. . . The basic solution, of course," Kim observed, "will be the promotion of the cultural revolution."[6] In order to bring about the cultural revolution, the party itself would have to be molded in the behavior patterns and ideology of the new society. The party must then lead the change in the society.

Whatever the term "cultural revolution" may have come to mean in China, in North Korea it clearly meant a "revolutionary" change in the political culture—both in values and behavior—of the population. From Kim Il Sung's point of view, such a change would come when the entire population had learned to think scientifically, using rational-analytical thought methods, and had acquired a knowledge of modern technology. This alone, in Kim's view, was in accord with the "scientific" social theory of Marxism-Leninism. The cultural revolution was to be promoted through the formal educational system, as well as through party ideological work.

With the reorganization of the educational system came an expansion of students at the higher educational levels. Although the number of students at the primary level *dropped* radically between 1956 when universal compulsory primary education was first introduced, and 1960, due to the low wartime birthrate, the students in universities had grown from 22,000 to 97,000. By the 1963–64 school year, North Korea had 214,000 students in the universities and 145,000 in higher technical schools.[7] (South Korea, by contrast, with more than twice North Korea's population, had only 112,900 students in colleges and universities in 1964.) This level began to decline after 1964, however, whether because smaller numbers of people in the age-group reached college level, or because of a reduction in the need for college-trained "cadres" once the first contingent had been produced is unclear. In 1964–1965 there were 185,000 students in colleges and universities and 156,000 in higher technical schools. By 1966–1967, the number of students in the universities had declined to 156,000.[8]

The formal educational system, however, was only one device for altering the political culture of the population, and scientific and technical education only one aspect of the new outlook to be inculcated. "The ideas of Marxism-Leninism and the lofty ethics of collectivism," as much as applied technology, would be needed to inspire a new outlook on the part of the populace.[9] "Rectification movements" to correct the ideological outlook of party members and the population at large had begun early. Among the techniques of "rectification" the most pervasive was the use of criticism and self-criticism, and public confessions. Kim Il Sung had said as early as 1946 that: "It is erroneous to believe that only educational institutions can train cadres . . . Criticism is education. Without it there can be no progress. It is the most important means of educating cadres."[10] By 1959, however, Kim's views on criticism had changed: "Educating people to rectify their mistakes of their own accord is the correct method of ideological examination. Instead, people are not educated but are threatened for their 'lack of Party spirit' and are pressed to confess their supposed wrongdoings. So they are compelled to criticize themselves, saying that everything is their fault. This sort ideological examination must be brought to an end."[11] The process of "rectification," Kim pointed out, should not be carried out in sudden waves of shock campaigns, but should be a steady, on-going process, to transform and educate the population in the new life style.

As the "vanguard" of the resocialization movement, party members were subjected to intensive education and indoctrination. Songdo College of Politics and Economics was organized as a central training college for party members, in addition to which one Communist University was established in each of the nine provinces, and a tenth in Pyongyang, under the direct management of the central committee of the KWP. The role of the party would be to direct the populace through organizing and mobilizing them for production, to explain the party programs, and to organize and direct political education. All party members themselves, divided into party cells, were obligated to attend party classes at least once a week.

The "social organizations" became known as the "transmission belts" for transferring party policy to the masses and reflecting mass views for the party. The most important of these organizations were the General Federation of Trade Unions (GFTU), with a membership of 1.72 million in 1962, the Agricultural Workers Union (AWU), with 2.3 million members in 1964,[12] the Socialist Working Youth League (SWYL) with a membership of 2.7 million in 1964, and the Korean Democratic Women's Union. The GFTU was composed of nine subunions, whose purpose along with that of the AWU, was the indoctrination of its members with Communist attitudes and concepts, and supervision of the achievement of output quotas. The SWYL served primarily as a training and recruiting ground for KWP members, and it was structured and operated in a fashion similar to the Korean Workers' Party. Unlike youth organizations in some of the other Communist states, such as the Komsomol in the Soviet Union, the membership of the league was not exclusive, but embraced virtually all (99.9 percent, according to official claims) young people between the ages of 14 and 30.[13] Women between the ages of 18 and 55 belonged to the KDWU, one prime purpose of which was to enlist the cooperation of mothers in the education of children in the new Communist life-style.

Another organization of immense importance was that of the Young Pioneers, organized somewhat on the model of scouts in non-Communist countries. Membership in the Young Pioneers was compulsory for children between the ages of 9 and 13. The Young Pioneers acted not only as a training ground for young people in the values of the state, but served to solidify a sense of peer-group unity. The Young Pioneers, as well as the SWYL, maintained group discipline, enforced compulsory school attendance among their members, and served as an institutional support for resisting family authority when the dictates of the state were in conflict with parental aims.[14]

All of these instrumentalities were used in the mobilization system in an effort to restructure the society. One of the purposes of mobilization was to increase economic production. Production itself served to build the economic independence of the nation, but its greatest significance, according to official doctrine, was in promoting a work ethic as a value in and of itself. In explaining the duty of teachers, Kim Il Sung told educational workers in 1961 that children must learn three loves: the love of the collective, the love of public property, and the love of labor. Love of labor was considered especially important in molding the character of the society, in contrast to the system of traditional values:

> In our country . . . many people used to think that the most lucky man was the one who led an idle life. When admiring a handsome child, people would remark that the child was destined for an idle life . . . Our forefathers, amidst their back-breaking toil, envied the idlers and wished that similar fortune might smile on them some day . . . Even now, some hold the wrong view that in communist society people will do no work at all. A communist society is not one in which people do not work.
>
> In communist society, the people will all work and live happily. As a matter of course, in communist society the development of technology will make man's work easier. . . However, even then labour will be needed. All wealth is the product of labour. Without labour a society cannot be maintained, nor can it advance.[15]

In the effort to increase economic production, the Ch'ŏllima movement was continued and strengthened—no longer on the mad scale of China's Great Leap, but as an instrumentation to promote continued increases in production. Each year, work teams were selected as "Ch'ŏllima teams" and given awards. The qualifications were not only the exceeding of work quotas, but a show of enthusiasm for the policies of the party. By 1965, 26,000 teams had been selected as Ch'ŏllima teams, and 980,000 workers had earned the honor.[16] The teams included both industrial and agricultural workers, as well as those in the educational, artistic, and other fields. Once selected, a team became a "model" for other teams, and therefore efforts were made to select at least one team in each large factory or collective farm, or other productive unit.

After establishing the "Ch'ŏngsan-li method" of party policy, designed primarily to strengthen guidance to the party units over-seeing the basic rural units of the society and eliminate the bureaucratic style of party work, another system was introduced when Kim Il Sung went to the Taean Electrical Appliance Plant in December 1961 to illustrate how to properly direct and administer industry.[17] The concept of going down to lower levels and personally investigating problems, and gaining the participation of the workers in resolving difficulties, was the central focus of this "Taean Work Method."

By the mid-1960's, the institutional and ideological tools for resocializing the population in the new values and behavior patterns were operating smoothly. Mass media, including newspapers, magazines, and radio, was used to reinforce organizational and mobilization techniques. Radio reached almost the entire population through a system of broadcasting loudspeakers in the towns, factories and on the city streets. The broadcasting system relayed only the broadcasts of the government radio station. In addition to the regular media, "cultural" activities—the arts, films, theater, literature, lectures—were used to reinforce the values being introduced to support the new system.

Because the party was designed as a principal resocializing force, one of the basic themes of the propaganda aimed at the populace was "Let Us Think and Act as the Party Does."[18] Other themes included the propagation of the concepts of "*chu-ch'e*" and the Ch'ŏllima movement, and the elimination of revisionism, factionalism "familyism" and other "isms" from the traditional past or outside influences which might counteract the resocialization process.

The carrying out of political resocialization and re-acculturation, like the previous carrying out of political consolidation, was soon to raise critical conflicts with external forces. Although Kim Il Sung had successfully consolidated his control over the system, and successfully consolidated the bases of political tools to support the system, North Korea was not yet in a position to be militarily or economically independent. The continued need for external inputs became abundantly clear when the coup d'etat occurred in South Korea in May 1961. Concerned that the new military government might be planning a march north, Kim traveled to both Moscow and Peking and concluded defense treaties in July 1961.[19]

The economic plan introduced at the Fourth Party Congress in 1961 had continued an emphasis on the building of an independent economic foundation for North Korea. Yet, to carry out the new Seven Year Plan, foreign economic assistance was essential. As with the previous economic plan, the Soviet Union objected to the unwillingness of the North Koreans to agree to coordinated planning with other bloc countries leading to an integrated economy among all the Communist countries. As with many of the American-South Korean disputes, the Soviet Union couched its objections in economic terms, while the North Koreans responded with political arguments.

The Soviet economic position was that integrated planning and an integrated economy among the bloc countries would take advantage of economics of scale, and of the necessity for locating given industries in areas where they would have the greatest comparative advantage. North Korea responded that this would clearly hinder its political independence. Since the Soviet Union had achieved a fully balanced economy already, it could not be adversely affected by any threat to cut off trade. But for an underdeveloped country to concentrate on only one or a few industries in which it would have a "comparative advantage" would be to subject it to the possibilities of economic blackmail.[20] The *Nodong Shinmun,* the official newspaper of the Korean

Worker's Party, asserted in 1963 that: "Economic independence is the basis of political independence. Economic dependence on foreign forces entails political dependence of those forces. Economic subordination leads to political subordination."[21] But the Soviet Union, with its own political system now fully consolidated and institutionalized, had developed a view of economics similar to that of the United States: as a science divorced from politics which could be understood only on its own self-contained rational terms. How could the North Koreans oppose rational, scientific, economic arguments with political emotionalism? The Soviet treatment of the North Koreans as economically "naive" touched off a bitter quarrel which developed into the most vitriolic of exchanges between the two nations to date. Even before the acerbic public rhetoric, however, the Soviet Union had severed its economic aid to North Korea, as illustrated by trade statistics for the years 1961–1963, which showed that all Soviet imports were paid for by North Korean exports.[22]

In October 1963, the North Koreans charged in an editorial in the *Nodong Shinmun* that the U.S.S.R. had attempted to use its economic and military assistance as a lever to control North Korean economic planning, and again reiterated that Soviet control of its economic development would deprive North Korea of its independence and sovereignty. *"It goes without saying that the loss of independence in economy will make it impossible for any country to maintain its genuine independence and sovereignty."*[23]

The greatest expressions of animosity did not appear in print until 1964. During June of that year, North Korea sponsored an "Asian Economic Seminar" in Pyongyang, attended by representatives of twenty-eight governments. Topics discussed included "Neo-Colonialism and the Asian Economy," and "Self-Reliant Recovery and Construction of an Independent National Economy."[24] The U.S.S.R. criticized the conference, charging the North Koreans with knowing nothing about the science of economics. The North Koreans were incensed, and responded in *Nodong Shinmun* on September 7, 1964: "What a slighting attitude of contempt and arrogance this is! What overbearing, insolent, and shameless nonsense it is! These are the words that can be used only by the great-power chauvinists who are in the habit of thinking that they are entitled to decide and order everything, others are all ignorant and they alone are learned."[25] The North Koreans went on to openly charge the Soviet Union with economic imperialism: "You furnished us with equipment . . . and other materials at prices much higher than the world-market prices and took away from us scores of tons of gold and quantities of valuable non-ferrous metals and raw materials at prices much lower than the world-market prices. Would it not be a reasonable attitude, when you talk about your 'aid' to us, to mention also that you took valuable materials produced by our people through arduous labor in the most difficult days of our life?"[26]

In a lucid lecture on North Korea's economic and political policies given at the Aliarcham Academy of Sciences in Indonesia in April 1965, Kim Il Sung explained the basis of his conflict with the Soviet Union:

> We by no means oppose economic co-operation between states, nor do we advocate building socialism in isolation. What we do reject is the big-power chauvinist tendency to hampering the independent and comprehensive development of the economies of other countries and, furthermore, to placing these economies under one's own control, by using the pretext of 'economic co-operation' and 'international division of labour.' We consider that co-operation should be based on the building of an independent national economy. . .[27]

The problem remained, however, that North Korea had not yet reached the stage where its economy could become viable in the absence of external inputs. Aid in the form of loans continued coming from China until 1964, but the Chinese were facing severe economic problems themselves and could not render much assistance.

North Korea's dispute with the U.S.S.R. weakened it not only economically, but militarily as well. North Korea was required to pay in full for all military equipment acquired from the U.S.S.R.

At the Fifth Plenum of the Fourth Party Congress, held December 10-14, 1962, defense was the primary topic on the agenda and it was suggested that economic plans would have to suffer for the sake of increased defense expenditures. In 1963, North Korea attacked the U.S.S.R. for its unwillingness to render military assistance, saying that "certain persons propagandize as though a certain country's armed forces alone were safeguarding the entire socialist camp . . . The defense of the socialist camp . . . should not rest on a certain weapon of the latest type alone . . . no socialist country should try to rely solely on the military power of another country . . . Hence it is important for all the socialist countries alike to possess the latest military technique and strengthen their defense power through mutual cooperation."[28]

As the conflict with the Soviet Union became acute, North Korea continued its internal consolidation in an effort to resist external pressures. In October 1962, elections were held once again to the "Supreme People's Assembly." The number of representatives was increased to 383, or 1:30,000 of population as opposed to the previous ratio of 1:50,000. In this election, the "black box" which had supposedly permitted an expression of disapproval of the proposed ballot, was eliminated. Now the government announced 100 percent approval of the slate by the electorate. The number of "representatives" of political parties and organizations other than the Workers' Party now totalled only 12 out of 383, as opposed to 37 out of 215 in the Second Assembly and 415 out of 572 in the First Assembly. Local elections were held in December 1963, once again without a "black box" alternative, and these results were also announced as 100 percent. The total number of deputies to the people's assemblies (the people's committees had become people's assemblies with the expansion of membership during the 1950's, and their "executive committees" took the name "people's committees") expanded from 64,650 to 87,070. Membership at all levels was increased: the village assembly members rose from 53,882 to 70,250, county members from 9,759 to 14,303, and provincial members more than doubled from 1,009 to 2,517. Meanwhile party membership continued

to rise, reaching 1.5 million in 1964, or approximately 12.4 percent
of the total population. Furthermore, by 1963, 15.1 percent of the
labor force were "office workers"—bureaucratic employees of the
Kim Il Sung regime. The purges that had been characteristic of earlier
periods were no longer in evidence; between the Fourth Party Congress
in 1961 and the special party conference convened in 1966, only
three high-level party members were removed from the party lists:
the chairman of the Red Cross Association, the chairman of the
Artists' Association, and the chairman of the Light Industry Commission—the first in 1961 and the other two in 1962.[29]

By 1963, North Korea was clearly experiencing difficulties in
meeting the goals of its Seven Year Plan, which was to extend
through 1967. None of the major products were able to meet the
levels of increase needed to meet the plan, and steel and textile
production had dropped below 1962 levels. Statistics for agriculture
were not even released. In 1964 the economy made an even poorer
showing, most statistics no longer being released, and those available
clearly falling far behind planned growth rates.[30] Most statistics for
1965 showed slight increases over the 1964 output levels, but the
output of some important products such as cement and chemical
fertilizers, which had been lower in 1964 than in 1963, declined
even further.[31]

As 1964 came to a close, assistance from China was also coming
to an end, and China was not in a position to renew its aid.
Krushchev's fall from power at that time created a face-saving
device with which the Soviets and the North Koreans could mend
their differences, although the new leadership included Leonid
Brezhnev, whose precipitation of the 1956 crisis in North Korea
could hardly have been forgotten by Kim Il Sung. In February
1965, Kosygin paid a visit to Pyongyang, and intercourse between
the two nations was renewed. A military assistance agreement was
concluded in May 1965, and an agreement on economic and
technical cooperation in June 1966.[32] The conclusion of these
agreements in no way indicated that North Korea was yielding
on the issue of the "independent economy." On the contrary,
on August 12, 1966, a long editorial in *Nodong Shinmun* strongly

reemphasized the necessity for North Korea to remain economically, politically, culturally, and even ideologically independent of the Soviet Union.

> The leadership of the revolution in each country must come from its own party and people. Revolution can neither be exported nor imported. While the revolution of each country is fulfilled in conjunction with the world revolution and is influenced by international factors, what is basic to the success of a revolution are the *internal factors.* Important as outside support is, it plays only a secondary role . . . [Emphasis added.]
>
> In carrying out revolution and construction, a country must give first place to its own internal strength, and second place to assistance from the outside. Even if outside aid is given to a country, it can be turned to good account only if the leadership of that country acts wisely.
>
> Mutual relations among Communist and Workers' Parties must be based on the principle of complete equality, sovereignty, mutual respect, noninterference in each others' internal affairs, and comradely assistance.[33]

In addition to North Korea's economic problems, another factor driving the Kim Il Sung government to seek a reconciliation with the U.S.S.R. was a growing strain in its relations with China. Although China was developing in a parallel fashion to North Korea, the Chinese system was facing serious problems unlike that of North Korea. Being relatively small, the North Korean system had proved much easier to organize than the vast society of China. North Korea had a pre-existing industrial base, extensive organizational assistance from the U.S.S.R. in early years, a four-year head start on the Chinese, and foreign economic assistance to North Korea had been in per capita amounts which no outside nation could conceivably have granted to China. By the mid-1960's, North Korea was a very effectively organized, industrialized, and considerably urbanized country. In 1963, 40.1 percent of North Korea's labor force was industrial, while 42.8 percent was agricultural, and industrial production accounted for 72 percent of the gross national product.[34] By 1967, 47.5 percent of North Korea's population lived in urban areas.[35] North Korea was rapidly on its way to becoming an urban-industrial society.

Having effectively consolidated its internal system, it had also moved ahead of China in the phase of institutionalization. The upheaval of China in its Cultural Revolution, and the cry to abandon technology for the "thought of Mao Tse-tung" were totally unattractive to the North Koreans. Kim Il Sung's ideal was vastly different: an orderly, organized society, schooled in modern science and technology, marching rapidly onward in organized fashion toward the goal of a modern, scientific, Marxist-Leninist society. North Korea was preparing to introduce universal compulsory technical education at the secondary level while the Red Guards in China were shouting anti-technological slogans. It was no wonder that the Red Guards began putting up anti-Kim Il Sung slogans, terming him a "fat revisionist." The North Koreans counterattacked. As they had previously condemned Soviet "revisionism," they now became equally critical of Chinese "dogmatism."

Kim was displeased with events in China for several reasons. First, by weakening China internally the upheavals weakened North Korea's defense posture—hence the hurried efforts to patch up relations with the U.S.S.R. Second, Chinese activity was embarassing to North Korean efforts to promote Marxist-Leninist development as a rational, scientific approach to the problems of development. Furthermore, China's interpretation of the meaning of "cultural revolution" could influence the use of the term in North Korea, and hamper efforts to bring about a revolution in the political culture on an orderly basis. The "Cultural Revolution" in China was not mentioned in the North Korean press throughout the period of upheaval.

North Korea's reconciliation with the U.S.S.R. came too late to salvage the goals of the Seven Year Plan. North Korea excused the failures which occurred as due to diversions to the defense budget, as it followed the policy announced in December 1962 at the Fifth Plenum of the Fourth Central Committee, to "make every soldier a political cadre, modernize the army, arm the populace, and turn the country into a fortress," even if economic goals had to suffer.[36] The 1962 decision to divert expenditures to defense had come after a North Korean delegation to Moscow in November 1962, headed by Defense Minister Kim Kwang-hyŏp, had failed to secure an agreement for Soviet military aid.[37] A national militia corps was created, whose claimed strength was 1,300,000. While North Korea in 1965 explained its economic setbacks by the diversion of funds in the defense budget,[38] in fact far larger sums were being spent on "socio-cultural" expenses in carrying out the cultural revolution, than on defense, during the period from 1961 through 1966. Budget allocations (by percentage) during that period were as follows:[39]

North Korean Expenditures as Percent of Budget, 1961-1966

Year	Economic Expenses	Socio-Cultural Expenses	Defense Expenses	Government Operations	Total
1961	73.3	21.1	2.6	3.0	100
1962	72.8	22.3	2.6	2.3	100
1963	74.0	21.3	1.9	2.8	100
1964	69.5	20.4	5.8	4.3	100
1965	68.7	19.1	8.0	4.3	100
1966	68.1	17.2	10.0	4.7	100

Only after China's new defense policy was announced by Lin Piao in his statement, "Long live the Victory of the People's War," in 1965, in which China seemed to imply that it would not become involved in the struggles of its allies, did North Korea become especially concerned.[40] In May 1966, Chou En-lai stated that "China will not take the initiative to provoke a war with the U.S."[41] Following this apparent Chinese commitment of noninvolvement, the defense expenses of North Korea increased threefold. Budget allocations during 1967-1971 concentrated heavily on defense:[42]

North Korean Expenditures as Percent of Budget, 1967-1971

Year	Economic Expenses	Socio-cultural Expenses	Defense Expenses	Government Operations	Total
1967	50.6	17.5	30.4	1.5	100
1968	48.9	17.2	32.4	1.5	100
1969	47.8	19.7	31	1.5	100
1970	50	17	31.5	1.5	100
1971	51.5	17	30	1.5	100

"Economic expenses" declined sharply as defense spending increased, but "socio-cultural" expenses remained steady, illustrating the commitment to cultural revolution at all costs.

The Fifth Congress of the Korean Workers' Party had initially been scheduled to meet in 1966. The congress was postponed, however (it was finally held in 1970), and instead the party called a "Special Conference," under the name of the 14th Plenum of the Fourth Central Committee. Unlike other regular Central Committee plenums, however, this conference, which met from October 5 to 12, was attended by representatives of the party from all levels, in the same manner as a party congress. A total of 1,275 delegates and 48 alternates attended.[43] One speculation concerning the reason for calling a conference rather than a congress was to avoid the necessity of inviting foreign delegations.[44]

Like the Third and Fourth Congresses before it, the 1966 conference marked a turning point in the process of North Korean development. Kim Il Sung unequivocally reiterated the party's independent stand with regard to other Communist parties. Another important aspect of the conference was the announcement that the Seven Year Plan would have to be extended for three additional years, to end in 1970. The conference also brought about some changes in the political leadership. The one remaining Soviet-Korean and the one remaining Yenan Korean in the political committee of the central committee were removed, as were the three remaining domestic Communist members; the one Yenan Korean and one domestic Communist who had been alternate members of the political committee were also dropped. The remaining members of the political committee of the central committee were all members of Kim Il Sung's Manchurian-Korean faction, or were new faces not previously known to have been affiliated with any faction. Furthermore, Kim Il Sung's younger brother, KimYong Ju, became director of party organization.

In addition to the personnel changes, a structural change was made: a six-man executive committee of the political committee was named. Of the six men in this new executive committee, all were members of Kim Il Sung's pre-1945 entourage. The members were Kim Il Sung, Ch'oë Yŏng-kŏn, Kim Il, Pak Kŭm-ch'ŏl, Yi Hyo-sun, and Kim Kwang-hyŏp.[45]

The conference, like a congress, also served to sum up achievement in development to that point, and to mark out the course for development in the years ahead. Reviewing the progress of the cultural revolution in North Korea, Kim Il Sung noted that: "With the progress of socialist construction in our country the ranks of the working class have grown speedily and the standards of their ideology and consciousness and of their culture and technique have risen markedly. Our working class has been successfully carrying out the historic mission of transforming the society and is displaying a high degree of revolutionary zeal and creative initiative in socialist construction."[46] However, Kim noted that the struggle against the "survivals of outdated ideas" must be kept up, for these survivals still remained and might re-emerge if intensive efforts were not continued: "The struggle against the remnants of outdated ideas . . . is an internal affair of the working people . . . and it is a task raised for educating and remoulding all the working people and leading them to communist society. . . . In our society today there exist no socio-economic and material sources for the emergence of outdated ideas, and the predominant ideology of our working people is the revolutionary ideas of Marxism-Leninism and the communist ideology. Accordingly, the outmoded ideological survivals can be overcome by persistent ideological education among the working people."[47]

Kim attacked both those "revisionists" who would relax the struggle to change the outlook of the society before the cultural revolution could be completed, and those "dogmatists" who would change the cultural revolution into a hostile and antagonistic struggle. The cultural revolution, in Kim's view, was clearly far from completed. With the working class now constituting as large a portion of the labor force as the peasant class, Kim noted they had now assumed the leading role in the revolution, in accordance with Marxist-Leninist theory.

The gap between the working class and the peasant class was seen by Kim as a major problem to be resolved through the proletarianization of the peasant class. Ultimately, this change would have to be achieved by extending the technological revolution to the countryside, along with the ideological and cultural revolutions.[48]

In continuing to carry out the "socialist revolution" Kim noted that support from other socialist countries was important, but that the Korean party would hold fast to its principle of independence in internal and external activities and continue to oppose "Right" and "Left" opportunism (Soviet revisionism and Chinese dogmatism), adhering instead to "pure" Marxism-Leninism.

By 1966, the process of the cultural revolution was in full swing. There were said to be 250,000 graduates of middle schools, technical schools, and higher technical schools, in addition to some 7,000 students who had been educated in the Soviet Union, Eastern Europe, China, and Cuba.[49] By far the greatest number of these students were educated in various areas of engineering, although some had been sent to the U.S.S.R. and Cuba to study political science. Those sent to China all studied textile manufacturing, the one area in which the North Koreans considered the Chinese more advanced. All of the instruments of the political system, in the meantime, had been mobilized to educate and remold the population in the idea system which would constitute the ideological underpinnings of the new political system.

This process of resocialization, like the process of consolidation before it, had met with external opposition. Kim Il Sung, relying on his concept of "chu-ch'e" had persisted in the face of external pressures from two different directions, losing external economic and military support for a time, but achieving the full mobilization of the resocialization process as a result.

The cultural revolution would continue in the period ahead, accompanied by a new trend to promote new elites in preparation for succession within and through the new political institutions of the system, and a new search for sources of legitimacy to support these institutions in the period of succession.

Institutionalization Phase II: Transformation for Succession and the Search for Legitimacy

The period following the 1966 party conference would continue to be characterized by "cultural revolution" even as efforts were begun to shift the generational base of the leadership and to find a source of legitimacy to support the institutionalization of the system in the process of the transition. As Cyril Black has pointed out, the necessary changes in the attitudes and behavior needed to support a new system ("the informal attributes of tradition and loyalty that hold together the fabric of society") may come about only after the leadership has "educated a generation or two of citizens to an acceptance of their politics."[50] In the late sixties both mobilization and indoctrination were intensified in an effort to completely resocialize the society into positively supporting and working through the institutions of the new system.

One serious problem in undertaking the cultural revolution was to be found in the ideology of Marxism-Leninism itself, for it did not provide specific guidelines for dealing with a number of the behavioral patterns of Korean society, such as "bureaucratism." It would be simple enough to assert that Marxism-Leninism implied that bureaucratism could not exist in a modern scientific society, but how should it be eliminated? The Chinese, facing an almost identical problem arising out of the same aspects of the Sinitic cultural heritage, chose to deal with it in a way quite different from that of Kim Il Sung. Who was to say that Kim was right and Mao wrong? The only explanation was that "circumstances" were different in the two societies, and therefore Marxism-Leninism must be applied "creatively to the particular circumstances in one's own society"—Kim Il Sung's definition of "*chu-ch'e.*"

Indeed, circumstances were quite different in China, where

Mao was using anti-bureaucratism as a justification for mobilizing the army and Red Guards to purge the party ranks, to more effectively consolidate control over his party. In North Korea, Kim's consolidation of control over the party was already complete. It would have made no more sense for him to attack his own party—his most effective pillar of support—than it would have made sense for Syngman Rhee in the South to attack his own police force during the period when it was his most important source of support. Kim's cultural revolution was not intended as a tool in an internal power struggle, but as an instrument of orderly resocialization of the society. But how could the North Korean regime justify the correctness of "*chu-ch'e*" itself? There was no explanation for insisting on adherence to Kim's idea of *chu ch'e* as opposed to the policies of Mao, or of Khrushchev-Brezhnev (the former labelled "dogmatism," and the latter labelled "revisionism") other than that the ideas of Kim Il Sung were *ipso facto* infallible. The external ideological interpretations of both China and the U.S.S.R. would have been dysfunctional if applied in the "particular circumstances" of North Korea, for North Korea was ahead of China in the stage of consolidation, yet far behind the U.S.S.R. in institutionalization. To prove Kim Il Sung infallible would be an essential task in supporting the North Korean cultural revolution. The result was the development of the "cult of Kim Il Sung."

The cult of Kim Il Sung was to serve two purposes besides providing support for the infallibility of *chu-ch'e,* and of Kim Il Sung's own interpretations as to how to get rid of the cultural deviations of traditional society with which Marxism-Leninism did not specifically deal. It would serve as a source of legitimacy for the new regime. By proving Kim Il Sung to be the true "Hero of the 20th Century" and "Leader of the 40 Million Korean People" (among the many new appellations soon to be appended to his lengthening title), one could prove that the new institutions, which were his own creations, were therefore clearly legitimate. It would also serve as a source of legitimacy for the succession of power—for if Kim's ideas were infallible, then his choice of a successor must therefore be correct. Conversely, to question the infallibility of Kim Il Sung would be to question the legitimacy of the new political system; such could not be tolerated. The party newspaper, *Nodong Shinmun,* summed up the inseparability of the system and the ideas of its leader:

> Apart from the revolutionary ideas and wise leadership of Comrade Kim Il Sung, we cannot think of the victorious development of the Communist movement in Korea and the restoration of the fatherland, the epochal changes which have taken place in our country, and the present-day happy life of our people, nor can we talk about the future develop- ment of our revolution and the ultimate victory of the cause of socialism and communism.
>
> The great revolutionary ideas . . . of Comrade Kim Il Sung, his original theories, methods and lines, the rich revolutionary achievements and experiences attained by him, and the immortal revolutionary traditions established by him are precious assets for the victory of the cause of socialism and communism in our country and the whole world and an outstanding contribution to enriching the treasure house of Marxism-Leninism and developing the world revolution. [51]

The cult of Kim Il Sung is said to have begun as early as 1956, when Kim Il Sung displayed his effective consolidation of control over the party. (*The Selected Works of Kim Il Sung* were first published in 1955.) It was after that that biographies and histories of his background began to be written. [52] Not until after that time was it openly admitted that his original name was not Kim Il Sung (that of the legendary hero), but Kim Sŏng-chu. Kim Il Sung is reported to have said about the personality cult in 1957 that "Criticism against the cult of the individual is a view of revisionism, and a plot of imperialists to split and break down the communist movement from inside by creating conflicts in the socialist camp." [53] In 1964, when North Korea was at odds with both China and the U.S.S.R., an intensification of the cult brought the publication of a large number of Kim Il Sung books. [54] The cult became most extreme after the October 1966 conference, at the same time that it was resolved to strengthen "*chu-ch'e*" and the cultural revolution.

In March 1967, a purge of some of Kim Il Sung's own Manchurian-Korean comrades at the upper levels was begun. Among those removed were Pak Kǔm-ch'ǒl and Yi Hyo-sun, both members of the Secretariat and of the political committee of the central committee, who ranked fourth and fifth, respectively, in the party hierarchy. Also removed were Yim Ch'un-ch'u, deputy chief of the South Korean Bureau of the KWP and an alternate member of the political committee, Kim To-man, a member of the Secretariat and director of the KWP Propaganda Department, Hǒ Sok-sun, director of the Education Department of the KWP Academy of Science and director of the KWP central committee's Internal Affairs Department, Ko Hyǒk, vice-premier in charge of Ideologies, and Yi Song-un, former chairman of the Pyongyang City Party Committee. Also missing after that time were the chairman of the two major "social" organizations, the General Federation of Trade Unions (GFTU) and the Socialist Working Youth League (SWYL). It was reported that in all about 100 party members at the upper levels were removed. Those dismissed were charged with being "bourgeois and revisionist elements" who "opposed the lines and policies of the party and [sought to] undermine its unity."[55] Apparently these members had opposed the intensification of political mobilization and the development of the Kim cult which was to come after the 1966 conference. Life-long personal associates of the leader were finding it increasingly difficult to treat him as a god.

Surveying the results of the purge, the party newspaper, *Nodong Shinmun*, editorialized: "The most important success made in the course of the struggle for implementing the resolutions of the Party Conference [October 1966] is that our revolutionary ranks have been consolidated as never before, politically and ideologically. The unitary Party ideas have been all the more firmly established within the whole Party and among the entire people, and the revolutionization of the Party membership and people has been pushed ahead."[56] Editorials of the *Nodong Shinmun* continued thereafter to stress the necessity to "proletarianize and revolutionize all members of society," insisting that it was essential to study more thoroughly the works of Kim Il Sung, in order to arm themselves with the unitary ideas of the party.

In May 1967, Kim Il Sung published a political thesis apparently
in response to criticisms that had been made against party policy.
Considerable theoretical discussion had been raised about the
problem of transition from socialism to communism, an aspect
of Marxist theory. In Kim's new work, entitled, "On the Questions
of the Period of Transition from Capitalism to Socialism and the
Dictatorship of the Proletariat," Kim asserted that the fact that
the bases of socialism had been constructed did not mean that the
dictatorship of the proletariat could be dispensed with. "It is
wrong to believe that the transition period will come to a close as soon
as the socialist revolution is achieved and the socialist system
established."[57] Kim explained that the stage of communism could
not be reached until the distinctions between the working class
and peasant class had been completely eliminated, so that there
were no longer separate classes in the country. Even then, the phase
of communism would not be reached until the technical revolution
had been achieved, placing everything on a scientific basis; furthermore
though communism had been achieved, the dictatorship of the
proletariat could not end until the revolution had been accomplished
on a worldwide scale—otherwise, opportunistic ideological trends
could creep in from without and destroy the socialist system by
reawakening old bourgeois ideas. North Koreans proclaimed his
theory the first scientific explanation of the transition from
capitalism to socialism.[58]

The chairman of the Party Control Committee reported to the
Fifth Congress that during 1968 and 1969 alone, two million copies
of the writings of Kim Il Sung had been published with party funds,
and distributed to all party members.[59] Libraries had also been
established with party funds to teach party members, and 30 million
copies of interpretations and analyses of Kim Il Sung's writings and
other reference books were published and distributed with the use
of party funds.[60] To illustrate the extent of the emphasis placed on
the "cultural revolution," the expenditures of the party for "outside
activities" in the year 1969, were reported to be thirty times the
amount spent in the year 1960.[61]

Intensification of the mobilization system, as well as the system of indoctrination (or "reeducation") was evident after 1966. A new, smaller production unit, the *punjo kwalliche* (subwork team management system) had been introduced on an experimental basis in 1965, and put into full-scale operation in 1966, reducing the size of the unit in the collectives to between 15 and 25 persons, making individual members of the team more directly accountable for failures to increase production. Vice Premier Kim Kwang-hyŏp reported in 1968 that this system made political control and indoctrination of the peasants easier.[62] Indoctrination, education, and remolding of the populace took precedence over all other policies, but coincidentally the mobilization of the population for increased production was considered to be one of the means of remolding their attitudes to value labor and production. Furthermore, by creating the economic base of communism (seen as a highly productive, advanced, automated technological state), economic production would eliminate the class distinctions which caused divergent political outlooks. Thus, economic and political policies coincided.

Along with the increased ideological and economic mobilization of the society, military mobilization was also stressed, as the third aspect of the policy of independence, or *"chu-ch'e"* which called for "independence in politics, self-reliance in economy, and self-defense in national defense."[63] Concurrently, military mobilization of the society could be used to support the Kim Il Sung legend of revolutionary activity. The program to arm the populace as a part of the people's militia encouraged the people to learn from the revolutionary experience of Kim Il Sung. In 1970, Kim Il Sung reported that, "One of the most significant achievements made in the strengthening of the defense power of the country during the period under review is that the entire people have been placed under arms and the whole country fortified. In our country the entire people know how to fire guns and are carrying arms with them."[64]

Political indoctrination in the military was also intensified. Defense spending was increased in 1967 to three times the 1966 budget, and political indoctrination in the military was stepped up.

Said Kim Il Sung reviewing the developments in the defense system between 1961 and 1970: "Especially during the period under review we took a number of radical actions for boosting the nation's defense capabilities . . . Our Party, first of all, has untiringly conducted politico-ideological education among the officers and men of the People's Army to give fullest play to the political and moral superiority of the People's Army as a revolutionary armed force."[65]

There were apparently some in the army who opposed Kim's line of "fortifying the whole country," however. A program to train each soldier to be capable of combatting 100 enemy soldiers, known as the "One to One Hundred" movement was introduced in September 1967. As if to prove to doubtful members of the army the reality of external threat requiring such intensive mobilization, the "spy ship" the U.S.S. *Pueblo* was captured in January 1968, in the midst of the mobilization campaign. In January 1969, several high-level military leaders were removed from their posts, including Kim Chang-pong, the minister of defense and a member of the political committee of the central committee, Hŏ Pong-hak, the chief of South Korean affairs and an alternate member of the political committee of the central committee, and Kim Chŏng-tae, the director of the Intelligence Bureau of the Ministry of Defense.[66] While not directly attacking these individuals, Kim Il Sung condemned those who were afraid of war ("infected with the revisionist ideological trend of warphobia"), pointing out that although "We are not in a position to compete with the developed countries in military-technical equipment . . . we are not required to do so" . . . "When all the people are under arms, when all the people hate the enemy, when all the people join in fighting against the aggressors, it is quite possible to defeat any enemy."[67] Following the purge of the "warphobiacs," the new surface-to-air missiles acquired from the Soviet Union were proven effective in the shooting down of the American "large-size spy plane 'EC-121'" on Kim Il Sung's birthday, April 15. The failure of the United States to retaliate was used to illustrate the fact that the enemy were "paper tigers," so there was nothing to fear.

Despite all efforts to mobilize the population, the cultural

revolution continued to meet difficulties. First Deputy Premier
Kim Il in 1968 criticized the workers as well as managers of the
production units, saying, "The fact that there were many who
showed passiveness and swerving and failed to devote all of their
zeal and wisdom to the party and the worker class, to the fatherland
and the people, when our party presented the new line of carrying
on economic construction and defense building in parallel, was,
in the final analysis, due largely to the fact that they had not
been revolutionized and proletarianized."[68] Kim Il Sung added in
September 1968, on the twentieth anniversary of the founding
of the North Korean state, "A society where the hostile classes
persist in insidious maneuverings, the corrosive action of old ideas
continues, there still remain distinctions between towns and the
countryside and the class distinctions between the working class
and peasantry, the industrialization of the country has not been
realized fully and the material and technical basis of socialism
has not been laid firmly cannot yet be called a completely
triumphant socialist society."[69] In an effort to overcome the
sluggishness in the cultural revolution, the regime invested almost
20 percent of the budget in 1969 in "socio-cultural" expenditures.[70]

In February 1969, *Nodong Shinmun* pointed out a basic problem
with the mobilization program. On the one hand, it was the people
in the countryside who would have to make the greatest sacrifices
during the initial period of development. "A certain amount of
funds has to be obtained from the rural areas for socialist industrialization for a certain period following the victory of the revolution."
On the other hand, however, it was the people in the countryside
who were least receptive to the socialist ideology which would
induce them to produce more: "It is the countryside where the
survivals and leftovers of the old society are found more than
anywhere else, and it is again the countryside where the materials
and technical foundations of socialism are the weakest. The lag of
the countryside behind the town, a leftover from the old society,
offers a foothold for the maneuvers of the hostile elements."[71]
Kim Il Sung went so far as to imply that so long as the "backward"
elements persisted in the countryside, some material incentives

might be necessary.[72] In November, the government newspaper
Minju Chosŏn emphasized the need to improve "logistic support"
(that is, food supplies, according to the content of the article)
to the local areas because, "only by satisfactorily looking after the
workers so as to free them from all inconveniences in their daily
life can we expect them to demonstrate a higher degree of revolutionary
enthusiasm."[73] The implication was that food shortages in the local
areas were tending to dampen "revolutionary enthusiasm."

By 1970, when the Fifth Congress of the Workers' Party was
held, 70 percent of the inhabitants of North Korea were under
thirty, and remembered nothing of the pre-1945 period, having
been brought up and educated under the new North Korean
political system.[74] In summing up the "Achievements in Cultural
Revolution," Kim's comments on the success and shortcomings
of the cultural revolution seemed somewhat contradictory. On the
one hand, he appeared to proclaim that the tasks of the cultural
revolution had been fulfilled: "With the successful fulfillment of
the tasks of the cultural revolution, our country has now turned
into a land of education where all the people, young and old, are
learning, into a land where science and socialist literature and art
are developing and efflorescing in an all-round way . . . The cultural
backwardness left over from the old society has been overcome
and the centuries-old desire of our people to lead a cultured and
happy life is coming true splendidly in the era of the Workers'
Party."[75] Kim pointed out that by 1970, North Korea had 497,000
trained engineers, assistant engineers, and specialists, and there were
129 universities and colleges, as compared with 78 in 1960. Also
by 1970, North Korea had 1,900,000 students in primary school,
1,300,000 students in compulsory middle-level technical schools
(up to age 16), 140,000 students in higher technical schools, and
160,000 students in colleges and universities.[76]

On the other hand, Kim Il Sung pointed out that some tasks
required considerable additional effort. Kim explained that the
task of primary importance in the cultural revolution was the
carrying out of public education and the training of national cadres.
The next task was the building up of the ranks of the working

class and the "revolutionizing and proletarianizing" of their outlook. The third task was the proletarianization of the peasantry. The first task had been fulfilled successfully, educating large numbers of the members of the younger generation "into able builders of socialism and communism," and training "large numbers of technicians and specialists." The second task, revolutionizing the working class, had also been carried out "credibly."[77] The proletarianizing of the peasant class, however, was another matter:

> In the rural areas of our country, erstwhile hired farm-hands are small in number and our peasantry consist chiefly of former poor and middle peasants. Accordingly, small proprietors' inclinations, egoism and other obsolete ideas are rooted deeply in their minds. The peasantry not only lag behind the working class technically and culturally, but are far behind ideologically. The socialist revolution has fundamentally altered the socio- economic position of the peasants and brought about a great change in their ideological consciousness, too, but the lag of the peasantry behind the advanced working class in ideology still remains one of the major conditions that engender the class distinctions between the working class and the peasantry class even after the establishment of the socialist system.[78]

In the process of carrying out the cultural revolution, a new generational base of leadership was rising through the party ranks, led by Kim Yong Ju, Kim Il Sung's younger brother, who was ten years his junior. Between the Fourth Party Congress in 1961 and the Fifth Party Congress in 1970, considerable change had taken place in the party leadership. Of the 85 regular members and 50 alternate members of the central committee in 1961, only 31 remained members of the new central committee. Of 117 full members of the new central committee, 71 were new to the top levels of leadership; of the 55 alternate members, 48 were new. Twenty regular and alternate members of the political committee had been removed.[79] Of the eleven members of the new political committee, five were carried over from the 1966 committee: Kim Il Sung, Ch'oë Yŏng-kŏn, Kim Il, Pak Sŏng-ch'ŏl, and Ch'oë

Hyŏn, while six new names had been added: Kim Yong Ju, O Chin-u
(promoted from alternate member to full member), Kim Tong-kyu
(promoted from alternate member to full member in 1968), Sŏ
Ch'ŏl, Kim Chung-nin (appointed alternate member in 1968,
promoted to full member, 1970), and Han Ik-su (appointed alternate
member in 1968,promoted to full member in 1970).[80] Of the four
alternate members of the political committee, one, Hyŏn Mu-kwang,
remained from the 1966 conference, and three were new: Chŏng
Chun-t'aek (appointed in 1968), Yang Hyŏng-sŏp, and Kim Man-kum.
Of the ten members of the new party secretariat, only the top three,
Kim Il Sung, Ch'oë Yŏng-kŏn, and Kim Il, remained of the group
appointed in 1966. The new members included: Kim Yong Ju,
O Chin-u, Kim Tong-kyu, Kim Chung-nin, Han Ik-su, Hyŏn Mu-
kwang, Yang Hyŏng-sŏp. As if to emphasize the turning over of the
generations, Kim Il Sung opened the Fifth Congress with a somber
recital of thirty-six names of "revolutionary comrades" who had
died since the Fourth Party Congress.[81]

Kim Yong Ju, 48 in 1970, emerged as the sixth ranking member
at the Fifth Congress; those ahead of him all were of the same age,
or older than Kim Il Sung. Two others, reputed to be his close friends,
were elevated along with him: Sŏ Ch'ŏl, aged 63, in charge of
ideological affairs, and Kim Tong-kyu, aged 55, in charge of international affairs.[82] These facts alone led to speculation that the
younger Kim was being groomed as his brother's successor.
Realistic political man that he was, however, Kim Il Sung could
not expect to promote his brother without seeing to it that Kim
Yong Ju built his own solid political base within the party. The
younger Kim was in a position to do just that, having been a member
of the party's organization bureau since 1954, section chief of the
organization department since 1957, and (secretariat-level) director
of the department of organization since 1966.[83] Before assuming
this role in the party, Kim Yong Ju had gone to the Soviet Union
in 1945 (when he was 23) to study in the department of political
economy of Moscow University, and in 1952 had gone through
training at the Higher Party School in Moscow.[84] By 1970, Kim
Yong Ju was being followed rapidly up the party ranks by others

educated abroad since independence. Of the 633 top ranking party members in 1968, 121, or about 20 percent, had been educated in the Soviet Union or Eastern Europe *since* 1945.[85] Other young members had been educated in the universities and party training centers at home. Steadily, under the organizational hand of Kim Yong Ju, the new breed had begun rising through the party ranks.

Emphasizing the need for continuing to raise new members through the ranks of the party, Kim Il Sung pointed out at the Fifth Congress:

> While giving Party members revolutionary education, we should steadily expand the ranks of the Party and continue to improve its qualitative make-up. In our country today, the new generation who have received a great deal of socialist education since the liberation are emerging as reliable masters of the country and playing an important role in all realms of the revolution and construction. The Party organizations should actively admit fine people from among the working-class youths. In this way, the qualitative composition of the Party ranks should be further improved and the ranks of its nuclei steadily expanded and our Party developed into a Party which is always vibrant with a revolutionary spirit.[86]

As if to ensure a smooth succession, several other members of the Kim family moved into important political posts in the party and government between 1966 and 1970. Kim Il Sung's wife, Kim Song-ae, emerged as a member of the central committee and head of the Democratic Women's Union; Ch'oë Hyŏn, the minister of defense and the fifth ranking member of the political committee was related to Kim Il Sung by marriage; Hŏ Tam, the minister of foreign affairs, was reported to be the husband of Kim's cousin; Hong Myŏng-hui, the vice president of the presidium of the Supreme People's Assembly, was Kim Il Sung's father-in-law; and Kang Yang-uk, another vice president of the presidium of the Supreme People's Assembly, was a relative of Kim Il Sung's father.[87]

The rise of Kim's family in political circles did more than simply guarantee the security of the power structure for the transition.

Kim Il Sung began to use his family for another purpose: to prove his personal legitimacy. Like Rhee in the South, Kim chose to draw on traditional legitimacy sources, by tracing his origin through a "legitimate" genealogy. Unlike Rhee, however, whose genealogy traced back to the Yi dynasty founder, Kim's genealogy showed him to be the "legitimate successor of revolutionary family lineage."[88] Explaining Kim's revolutionary family origins, one official North Korean publication reported:

> The family of Comrade Kim Il Sung is a patriotic and revolutionary family that have fought from generation to generation for the independence of the country and the freedom and liberation of the people against foreign aggressors.
>
> His great-grandfather Mr. Kim Ung U was a patriot who led the battle for sinking the pirate ship "General Sherman" dispatched by the U.S. aggressors as a feeler for their aggression of our country in 1866.
>
> His grandfather Mr. Kim Bo Hyon and his grandmother Mrs. Li Bo Ik, too, were patriots who, backing the revolutionary struggle of their sons and grandsons, remained profoundly true to their national principles without yielding to the harsh repression and persecution by the Japanese imperialists and fought tenaciously against the aggressors.
>
> His father Mr. Kim Hyong Jik was a pioneer and outstanding leader of the national-liberation movement in our country. He had a strong patriotic anti-Japanese spirit and extraordinary talents and noble qualities . . .
>
> Mrs. Kang Ban Sok, mother of Comrade Kim Il Sung, was also endowed with remarkable talents, a kind heart and strong character, and she was an anti-Japanese revolutionary fighter who fought unyieldingly against the foes. . . .
>
> Mr. Kim Hyong Gwon, uncle of Comrade Kim Il Sung, too, was an ardent revolutionary fighter and staunch Communist who joined in the revolutionary struggle in his early years for the restoration of the fatherland. . . .
>
> The two younger brothers of Comrade Kim Il Sung were also Communists who took part in the anti-Japanese struggle in their early years and fought stoutly.
>
> His younger brother Comrade Kim Chol Ju was an inde-

fatigable revolutionary fighter who . . . died a heroic death in
1935 fighting in arms against Japanese imperialism.

His cousin Comrade Kim Won Ju, too. . . .

Mr. Kang Don Uk, grandfather of Comrade Kim Il Sung
on the mother's side, and Mr. Kang Jin Sok, his uncle on
the mother's side, were also anti-Japanese fighters who fought
fiercely for the restoration of the fatherland.[89]

Clearly, if Kim Il Sung was the "legitimate successor" of such an
impressive family lineage, his brother was as well. The legitimacy of
the succession was clear. But who would succeed Kim's brother?
Kim is reported to have two sons by his first wife (who died in
1949), although they have as yet not been mentioned in official
publications.[90] It should be emphasized, of course, that Kim Il
Sung himself was far from ready to leave the scene. Only thirty-
three when he came to power in 1945, he was not to celebrate his
60th birthday until 1972. Even then, he was still ten years younger
than Syngman Rhee had been when he returned to Korea in 1945.
Although attacking the "outmoded ideas" and "remnants" of
Confucian society, including "familyism," Kim Il Sung nonetheless
turned to the traditional notions of Confucian genealogy to reinforce
his claim to legitimacy as a leader.

Aside from the revolutionary family genealogy, the party historians
began to build up and exaggerate the story of Kim Il Sung's early
participation in the anti-Japanese guerrilla movement in Manchuria.
Although Kim was actually a member of the Chinese Communist
forces there, he was always depicted as a leader of the "Korean"
anti-Japanese forces, as a great revolutionary "General" (he was in
fact only 29 in 1941 when he and his unit retreated, defeated, into
the Soviet Union, where they entered a training school and ceased
fighting the Japanese).[91] The partially fabricated story of Kim's
revolutionary experience, which now depicts him as having single-
handedly defeated the Japanese in World War II (the story not only
does not refer to his association with the Chinese and Russians, but
does not mention the American involvement in the defeat of Japan),
has become required reading throughout North Korea's schools,
party training schools, and special "leader study centers" which

have been established in industries and communes. Between the
Fourth and Fifth Congresses, 39 million copies of the *Selected
Works of Kim Il Sung* were published (although there were only
14 million people in North Korea, of whom 6.6 million were under
age 14); and 8.8 million copies of the *History of the Revolutionary
Activities of Comrade Kim Il Sung* were also published along with
45.5 million copies of other "revolutionary guidance" books.
The total expenditure for publications in 1969 was twice that
of 1960.[92] Party members were required to spend a minimum of
two hours per day reading the life and works of Kim Il Sung. In
1967 a special re-training institute for party members was established,
and in the year 1969 alone, more than 500,000 party members
returned to school for a one-month re-education in the ideas of
Kim Il Sung.[93]

The cult of Kim had reached such an extreme by 1970, that
any mention of him in print had to be followed by a standardized
list of adjectives, repeated with each repetition of his name. Thus,
the following passage appeared in the party newspaper in bold-
face type describing the re-election of Kim Il Sung as general
secretary of the party at the Fifth Congress:

> When it was announced that Comrade Kim Il Sung, the
> founder of our Party, peerless patriot, national hero, ever-
> victorious, iron-willed brilliant commander, one of the
> outstanding leaders of the international communist movement
> and working-class movement and the great Leader of our Party
> and the 40 million Korean people, had been elected General
> Secretary of the Central Committee of the Party, the entire
> delegates to the Congress and the observers all rose and
> loudly shouted 'Long live Comrade Kim Il Sung, the great
> Leader!' with overwhelming joy and emotion.[94]

Exactly the same adulatory words, in the same order, appeared
after each mention of the leader's name. A Nigerian official visitor
to North Korea observed upon his return home in 1969, "I saw
'God' in North Korea," illustrating the ludicrous extremes of the
Kim Il Sung personality cult.[95]

The personality cult, his "revolutionary genealogy," and his supposed past feats of patriotic heroism are not all that Kim Il Sung relies on to promote his claim to legitimacy, however. Even more important is his proposition that he can unify Korea, drawing on the vibrant sense of nationalism among the Korean people to support his leadership. Indeed, as time passes, it becomes increasingly difficult to separate the cultural revolution, the cult of Kim, and the issue of national unification in North Korean policies. The cultural revolution of the Korean people cannot be carried out so long as two-thirds of the people remain outside of Kim's system of control. As long as the Southern government continues to offer an alternative magnet of loyalty and provides an alternative theory of rule which may be attractive to some North Koreans, especially because of their desire for national unification, the cultural revolution in the north cannot succeed, and the claim to legitimacy of the northern leadership cannot be permanently established. If Kim is the legitimate leader of Korea, why does he rule fewer than one third of the Korean people? Unification is necessary to establish the legitimacy of the North Korean political system.

Kim Il Sung has long claimed that unification can come only through a "revolution" in the South. Said Kim Il Sung reporting to the Fifth Congress in November 1970 on the "South Korean Revolution and Unification of the Fatherland,"

> Comrades,
> The South Korean revolution is a component part of the whole Korean revolution. For the achievement of the nation-wide victory of the Korean revolution, it is essential to forcefully push ahead with socialist construction in the northern half of the Republic and, at the same time, further advance the revolutionary struggle in South Korea.
> The basic task of the revolution is to drive the U.S. imperialist forces of aggression out of South Korea and eliminate their colonial domination and to overthrow the military fascist dictatorship and establish a progressive social system . . .
> To unify the divided fatherland is the greatest national task

for the entire Korean people at the present stage and the most pressing task the solution of which brooks not a moment's delay.[96]

As North Korean political and military mobilization increased following the October 1966 party conference, so did North Korean infiltration into the South, in an effort to set up a revolutionary organization on the pattern of the NLF in South Vietnam. While infiltration incidents were estimated at 50 in 1966, the number rose to 543 in 1967 and 1,247 in 1968.[97] A small group of agents trained by North Korea did succeed in setting up a secret organization in South Korea named the "Revolutionary Party for Reunification," but they were soon arrested and executed.[98] As late as October 1971, South Korea announced the arrest of three more groups totaling ten individuals who had been assigned by North Korea to reconstruct the Revolutionary Party for Reunification (RPR).[99] In 1968 one infiltrator, the only surviving member of a suicide team sent to assassinate President Park, explained that the 124th Unit of the (North) Korean People's Army had been reorganized into a 2,400 all-officer unit, divided into eight divisions, each assigned to one province in the South.[100]

In November 1968 a group of 120 North Koreans landed by sea on the eastern coast of South Korea, and dispersed into the South. It took 40,000 South Korean soldiers several months to locate and capture or kill them all.[101] After 1968, such infiltration efforts declined markedly (perhaps as a result of the January 1969 purge of the military leadership and the concurrent change of tactics), but the emphasis on the necessity of "revolution" in the South was not changed. From Kim Il Sung's ideological standpoint, only a successful extension of the Communist system to the South could guarantee the successful establishment of his ideal system in the North. Although Kim continued to call for "peaceful unification," he noted that "It is a historic lesson of the anti-Japanese national liberation struggle in our country that . . . the most decisive and highest form of struggle for freedom . . . is revolutionary violence."[10] Unification must be achieved, he noted, "in our generation."[103]

Efforts to maintain the existing political consolidation continued through the period of 1966 to 1970. In 1965, a resident registration program had been initiated, and this was stepped up in 1966 and completed in 1967. All residents were provided with dog-tag-like chains bearing pockets containing up to fourteen different identification cards for the collectives and professional and "social" organizations, as well as their residency-registration certificates.[104] The party was putting forth all efforts to establish organizational as well as ideological control over the populace. By 1970, there were 3,288,000 employees in the industrial labor force, of whom 2,200,000 were members of the General Federation of Trade Unions. The party was said to have a membership of 1,700,000, and its affiliated Socialist Working Youth League (ages 14-30) a membership of 2,700,000, while the Young Pioneers (ages 9-13) totalled 2,300,000.[105]

Elections to the Supreme People's Assembly and to local governments were both held in November of 1967. Elections followed the familiar pattern of a government-sponsored slate, with no option to vote either for other candidates, or, since 1962, against the slate. In both elections the government announced a 100 percent approval of the slates. Membership in the Supreme People's Assembly was increased to 457 (the Third Assembly, elected in 1962, had a membership of 383). Of these, 442 represented the Korean Workers' Party, four the Ch'ŏndokyo Young Friends Party, while the "representation" of the Chosŏn Democratic Party—the party of Christian-nationalists in 1945, which had long since been an organization in name only—had declined to only one member. One member each was elected from the Working People's Party, the Democratic Independence Party, and the Buddhist Alliance. A significant addition were seven representatives of the Chae Ilbon Chosŏnin yŏnmaeng ("Choryŏn"), the General Association of Korean Residents in Japan.[106]

As North Korea pushed its "chu-ch'e" theme and its cultural revolution, it minimized contacts with China and the U.S.S.R., especially the former, to reduce any dysfunctional impact from its external relations. Relations with China reached a low point following Chinese Red Guard criticisms of Kim Il Sung. In 1967, North Korean embassy officials abroad retorted to what they called Chinese "slanders" saying that the Chinese would be held responsible for "all possible consequences" resulting from the attacks.[107] Remarked one official stationed in Cuba, "It seems that some who like to defame the living conditions in our country and close their eyes to reality do not live better than we do,"[108] as if to remind the Chinese that North Korea had been more successful than China in its economic achievements, especially in industrialization. When the Chinese journal *Wen-ko T'ung-hsun* said in its issue of February 15, 1968, that Kim Il Sung was "an out-and-out counterrevolutionary revisionist of the Korean revisionist clique as well as a millionaire, an aristocrat, and a leading bourgeois element in Korea," North Koreans did not respond. China and North Korea moved close to an open split, as North Korea refused to cut off relations with the U.S.S.R. despite the Chinese admonition that "All *true* revolutionaries must draw a clear line of demarcation between themselves and the modern revisionists."[109] Unlike the Russians, however, the Chinese were not offering economic assistance, badly needed by the North Koreans to complete the extended Seven Year Plan in 1970.

Relations with the U.S.S.R., on the other hand, continued to be more than simply "correct," but by no means overly cordial. From 1967 through 1968, the U.S.S.R. was said to have supplied North Korea with 250 of its 500 military airplanes, and between 1965 and 1968 with eight of its ten missile bases.[110] By 1971, the North-South air power ratio was 2:1, North Korea having 800 airplanes of which 500 were MIG fighter-bombers, and South Korea having a total of only 350 aircraft.[111] Also by 1971, North Korea had 30 missile bases.[112] For a time, the relationship with the U.S.S.R. was clearly more useful in terms of the needed input of external tools than was the relationship with the P.R.C.

By 1969, however, a reversal in the trend was evident, when China warmly endorsed North Korea's shooting down of the American EC-121, while the Soviet Union came to the aid of the United States in an effort to search for survivors, evidently determined to show that the U.S.S.R. had no hand in the attack on the American aircraft over international waters.[113] A few weeks later, the chairman of the presidium of the U.S.S.R. Supreme Soviet, Nikolai V. Podgorny arrived in Pyongyang, accompanied by V. V. Kuznetsov, first deputy minister of foreign affairs, as well as the chairman of the maritime committee, and the vice chairman of the state committee on economic relations. The nature of the discussions was not revealed, although Podgorny emphasized in his public speech that "We resolutely advocate reduction of tension in the Far East and peace and security in that area."[114] In June, the North Korean minister of foreign trade, in an article in *Minju Choson* remarked that the "developed socialist countries . . . should give more material assistance with no political strings attached or no selfish motives to the economically backward countries which oppose imperialism."[115] North Korea did not attend a summit meeting of Communist parties in Moscow in June.[116]

As Soviet Military and economic aid drew toward a close, relations between China and North Korea perceptibly warmed while those with the U.S.S.R. cooled commensurately. Chinese Premier Chou En-lai made a state visit to North Korea in April 1970, and by autumn it was clear which ally was being given precedence. China's congratulatory message to the Fifth Congress was the first to be announced at the meeting, followed by that of the Viet Cong and Laotian parties, on the first day of the meeting. The greetings of the U.S.S.R. were the fourteenth to be read, preceded on the third day by greetings from the Communist parties of Mongolia, Burma, Thailand, and Yemen.[117] After Soviet aid came to an end in 1971, China agreed to grant free military assistance to North Korea, albeit in an unspecified amount.[118]

In February 1971, apparently fearing the possibility of an influx of "liberal" ideas from Eastern Europe undermining its cultural revolution, and angry with the Soviet Union for abandoning the "world revolution," North Korea lashed out in a lengthy editorial statement published in every North Korean newspaper, making a bitter attack upon "revisionism." The article, entitled "Let Us Uphold the Dictatorship of the Proletariat and Proletarian Democracy," decried in anguished tones the trend of "liberalization" in other Communist countries.

Today, the revisionists, the betrayers of the revolution,
dead set against the dictatorship of the proletariat, are trying
by hook or by crook to befog the class line between proletarian
democracy and bourgeois democracy and revive bourgeois
democracy under the slogan of what they call 'liberalization'
and 'democratic development' . . . The reactionary ideological
and cultural infiltration of the U.S. imperialists and the
injurious role of revisionism have done harm to some countries
today. In these countries, bourgeois ideologies and culture
and the bourgeois way of life intruding from outside are
spreading and, under their influence, all brands of bourgeois
elements are reviving and such antiquated ideas as individualism
and selfishness are further fostered. . . .

'Revisionist democracy' is no more than bourgeois democracy
smuggled into socialist society . . . Proletarian democracy is
democracy every inch for the working class and other working
people. Under socialism one is allowed to speak and act only
within the framework of the interests of the revolutionary
class and of the revolution. If the class character of proletarian
democracy is denied and everyone is given freedom to speak
and act as he pleases under socialism, this would mean granting
the counter-revolutionaries and the anti-socialists 'freedom' to
maneuver unhindered and bring bourgeois democracy into
socialist society.[119]

Despite its anti-revisionist tirade and the termination of Soviet aid,
however, North Korea did not make any attempt to break off ties
with the U.S.S.R., remaining "correct" in all its relations. The
Soviet-Korean defense treaty was permitted to be automatically
renewed in 1971 for another five-year period.

While continuing to experience difficulties in dealing with
external inputs from the U.S.S.R., China, and other Communist
countries, North Korea began to mobilize some of its political
tools in an effort to exert some influence external to its borders.
Having consolidated its system internally, it could turn some of
its attention outward. Aside from its efforts toward South Korea,
which were singularly ineffective, North Korea began seeking other
channels for external influence. Since North Korea did not belong

to any organization in the U.N.-sponsored international system, it echoed the view of Sukarno of Indonesia that the U.N. organization was simply a means for the "Old Established Forces" to seek to dominate the "New Emerging Forces." (Indeed, Kim Il Sung and Sukarno had exchanged state visits, Kim's only venture into the non-Communist world.) The diplomatic—and more often undiplomatic—campaign of the North Koreans in the international arena had a three-fold purpose: to gain international endorsement to establish its claim to legitimacy with its own people, to find indirect methods of communication with and influence over the people of South Korea, and to promote the "world revolution." Its efforts to gain international recognition had some success: by 1971 North Korea was recognized by forty-eight countries, of whom it had exchanged ambassadors with thirty-five, consuls general with five, and official representatives with eight.[120]

North Korea's most important means of indirect communication with South Koreans was through its influence over Koreans in Japan, through the North Korean-financed General Association of Koreans in Japan (Chōsen Soren), with a membership of 350,000 of the 600,000 Korean residents in Japan. Between 1957 and 1967, North Korea had sent ¥6,318,401,793 to finance scholarships for Koreans in Japan and other expenses of the association. These efforts paid off in the repatriation to North Korea of 88,000 Koreans from Japan over a period of years, a propaganda victory for the Northern regime.[121] Koreans in Japan, suffering considerable discrimination and generally of low socio-economic status, were a fertile target for North Korean propaganda.[122] Other expatriots were less ready targets. As one analyst of the propaganda materials received by Koreans in Canada noted, more than 70 percent of the 5,000 Koreans in Canada were university graduates, with almost one-fourth of the heads of families holders of Ph.D. or M.D. degrees.[123] They were unlikely to be interested either in stories of "workers and peasants" or in the cult of Kim Il Sung.[124] The same was generally true of the approximately 250,000 Koreans in the United States. Some Korean students in Europe, however, many of them unable to find employment to provide for their living expenses while studying, were receptive to North Korean offers of financial assistance to complete their studies. A number of such students were arrested by South Korean intelligence agents in Europe in 1967, and taken home to stand trial for dealing with the enemy.[125]

North Korea's efforts to promote "world revolution" were the least effective of its international endeavors. It was reported that an international guerrilla warfare training center was established in North Korea in 1966, for the training of about 2,000 young people from more than 25 countries of Asia, Africa, and Latin America. Mexico arrested 19 members of a 50-member group in March 1971, whom the Mexican government said had been trained in North Korea.[126] The North Korean mission in India was accused of intervening in Indian domestic politics.[127] The North Korean mission in Ceylon was reportedly involved with the insurgents who attempted to overthrow Ceylon's government, and the D.P.R.K. ambassador and his staff were expelled from Ceylon on April 16, 1971.[128] North Korea's more successful endeavors were in support of existing governments: it sent a considerable amount of assistance to North Vietnam, and reportedly sent arms and ammunition to Pakistan during the Pakistan-India conflict.[129] North Korea clearly had not given up hope for a "world revolution."

By 1961, at the beginning of the period under review, the system in North Korea had already been consolidated, with all instruments of politics concentrated in the hands of those who were committed to support of the system. Whatever dissension may have arisen within the system in the period to follow, was not in the form of a challenge to the basic structure of the political system. During the 1960's, the task was no longer to consolidate the political system, but to use the already established bases to mobilize and re-educate the society at large in an acceptance of the new system; to gain their positive participation within the new institutions so that the insitutional framework, combined with the new ideological education, would bring about an alteration of their political behavior eliminating traditional behavior patterns which were considered dysfunctional for the development of a modern political system.

Although the consolidation over internal political tools had been completed, the North Korean system was not as yet in a position where it could completely isolate itself from reliance on external inputs. As late as 1970, North Korea was explaining that it had yet to obtain sufficient self-reliance in its economy. The Six Year Plan, introduced at the Fifth Congress, aimed at the achievement of an economy which would be 60-70 percent self-sufficient by 1976. By "self-sufficient," North Korea meant that it would not have to rely on inputs of aid or loans, and that it could exist even if trade should be cut off. (By 1968, 15 percent of North Korea's trade was with the West, and the portion was rapidly increasing.)[130] That North Korea was still militarily dependent on its neighbors was evidenced by the fact that its defense treaty with the U.S.S.R. was permitted to be renewed automatically (the defense treaty with China was for an unlimited period, though it had provisions for abrogation), and by the fact that North Korea felt compelled to seek Chinese military aid in 1971. It was through its internal organization that the system had become most independent of external factors. Divided loyalties were no longer present in the party. Ideologically, the government had taken great pains to isolate its citizenry from foreign influences: students were brought home from abroad for "re-education" and foreign publications and source materials were not allowed into the country. When the U.S.S.R. had discontinued technical assistance, the North Koreans had even advocated developing an "independent technology."

The greatest problem in achieving success in resocialization had been the dysfunctional influence of external factors. External inputs were needed to supplement weak internal tools, yet they often counteracted the goals of the leadership. The Soviet Union was already a fully institutionalized system, and no longer perceived the need to consolidate the bases of the system, much less to carry out a "cultural revolution." Since the U.S.S.R. had long been looked upon as the "motherland of socialism," its arguments had considerable appeal. Furthermore, the "rational" basis of the arguments was attractive to those advocating the creation of a "scientific" society. To avoid the attraction of dysfunctional Soviet ideas, the North Korean society had to be sealed off from Soviet influence. Films, books, and other materials from the U.S.S.R. were banned in North Korea. Yet the North Korean regime could find little "rational" basis for a counterargument, and fell back on insisting on "*chu-ch'e*" because it was the idea of Kim Il Sung and hence a necessary truth.

Matters were complicated even further when China began using the concept of "cultural revolution" to further her consolidation of power. North Korea had already consolidated its political bases—in part because Chinese support had assisted in resisting Soviet efforts to reverse the consolidation process in the name of "de-Stalinization." Now that its base was consolidated, North Korea had less to fear from the dysfunctional effects of external economic inputs from the U.S.S.R. than it had to fear from the ideological inputs from the two systems. North Korea eagerly accepted the renewal of economic assistance from the U.S.S.R. after the fall of Khrushchev, so long as the U.S.S.R. did not insist on "integrated planning." From the Chinese perspective, the North Korean willingness to return to normal economic relations with the U.S.S.R. was viewed as a "revisionist" tendency. The Red Guards, participants in the Chinese "cultural revolution" rather than its formulators, took the ideological content of the movement seriously. Attacking their own party functionaries in the name of "anti-bureaucratism," they could not understand the failure of the North Koreans to follow suit, and hence charged the North Korean government with being "revisionist." The North Koreans in turn, having consolidated effective organizational control over their own society, were unable to comprehend the inability of the Chinese government to control some of the activities of the Red Guards, and held the government itself accountable for their actions. When the upheaval of the Chinese "cultural revolution" came to an end, with the Chinese system more effectively consolidated, the divergence in perspective declined, and the two governments were able to restore amicable relations.

The external origin of the Communist ideology had become an increasingly serious problem. In both China and North Korea, as it became necessary to justify interpretations which were highly divergent from those of the Soviet Union, "personality cults" emerged, centering around Mao Tse-tung and Kim Il Sung. In each society, if the words of the leader were in themselves infallible, they could not be questioned. North Korean Workers' Party Secretariat member and alternate member of the political committee, Yang Hyŏng-sŏp, newly elevated from the Hwanghae Namdo provincial committee, explained the North Korean leadership theory at the Fifth Congress:

> An outstanding leader is the sole center of unity and cohesion which rallies the Party, class and masses as one . . . Neither the guiding role of the Party nor the class leadership of the working class over the popular masses in the revolutionary struggle can be realized apart from the leadership of the leader.
>
> As shown by the whole historic course of the communist movement and working class movement, the opportunists of all complexions concentrated the spearhead of all their attacks on slandering the authority and prestige of the leader, the brain of revolution, and weakening his influence . . . Hence, attitude toward the leader is the most important criterion in distinguishing a genuine revolutionary from an opportunist. [131]

By 1971, the North Korean government, party, and other organs had become considerably regularized, with a new generation committed to the system rising through the ranks of these organizations, now regular channels for upward mobility through the system. The system had become "normalized."

The system had not, however, been fully legitimized. "Hostile elements" remained in the countryside, noted Kim Il Sung, hoping for a restoration of the old system. The greatest threat to establishing a permanent claim to legitimacy remained the stubborn refusal of those in the South to submit to the leadership of Kim Il Sung. Only through unification under Kim's leadership could legitimacy for his system be achieved. Increasingly, the goals of the system were centering upon the necessity for national unification.

Chapter IX

SUMMARY AND CONCLUSIONS

During the almost three decades since Korea was divided into two competing sectors in 1945, two political systems have been developing in a society still considered, by all participants, to be a single nation. The process of establishing a new political system involves a consolidation by a leadership group over the bases of power in the society, followed by the reshaping of behavior patterns in the society to conform to the new institutions and the acceptance of these new patterns of political institutions and behavior as legitimate. Clearly, by these criteria, the North Korean political system has achieved a greater degree of consolidation and has become more firmly established than the series of systems which various leadership groups have attempted to establish in the South.

The fact that the Northern system was more effective in achieving these goals does not imply that the Northern method was superior, for this consolidation was influenced by many factors which were beyond the control of the various leadership groups. Nor is this interpretation intended to imply that a democratic system could not be established in Korean society. The writer feels that despite developments to date, a combination of favorable external factors with a leadership which possessed both strong legitimacy claims and an understanding of the necessity for consolidating democratic bases of support, could lead to the successful establishment of a democratic system. Unfortunately, such a possibility cannot be proved by the failures of the past, because this favorable combination of factors did not exist. Additionally, the fact that the North Korean leadership had more success in getting its system implanted in the society should not be taken as implying any superiority in the *form* of system established. It may be that a democratic system would be more difficult to establish, but more functional once established. The account and analysis on the preceding pages has dealt only with the relative success in establishing a new system, not with the relative merits of the alternative structures of political order once established. Since neither system was fully institutionalized at the time of writing, such a comparison could not be empirically made.

The division of the country itself created some of the factors which contributed to the greater success of the Northern system in its consolidation efforts, for the Northern regime did not have to deal with the most conservative groupings—the Japanese-trained administrative personnel and police, the greater portion of the landlord elite, or the numerous traditional-style power seekers who normally centered their activities in the capital city of Seoul. On the other hand, the fact that most of the population, as well as the traditional national capital, was in the South did present the North with a serious legitimacy problem.

More than the division, the three-year occupation of the two sectors by the two superpowers who followed different policies of rule left the two systems in vastly divergent political circumstances. While the Soviet Union had worked effectively to assist the consolidation of the base of the political system supporting Kim Il Sung, the United States, during the American Military Government period, had worked to prevent the consolidation of political power by Syngman Rhee. Although he succeeded in clinging to leadership, Rhee's political bases were seriously eroded by 1948. Thus the two systems began, at independence in 1948, at essentially different stages of political consolidation.

The full support of the United States for the South Korean political system during the war reversed its spiral of disintegration. The failure of the U.S.S.R. to give all-out military support to the North ultimately resulted in the breakdown of Soviet controls, though this was possible in large part because of the continued military support of China for the Northern regime. Although the war permitted a reconsolidation of power by Syngman Rhee, his power base remained insufficient to resist external challenges in the late 1950's, leading to his ultimate fall in 1960. Kim Il Sung's power base, on the contrary, was strong enough by the mid-1950's to resist external challenges, and he used the conflict with the Soviet Union to boost the nationalist legitimacy of the regime.

While South Korea continued to wrestle with the task of consolidating political power during the 1960's, North Korea, its bases consolidated, was seeking to reshape the society into the mold of its new institutions, channel political change through the system, and prepare for a smooth transition when the time for political succession should arise.

A consolidation of power was not fully achieved in South Korea under any of the three republics. Even today, support of the system by the instruments of force is not certain should circumstances bring about a change of leadership, although Park clearly has effective control for the present. Resources of funds for political use remain highly irregular. Except for the bureaucracy and the army, organizations (including the Korean CIA) continue to exist as clusters of personal groups without institutional regularity—highly fluid, and subject to collapse with the disappearance or defection of individual leaders. Although the organizations at the top are extremely powerful, and under the firm control of the present leadership, they do not penetrate the society deeply and loyalty to the current leadership is not necessarily transferable to a successor. No coherent ideology binds the system together. Lacking consolidation, the system had not been institutionalized by the end of 1971, and even those who operated the irregular funding system admitted the illegitimacy of the methods they were required to employ, and resented the role they had to play in "corruption," since this conflicted with the values the system itself claimed to endorse. The fact that the values inculcated by the system through the educational institutions and the media had to be undermined to make the system work created much discomfort and disaffection from the system. Yet the cause of the political irregularities was not depravity of leadership or "degeneracy" of the national character. The fault lay, rather, in the inability of the leaders to consolidate and construct a viable developmental system. The incoherence of the system fostered the behavior patterns so much disliked by participants and observers alike. The forms of political behavior which had emerged from the Yi dynasty, and which all perceived as dysfunctional for a modern system, were perpetuated rather than altered by the continuing instability of the system.

The consolidation of the system in the North has presented a striking contrast. With consolidation effectively achieved, the leadership has undertaken a monumental effort to mobilize the populace through institutional means as well as through indoctrination and re-education. Since the retraining effort has been in full swing only since the early sixties, the leadership itself admits that much of the population has not yet been effectively resocialized. Thus, it would be premature to characterize the Northern system as institutionalized. Its claim to legitimacy remains shaky. Will an increasingly technocratic society accept a source of legitimacy based on the cult of personality—especially the cult of an individual considerably less educated than the system's emerging younger leaders? Yet clearly the system is fully consolidated and there exist no independent sources of political tools which can be mobilized to overturn the system. If change is to take place, it must take place within the framework of the system itself.

The study of both South and North Korea has illustrated many points common to the politics of development. External factors played a crucial role in both systems, both in supporting and opposing the political consolidation efforts of the leadership groups. In both cases, the actions of the external powers were shaped by those powers' own political mythologies, often having dysfunctional results in the subject system. When the U.S.S.R. used de-Stalinization as a tool to intervene in the North, it posed a threat to consolidation of the system and was successfully resisted by internal forces. When the United States intervened in the South in the name of democracy, it tended to undermine efforts to consolidate effective internal bases of support, perpetuating the dependence of the Southern system on external support at the same time that the United States frequently chided the Southern leadership for its continued dependence on U.S. aid and military assistance.

One factor common to both the Soviet and American leadership in dealing with the two Korean systems was the absolute confidence on the part of those controlling the external factors in their own superior capacity to interpret the needs of the subject system. When a clash occurred between the external and internal interpretations as to the needs of the system, the external powers invariably saw it as a reflection of the lack of knowledge or understanding— or of sincerity and integrity—on the part of the Korean leadership. This was perhaps inevitable since both sectors claimed to be patterning their political system after that of the sponsoring power. Naturally, the leaders of the sponsoring powers would consider themselves more expert in the workings of their own system—which the Koreans professed to be copying—than the Koreans themselves would be. Yet the Americans and post-Stalin Soviet leadership viewed politics from the perspective of established rather than developmental systems, and thus did not perceive, as did the indigenous leaders, the necessity to consolidate and institutionalize the new political order.

In both sectors, leaders faced the necessity of maintaining effective political control over the instruments of force, as was illustrated by attempted or successful military coups (the North apparently having narrowly averted a coup in 1958). Both leadership groups also found that the necessity for political funding required a financing of politics by the productive resources of the system— in both cases primarily the manufacturing sector. North Korea handled the problem in the most obvious manner: by state ownership which turned over the profits of production directly to the government and open government financing of political activity. South Korea, avoiding direct state financing which had been deemed contrary to a democratic system, ended up achieving the same results through an elaborate system of payoffs and kickbacks. The difficulty with the kickback system was that the necessity of secrecy prevented any regularized means of control, resulting in undesirable leakages which undermined the effectiveness of the system and led to considerable resentment by the populace at the ostentatious wealth of many high-level officials.

Both sectors set about building political organizations to penetrate the society. In the North, such organization was assisted by the sponsoring power in the initial stages of consolidation. By the time an establishment leadership came to power in the U.S.S.R. and sought to counteract the policies of its predecessor, the organizational base of the North Korean system was already strong enough to resist the challenge. In the South, large-scale political organization was viewed with suspicion by the sponsoring power, and the American Military Government worked to undermine both the Communist organizational base and the nationalist organizational system initially constructed by Rhee, and to substitute a "coalition" of leaders unsupported by any organizational structures. The later organizational efforts of Kim Jong Pil were also undermined when his new party had to reabsorb the leadership of prior eras in order to compete in elections, and became fractionated by the competition between the new and old leadership groups. The only organization given solid support by the United States was the Korean army, and U.S. pressure to reduce the size of that organization was a factor in the army coup. Like all developmental systems, both sectors of Korea felt the need to build strong political organization, and in both sectors such needs came into conflict with the ideological self-image of the established leadership of the sponsoring powers, as the regimes in the two sectors sought to shift from reliance on external to internal bases.

Ideology became an essential element in the structure of power. Both sectors chose to adopt one ready-made from the sponsoring power. Both learned belatedly that use of externally-provided idea systems would lead to conflicting interpretations over application of the ideology, and to clashes with the sponsoring power. North Korea sought to meet the challenge by adapting the ideology through the "thought of Kim Il Sung." South Koreans tended instead to condemn themselves for being "too backward" to conform to the foreign ideology, an attitude crushing to national pride.[1] The later decision to stick to "economic development" as the national ideology temporarily reversed this feeling, as South Korea proved itself successful in achieving its economic goals, leading to a temporary upsurge in national pride. Such an "ideology" ultimately proved

338

empty, however, as economic accomplishments ran into snags with
the reversal of previously favorable external supports to economic
growth, and the society once again appeared devoid of purpose and
goals.

Starting with the same political culture, leadership groups in
both sectors met with similar challenges from the traditional
behavioral patterns: factionalism, bureaucratism, family-centrism,
and so forth. North Korea sought to build a mobilization system
to resocialize the populace and alter the traditional behavior patterns
derived from the Yi dynasty system; South Korean leaders, while
condemning the dysfunctional behavior patterns, remained too
preoccupied with the consolidation phase of the system's development
to be able to work toward effective alteration of the patterns of
behavior. The very absence of consolidation, on the contrary,
fostered the continuation of these patterns. Although extrinsic
factors such as educational development and urbanization, for
example, worked to undermine the extended family system, the
insecurity of the society tended to perpetuate the continued reliance
upon the family as the only effective institution for maintaining
economic security, with each member being required to support
the unemployed members of the family or to assist them in gaining
employment. Without effective alternative channels through which
to achieve individual needs, the family and personal faction-groups
remained the only elements of the society which promised a sufficien
degree of permanence to permit the individual to rely upon them
for security.

Both initial leadership groups sought to tie their legitimacy to
the national political mythology. Rhee's strong links with both
traditional sources of legitimacy and the reform and independence
movements of the past, as well as the apparent succession from
the last monarch to the Korean Provisional Government which
Rhee headed, established at the time of the emperor's death,
provided strong ties of legitimacy and continuity for the First
Republic. In the North, Kim Il Sung's claim to legitimacy through
the guerrilla movement in Manchuria seemed pale by comparison.
The overthrow of Rhee, however, took the form of a repudiation

of the link with legitimacy which led backward through Rhee to the independence movement, the monarchy, and the reformist movements of the nineteenth century. The new leadership which ultimately emerged in the South had its pre-independence ties with the Japanese military in Manchuria and could claim no links with the traditional system or the independence movement.

The extrinsic factors, which are often used as measures of "development," advanced markedly under both systems, with both shifting from a society 80 percent rural to one 50 percent urban, from less than 20 percent literacy to more than 90 percent

South-North Comparative Economic Indicators, 1969-70

Indicator	Unit	South	North	Ratio
Population	Millions	31.14	14.05	1:0.45
GNP, 1969	Billions of U.S. dollars	6.07	2.95	1:0.48
GNP, 1970	Billions of U.S. dollars	6.99	3.14	1:0.45
Per capita income, 1969*	U.S. dollars	195	210	1:1.07
Per capita income, 1970*	U.S. dollars	223	217	1:0.97
Average annual rate of growth of GNP, 1967-1969**	Percentage increase	12.6	8.6	1:0.68
Total Industrial production, by value, 1969	Billions of U.S. dollars	1.22	1.95	1:1.59
Annual rate of industrial growth, 1969***	Percentage increase	24.1	12.7	1:0.52

* As calculated by South Korea. Other figures indicate North Korea still slightly ahead in per capita income.
** It should be noted that these were the peak growth years for South Korea, while North Korea was just coming out of an economic slump.
*** 1969 was South Korea's highest growth year during the period under study. (Statistics indicate this rate of growth was exceeded in 1973.)

literacy, and to rapidly industrializing economies. Economically, statistics for 1969-1970 showed the North still more advanced than the South, but with the South developing at a more rapid rate, implying that it would soon overtake the North. Thus, as can be seen in the preceding table, the average annual rate of GNP growth in South Korea during 1967-1969 was 12.6 percent, as compared with 8.6 percent for North Korea. South Korea's 1970 GNP of $6.99 billion was more than twice that of the North, which was $3.14 billion, but was approximately equal on a per capita basis—both the GNP and population of the North being 45 percent of the South's level. On the other hand, according to South Korean figures, the North still had industrial production valued at more than one and one-half times that of the South.[2]

The fact that North Korea succeeded in political consolidation during the period under study, whereas the South did not, does not imply that the consolidation methods of North Korea are superior to more open or democratic methods. The contrasting role of external factors—supporting consolidation in the initial stages in the North, opposing consolidation during that period in the South—appears to have been more important in the success of the North's efforts than were the contrasting methods of consolidation. Indeed, the heavy use of force in the North was largely necessitated by the lack of a strong claim to legitimacy on the part of the Northern leadership. In the South under the First Republic, where Rhee embodied multiple sources of legitimacy and initially acted as a magnet drawing in support, consolidation might have been successful with a minimum amount of force and a maximum amount of voluntarism if it could have been completed within the first few years, as it was in the North. What the comparison does show is that political consolidation by *some* method is a necessary precondition for further development.

On October 17, 1972, President Park Chung Hee declared martial law, dissolved the National Assembly, and suspended the constitution.[3] On November 21, a new constitution giving the president broad powers was approved in a national referendum, while the country was still under martial law.[4] The new constitution gave the president the power to appoint one-third of the National Assembly (it did not go so far as General Hodge of the American Military Government had done in appointing one-half of the Assembly), as well as virtual control over the courts (which had been, up to that date, developing a considerable degree of judicial independence). It also extended the presidential term to six years, and imposed no limitations on the number of terms which the president could serve. President Park was re-elected on December 23, 1972, through a new system of "indirect elections" involving a series of local councils.[5] Clearly, the election was under governmental control—and, increasingly, government meant the powerful Korean CIA organization. Park called the new system "Koreanized democracy." Unlike the period when he first came to power, the United States no longer had the power it had possessed within Korean society. When the military seized power in 1961, the United States provided more than one half of the Korean budget through economic aid, and 72.4 percent of the defense expenditures;[6] by 1971, economic aid had been discontinued and military aid made up only 10 percent of the defense expenditures.[7] Furthermore, American troops were already scheduled to be withdrawn, regardless of developments in Korea. Thus, the economic clout that the United States had possessed in 1963, by which it had forced Park Chung Hee to reverse his decision to extend military rule, no longer existed. Park could now attempt a new political consolidation without effective resistance from external sources.

Are Park's new consolidation efforts likely to succeed? At the time of writing, it is difficult to say. It should be pointed out that unlike the generally grudging welcome which the military coup-makers faced in 1961, when they moved in with a revolutionary élan to clean up the chaos and corruption of the preceding regime, the militant "reforms" introduced by the twelve-year-old Park government met with only wary submission. No organizations, sources of funding, or instruments of force were available to challenge the new efforts at consolidation, yet it was disapproved not only by opposition politicians but by those in Park's own party who had been jockeying for the succession. Although the North Korean regime had succeeded in imposing a consolidation on the North by heavy reliance on the instruments of force, it had done so with strong external assistance (both from the U.S.S.R. and from China), through a sweeping land reform which gave the regime a reserve of peasant support (then the majority of the population), and through reliance on a disciplined party elite and systematic well-inculcated ideology. Furthermore, Kim Il Sung had possessed at least a semblance of a claim to nationalist legitimacy, despite the propaganda fabrications. These elements were missing to assist a consolidation by coercion in the South.

North Korea also introduced a new constitution at the end of 1972, which was adopted by the Supreme People's Assembly on December 28.[8] Elections to the new Supreme People's Assembly were held on December 12,[9] and following the adoption of the new constitution Kim Il Sung was elected president of the DPRK, the new post for the head of state.[10] Unlike the new constitution in the South, which represented another effort to begin the consolidation process, the new North Korean constitution was designed to reflect the developments already achieved, and to merge the institutional and leadership legitimacy claims of the Northern regime. The former Soviet-style constitution was replaced with one which was said to have been "conceived and authored in person by the great Leader President Kim Il Sung."[11] Provisions of the new constitution included guidance by "*chu-ch'e*," the great "Chongsan-*li* spirit," and the "Ch'ŏllima Movement" and the carrying out of the cultural revolution. Article 38 provided that "The State eliminates the way of life inherited from the old society and introduces the new socialist way of life in all fields." New "rights" such as the right to work, the right to education, and the right to free medical care were embodied in the constitution. The new framework more closely embodied the actual values and institutions of the regime. This constitution was hailed by the Northern press as unique, and as the most advanced socialist constitution in existence, "embodying the Leader's *chu-ch'e*-based idea of state construction in a comprehensive way." [12]

The new Southern and Northern constitutions introduced at the close of 1972 had two features in common, though their provisions continued to be entirely different. First, both rejected the models of the sponsoring powers, the United States and the Soviet Union, choosing instead "Korean Democracy" in the South, and "Korean Socialism" in the North, creating political structures distinct from the models they had originally sought to emulate. Second, both deleted many of the provisions which had long been inoperative in their respective systems, shedding at least the hypocrisy of a constitution that the political leadership had no intention of following. Whether these provisions would act to insulate them from external influences remained to be seen.

In the modern world, the two governments may find it difficult indeed to maintain sufficient isolation to preserve systems heavily reliant on coercion. The North has found that it must even barricade itself against Soviet "liberalizing" influences, as the U.S.S.R. has begun, grudgingly, to yield to the human demands of its people. In the South, given the continuous interaction with the United States and Japan, both democratic systems, such isolation seems impossible even for a brief period of time. It would be more realistic for both to recognize these demands and needs of human nature which in the longrun will have to be embodied in a system in order for it to achieve permanent legitimacy in the modern world of international interaction. When both have come to recognize that they can never permanently isolate themselves from the attractive ideas of fundamental human rights and civil liberties prevailing in other political systems, they may find the barriers to cooperation lessened, and may turn their attention to the problem of national unification, as expressed in their historic agreement of July 4, 1972, to seek reunification through peaceful means.

NOTES

Abbreviations Used in the Notes

Pukhan ch'ongkam
Pukhan nyŏn'gam kanhaeng wiwŏn-hoë, *Pukhan ch'ongkam*

Pukkwe
Nae-oë munje yon'guso, *Pukkwe-ŭi p'apol t'u-jaeng-sa*

SCAP Summation
Supreme Commander for the Allied Powers, *Summation of Non-Military Activities in Japan and Korea, 1946-47*

SKIG, Activities
United States Armed Forces in Korea, *South Korean Interim Government Activities*

Song Chin-u Biography
Koha sŏnsaeng chonki p'yonch'an wiwŏnhoë p'yŏn, *Koha Song Chin-u sŏnsaeng-chŏn*

Third Congress Documents
Chosŏn nodong-dang chaesam-hoë taehoë munhŏn

Tōkei nempō
Chōsen Sōtakfu Tōkei nempō

UNCURK Report
United Nations, *Report of the United Nations Commission for the Unification and Rehabilitation of Korea*

USAMGIK, Summation
United States Army Military Government in Korea, *Summation of Activities*

Yŏ Un-hyŏng sŏnsaeng
Yi Man-gyu, *Yŏ Un-hyŏng sŏnsaeng t'ujaeng-sa*

Introduction

1. This framework of analysis is elaborated in much greater detail in the writer's [Joungwon A. Kim] article, "The Politics of Predevelopment,"

345

Comparative Politics 5.2: 211-235 (January 1973). The writer is indebted to Zbigniew Brzezinski, W. Howard Wriggins, and Dankwart A. Rustow for their valuable comments and assistance during the preparation of that article.

I. The Bases for Development in Korea, 1945

1. The date of the Japanese announcement of surrender was August 15, 1945, in Japan and Korea. Because of the time difference, it was August 14 in the United States.

2. The American Military Government recorded 887,836 Japanese departing from Korea between October 1, 1945 and December 31, 1948. The 1944 census of Japanese in Korea had shown a population of 708,448. United States Army Forces in Korea, *Republic of Korea, Economic Summation*, no. 36:4 (November-December, 1948); Results of 1944 census, Chōsen Government-General, May 1944, as cited in George M. McCune, *Korea Today* (Cambridge, Mass., 1950), p. 331.

3. Government-General of Chōsen, *Annual Report on the Administration of Chōsen*, 1944 (Seoul, 1944).

4. Koryŏ taehakkyo minjok munhwa yŏn'guso, *Han'guk munhwa-sa taekae*, vol. 2: *Chŏngch'i Kyŏngchae-sa* (Seoul, 1965), p. 167.

5. Lucian W. Pye, *The Spirit of Chinese Politics* (Cambridge, Mass., 1968), p. 18n.

6. Edwin O. Reischauer, and John K. Fairbank, *East Asia: The Great Tradition* (Boston, 1960), p. 117.

7. John K. Fairbank, Edwin O. Reischauer, and Albert M. Craig, *East Asia: The Modern Transformation* (Boston, 1965), pp. 462-463.

8. Gregory Henderson, *Korea: The Politics of the Vortex* (Cambridge, Mass., 1968), p. 63.

9. See an account of the rebellion in Benjamin B. Weems, *Reform, Rebellion, and the Heavenly Way* (Tucson, Ariz., 1964).

10. *Chingbo munhŏn piko*, vol. 161, pt. 1.

11.   Han Woo-keun, *The History of Korea*, Lee Kyung-shik, trans. and Grafton K. Mintz, ed. (Seoul, 1970), p. 344.

12.   See Syngman Rhee (Yi Sŭng-man), *Tongnip chŏngshin* (Seoul, 1904, first published San Francisco, 1908); Kim Il Sung (Kim Il-sŏng), *Kim Il-sŏng sŏnjip*, vols. 1-6 (Pyongyang, 1960-63); Park Chung Hee (Pak Chŏng-hui), *Our Nation's Path* (Seoul, 1962).

13.   *Third Congress Documents*, p. 104.

14.   Park Chung Hee, *Our Nation's Path*, p. 9.

15.   Syngman Rhee, *Tongnip chŏngshin*, p. 37.

16.   Kim Il Song, *Kim Il-sŏng sŏnjip*, IV, 244.

17.   Park Chung Hee, *Our Nation's Path*, 49.

18.   Kim Il Sung, *Kim Il-Sŏng sŏnjip*, IV, 244.

19.   Park Chung Hee, *Our Nation's Path*, pp. 16-17.

20.   Syngman Rhee, *Tongnip chŏngshin*, p. 35.

21.   Kim Il Sung, *The Selected Works of Kim Il Sung*, English ed. (Pyongyang, 1965), II, 516, Speech of April 14, 1965, at Aliarcham Academy of Social Sciences of Indonesia.

22.   Park Chung Hee, *Our Nation's Path*, pp. 71-76.

23.   Syngman Rhee, *Tongnip chŏngshin*, p. 37.

24.   Kim Il Sung, *Kim Il-sŏng sŏnjip*, IV, 238-253.

25.   Park Chung Hee, *Our Nation's Path*, pp. 212-214.

26.   James Willard Hurst, *Law and the Conditions of Freedom in the Nineteenth Century United States* (Madison, Wisconsin, 1956).

27.   Koreans made up 18 percent of the higher burearucracy and 32.2 percent of the middle bureaucracy in 1942. *Tōkei nempō*.

28. Henderson, p. 63; 36,000 Tonghaks were reported killed in one area
     in a two-month period. Hwang Hyŏn, *Maech'ŏn yarok*, no. 1:167
     (Seoul, 1955).

29. In 1908. Headquarter, Japanese Garrison Army in Korea, *Bōto
     tōbatsushi* (Seoul, 1913), Appendix, Table 2.

30. *Yŏ Un-hyŏng sŏnsaeng*, p. 170.

31. Robert A. Scalapino and Lee Chong-Sik, "The Origins of the Korean
     Communist Movement," *The Journal of Asian Studies*, 20.1:9-31
     (November 1960), 20.2:149-167 (February 1961).

32. Data for 1911, 1928, and 1939, from Office of the Overseas Minister,
     Takumu tōkei, 1939; for 1944 from *Annual Report on the Admin-
     istration of Chōsen 1944.*

33. *Tōkei nempō, 1942.*

34. *Tōkei nempō, 1910 and 1914.*

35. *Tōkei nempō, 1942.*

36. *Tōkei nempō, 1910 and 1943.*

37. Government-General of Chōsen, *Annual Report, 1934-35*, p. 213.

38. George M. McCune, "Korea's Postwar Political Problems" (Secretariat
     Paper No. 2, Institute of Pacific Relations, Tenth Conference, New
     York 1947), pp. 4-5.

39. *Survey of Korea*, comp. Military Intelligence Service, War Department
     General Staff (Washington, D.C., June 15, 1943), p. 177.

40. *Survey of Korea*, p. 262; *Tōkei nempō, 1938*, pp. 168-169.

41. *Tōkei nempō*, 1916 and 1942.

42. *Survey of Korea*, pp. 68-80.

43. Government-General of Chōsen, *Annual Report, 1912-1913*, and
     1934-1935.

44. Andrew J. Grajdanzev, *Modern Korea* (New York, 1944), p. 161;
     Charles N. Henning, "Korea: Looking Forward to an Altered Political
     and Economic Status," *Foreign Commerce Weekly* (January 1, 1944),
     p. 8.

45. For a history of the Ch'ŏndokyo, see Weems.

46. One useful history of the Korean Communist Party is Suh Dae-Sook,
     The Korean Communist Movement, 1918-1948 (Princeton, 1967).
     For the Korean Communist movement outside of Korea, see
     Scalapino and Lee.

47. Government-General of Tyosen, *Annual Report on Administration
     of Tyosen, 1937-38* (Keizyo [Seoul] , December, 1938), p. 106.

48. Suh Dae-Sook, *The Korean Communist Movement, 1918-1948*, p. 72.

49. J.O.P. Bland, *Li Hung-chang* (London, 1917), p. 160.

50. A copy of the American-Korean treaty of 1882, and of the 1905
     appeal, signed by both P.K. Yoon and Syngman Rhee, are printed in
     the appendix of F.A. McKenzie, *The Tragedy of Korea* (London,
     1908), pp. 279-281 and 311-312.

51. *The New York Times* (March 9, 1919).

52. United States Department of State, *The Conferences at Malta and
     Yalta* (Washington, D.C., 1960), pp. 336-339.

53. Kim Kyu-sik, "The Asiatic Revolutionary Movement and Imperialism,"
     Communist Review, 3.3:137-147 (July 1922).

54. Government-General of Chōsen, *Annual Report, 1912-13*, p. 18.

55. Government-General of Chōsen, *Annual Report, 1912-13*, p. 18,
     Annual Report, 1921-22, p. 16, *Annual Report, 1922-23*, pp. 15-16;
     Survey of Korea, pp. 58-59; *Korea Economic Mission*, United States
     Department of State, June 1947, as quoted in McCune, *Korea Today*,
     p. 328.

56. USAMGIK, *Summation* no. 36:4 (November-December, 1948).

57.   Scalapino and Lee.

58.   *Survey of Korea*, p. 59.

59.   Japanese Ministry of Internal Affairs, *Tokkō Geppō* (Tokyo, June 1945).

60.   Harry S. Truman, *Memoirs* (Garden City, New York, 1955), I, 316-317.

61.   "Habarosuku ya-ei gakkō no jōkyō," *Gaiji geppō* (November 1942), pp. 85-86; "Hokuman chiku kyōsan-hi kenkyō jiken," *Gaiji geppō* (November 1943), pp. 125-131; "Kin Nichi Sei no katsudō jōkyō *Tokkō gaiji geppō* (November 1944), pp. 76-78.

62.   Philip Rudolph, *North Korea's Political and Economic Structure* (New York, 1959), p. 26; Glenn D. Paige, *The Korean People's Democratic Republic* (Stanford, 1966), p. 57.

63.   *Survey of Korea*, p. 109, gives the figure as 500. See also Chang Chun-ha, "Kanŭng ch'ŏngsunŭn yangcha t'angnyuro," *Sassanggye* 8.12:252-267 (December 1960).

64.   United States Department of State, *The Conferences at Malta and Yalta*, pp. 336-339.

65.   Government-General of Chōsen, *Annual Report, 1921-22*, p. 261; *Dong-A nyŏn'gam*, p. 963.

66.   *Survey of Korea*, p. 57.

67.   *Dong-A nyŏn'gam*, p. 963, and *Pukkwe hyŏnhwang* (Seoul, March 1971), p. 211.

68.   Government-General of Chōsen, *Annual Report, 1942*.

69.   Census of 1944, as cited in McCune, *Korea Today*, p. 334.

70.   *Survey of Korea*, p. 82.

71.   George M. McCune, "Essential Unity of the Korean Economy," *Korean Economic Digest* (January, 1946), p. 7.

72. Ibid.

73. Ibid., pp. 3-8.

74. Yi Wŏn-sun, *Ingan Yi Sŭng-man* (Seoul, 1965), pp. 27-28; Yi Yu,
     "Korea's Political Dilemma." Unpublished manuscript (New York,
     1965), p. 102, Robert T. Oliver, *Syngman Rhee: The Man behind
     the Myth* (New York, 1954), p. 337.

75. Sŏ Chŏng-chu, *Yi Sŭng-man Paksa chŏn* (Seoul, 1949).

76. *The Independent* (March 11, 1898). This newspaper was published by
     the Independence Club in English and Korean. Its Korean title was *Tongnip
     shinmun*. This issue reports the demonstration and reprints a petition
     to the king signed by Syngman Rhee.

77. Shin Hung-u, "Ri shōban o kataru," *Shisō ihō* no. 16 (September 1938).
     This is a Japanese report of the interrogation of Shin Hung-u, who had
     been Syngman Rhee's cellmate in prison. The interrogation was under-
     taken in the late 1930's. See also Yi Wŏn-sun, p. 69.

78. Syngman Rhee, *Tongnip chŏngshin*.

79. Syngman Rhee, *Japan Inside Out* (London, 1942), p. viii. See also
     Oliver, p. 81.

80. Interview with Park Chan-il, former presidential secretary in Washing-
     ton, D.C., January 1967.

81. Yi Wŏn-sun, pp. 111-112; Oliver, pp. 84-90; F.A. McKenzie, pp. 311-
     312, reprints the petition addressed to President Roosevelt and signed
     by Syngman Rhee and P.K. Yoon.

82. Yi Wŏn-sun, pp. 130, 132, 140; Oliver, p. 100.

83. Lee Chong-Sik, *The Politics of Korean Nationalism* (Berkeley, Calif.,
     1963), p. 132.

84. Ibid., p. 130.

85. Taekunch'al-ch'ŏng susaguk, *Chwa-ik sagŏn sillok* (Seoul, 1964), I,
     35-38; Chŏn Kwan-u, *Dong-A nyŏn'gam, 1967* (Seoul, 1967), pp. 41-42.

86. Richard D. Robinson, "Korea—Betrayal of a Nation." Unpublished manuscript (1947), p. 121.

87. Oliver, p. 4.

88. United Korean Committee in America, *Korean Liberty Conference* (Washington, D.C., 1942), p. 74. Syngman Rhee said, "Dr. Line will now read the Declaration of Independence, the original of which was engraved on a block of wood from which thousands of copies were made and circulated throughout three hundred cities and towns of Korea. The original was brought to this country by Mr. McRae who happened to be in Seoul at that time. He brought it in, in the bottom of his shoe, and when he arrived in Honolulu published it to the world and returned the copy to me."

89. Sŏ Chŏng-chu; Yi Wŏn-sun; Warren Y. Kim, *Fifty-Year History of Koreans in America* (Reedley, Calif., 1959).

90. Interview with Kingsley K. Lyu, former Korean missionary in Hawaii for the Methodist church, later editor of *Pacific Weekly* (newspaper of the Tongjihoë organization), and subsequently Korean broadcaster, Office of War Information (OWI). In Washington, D.C., January 14, 1967.

91. According to Robinson, drawn from U.S. Army intelligence files while Robinson was preparing the official history of the American Military Government in Korea.

92. Some biographical information on Kim Il Sung can be found in *Gendai Chōsen jinmei jiten* comp. Asian Bureau, Ministry of Foreign Affairs (Tokyo, 1962); *Kibon chŏngbo;* Yi Puk, *Kim Il-sŏng wijo-sa* (Seoul, 1950), and in English, Suh Dae-Sook, *The Korean Communist Movement*; Lee Chong-Sik, "Kim Il-song of North Korea," *Asian Survey* (June 1967), pp. 374-382. Official North Korean sources which exaggerate and often fabricate, include Chosŏn nodong-dang chung'ang wiwŏn-hoë jiksok tan'yŏksa yŏn'guso, *Hangil ppalchisan ch'amkajadŭl-ŭi hoësang-ki* (Pyongyang, 1961), vols. 1-4; *Han'gil mujang t'ujaeng chŏnjŏkchi-rŭl ch'ajo-sŏ* (Pyongyang, 1960); Han Sŏl-ya, *Hero General Kim Il Sung* (Tokyo, 1962); Im Ch'un-ch'u, *Hangil mujang t'ujaeng shiki-rŭl hoësang hayŏ* (Pyongyang, 1960), and Baik Bong, *Kim Il Sung Biography* (Tokyo, 1969-70), vols. 1-3.

93. At least, he was using the name by 1935. See Archives of the Japanese Ministry of Foreign Affairs, microfilm, Library of Congress, reels S.P. 104-6, pp. 9390-9420.

94. Japanese Ministry of Foreign Affairs, *Gendai toa jinmei-kan* (Tokyo, 1950), p. 101.

95. Hatano Kenishi, ed., *Chūgoku kyōsanto 1937 nen shi* (Tokyo, 1938), pp. 815-824.

96. Inmul Han'guk-sa pyonchan-hoë, ed., *Inmul Han'guk-sa* (Seoul, 1965), pp. 290-293.

97. Ibid.

98. Spencer J. Palmer, ed., *Korean-American Relations* (Berkeley, 1963), vol. 2.

99. Kim Koo, *Paekbŏm ilji: Kim Ku chasŏjŏn* (Seoul, 1947), pp. 52-67.

100. Some background sources on Kim Koo include ibid., and Ku Cha-pung, "Kim Ku," in Yim Sun-buk, et al., *Chongkae yahwha* (Seoul, 1966), pp. 22-59; O Chae-sik, *Han'guk kŭnse wiinŏn* (Seoul, 1948), pp. 94-104; Om Hang-sŏp, *Kim Ku Sŏnsaeng hyŏltu-sa* (Seoul, 1946); and *Inmul Han'guk-sa*, V, 225-238.

101. Kim Koo, *Paekbŏm ilji*, p. 290.

102. Ibid.

103. Ibid., pp. 299-305.

104. *The New York Times* (April 29, 1932).

105. Kim Koo, *Paekbŏm ilji*, pp. 322-324.

106. Hyŏn Sang-yun, "Sam-il undong-ŭi hoë-sang," *Shinch'ŏnji*, 1.2:230-237 (March 1946).

107. *Song Chin-u Biography*, p. 53.

108. *Gendai Chōsen jinmei jiten*, p. 110.

109. *Song Chin-u Biography.*

110. Hyŏn Sang-yun.

111. *Gendai Chōsen jinmei jiten*, p. 202.

112. *Shisō ihō*, 4: 135 (September 1935).

113. One source on Yŏ Un-hyŏng's background is Yi Man-gyu, *Yŏ Un-hyŏng sŏnsaeng.*

114. Kim Chong-pŏm, and Kim Tong-un, *Haebang chŏnhu-ŭi Chosŏn chinsang* (Seoul, 1945), p. 65; *Gendai Chōsen jinmei jiten*, p. 110.

115. Korean Government-General, High Court, Prosecutor's Bureau, "Ro Unkyō chōsaho," in *Chōsen shisō undō chōsa shiryō*, no. 2:12 (March 1933).

116. Kim Chong-pŏm and Kim Tong-un, p. 46; Yŏ Un-hong, *Yŏ Un-hyŏng* (Seoul, 1967), p. 123. (Yŏ Un-hong was the brother of Yŏ Un-hyong).

117. "Kyōsan shugi senjin Pak Hŏn-yŏng no taiho ni kansuruken," Japanese Ministry of Foreign Affairs Archives (Library of Congress microfilms), Reel S. 403.

118. Suh Dae-Sook, *The Korean Communist Movement*, p. 72.

119. *Gendai Chōsen jinmei jiten*, p. 250.

120. Chang Pok-sŏng, *Chosŏn kongsan-dang p'ajaeng-sa* (Seoul, 1949), p. 49.

121. *Gendai Chōsen jinmei jiten*, p. 238.

122. *Pukhan ch'ongkam* (Seoul, 1968).

123. Suh Dae-Sook, *The Korean Communist Movement,* p. 303.

II. The Struggle for Power in South Korea, 1945-1948

1. Kim Chun-yŏn, *Tongnip nosŏn* (Seoul, 1947), pp. 2-6; also, Secret Report of H. Merill Benninghoff, Foreign Service Officer, Political Advisor to the Secretary of State on Political Movements in Korea, 29 September 1946, unclassified secret document, and Personalities and Chronology, unclassified secret document.

2. Kim Chun-yŏn; and interview with Mr. Kim, Seoul, August 1, 1968. Mr. Kim was one of Mr. Song's close friends.

3. Song Chin-u, radio broadcast, December 21, 1946.

4. Yi Yu.

5. Yi Ki-ha, *Han'guk chŏngdang paltal-sa* (Seoul, 1961), pp. 19-24.

6. Henderson, p. 115. Yŏ's supporters denied that he had received any subsidy, but it is hard to imagine that the Japanese expected him to keep order without any means of financing it. It is generally believed that he received about ¥700,000, not a large sum for such a purpose.

7. Yi Ki-ha, pp. 39-44.

8. Henderson, p. 115.

9. Yi Ki-ha, p. 49.

10. Chang Pok-sŏng, p. 49.

11. Yi Man-gyu, *Chosŏn kyoë-uk-sa* (Seoul, 1950), p. 221.

12. Yi Man-gyu, *Yŏ Un-hyŏng sŏnsaeng*, p. 156.

13. Yamana Mikio, *Chōsen sotoku-fu shusei no kiroku* (Tokyo, 1956), pp. 1-41; Yi Man-gyu, *Yŏ Un-hyŏng sŏnsaeng*, pp. 261-263; *Chosŏn haeban nyŏnbo, 1946* (Seoul, 1946), pp. 179-228.

14. Yi Ki-ha, p. 44.

15. Interview with Professor Byung Guk Kim (Chairman, Department of Economics, Sŏkwang University, Seoul), in Washington, D.C., December 1968.

16. Yi Man-gyu, *Yŏ Un-hyŏng sŏnsaeng*, pp. 235-236.

17. No less than Kim Il Sung later confirmed that the Communists in South Korea had been responsible for naming Syngman Rhee president of the People's Republic, a move which he bitterly condemned: "They [the 'Pak Hŏn-yŏng clique'] proclaimed that they would make Syngman Rhee . . . the president of the 'People's Republic' framed up behind the scenes." *Third Congress Documents*, p. 9.

18. Taekunch'al-ch'ŏng susaguk, *Chwa-ik sagŏn sillok*, I, 35-38.

19. E. Grant Meade, *American Military Government in Korea* (New York, 1951), p. 162.

20. Robinson. Mr. Robinson obtained his information from American intelligence files, while preparing the official history of the American Military Government.

21. Ibid.

22. USAMGIK, *Summation*, no. 14 (November, 1946); also, *The New York Times* (May 11, 1946).

23. An Chae-hong, for example, after his resignation as vice chairman of the committee, formed a small party called the Nationalist Party.

24. "Gradualists" here refers to those who advocated gradual means of achieving independence (e.g., building internal economic and organizational strength), whereas "activists" refers to those who advocated direct action and open resistance. In general, the gradualists were older, wealthier, and more conservative, but the line between the two was often blurred. Some post-1945 gradualists had started as Communists.

25. Ch'ŏn Kwan-u, p. 41; Han T'ae-su, *Han'guk chongdang-sa* (Seoul, 1961), p. 63.

26. Chayu-dang chung'ang tangbu sŏnchon wiwŏnhoë, *Minju-dang-ŭi punpa naemak* (Seoul, 1959), p. 14; Meade, p. 162.

27. Ch'ŏn Kwan-u, pp. 41-42.

28. United States Department of State, *The Conferences at Malta and Yalta*, pp. 336-339.

29. Interview with the Korean broadcaster for O.W.I. at the time, Mr. Kingsley K. Lyu, Washington, D.C., January 28, 1967.

30. Carl Berger, *The Korea Knot: A Military-Political History* (Philadelphia, 1964), from *History of USAFIK* [United States Army Forces in Korea], pt. II, ch. 4, p. 88; General Hodge informed the State Department that after this decision it would be difficult if not impossible to implement further policy directives in Korea; see also *Dong-A Ilbo* (December 29, 1945).

31. Harry S. Truman, *Memoirs* (Garden City, N.Y., 1955), II, 319.

32. Berger.

33. For example, see the editorials in *Dong-A Ilbo* (December 29-31, 1945). Most Korean nationalists had no less reason to be suspicious of the intentions of the United States than of Russia, Japan, or any other country which might take over the rule of Korea.

34. Pak Mun-ok, *Haengchŏng-hak* (Seoul, 1962), p. 241; Bertran D. Sarafan, "Military Government: Korea," *Far Eastern Survey* (November 1946), p. 350. Sarafan was with the Military Government in Korea.

35. A very interesting study of this American policy is Lee Won Sul, "The Impact of the United States Occupation Policy on the Socio-Political Structure of South Korea, 1945-1948" (Ph.D. dissertation, Western Reserve University, 1961).

36. Hong Chŏng-in, "Konchŏng-ŭi ponsilkwa kuŭi," *Shinch'ŏnji* (December 1946), pp. 8-15.

37. United Nations Document A/575, vol. I, 3 sess., suppl. 9, p. 117;

Dong-A Ilbo (November 14, 1947). When nationalists attacked this policy, the AMG reportedly defended it by saying, "They have good experience and are working well. If we expel them, it is reasonable to conclude that they will join a movement against the military government." *Dong-A Ilbo* (November 20, 23, 1946).

38.   Interview with Dr. E.A.J. Johnson, American civil administrator in Korea, in Washington, D.C., November 30, 1966.

39.   United States Army Forces in Korea, *Republic of Korea Economic Summation*, no. 36: 7-9.

40.   Ibid.

41.   USAMGIK, *Summation*, no. 7:13 (April 1946).

42.   The AMG declared that "United States policy prohibits official recognition or utilization for political purposes of any so-called Korean provisional government or other political organization by the United States Forces." SCAP *Summation*, 1: 117.

43.   Berger, quotes from *The History of USAFIK*, pt. II, ch. 1, pp. 33-34; "It is clear that the State Department had doubts as to Rhee's value in bringing order to the excited political scene there. He had been a steady critic of the department and U.S. policies, and furthermore he was in his seventieth year and had been away from his homeland for many years." Henderson, p. 128, Oliver, p. 210, and Yi Wŏn-sun, pp. 258-260, recount Rhee's difficulties in trying to return to Korea.

44.   Henderson, pp. 128-129, tells this little-known story. Mr. Henderson was cultural attaché with the United States Embassy in Seoul for many years.

45.   As quoted in *The New York Times* (October 21, 1945).

46.   Letter to Dr. Robert Oliver, October 21, 1945.

47.   The main outline of this strategy was suggested in his letter to Dr. Oliver, ibid.

48.   Ch'ŏn Kwan-u, p. 42.

49. Taekunch'al-ch'ŏng susaguk, *Chwa-ik sagŏn sillok*, p. 55.

50. Kim Chŏng-pom and Kim Tong-un, p. 152.

51. *Dong-A Ilbo* (November 19, 1945).

52. SCAP, *Summation*, 2: 183 (November 1945), 3:8 (December 1945).

53. Kim Chŏng-pom and Kim Tong-un.

54. Yi Ki-ha, p. 86.

55. *Chosŏn Inminbo* (November 29, 1945). The *Chosŏn Inminbo* was the news organ of the Communist Party in Seoul during 1945 and 1946, and was one of the first publications after the Japanese surrender.

56. *The New York Times* (December 6, 1945).

57. Robinson, p. 62. Mr. Robinson was present at the meeting, which was also reported in the *Chosŏn Inminbo*, the Communist Party newspaper, on December 17, 1945. Knowing the explosiveness of the issue of cooperation with these men, Rhee reportedly denied that the meeting had taken place.

58. *Dong-A Ilbo* (December 6, 1945).

59. *United States Department of State Bulletin* (December 30, 1945), p. 1030.

60. *Dong-A Ilbo* (December 29, 1945).

61. Robinson, p. 62. See accounts also in *The New York Times* (January 1, 1946), *Dong-A Ilbo* (December 28, 1945-January 4, 1946).

62. Tsuboe Senji, *Nansen no kaihō jūnen* (Tokyo, 1956), pp. 84-85.

63. Robinson, p. 26.

64. *Seoul Shinmun* (December 30, 1945).

65. Interview with Dr. Johnson, see note 38.

66. *Dong-A Ilbo* (December 30, 1945).

67. Rhee had been trying to put pressure on the government in Washington
     throughout November and December of 1945, by means of his lobby-
     ing organization left behind in the United States, as well as friends in
     the United States press and army. In his letter of October 21 to Dr.
     Oliver, one of his associates in the United States, he wrote that General
     Hodge had sent him a copy of a letter to the State Department urging
     a change in the "earlier policy" (i.e., trusteeship). President Truman
     mentions this letter from Hodge in his *Memoirs*, II, 318.

68. Robinson indicates that Army intelligence intercepted a copy of the
     orders at the 38th parallel; *United States Army Area Handbook for
     Korea* (Washington, D.C., 1964), p. 38, also mentions these orders.

69. Richard C. Allen [pseud.], *Korea's Syngman Rhee: An Unauthorized
     Portrait* (Rutland, Vermont, 1960), p. 90.

70. Yi Ki-ha, p. 93; *Dong-A Ilbo* (January 5, 1945).

71. USAMGIK, *Summation*, 6:9 (March 1946).

72. *Taehan Min'guk chŏngdang'sa*, ed. Chung'ang sŏnko kwalli wiwŏn-hoĕ
     (Seoul, 1964), pp. 97-99.

73. United States Army Forces in Korea, HQ XXIV Corps, G-2 Section,
     The National Society for the Rapid Realization of Independence,
     July 1, 1946, unclassified document, pp. 1-10.

74. Meade, p. 163, points out that by July 1, 1946, for the first time the
     nationalists had become the most powerful group at the local level.
     Meade was a local officer of the American Military Government in
     Cholla-namdo Province.

75. As quoted in Yi Ki-ha, p. 111.

76. As quoted in Han T'ae-su, *Han'guk chongdang-sa*, pp. 78-79.

77. USAMGIK, *Summation*, 8: 27 (May 1946), 14: 24 (November 1946).
     The financial officer of the Korean Communist Party was sentenced to
     life imprisonment for the counterfeiting of ¥12,000,000.

78. Robinson, pp. 113-114, from American intelligence reports; see also
     detailed reports in *Dong-A Ilbo* (March 6-9, 11, 13, 14, and 20, 1948),
     and General Hodge's statement of October 20, 1947, that "The close
     tie-in of the North Korean Labor Party [successor to the North Korean
     Communist Party] and the North Korean People's Committees [govern-
     ing organs in the North] with the leadership and activities of the South
     Korean Labor Party [successor to the South Korean Communist Party]
     and its satellites in the continuing efforts to disturb the peace of South
     Korea is so well established as no longer to require surmise on the part
     of South Koreans or the American command." *The New York Times*
     (October 21, 1947).

79. Both Henderson, p. 170, and Robinson, who had access to confidential
     materials, mention these orders, and Dr. E.A.J. Johnson, the American
     civil administrator in Korea, pointed out that "Our instructions were
     to build a government of the 'center.'" Interview with Dr. Johnson,
     see note 38.

80. For an account of the Joint Commission meetings, see United States
     Department of State, *Korea's Independence*, Far Eastern Series 18
     (October 1947).

81. USAMGIK, *Summation*, no. 6 (March 1946).

82. Akira Sakamoto, *Report on the State of Public Order* (October 1945),
     p. 3.

83. Meade, p. 65.

84. USAMGIK, *Summation* 13:16-18 (October 1946); *Dong-A Ilbo*
     (October 1946).

85. Ibid., 9:21 (June 1946).

86. Interview with American civil administrator, Dr. E.A.J. Johnson, see
     note 38.

87. USAMGIK, *Summation* 13:16-18 (October 1946).

88. Ibid., 16:11-26 (January 1947).

89. Bank of Korea, Research Department, *Chosŏn kyŏngche nyŏnbo, 1948* (Seoul, 1948), p. 9.

90. USAMGIK, *Summation* 27: 209 (December, 1947); *Far East Stars and Stripes Weekly* (June 15, 1947), and *Time* (June 30, 1947), pp. 25-26, pointed out the financing of the group by the United States, a well-known fact. See Henderson, p. 141, and Robinson, pp. 249-55. Syngman Rhee's former press secretary stated that these funds came from General MacArthur's headquarters in Tokyo, and not from the American Military Government in Seoul, which was under instructions *not* to support the nationalists. Interview with Dr. Choi Kee Il, Washington, D.C., December 20, 1966. However, the AMG reported the sums budgeted for the youth corps in the *Summation*.

91. Kim Sŭng-shik, ed., *Chosŏn nyŏn'gam*, 1947 (Seoul, 1946), p. 250.

92. USAMGIK, *Summation* 13: 23-26 (October 1946).

93. Ibid., 15:59 (December 1946).

94. Ibid., 27:32 (December 1947).

95. Ibid., 27:4 (December 1947) and 36:4 (November-December 1948).

96. Ibid., 13:24 (October 1946).

97. Ibid., 9:20 (June 1946).

98. General Hodge, press release, August 22, 1947, as cited in George McCune, p. 87, and *Dong-A Ilbo* (October 4, 5, and 6, 1948).

99. USAMGIK, *Summation* 13:16 (October 1946).

100. Ibid.

101. Yi Man-gyu, *Yŏ Un-hyŏng sŏnsaeng*; Han T'ae-su, *Han'guk chong-dang-sa*, p. 68.

102. USAMGIK, *Summation* 12:11 (September 1946); Ordinance No. 11S, as cited in *The Voice of Korea*, November 16, 1946.

103. Ibid., and *Dong-A Ilbo* (October 9, 1946).

104. Meade, p. 187.

105. *Dong-A Ilbo* (October 9, 1945); McCune, *Korea Today*, pp. 78-79.

106. USAMGIK, *Summation* 15:13 (December 1946).

107. Ibid.

108. Ibid., p. 14.

109. In fact, news of Rhee's suggestion of separate independence reached the Western press as early as June 1946 (*The New York Times* [June 9, 1946]) although Rhee did not press the issue in Korea until some time later.

110. Dr. Johnson, interview, see note 38.

111. Ibid.

112. This interpretation of Robinson, pp. 184-186, was drawn from American intelligence reports.

113. This interpretation, as told by Rhee's friend Dr. Robert Oliver (interview, January 14, 1967), is allegedly based on Rhee's own account.

114. The coup attempt is mentioned in USAMGIK, *Summation* 18:12 (March 1947).

115. Allen, *Korea's Syngman Rhee*, pp. 89-90.

116. Robinson, p. 196.

117. Ibid., p. 205.

118. *The New York Times* (April 12, 1947).

119. Dr. Johnson, American civil administrator, interview, see note 38.

120. United States Department of State, *Korea's Independence*, pp. 32-54.

121. Interview with Dr. Choi Kee Il, Rhee's press secretary, 1945-1947, December 1966, Washington, D.C.

122. Chang Taek-sang, in Yi Pŏm-sŏk, et al., *Sasil-ŭi chŏnburŭl kisulhanda* (Seoul, 1966), p. 107.

123. Robinson, p. 228.

124. United States Department of State, *Korea's Independence*, p. 56.

125. Interview with Dr. Anderson, November 29, 1966.

126. Dr. Johnson, interview, see note 38.

127. Ibid.

128. Yim Sun-buk, et al., p. 273.

129. *United States Department of State Bulletin*, March 7, 1948, pp. 247–298; United Nations Document A/Ac, 18/31.

130. United Nations Document, A/575, add. 2, p. 90; Han T'ae-su, *Han'guk chongdang-sa*, p. 99.

131. Kim Koo, *Paekbŏm ilji*, app. 1-9.

132. Chi Hon-mo, *Choëhuŭi paekbŏm* (Seoul, 1960), pp. 28-29.

133. For example, Lyu, in an interview (see note 29) tells of Rhee's bitter reaction when Koreans in Hawaii sent funds to Kim Koo for his terrorist activities in the 1930's.

134. USAFIK, *SKIG Activities*, 27:205 (December 1947).

135. Richard E. Lauterbach, *History of the American Military Government in Korea*, Korean ed. (Seoul, 1948), p. 46.

136. *Haebang isipnyŏn* (Seoul, 1956), p. 74.

137. Detailed reports of the trial were carried in *Dong-A Ilbo*.

138. Yi Tong-su, in O Sso-paek, *Haebang isipnyŏn* (Seoul, 1965), pp. 294–296.

139. Ch'oë Sŏng-puk, "Pyongyang nampuk hyŏpsang-ŭi insang," *Shinch'ŏnji* 4-5:62-71 (May 1948); Sŏl Kuk-hwan, "Nampuk hoëdamg suhaengki," *Shinch'ŏnji* 4-5:72-81 (May 1948).

140. As quoted in *Dong-A Ilbo* (May 7, 1948).

141. McCune, *Korea Today*, p. 147.

142. UN Document A/AC, 19/80, p. 121; *Taehan Min'guk sŏnko-sa*.

143. E.g., see *Dong-A Ilbo* (May 18, 1948).

144. United Nations General Assembly, resolution 195 (III), December 12, 1948.

145. *Taehan Min'guk sŏnko-sa*, p. 388.

146. USAMGIK, *Summation* 27:13 and 73 (December 1947).

147. Ibid., p. 139.

148. Bank of Korea, *Economic Statistics Yearbook, 1968* (Seoul, 1968), p. 6.

III. Consolidation of Power in North Korea, 1945-1948

1. North Koreans call this the period of "consolidation of the democratic base." See *Political Survey of the DPRK, 1945-1960* (Pyongyang, 1960).

2. United States Department of State, *North Korea: A Case Study in the Techniques of Takeover* (Washington, D.C., 1961), p. 12.

3. Rudolph, p. 26; Paige, "The Communist System: The North Korean Party State" (Draft, 1964), p. 22; Paige, *Korean People's Democratic Republic*, p. 57.

4. Tsuboe Senji, *Chōsen minzoku tokuritsu undōhisi* (Tokyo, 1959), p. 24; Kim Ch'ang-sun, *Yŏksa-ui chŭng'in* (Seoul, 1936).

5. Japanese Ministry of Foreign Affairs, p. 101; Robinson, from American intelligence.

6. Ibid., and Tsubōe Senji, *Hokusen no kaihō jūnen* (Tokyo, 1956), pp. 24-26.

7. Tsubōe Senji, *Hokusen*; *Pukkwe*.

8. Scalapino and Lee, pp. 9-31.

9. Japanese Ministry of Home Affairs, Security Division, *Tokkō Geppō* (Tokyo, June 1945).

10. Chosŏn haebang nyŏnbo ch'ulp'anbu, *Chosŏn haebang ilnyŏn-sa* (Seoul, 1946), p. 80.

11. Kim Il Sung, *Kim Il-sŏng sŏnjip*, II, 127; also quoted in N.K. Vaintsvaig and V.V. Lezin, *Koreiskaya Narodno-Demokratisheskaya Respublika* (Moscow, 1964), pp. 212-213.

12. *Pukkwe*.

13. Kim Ch'ang-sun, *Pukhan siponyŏn-sa* (Seoul, 1961).

14. Rudolph, p. 9, from *Krasnoe Znamia* (Vladivostok, August 31, 1945), p. 4.

15. Lee Won Sul.

16. Chosŏn haebang nyŏnbo ch'ulp'anbu, *Chosŏn haebang ilnyŏn-sa* (Seoul, 1946), p. 390; Rudolph, p. 10 from Shabsina, F.I., *Ocherbi noveishei istorii Korei*: 1945-1953 (Moscow: Godussarstvennoe Izdatel'stvo Politicheskoi Literary, 1958), p. 45.

17. Chŏngbo-kuk Oëmu-pu, *Pukhan isipnyŏn* (Seoul, 1965).

18. Kim Ch'ang-sun, *Pukhan*, p. 190.

19. *Pukkwe*.

20. Rudolph, from B.V. Shchetinin, "Vozniknovenie narodnykh komitetov v severnoi Korei," *Sovetskoe Gosudarstvo i Provo*, no. 4: 67-72 (1947).

21. Ibid.

22. *Taehan Minguk chŏngdang-sa*, p. 470.

23. Tsuboe Senji, *Hokusen*, pp. 36-39, and Kim Ch'ang-sun, *Pukhan*, p. 66.

24. *Pukkwe*.

25. Kim Ch'ang-sun, *Yŏksa-ŭi*, pp. 200-240; Kim Ch'ang-sun, *Pukhan*; Tsuboe Senji, *Hokusen*, pp. 2-51; Han Chae-dok, *Kim Il-sŏng-ŭl kobalhanda* (Seoul, 1965).

26. *Pukhan ch'ongkam*; Chŏngbo-kuk Oëmu-pu, *Pukhan isipnyŏn*, p. 52, gives the date as October 13.

27. *Pukkwe*.

28. There is some disagreement in sources here; official North Korean sources now say that Kim Il Sung was elected to chair the committee at this time, but others, including South Korean intelligence, indicate that he did not achieve this post until December. Since he was not publicly introduced until after the party organization meeting (October 14), the latter would seem more likely. See *Chosŏn chung'ang nyŏn'gam, 1949* (Pyongyang, 1949), p. 715; Kim Ch'ang-sun, *Pukhan*; Chŏngbo-kuk Oëmu-pu, *Pukhan isipnyŏn*, p. 9; *Taehan Min'guk sŏnko sa*, p. 470; and Rudolph, p. 25, from Indian Communist sources, for the earlier date, and Tsuboe Senji, *Hokusen*; *Kibon ch'ŏngbo*; and Oh Che-do, "The Communist Plot Against Korea," manuscript (August 8, 1959) p. 12, for the latter date.

29. Kim Ch'ang-sun, *Pukhan*.

30. Han Im-hyŏk, *Kim Il-sŏng tongji-ŭi wihan Chosŏn kongsan-dang ch'anggon* (Pyongyang, 1961), p. 32; Dae-sook Suh, "North Korea: Emergence of an Elite Group," in Richard F. Staar, ed., *Aspects of Modern Communism* (Columbia, S.C., 1965), p. 324.

31. U.S. Department of State, *Techniques of Takeover*, p. 13.

32. Anna Louise Strong, "I Saw the North Koreans" (Los Angeles, July 16, 1950), p. 8. Miss Strong reports that Kim Il Sung told her this in a personal interview.

33.   "Kim Il-sŏng chaggun pudae-wa Chosŏn wiyonggyun-ŭi chunggyon kanbu chuadam-hoë, *Shinch'ŏnji* (Seoul, March 1943), pp. 230-237.

34.   *Chosŏn chung'ang nyŏn'gam*, 1949, p. 63.

35.   The background of these leaders is from *Kibon chŏngbo*; Kim Il did not fight with Kim Il Sung in Manchuria, but apparently joined him in the U.S.S.R.

36.   Kim Il Sung's name, as we have seen, was Kim Sŏng-chu; Kim Ch'aek's was originally Kim Chae-min, Kim Il's was Kim T'ae-chŏn, and Ch'oë Yŏng-gŏn's was Ch'oë Sŏk-ch'on.

37.   Yi Ki-ha, p. 154.

38.   Chŏngbo-kuk Oëmu-pu, *Pukhan isipnyŏn*, p. 101.

39.   *Kibon chŏngbo*; *Pukhan ch'ongkam* gives the date as December 17.

40.   Tsubōe Senji, *Hokusen*.

41.   F.I. Shabshina, *Narodnoe vosstanovlenie 1919 goda v Koree* (Moscow, 1952), p. 105.

42.   Kim Ch'ang-sun, *Pukhan*, p. 71.

43.   Ibid.

44.   *Pukkwe*, p. 17.

45.   Chŏngbo-kuk Oëmu-pu, *Pukhan isipnyŏn*, p. 101.

46.   *UNCURK Report*.

47.   *Kin Nichisei Senshu*, p. 217.

48.   Kim Ch'ang-sun, *Pukhan*, p. 192.

49.   Ibid.

50.   *Pukkwe*, p. 17.

51.   Rudolph, p. 37.

52.   Ibid., from *UNCURK Report*.

53.   See land distribution statistics in North Korea as of 1938, in Andrew J. Grajdanzev, "Korea Divided," *Far Eastern Survey* (October 10, 1945), p. 282.

54.   *Kin Nichisei Senshu*, p. 217.

55.   Grajdanzev, "Korea Divided," p. 282.

56.   Kim Il Sung, *The Selected Works of Kim Il Sung*, II, 301.

57.   *Kin Nichisei Senshu*, Supplemental Volume, p. 115.

58.   U.S. Department of State, *Techniques of Takeover*, p. 56.

59.   Ibid., p. 57.

60.   See Lee Chong-Sik, "Land Reform, Collectivisation and the Peasants in North Korea," *The China Quarterly*, no. 14:65-81 (April-June 1963), for a description of the procedures used in carrying out the land reform.

61.   *Kin Nichisei Senshu*, supplemental volume, p. 115.

62.   Rudolph, p. 48.

63.   Grajdanzev, *Modern Korea*, pp. 113-114.

64.   Rudolph, from *UNCURK Report*, p. 28; and U.S. Department of State, *Techniques of Takeover*, p. 57.

65.   *Inmin chŏnggwŏn-ŭi suripkwa kŭui konggohwarul wihan* (Pyongyang, 1958), p. 35.

66.   E.A. Pigulevskaia, *Koreiskii narod v bor'be za nezavisimost' i demokratiiu* (Moscow, 1952), p. 174.

67.   *Kibon chŏngbo*.

68. Kim Ch'ang-sun, *Pukhan*.

69. Suh Dae-sook, "North Korea: Emergence of an Elite Group," p. 303.

70. Han T'ae-su, *Han'guk chongdang-sa*, p. 99.

71. Kim Ch'ang-sun, *Pukhan*. Kim Ch'ang-sun was a domestic Communist in the North who later fled South. Though his accounts are naturally biased, the factual material is generally corroborated by other sources.

72. Ibid.

73. Chŏson haebang nyŏnbo ch'ulp'anbu, *Chosŏn haebang ilnyŏn-sa*, pp. 455-456.

74. Kim Il Sung, *Kim Il-sŏng sŏnjip*, I, 81-82.

75. E.A. Pigulevskaia, and F.I. Shabshina, from Rudolph, p. 27. Before the merger, the number of Communists was 134,000. The total Worker's Party members after the merger is said to have been 366,000. This would mean that there were 232,000 members of the New People's Party.

76. Kim Ch'ang-sun, *Pukhan*, pp. 99-101.

77. Ibid., p. 101.

78. Chosŏn haebang nyŏnbo ch'ulp'anbu, *Chosŏn haebang ilnyŏn-sa*, pp. 456-457.

79. Ibid.

80. Kim Il Sung, *Kim Il-sŏnjip*, VI, 47-48.

81. *Pukhan ch'ongkam*, p. 123.

82. V.A. Kim, *Gosudarstvennyi stroi Koreiskoi Narodno-Demokraticheskoi Respubliki* (Moscow, 1955), p. 52, gives the number as 750,000.

83. *Kin Nichisei Senshu*, I, 64.

84. *Trud* (May 24, 1947), as translated in *Soviet Press Translations* 2:70-74 (August 1947).

85. Yi Chŏl-chu, *Pukŭi yaesulin* (Seoul, 1965), p. 131.

86. U.S. Department of State, *Techniques of Takeover*, p. 88.

87. Ibid., p. 87.

88. Ibid.

89. Kiwon Chung, "The North Korean People's Army and the Party,"
The China Quarterly (April-June 1963), pp. 105-124.

90. Kim Ch'ang-sun, *Pukhan*, pp. 61-65.

91. Ibid.

92. Edwin W. Pauley, *Report on Japanese Assets in Soviet-Occupied Korea
to the President of the United States, June 1946* (unclassified November 8, 1949), p. 119.

93. Kiwon Chung, p. 107.

94. U.S. Department of State, *Techniques of Takeover*, p. 114.

95. Ibid., p. 12.

96. Chosŏn haebang nyŏnbo ch'ulp'anbu, *Chosŏn haebang ilnyŏn-sa*, p. 128.

97. As quoted in *The Voice of Korea* (October 16, 1948). *The Voice of
Korea*, published by a Korean in the United States, was a left-oriented,
non-Communist publication, critical of both Northern and Southern
regimes.

98. *Inmin chŏnggwŏn-ŭi suripkwa*, p. 42.

99. McCune, *Korea Today*, p. 174. See P. Ivanov, "Election Results for
the People's Committees of Northern Korea," *Izvestia* (November 16,
1946); and V. Smolensky, "The Situation in Korea," as translated in
Soviet Press Translations (December 14, 1946 and March 15, 1947),
Far Eastern Institute, University of Washington, Seattle, Washington.

100. *Inmin chŏnggwŏn-ŭi suripkwa*, p. 44.

101. McCune, *Korea Today*, p. 177.

102. Rudolph, p. 14, from V.A. Kim, pp. 56-59.

103. SKIG, *Activities* (April 1948), p. 5.

104. *First Part of the Report of the United Nations Temporary Commission on Korea* (New York: General Assembly, Official Records, 3rd sess., supp. 9, A/575, 1948), pt. I, p. 23.

105. U.S. Department of State, *Techniques of Takeover*, p. 8.

106. Pak Tong-un, *Pukhan t'ongchi kiguron* (Seoul, 1964), p. 23.

107. Ibid., and Rudolph, p. 17.

108. Kim Il Sung, *Kim Il-sŏng sŏnjip*, I., 268.

109. McCune, *Korea Today*, p. 53.

110. U.S. Department of State, *Techniques of Takeover*, p. 14.

111. Such as O Ki-sŏp, Chŏng Tal-hŏn, and Ch'oë Yong-tal. See Kim Il Sung's criticism of these and other followers at the Second Congress of the Korean Workers' Party, March 29, 1948. Kim Il Sung, *Kim Il-sŏng sŏnjip*, II, 181-186.

112. E.g., see Kim's report on "The Struggle for Consolidation of the Party," at the Third Congress of 1956, in *Third Congress Documents*, pp. 78-83.

113. Kim Il Sung, *Kim Il-sŏng sŏnjip*, VI, 47-48.

114. *Pukhan ch'ongkam*, p. 123.

115. Kim Ch'ang-sun, *Pukhan*. The reference to a "frog in a well" was also made by Mao Tse-tung, on December 27, 1935, when he said, "In approaching a problem, a Marxist should see the whole as well as the parts. A frog in a well says, 'The sky is no bigger than the mouth of the well.' That is untrue for the sky is not just the size of the mouth of the

well. If it said, 'a part of the sky is the size of the mouth of a well,' then that would be true, for it tallies with the facts." Mao Tse-tung, *Selected Works*, English ed. (Peking, 1953), I, 159. In fact, the phrase, which is now quoted as one of Mao's great thoughts in "the little red book" of *Quotations of Chairman Mao Tse-tung*, is a traditional proverb which both were quoting.

116. Kim Il Sung, *Kim Il-sŏng sŏnjip*, VI, 47-48. Later figures give the membership as 750,000 at that time.

117. U.S. Department of State, *Techniques of Takeover*, p. 39.

118. Kiwon Chung, p. 107.

119. Rudolph, p 37

120. Ibid., p. 38, from North Korean radio broadcast, February 20, 1948.

121. U.S. Department of State, *Techniques of Takeover*, p. 52.

122. Ibid., p. 101.

123. Ibid.

124. Ibid.

125. Kim Ch'ang-sun, *Pukhan*, p. 54.

126. *Education and Culture in the DPRK* (Pyongyang, 1953), p. 8.

127. L.N. Karshinov, *Socialist Industrialization in the Korean Democratic People's Republic*, tr. Glenn D. Paige (Moscow, 1960), p. 6; Sang-hak Kim, *Development of Socialist Industry in the D.P.R.K.* (Pyongyang, 1958), pp. 14-16.

128. See Joungwon A. Kim, "North Korea's Economic Progress, 1946-1963," monograph reproduced by the United States Department of State, April 1964, p. 10.

129. U.S. Department of State, *Techniques of Takeover*, p. 7.

IV. Attempted Introduction of the First Republic in South Korea, 1948-1960

1. The assembly was to be composed of 200 members, but elections were not held in two districts in Cheju Province due to outbreaks of violence in that area. Han Chŏng-il, *Han'guk chŏngch'i haengchŏngrŏn* (Seoul, 1969), p. 168.

2. *Kukhoë sipnyŏnji*, ed. Taehan Min'guk kukhoë minŭiwon samuchŏ (Seoul, 1958), pp. 85-87.

3. *Kukhoëbo* 1.1:m.p. (n.d.); Yu Chin-o, *Minju chŏngchiae-ŭi kil* (Seoul, 1963), p. 137.

4. Quoted by Oliver, p. 272; see also McCune, *Korea Today*, p. 244, who attributes the strength of the presidential role to Rhee's intervention in the constitution-making process.

5. According to Yi Pŏm-sŏk, who conveyed the request from the KDP to Rhee. Yi Pŏm-sŏk, et al., *Sasil-ŭi chŏnburul kisulhanda* (Seoul, 1966), pp. 85-88. See also Han T'ae-su, *Han'guk chongdang-sa*, p. 113.

6. Personal letter from Syngman Rhee to Robert T. Oliver, July 28, 1948.

7. The United Nations did recognize the South Korean government as the "only lawful government" in Korea on December 12, 1948, by General Assembly Resolution 195 (III), and this was an important step in laying the groundwork for United Nations defense of South Korea in the Korean War, in view of the fact that the attack from the north directly challenged this UN resolution.

8. Letter to Dr. Oliver, see note 6. Dr. Rhee dictated the letter to his wife, who wrote it in the third person. To make the meaning clear, the writer has substituted "[I]" where Mrs. Rhee wrote "Dr." Since Mrs. Rhee spelled the personal names according to a different transliteration system, the McCune-Reischauer system of spelling is inserted in brackets where appropriate. (See preface.)

9. Yi Pŏm-sŏk, pp. 85-88; Han T'ae-su, *Han'guk chongdang-sa*, p. 113.

10. Ibid.

11. Louise Yim, *My Forty Year Fight for Korea* (New York, 1951).

12. Interview with Dr. Robert T. Oliver (Professor of Speech, Pennsylvania State College). Dr. Oliver was a friend of Syngman Rhee who worked with the Korean Commission in Washington, 1942-1945, and later with the Korean Research and Information Office. He is the author of Rhee's English-language (authorized) biography. In State College, Pennsylvania, January 14, 1967.

13. UN Document A/AC, 19/30, add. 1, p. 22, noted, "There was widespread criticism of the personnel appointed to the Cabinet and the opinion was expressed that the President had failed to utilize fully the best talents available." The *Dong-A Ilbo*, on August 7, 1948, in a front page editorial, had said, "Syngman Rhee made a mistake in not selecting good leaders for the Cabinet."

14. Han T'ae-su, *Han'guk chongdang-sa*, p. 113.

15. *Kukhoë sokkirok* [Minutes of the National Assembly], September 7, 1948, 1 Sess., p. 1117. Also Kim Chin-hak and Han Chŏl-yong, *Chaehŏn kukhoë-sa* (Seoul, 1954), p. 72; *Kwanbo* [Gazette], no. 5, September 22, 1948.

16. *Kukhoë sokkirok*, September 7, 1948, p. 1122.

17. *Chae samhoë kukhoë imsi hoëŭi sokkirok*, no. 1 and no. 2 (May 21, 1949). *Dong-A Ilbo* (June 23, 1949).

18. *Dong-A Ilbo* (February 16, 1950). *Yi Sŭng-man taet'ŏngyŏng-ŭi tamhwajip* (Seoul, 1951), pp. 30-31.

19. *Chae yukhoë kukhoë chongki hoëŭi sokkirok*, no. 48 (March 9, 1950).

20. *Dong-A Ilbo* (March 19, 1950).

21. Han'guk hyŏngmyŏng chaep'an-sa p'yŏnch'an wiwŏnhoë, *Han'guk hyŏngmyŏng chaep'an-sa* (Seoul, 1962), I, 39.

22. Han T'ae-su, *Han'guk chongdang-sa*, p. 119.

23. John W. Connelly, Jr., "Report on Economic Provisions of the Constitution of the Republic of Korea," Memorandum prepared for Mr. Morris Wolf, General Counsel, FDA, Washington, D.C., March 24, 1954.

24. Rhee's reluctance to raise taxes was noted with strong disapproval by his American economic advisers, who did not take into account the funds collected by unofficial means. For example, Dr. Wilhelm Anderson, economic adviser to the Rhee government, indicated the lack of economic wisdom in this low-tax policy. Interview, Washington, D.C., November 29, 1966. The Secretary of State sharply reprimanded Rhee for his unwillingness to raise taxes, in a note, as reported in *The New York Times* (April 8, 1950).

25. Henderson, p. 142.

26. *Handbook of Korea* (Seoul, 1955), p. 167. By March 1, 1951, 1,029,000 acres had been redistributed.

27. *Chae yukhoë kukhoë chongki hoëǔi sokkirok*, no. 435; *Taehan nyŏn'gam* (Seoul, 1955), pp. 426-429; *Kyŏngcherok taesajŏn* (Seoul, 1964), p. 1493.

28. Yi Pyŏng-do, et al., eds., *Haebang isipnyŏn* (Seoul, 1965); *Dong-A Ilbo* (October 22, 1948).

29. *Seoul Shinmun* (October 21 and November 11, 1948). *The New York Times* (October 27, 1948).

30. *Kukhoë sokkirok*, 1 sess., no. 89, October 27, 1948, pp. 641-660.

31. Sŏn Chang-mu, *Yikosi chinsang ida* (Seoul, 1966), p. 59.

32. Ibid. Rhee's statement about Kim Koo was reported in *The New York Times* (July 1, 1949).

33. When Secretary of State Dean Acheson drew his famous "defense perimeter" excluding Korea in January 1950, he indicated that it would be the policy of the United States to promote economic stability in those areas not included in U.S. defense plans.

34. According to Dr. E.A.J. Johnson , interview (see chap. 2, note 38), who both formulated the proposal and named the minister. (He was never given the title "minister" in the Korean language and was not announced as a member of the cabinet.)

35. Interview with Dr. Johnson, see chap. 2, note 38.

36. Interview with Dr. Wilhelm Anderson, chairman, National Economic Board, American Military Government in Korea (1946-1947); Chief Economic Adviser to Korea (1947-1949); in Washington, D.C., November 29, 1966.

37. Ibid.

38. Ibid.

39. *Dong-A Ilbo* (January 3, 1949).

40. *Chae ohoë kukhoë imsi kukhoë sokkirok* (Seoul, 1959), no. 29; *Dong-A Ilbo* (May 10, 1950).

41. *The New York Times* (April 8, 1950); *Dong-A Ilbo* (April 9, 1950).

42. *Chae yukhoë kukhoë chŏngki hoŭi sokkirok*, no. 11 (January 21, 1950); *The New York Times* (January 20, 1950).

43. *The New York Times* (April 8, 1950); *Dong-A Ilbo* (April 9, 1950).

44. *Dong-A Ilbo* (April 12, 1950). In response to questions at a press conference in Korea a year and one half before, the American Economic Assistance representative, Cyrus Vance, had stated categorically that economic aid would not be used for "political intervention in South Korea." *Dong-A Ilbo* (October 12, 1948).

45. *Korea Annual, 1967* (Seoul, 1967), p. 165; The Bank of Korea, *Economic Statistics Yearbook 1967* (Seoul, 1968), p. 294.

46. *Dong-A Ilbo* (April 22, 1949).

47. *United States Department of State Bulletin* (January 23, 1950), pp. 111-116. Statement made at the National Press Club, January 12, 1950.

48. *Kukhoë sokkirok* (December 29, 1948).

49. *Gendai Chōsen jinmei jiten,* appendix, p. 45. Shin Sung-mo then became home minister in December 1948, but resigned in March 1949. Yin Pyŏng-jik became foreign minister and remained in that post until April 1951.

50.   *Dong-A Ilbo* (February 22, 1949).

51.   Ibid. (March 22, 1949).

52.   Ibid. (May 28, 1949).

53.   As *The New York Times* indicated, "95 percent of the officers in the South Korean Army are men chosen by Americans." May 30, 1950.

54.   W.D. Reeve, *The Republic of Korea: A Political and Economic Study* (London, 1963), p. 31.

55.   Truman, *Memoirs*, II, 454.

56.   The system is described in Yi Yu, pp. 104-113, and Henderson, p. 349.

57.   The system of corruption in the Korean Army during the war was laid bare at the "purge" proceedings of the "Korean Revolutionary Court," in 1961, following the coup d'etat, during which numerous officers were dismissed from the army for their involvement in this activity. Han'guk hyŏngmyŏng chaepan-sa pyŏnchon wiwŏnhoë, *Han'guk hyŏngmyŏng chaep'an-sa* (Seoul, 1962), vols. 1-4.

58.   Yi Pyŏng-do, p. 82. Kim was head of the investigating agency from 1951 until 1956, when he was assassinated by an army colonel who worked under him.

59.   Allen, *Korea's Syngman Rhee*, p. 154.

60.   *Han'guk kunsa hyŏngmyŏng-sa* (Seoul, 1962), pp. 80-81; Song Kŏn-ho, "Chŏngch'i chagŭm-kwa chaepŏl," *Chŏngkyŏng yŏn'gu*, pp. 247-255 (March-April, 1965); Choë Tan-yŏng, "Han'guk-ŭi chŏng-kwa chŏngch'i chagŭm," *Chŏngkyŏng yŏn'gu* (March-April, 1965), pp. 239-246.

61.   *The Korean Republic* (September 10, 1953).

62.   *Han'guk kunsa hyŏngmyŏng-sa*, I, 28, gives the following count: unaffiliated, 85; Rhee followers, 53; Kim Sŏng-su followers (DNP), 29; Yi Chŏng-chon followers, 14; Yi Pŏm-sŏk followers (Youth Corps), 6; others, 11; total, 198.

63.   *Kukhoë sipnyŏnji*, appendix between pp. 92-93.

64. A useful study of the development of the Liberal Party is Kim Chong Hoon, "The Rise and Fall of the Liberal Party in Korea: 1951-1960." M.A. thesis, George Washington University, 1961.

65. *Gendai Chōsen jinmei jiten*, appendix. He remained home minister until July, 1952.

66. Kim Chong Hoon, p. 78.

67. *Taehan Min'guk sŏnko-sa*, p. 314.

68. *Kukhoë chŏnggi hoëŭi sokkirok* (November 30, 1951 and January 18, 1952).

69. Ibid.

70. *Yŏng Nam Ilbo* (May 23 and 24, 1952); *Pusan Ilbo* (June 27, 1952).

71. Ibid.

72. Ma Han, *Han'guk chŏngch'i-ŭi ch'ongpipan* (Seoul, 1960), p. 111.

73. *Dong-A Ilbo* (May 26, 1952).

74. Han T'ae-su, *Han'guk chongdang-sa*, p. 135.

75. Ibid.

76. While there is no proof that Syngman Rhee did not order Yi Pŏm-sŏk to use the police force in such an overt manner to force through the constitutional amendments, in view of Syngman Rhee's commitment to promoting international endorsement for his government as a crucial pillar of its survival, such an action on his part would seem extremely foolhardy. The international uproar which followed the police action in South Korea could easily have been anticipated by one so sensitive to international opinion as Rhee, and the act did more to undermine international respect for his government abroad than had been gained by all of his previous efforts to secure international endorsement.

77. *Taehan Min'guk chŏngdang-sa*, p. 604.

78. *Taehan Min'guk sŏnko-sa*, p. 474.

79. *Taehan Min'guk chŏngdang-sa*, p. 561.

80. "Sam-il undong-ŭi hoë-sang," *Shinch'ŏnji*, 1.1:28-29 (March 1946) speaks of Han's role in organizing.

81. *Taehan Min'guk sŏnko-sa*, p. 316.

82. Ibid.

83. *The New York Times* (August 10, 1952).

84. *Taehan Min'guk sŏnko-sa*, p. 314.

85. Ibid.

86. Yi Yu, p. 152.

87. Ibid.

88. *Kukhoë sipnyŏnji*, p. 91; *Taehan Min'guk sŏnko-sa*, p. 408. Of the 203 members elected to the third assembly, 114 were members of the Liberal Party, 15 of the DNP, 67 were unaffiliated, 3 of the National Society, 3 of the Korean Nationalist Party, and 1 other.

89. *Kukhoë hoëŭi sokkirok*, November 27, 1954; Mun Hong-ju, "Uri nara hŏnpŏp-sa," *Chŏngkyŏng yŏn'gu* (July 1965), pp. 11-23.

90. Ibid.

91. *Kukhoë imsi hoëŭi sokkirok*, 19th sess., no. 91, November 29, 1954; Pak Il-kyŏng, "Han'guk chŏngbu hyŏng taeŭi pyŏnchŏn," *Chŏngkyŏng yŏn'gu* 1.7:78-91 (August 1965).

92. *Han'guk kunsa hyŏngmyŏng-sa*, pp. 79-80.

93. *Taehan Min'guk sŏnko-sa*, p. 318.

94. Yi Wŏn-sun, p. 29.

95. *Taehan Min'guk sŏnko-sa*, p. 688.

96. Henderson, p. 259. Mr. Henderson was cultural attaché with the American Embassy in Seoul in 1952.

97. Ibid.

98. Rhee's statement to UNCURK, as quoted in Seymour M. Vinocour, "Syngman Rhee: Spokesman for Korea (June 23, 1951–October 8, 1952): A Case Study in International Speaking." Ph.D. dissertation, Pennsylvania State College, 1953, appendix.

99. Hahn Bae-ho and Kim Kyu-taik, *Intergroup Conflicts and Political Decision-Making in Korea* (Seoul, 1965), p. 32.

100. Interview with Dr. Robert T. Oliver, see note 12.

101. Dong-A Ilbo sa, *Dong-A nyŏn'gam, 1969*, p. 963.

102. Ibid.

103. Statistics for 1947 from *Taehan nyŏn'gam, 1952* (Seoul, 1952), pp. 402-403, and for 1956 from *Taehan Min'guk t'onggye nyŏn'gam 1960* (Seoul, 1960), pp. 414-415.

104. Kim Wŏn-su, "Shinmun tongshin kiŏp kyŏng'yŏng shiltae chosa boko," *Seoul Taehakkyo shinmun yŏnkusŏ hakpo* (Seoul, 1965), pp. 123-134.

105. *Taehan Min'guk sŏnko-sa*, p. 688.

106. Kukhoë tosŏkwan ippŏp chosaguk, *Kukhoë tosŏkwan ippŏp chosaguk chamgosŏ* (August 28, 1969), p. 11.

107. *Korea Annual 1968* (Seoul, 1968), p. 187.

108. Kim Kwan Bong, *The Korea-Japan Treaty Crisis and the Instability of the Korean Political System* (New York, 1971), p. 32.

109. Bank of Korea, *Kungmin sodŏk nyŏnbo, 1968* (Seoul, 1968); Bank of Korea, *Chosa wŏlbo* (December 1961).

110. *Korea Annual, 1964*, p. 288.

111. Kim Sŏk-yŏng, *Panmunjŏm* (Seoul, 1972), p. 344.

112. *The New York Times* (June 3, 1952).

113. Ibid. (June 13, 1952).

114. The most notorious of the accounts of the "human curtain" is Kim
     Sŏk-yun, *Kyŏngmudae-ŭi pimil* (Seoul, 1961), written by a former
     secretary to Rhee. See also the best-selling Korean novel by Han Un-sa,
     "Chaldoë kapnida" (Seoul, 1968), a fictionalized account of the "human
     curtain" which became a famous radio series.

115. Domestic press conference, May 26, 1956, as quoted in *Korea Flaming
     High* (Seoul, 1960), IV, 11.

116. Interview with Yi Hyŏng, former reporter for the *Han'guk Ilbo* news-
     paper, in New York, January 14, 1967. The reporter referred to was
     Cho Se-yong of the *Chung'ang Ilbo* and the incident occurred in 1957.

117. *Dong-A Ilbo* (June 27, 1958).

118. Domestic press conference, February 3, 1959, as quoted in *Korea
     Flaming High*, IV, 162.

119. Ibid.

120. Answer to question from Mr. Charles Chin, Associated Press, Foreign
     Press Conference, June 27, 1958, as quoted in *Korea Flaming High*,
     IV, 104-105.

121. *Han'guk Ilbo* (April 1, 1958).

122. Ibid. (January 5, 1959).

123. *The New York Times* (April 28, 1960); see also detailed reports on the
     operation of the system of political financing in *Han'guk hyŏngmyŏng
     chaepan'sa*, pp. 92-98; Ch'oë Tan-yong, pp. 239-246; Song Kŏn-ho,
     pp. 247-255; and Nam Chae-hi, "Chŏngdang unyŏng-kwa tangchaejŏng,"
     Chŏngkyŏng yŏn'gu (February 1967), pp. 132-137.

124. *Han'guk kunsa hyŏngmyŏng-sa*, pp. 100-102, and 140-141; Y Tong-
     hwan, "Chŏngch'i chagŭmŭi amnyŏk," *Sassanggye* (March 1960),
     pp. 68-79.

125. *Han'guk kunsa hyŏngmyŏng-sa*, I, 140-141.

126. Yi Tong-hwan, "Kkekkuthan ŭnhaeng-ŭl mandŭlja," *Sassanggye* (May 1960), pp. 26-39.

127. Wu Pyŏng-kyu, "Kundae naeŭi inkan kwŏn kewajihwa," *Sassanggye* (November 1960), pp. 254-263.

128. Kim Se-jin, *The Politics of Military Revolution in Korea* (Chapel Hill, N.C., 1971), p. 85.

129. Bank of Korea, *Chosa wŏlbo* (December 1961), *Korea Annual 1964*, p. 288.

130. Yi Yu, p. 173; Yi Tong-hwan, "Chongch'i chagŭmŭi amnyŏk"; interview with Dr. Kyu Hong Chyun, former administrative secretary to Syngman Rhee, who said he was informed by Cho Pyŏng-ok. Many former DP members have confirmed this in interviews.

131. *Han'guk kunsa hyŏngmyŏng-sa*, pp. 140-141.

132. Yu Sŭng-t'aek, "Kim Chang-yong-ŭi choëhu," in O So-paek, ed., *Haebang isipnyŏn: Kirok p'yŏn* (Seoul, 1965), pp. 455-488.

133. Yi Yu, p. 221.

134. *Han'guk Ilbo* (August 9, 1956).

135. *Han'guk Ilbo* (August 14, 1956).

136. Ibid. (August 15, 1956).

137. *Han'guk Ilbo* (January 3, 1958).

138. *Korea Annual*, 1964, pp. 540-541, from Economic Planning Board, based on population survey, December 1, 1962; 1944 figures from McCune, *Korea Today*, p. 334, from 1944 Census.

139. Ibid.

140. National Assembly Library, Legislative Reference Service, *Special Report* (August 27, 1969).

141. Sŏul taehakkyo, *Sŏul taehakkyo shinmun yŏnguso hakpo* (Seoul, 1965), II, 123-134.

142. *Kukhoë imsi hoëŭi sokkirok* (April 18, 1957). A similar organization, called "inminban" was formed in the North.

143. *Han'guk hyŏngmyŏng chaepan-sa*, pp. 97-100.

144. *The New York Times* (January 17, 1959).

145. Ibid. (January 18, 1959).

146. Ibid. (January 21, 1959).

147. Ibid. (January 25, 1959).

148. Ibid. (May 2, 1959).

149. *Korea Annual, 1964*, p. 579.

150. Bureau of Statistics, Economic Planning Board, Republic of Korea, *Korea Statistical Yearbook, 1962* (Seoul, 1962).

151. Chu Sock Kyon, "Why American Aid Failed," *Korean Quarterly* 4.1:81-93 (Autumn, 1960).

152. *Korea Annual, 1964*, p. 288.

153. Ibid.

154. Statistics Bureau, Ministry of Home Affairs, *Chae sa-hoë Taehan Min'guk t'onggye nyŏn'gam* (Seoul, 1957), pp. 26-27; Statistics Bureau, *Chae ch'il-hoë Taehan Min'guk t'onggye nyŏn'gam* (Seoul, 1960), pp. 20-21.

155. E.g., *Han'guk Ilbo* (January 5, 1959).

156. *Dong-A Ilbo* (July 30, 1956); *Korea Times* (July 30, 1956).

157. *Kukhoë sokkirok* (July 30, 1956); *Korea Times* (July 31, 1956).

158. *Kyunghyang Shinmun* (August 1, 1956); *Korea Times* (August 1, 1956).

159. Yi Yu, p. 135.

160. Ibid.; *Han'guk kunsa hyŏngmyŏng-sa*, I, 102-103; *Dong-A Ilbo* (February 16, 1960).

161. The election law provided that a candidate could not be replaced if he died during the campaign. The Liberal Party had proposed that this be changed in 1959, but the Democratic Party had refused to accept the proposal, assuming that Rhee would be the most likely person to die, in view of his advanced age. When their candidate died, therefore, they were stuck with their own policy. Kwan-bong Kim, p. 229.

162. *Taehan Min'guk sŏnko-sa*, p. 341.

163. *Dong-A Ilbo* (February 13 and 20, 1960).

164. *Dong-A Ilbo* (March 17, 1960).

165. *Han'guk kunsa hyŏngmyŏng chaep'an-sa, I,* 155-163.

166. Minju Han'guk hyŏngmyŏng-sa p'yonch'an wiwonhoe, *Minju Han'guk hyŏngmyŏng-sa* (Seoul, 1962), p. 9, gives the number killed as 101, *Dong-A Ilbo* (April 21, 1960), indicates the number of deaths was 97. Some may have subsequently died of wounds.

167. *The New York Times* (April 27, 1960).

168. C.I. Eugene Kim and Kim Ke Soo, "The April 1960 Korean Student Movement," *The Western Political Quarterly* (March 1964), pp. 83-92.

169. Yi Pŏm-sŏk, et al., selection by General Song, p. 470.

170. Ibid.

171. Ibid.

172. C.I. Eugene Kim and Kim Ke Soo.

173. Ibid.

174. Ibid.

V. Reconsolidation and Establishment of a "Socialist" Political System in North Korea, 1948-1961

1. *Pukhan ch'ongkam*, p. 125.

2. Rudolph, pp. 17-18.

3. McCune, *Korea Today*, p. 274.

4. *Pukhan ch'ongkam*, p. 125.

5. Ibid.

6. Kim Il Sung later married Hong's daughter after his first wife died in 1949.

7. Backgrounds of the participants in the North Korean government and party are drawn primarily from *Kibon chŏngbo*. The South Koreans were: Pak Hŏn-yŏng, Hong Myŏng-hŭi (to become Kim Il Sung's father-in-law soon thereafter), Chŏng Chun-t'aek (one of Kim Il Sung's partisan comrades), Pak Mun-gyu, Hŏ Chŏng-suk, Paek Nam-un, Yi Pyŏng-nam, and Yi Sŭng-hwa.

8. Miss Hŏ (who had studied law in Japan, and spent 1927-1928 in the United States) was later to become the minister of justice and then the chief justice of the North Korean Supreme Court, before being purged in 1961.

9. *Pravda* (February 5, 1949).

10. "Special cities" are cities administered on the same level as provinces, rather than placed under provincial administration. In 1949, North Korea had only one special city (Pyongyang). Since then a second special city (Hamhŭng) has been added. The same system exists in the South, where Seoul was originally the only "special city" but Pusan was later added.

11. *Pukhan ch'ongkam*, p. 149.

12. V.A. Kim, pp. 76-78.

13. Rudolph, p. 49.

14. Pak Tong-un, p. 204.

15. Kim Ch'ang-sun, *Pukhan*, p. 233.

16. Chŏngbo-kuk Oëmu-pu, *Pukhan isipnyŏn*.

17. Kim Il Sung, *Kim Il-sŏng sŏnjip*, VI, 269.

18. *Kibon chŏngbo.*

19. Kim Il Sung, *Kim Il-sŏng sŏnjip*, II, 151-152.

20. Ibid.

21. *Third Congress Documents*, p. 78.

22. *Pukhan ch'ongkam*, p. 146.

23. Ibid.

24. Rudolph, p. 40.

25. *Postwar Rehabilitation and Development of the National Economy in the Democratic People's Republic of Korea* (Pyongyang, 1957), p. 58.

26. See Joungwon A. Kim, "North Korea's Economic Progress."

27. Paige, *The Korean People's Democratic Republic*, pp. 31-32.

28. *Han'guk chŏngjaeng-sa* (Seoul, 1967), p. 729.

29. *Korea Annual, 1967*, p. 187.

30. U.S. Department of State, *Techniques of Takeover*, p. 85.

31. Kim Il Sung, *Kim Il-sŏng sŏnjip*, I, 371-377.

32. U.S. Department of State, *Techniques of Takeover*, p. 85.

33. Kim Sam-kyu, *Konnichi no Chōsen* (Tokyo, 1956), pp. 34-35.

34. See, for example, *Democratic People's Republic of Korea* (Pyongyang, 1958), pp. 93-95, which outlines and even charts the "enemy's attack plan," and such books as Irving F. Stone, *The Hidden History of the Korean War* (New York, 1952), which suggests that the U.S. military and South Korea deliberately lured North Korea into the attack (which proves what?), and Wilfred G. Burchett, *Again Korea* (New York, 1967), which adheres to the North Korean line. For a South Korean version, see Oh Che-do.

35. Kim Sam-kyu, pp. 32-44 (this writer is a Korean neutralist who resides in Japan); *Seoul Shinmun* (May 14, 1949).

36. Statement of Secretary of State Dean Acheson at the National Press Club, January 12, 1950. *United States Department of State Bulletin* (January 23, 1950), pp. 111-116.

37. *The New York Times* (October 18, 1949).

38. U.S. Department of State, *Korea's Independence*, p. 118.

39. Kim Il Sung, *Kim Il-sŏng sŏnjip*, IV, 330-331.

40. U.S. Department of State, *Korea's Independence*.

41. Kim Il Sung was much later to charge the U.S.S.R. with having practiced economic imperialism—importing from North Korea its basic raw materials and metals for prices far below the normal world market value, and then exporting goods to North Korea at prices far above the world market prices. *Nodong Shinmun* (September 7, 1964).

42. Kim Sang-hak, p. 16.

43. *Chosŏn chung'ang nyŏn'gam, 1961* (Pyongyang, 1961), p. 321.

44. *Chosŏn chung'ang nyŏn'gam, 1951-52* (Pyongyang, 1952), p. 82.

45. V.A. Kim, pp. 153-154.

46. For background on the Chinese intervention in the Korean War, see Allen S. Whiting, *China Crosses the Yalu: The Decision to Enter the Korean War* (New York, 1960). For South and North Korean versions see *Pukhan ch'ongkam*, p. 964, and *Democratic People's Republic of Korea*, p. 100.

47. Kim Il Sung, *Kim Il-sŏng sŏnjip*, IV, 358.

48. Kim Ch'ang-sun, *Pukhan*, p. 131.

49. Kim Il Sung, *Kim Il-sŏng sŏnjip*, III, 137-140.

50. Ibid., III, 196.

51. Kim Ch'ang-sun, *Pukhan*, p. 59.

52. *Pukkwe*, p. 41.

53. Chŏngbo-kuk Oëmu-pu, *Pukhan isipnyŏn*, p. 61.

54. Kim Ch'ang-sun, *Pukhan*, p. 131.

55. *Kibon chŏngbo*.

56. Tsubōe Senji, *Hokusen*, p. 86.

57. *The New York Times* (June 24, 1951).

58. Pang In-hu, *Pukhan Chosŏn nodong-dang-ŭi hyŏngsŏng kwa palchŏn* (Seoul, 1967), p. 146.

59. *Puknodang chae i-ch'a chŏndang taehoë hoëŭirok* (Pyongyang, 1948), p. 258.

60. Kim Il Sung, *Kim Il-sŏng sŏnjip*, III, 295-297.

61. Ibid., IV, 358-359.

62. Yi Pyŏng-do, et al., p. 661.

63. *Kibon chŏngbo*.

64. Rudolph, p. 20.

65. Chosŏn minjujui inmin konghwaguk ch'oëgo chaep'anso, *Michaegukjui kanch'ŏp Pak Hŏn-yŏng, Yi Sung-yŏp, to tang-ŭi Chosŏn minjujŭi inmin konghwaguk chŏngkwŏn chŏnpok ŭnmo-wa kanch'ŏp sakŏn kongp'an munhŏn* (Pyongyang, 1956), pp. 159-160.

66. Ibid., p. 102.

67. *Pukkwe*, p. 136.

68. Chŏngbo-kuk Oëmu-pu, *Pukhan isipnyŏn*, p. 62. Among prominent South Korean members purged, in addition to Pak Hŏn-yŏng and Yi Sung-yŏp, were Pae Ch'ŏl, Pak Sŭng-wŏn, Yun Sun-tal, Cho Il-hong,

Im Hwa, Yi Wŏn-cho, Maeng Chŏng-ho, Yi Kang-kuk, Sŏl Chŏng-sik, Paek Hyŏng-pok, Cho Yong-pok, and Yu Yŏng-chun.

69. *Pukkwe*, p. 22.

70. Ibid., p. 24.

71. *Kibon chŏngbo*, p. 170.

72. *Development of the National Economy and Culture of the People's Democratic Republic of Korea, 1946-1959* (Washington, D.C., October 31, 1960), pp. 30-31.

73. *Postwar Rehabilitation and Development of the National Economy of the Democratic People's Republic of Korea* (Pyongyang, 1957), p. 8.

74. North Korea's population, according to official statistics, was 8,491,000 on January 1, 1953, as compared with 9,622,000 at the end of 1949. By 1953, only 46.9 percent of the population was male. *Chosŏn chung'ang nyŏn'gam*, 1961, p. 321.

75. Vsevolod Holubnychy, "Soviet Economic Aid to North Korea," *Bulletin of the Institute for the Study of the U.S.S.R.* 4.1:19 (January 1957).

76. *Chosŏn chung'ang nyŏn'gam*, 1961, pp. 339-340.

77. Kim Il Sung, *Kim Il-sŏng sŏnjip*, IV, 177.

78. *Chosŏn chung'ang nyŏn'gam, 1959* (Pyongyang, 1959), p. 322.

79. Ibid.

80. Kim Il Sung, *The Selected Works of Kim Il Sung* (Pyongyang, 1965), II, 522.

81. See Joungwon A. Kim, "Soviet Policy in North Korea," *World Politics*, vol. 22 (January 1970), pp. 237-251.

82. If we accept Kim Il Sung's figures that there were 600,000 members in 1950, of whom 300,000 had been purged by September 1951 when he intervened to stop the purge, and an additional 450,000 were added between 1951 and 1953.

83. *Chosŏn nodong-dang chaesamcha taehoë chuyo munhŏnjip*, p. 71.

84. Ibid., p. 84.

85. Ibid.

86. *Chosŏn chung'ang nyŏn'gam*, 1959, p. 330.

87. Ibid.

88. Kim Il Sung, *Kim Il-sŏng sŏnjip*, IV, 267-268.

89. Ibid., pp. 335-336.

90. Kim Il Sung, *Kim Il-sŏng sŏnjip*, IV, 326.

91. Ibid., p. 336.

92. *Kibon chŏngbo*, p. 397.

93. South Korea figures from *Dong-A nyŏn'gam, 1969*, p. 963; North Korea figures from *Pukhan ch'ongkam*, p. 36.

94. South Korea had 90,104 students in colleges and universities in 1956. *Taehan Min'guk t'onggye nyŏn'gam, 1960*, pp. 414-415. North Korea had 22,458 students in colleges and universities during the same year. *Chosŏn chung'ang nyŏn'gam*, 1959, p. 41.

95. Statistics on South Korea's employed work force, from which the percentages are derived, are from Naemupu t'ongkaeguk, *Chae sahwae Taehan Min'guk t'onggye nyŏn'gam* (Seoul, 1957), pp. 26-27. The percentage statistics for North Korea's employed labor force are from *Chosŏn chung'ang nyŏn'gam*, 1961, p. 321.

96. *Chosŏn nodong-dang chaesam-ch'a taehoë chuyo munhŏnjip*, p. 348.

97. Ibid.

98. Ibid., p. 350.

99. *Nodong Shinmun*, October 28, 1963.

100. Figures on economic assistance to North Korea are from Han'guk

chung'ang chŏngbo-pu, *Pukkwe hyŏnhwang* (Seoul, March 1971), pp. 152-154. See also Japan External Trade Organization, *How to Approach the China Market* (Tokyo, 1972), p. 52.

101. *Pukkwe*.

102. Kim Il Sung, *The Selected Works of Kim Il Sung*, pp. 579-80. Emphasis added.

103. *Pukhan ch'ongkam*, p. 146.

104. Ibid., p. 125.

105. *Chosŏn chung'ang nyŏn'gam*, 1961, p. 321.

106. Exact figures on the size of the bureaucracy are not available. However, percentages are given on office workers, and since by 1958 the economy was classified as fully "socialized" these office workers were all bureaucratic employees of the regime. According to these figures, 8.5 percent of the working population were office workers in 1953 and 13.6 percent in 1956. In 1959, when the next statistics became available, they made up 13.4 percent, but this was after the initiation of the Ch'ŏllima Movement when 50 percent of their number was said to have been diverted into the industrial work force. *Chosŏn chung'ang nyŏn'gam*, 1961, p. 321.

107. Yi Tong-chun, *Hwansang kwa hyŏnsil* (Seoul, 1961). Mr. Lee (Yi) was a *Pravda* correspondent in Pyongyang before his defection to the South.

108. Kim Il Sung, *Modon munje haeyŏreso chungsim kokirŭl t'unt'unhi t'ŭrŏ chapko kŭe yŏgyanggŭl* (Pyongyang, 1959), p. 12.

109. *Pukkwe hyŏnhwang*, p. 153.

110. Yi Tong-chun, p. 218.

111. See Lee Chong-Sik, "Land Reform, Collectivisation, and the Peasants in North Korea."

112. See Joungwon A. Kim, "The 'Peak of Socialism' in North Korea: The Five and Seven Year Plans," *Asian Survey* 5:225-269 (May 1965).

113. *Pukkwe hyŏnhwang*, p. 152.

114. Kim Sam-kyu, "Senri no koma undōno haikei," *Korea Review* 3:4-5 (September 1959).

115. *Documents of the Fourth Congress of the Workers' Party of Korea* (Pyongyang, 1961), p. 103.

116. *Tongnip chŏngshin*, p. 93.

117. Kim Il Sung, *Kim Il-sŏng sŏnjip*, IV, 379.

118. *Tongnip chŏngshin*, p. 33.

119. This and the statistics which follow are from the following sources: *Pukhan ch'ongkam*, pp. 123, 146; *Chosŏn chung'ang nyŏn'gam, 1961*; Economic Planning Board, *First Five Year Economic Development Plan* (Seoul, June 1964); *Tong-a nyŏn'gam, 1969*, p. 963; *Toitsu Chōsen nenkan, 1968*, p. 553; Legislative Reference Service, National Assembly Library, Republic of Korea, *Special Report*, August 27, 1969.

120. *Kibon chŏngbo*, p. 170.

VI. Attempted Introduction of the Second Republic in South Korea, 1960-1961

1. *Kyunghyang Shinmun* (June 2, 1960).

2. *Han'guk nyŏn'gam, 1961* (Seoul, 1961), p. 51.

3. Ibid.

4. The text of the 1960 constitution appears in *Military Revolution in Korea*, ed. Secretariat of the Supreme Council for National Reconstruction (Seoul, 1961), pp. 113-148.

5. Ibid.

6. *Taehan Min'guk chŏngdang-sa*, pp. 607-608.

7. Sŏ Pyŏng-jo, *Chukwŏnjaŭi chŭngŏn: Han'guk taeŭi chŏngch'i-sa* (Seoul, 1963), pp. 365-366.

8.   *Taehan Min'guk chŏngdang-sa*, p. 193; *Dong-A Ilbo* (August 19, 1960).

9.   For a history of the *Hŭngsadan*, see Hŭngsadan-sa pyŏnchan wiwŏnhoë, *Hŭngsadan osipnyŏn-sa* (Seoul, 1964).

10. C.I. Eugene Kim and Kim Ke-soo, pp. 83–92.

11. Sŏ Pyŏng-jo, p. 377.

12. Lee Hahn-Been, *Korea: Time, Change, and Administration* (Honolulu, 1968), p. 129.

13. Ibid. See also Kim Sang-cho, "Naegak chaekimjae-ŭi palso pyongchil hako itda," *Sassanggye* (December 1960), pp. 46–51.

14. *Dong-A Ilbo* (November 8–9, 1960); see Han T'ae-yun, "Kungmu chŏngnikun," *Sassanggye* (October 1960), pp. 30–37.

15. Yun Po-sŏn in Yi Pŏm-sŏk, et al., p. 300.

16. *Dong-A Ilbo* (May 4, 1961).

17. Henderson, p. 178.

18. Lee Hahn-Been, p. 138.

19. Hahn Bae-ho and Kim Kyu-taik, "Korean Political Leaders (1952–1962): Their Social Origins and Skills," *Asian Survey* (July 1963), pp. 305–323.

20. *Dong-A Ilbo* (December 28, 1960).

21. Richard C. Allen, "South Korea: The New Regime," *Pacific Affairs*, 34.1: 54 (Spring 1961).

22. Stephen Bradner, "Korea: Experiment and Instability," *Japan Quarterly*, 8.4: 414 (October-December 1961). See also Han Nae Bok, "April Anniversary in Korea," *Far Eastern Economic Review* (May 4, 1961), p. 208, where Han Nae Bok estimates the number at 1.2 million participants.

23. *Military Revolution in Korea*, p. 15, based on a count of 1,835 demonstrations and 969,630 participants.

24. Chang Myŏn, "Chang Myŏn p'yŏn" in Yi Pŏm-sŏk, et al., pp. 382-383.

25. *Han'guk Ilbo* (October 15, 1960).

26. Civil Rights Law, no. 587, December 21, 1960, as printed in Ch'ŏngyang yukpŏp p'yŏnch'an wiwŏnhoë, *Yukpŏp chŏnsŏ* (Seoul, 1961), pp. 28-30.

27. *Kyunghyang Shinmun* (December 31, 1960).

28. *Han'guk hyŏngmyŏng chaep'an-sa*, pt. 1, p. 258.

29. Ibid.

30. A random poll of 377 students at Korea University in 1961 found that 86 percent felt that Western democracy was inapplicable to Korea. Forty percent of these chose the response "We are not prepared," while another 30 percent responded that because of the "socio-cultural gap" between Korea and the West, the principles of democracy could not yet be realized in Korea. See Hong Sŏng-chik, "Taehaksaeng'un muŏsŭl saeng'gakhakko itna?" *Sassanggya* (April 1962), p. 122.

31. *Chung'ang sŏnko kwalli wiwŏn-hoë*, pp. 433-434.

32. *Dong-A Ilbo* (December 28, 1960).

33. *Hapdong nyŏn'gam, 1964* (Seoul, 1964), p. 43; *Dong-A Ilbo* (May 4, 7, 13, 1961).

34. Kukhoë tongil yŏn'gu t'ukpŏl wiwŏnhoë, *Tongil paksŏ* (Seoul, 1967), p. 291.

35. Kyŏngche kaeŭewon, *Kyŏngche paksŏ* (Seoul, 1963), pp. 2-3; Han Nae Bok, "Readjusting the Rate," *Far Eastern Economic Review* (February 23, 1961), pp. 335-337; *Minŭiwŏn hoëŭirok*, 38 sess. 32 meeting, February 27, 1961, p. 1.

36. Han'guk unhaeng chosabu, *Kyŏngchae tonggye nyŏnbo* (Seoul, 1963), pp. 2-3.

37. *Minŭiwŏn hoëüirok*, 38 sess., 32 meeting, February 2, 1961, p. 8; Han Nae Bok, "April Anniversary," pp. 208-211.

38. *Han'guk kunsa hyŏngmyŏng-sa*, I, p. 124.

39. One deal known to have been concluded for the purpose of bringing in funds to the party was an arrangement between a government minister and a Japanese firm to sell Korean tungsten to the Japanese far below the market value in exchange for a large bribe paid to the minister, presumably for party activities. *Minŭiwŏn hoëüirok*, 38 sess., 34 meeting, March 2, 1961, pp. 3-31; *Dong-A Ilbo* (March 7 and 15, 1961).

40. *Kyŏngchae paksŏ*, p. 52.

41. *Dong-A Ilbo* (March 14, and May 7, 1961).

42. Han Nae Bok, "April Anniversary," p. 208.

43. *Han'guk hyŏngmyŏng chaep'an-sa*, pt. 1, p. 258.

44. *Han'guk kunsa hyŏngmyŏng*, p. 47.

45. Interview with Lt. Gen. Ch'oë Kyŏng-rok in 1964, cited in Kim Se Jin, *Military Revolution in Korea* (Ph.D. dissertation, University of Massachusetts, 1966), p. 173.

46. *Hapdong nyŏn'gam, 1961* (Seoul, 1961), pp. 152-153.

47. Ibid.

48. Lee Hahn-Been, p. 97.

49. *Dong-A Ilbo* (February 18, 1961).

50. Wu Pyŏng-kyu, pp. 254-263.

51. David C. Cole and Princeton N. Lyman, *Korean Development: The Interplay of Politics and Economics* (Cambridge, Mass., 1971), p. 274, fn 5.

52. Ibid.

53. *Han'guk hyŏngmyŏng chaep'an-sa*, I, 914-916; Wu Pyŏng-gyu, pp. 254-263.

54. *Han'guk kunsa hyŏngmyŏng-sa*, pp. 195-196; *Hapdong nyŏn'gam, 1961*, p. 135.

55. Daniel Wolfstone, "The Generals Strike," *Far Eastern Economic Review* (May 25, 1961), p. 348.

56. Kang In-sŏp, "Yuksa p'algi seng," *Shindong-a* (September 1964), pp. 170-198.

57. Hahn Bae-ho and Kim Kyu-taik, "Korean Political Leaders," p. 309.

58. Ibid.

59. *Han'guk hyŏngmyŏng chaep'an-sa*, p. 248.

60. Hong Sŏng-chik, "Taehaksaeng'un . . ," p. 122; Hong Sung Chick, *The Intellectual and Modernization: A Study of Korean Attitudes* (Seoul, 1967).

61. Hahm Pyong Choon, "Politics of Melancholy: The Recent Experiences of the Korean Polity," unpublished paper prepared for the Peace Corps

62. Hong Sŏng-chik, "Taehaksaeng'un . . ," p. 122; Hong Sung Chick, *The Intellectual and Modernization.*

63. Hong Sung Chick, *The Intellectual and Modernization*, p. 194.

64. Hahn Bae-ho and Kim Kyu-taik, p. 316.

65. Ibid., p. 322.

66. Ibid.

VII. Military Rule and the Third Republic in South Korea, 1961-1971

1. Kang In-sŏp, "Minjudang chŏngwŏn ch'oëhu-ŭi nal," *Shindong-a* (May 1965), pp. 100-101.

2.   Ibid.

3.   Koreans, who are fascinated by intrigue, love to speculate about whether
      the United States in fact planned the coup, especially in view of parallel
      events in Vietnam and Indonesia (and later Cambodia?). If so, it would
      have had to have been done by the CIA without the approval of the
      State Department, the U.S. Command in Korea, and without the endorse-
      ment of President Kennedy, whose attitude toward the coup-makers
      was very unreceptive. Such a situation seems unlikely. Yet the circum-
      stantial factors pointing to the U.S. involvement are interesting: the
      Korean students had agreed to meet with North Koreans at Panmunjom
      four days after the coup occurred; the coup in Vietnam was clearly
      encouraged and endorsed by the United States, one reason apparently
      being that Ngo Dinh Nhu was trying to make a secret rapprochement
      with North Vietnam; the coup in Indonesia occurred because the
      Communists were becoming overly-powerful (and in Cambodia,
      Sinhanouk was not taking sufficiently strong measures against the
      Viet Cong). Marshall Green was stationed in Korea at the time of the
      Korean coup and in Indonesia at the time of the Indonesian coup.
      Kim Jong Pil, who engineered the coup, was in Korean Army intelli-
      gence. His "CIA," created as the initial instrument of organization
      after the coup, was based on the core of the Army intelligence group,
      and developed a direct link with the U.S. CIA for intelligence pur-
      poses. Furthermore, plans for the coup had begun before the overthrow
      of Rhee, the charismatic nationalist leadership symbol, and the other
      Asian coups were carried out against similar leaders: Diem, Sukarno,
      and Sihanouk. Many Koreans, who are very skeptical of accidental
      coincidences, visualize this as a part of a grand anti-Communist strategy
      being conducted by the CIA, with Mr. Green as a super-strategist. In
      view of the CIA-sponsored invasion of Cuba later in 1961, and the
      obvious American endorsement of the coup against Diem in South
      Vietnam, the theory is not unreasonable. However, it seems dubious
      in view of the apparent American satisfaction with the Chang govern-
      ment, and the icy reception given to the military regime.

4.   U.S. Department of State, *A Historical Summary of United States-
      Korean Relations* (Washington, 1962), p. 135.

5.   Ibid.

6.   Oh, p. 111.

7. Ibid., p. 112.

8. Ibid.

9. *Han'guk kunsa hyŏngmyŏng-sa*, I, 252. Also Walter Briggs, "The Military Revolution in Korea: Its Leader and Achievements," *Koreana Quarterly*, 5:31-32 (Summer 1963).

10. *The Korea Times* (May 18, 1961).

11. Minju Han'guk hyŏngmyŏng ch'ŏng-sa p'yŏnch'an wiwŏnhoë, *Minju Han'guk hyŏngmyŏng ch'ŏng-sa* (Seoul, 1961).

12. *Dong-A Ilbo* (May 31, 1961).

13. U.S. Department of State, *American Foreign Policy: Current Documents, 1961* (Washington, D.C., 1965), p. 974.

14. United Press International (May 19, 1961).

15. U.S. Department of State, *American Foreign Policy*, p. 975.

16. Mun Myŏng-ho, "Yaebiyŏk changsŏngdŭl," *Shindong-a* (December 1967), pp. 132-152.

17 See Kim Se Jin, "Military Revolution in Korea," p. 180.

18. *Han'guk kunsa hyŏngmyŏng-sa*, I, 915.

19. Ibid.

20. Paek Nam-ju, ed., *Hyŏngmyŏng chidoja Pak Chŏng-hŭi-ron* (Seoul, 1969), pp. 39-42.

21. The Officers Candidate School became the Korean Military Academy when it was converted into a four-year institution. The classes are numbered consecutively from the first class trained at the OCS. As previously noted (Chapter VI), the earliest classes received only a few weeks of training, whereas by the middle of the Korean War cadets were receiving four years of intensive training.

22. Henderson.

23. Kim Kyŏng-rae, "Chŏnhyangja-nya, ani-nya?" *Sassanggye* (October 1963), pp. 102-110; *The New York Times* (May 20, 1961).

24. *Minju Han'guk hyŏngmyŏng ch'ŏng-sa*, p. 130; *The New York Times* (May 23, 1961).

25. *Minju Han'guk hyŏngmyŏng ch'ŏng-sa*, p. 351.

26. Ibid., p. 353.

27. Ibid., pp. 353 and 358.

28. *Han'guk Ilbo* (June 4, 1969).

29. *Han'guk hyŏngmyŏng chaep'an-sa*, p. 963.

30. Ibid., p. 980.

31. Kim Se Jin, "Military Revolution in Korea," pp. 149-156.

32. Ibid., p. 155.

33. *The New York Times* (June 7, 1961).

34. *Han'guk Ilbo* (May 22, 1961).

35. Kim Se Jin, "Military Revolution in Korea," p. 81.

36. *The New York Times* (May 29, 1961).

37. O Ŭng-hwan, "Korich'ae chŏngni" in *Haebang isipnyŏn* (Seoul, 1965), pp. 656-657.

38. Park Chung Hee, *The Country, The Revolution and I* (Seoul, 1962), p. 63.

39. Kim Se Jin, "Military Revolution in Korea," p. 12.

40. *Dong-A Ilbo* (May 28, 1961).

41. "Minju-jŭi wa kunsa hyŏngmyŏng," *Sassanggye*, 9:4 (June 1961).

42. *Koreana Quarterly* (Summer 1961), pp. 7-17.

43. *The Philadelphia Inquirer* (July 5, 1961).

44. *Korea Annual, 1969* (Seoul, 1969), p. 109.

45. Berger, p. 209.

46. *Korean Report*, 1.4:2 (October 1961).

47. *The New York Times* (November 16, 1961).

48. *Han'guk kunsa hyŏngmyŏng-sa*, II, 610.

49. Kim Kwan Bong, p. 16.

50. *Han'guk kunsa hyŏngmyŏng-sa*, II, 610.

51. Kim Se Jin, *The Politics of Military Revolution in Korea*, p. 232.

52. *Koreana Quarterly* (Summer 1961), p. 7.

53. *Minju Han'guk hyŏngmyŏng ch'ŏng-sa*, p. 131.

54. Kim Kwan Bong, p. 158.

55. *Minju Han'guk hyŏngmyŏng ch'ŏng-sa*, p. 130.

56. Kim Yŏng-su, "Minju konghwa-dang sajŏn chojik," *Shindong-a* (November 1964), pp. 168-173.

57. It has also been pointed out that it resembled the structure of the Kuomintang (KMT) of Taiwan, but since both the North Korean Workers' Party and the KMT were patterned after the Communist Party of the Soviet Union, the parallel is not surprising. The KMT was built in the 1920's with Soviet organizational advice. See Cole and Lyman, p. 41, and Henderson, p. 305, for the suggestion that the DRP was patterned after the KMT rather than after the KWP of the North.

58. *The DRP Bulletin*, 1.10: 25-28 (December 1966).

59. Kim Kyŏng-rae, "Chŏnhyangja, ani-nya?" pp. 102-110.

60. Ibid.

61. *Han'guk kunsa hyŏngmyŏng-sa*, IB, 652-653.

62. *Taehan Min'guk chŏngdang-sa*, p. 258.

63. Kim Se Jin, "Military Revolution in Korea," pp. 149-156.

64. *Taehan Min'guk chŏngdang-sa*, p. 204.

65. Ibid., p. 205.

66. *Dong-A Ilbo* (June 16, 1962).

67. Economic Planning Board, Republic of Korea, *Summary Draft of the Five Year Economic Plan (1962-1966)*, (Seoul, 1961), p. 24.

68. Reeve, p. 168.

69. Oh, p. 142.

70. *Han'guk Ilbo* (September 25, 1963); *Korea Annual, 1964*, p. 137. See also Sohn Jae-Souck, "The Role of the Military in the Republic of Korea," paper presented to the International Sociological Association, Evian, France. 1966.

71. *The New York Times* (April 7, 1963); *Time* (April 19, 1963); *Newsweek* (April 22, 1963); *The New York Times* (February 15, 1968).

72. Kim Kwan Bong, p. 56.

73. *Kukhoë hoëŭirok*, 40 sess., February 10, 1964, p. 4; *Hanil hoëdam paeksŏ*, p. 49.

74. *Chosŏn Ilbo* and *Dong-A Ilbo* (March 27, 1967); *Korea Annual, 1965*, pp. 16-18.

75. *Chosŏn Ilbo* (July 29, 1965 and August 11, 1965).

76. *Hŏnpŏp kahunan haesŏl* (Seoul, 1962).

77. *Taehan Min'guk sŏnko-sa*, p. 392.

78. "Nation's First Referendum Approves New Constitution," *Korean Report*, 2:3 (November-December, 1962).

79. Hong Soon-il, "On Current Political Phenomena," *Korean Affairs*, 2.1:98 (1963).

80. *Han'guk kunsa hyŏngmyŏng-sa*, IB, 662-664.

81. *Korean Republic Weekly* (January 2, 1963).

82. *Minju konghwa-dang sa nyŏn-sa*, p. 35.

83. *Taehan Min'guk chŏngdang-su*, p. 258.

84. Ibid.

85. *Taehan Min'guk sŏnko-sa*, p. 398.

86. Kim Kyŏng-rae, "Chŏnhyangja-nya, ani-nya?" pp. 102-110.

87. *Taehan Min'guk sŏnko-sa*, p. 393.

88. Yu Hyŏk-in, "Pak Taet'ongnyŏng-ŭl umjigi-nun salamdŭl," *Shindong-a* (October 1964), pp. 158-159.

89. Ibid.

90. *Han'guk kunsa hyŏngmyŏng-sa*, I, 73-74.

91. *Kyunghyang Shinmun* (February 18, 1963).

92. United Press International, Washington, D.C., February 18, 1963.

93. Han T'ae-su, *Hyŏndae Han'guk chŏngchiron* (Seoul, 1968), p. 204.

94. Kim Kyŏng-rae, "Chŏnhwanjŏm-ŭi sum chŏngdangdŭl," *Sassanggye* (December 1963), pp. 49-50; Berger, p. 214.

95. *The New York Times* (April 3, 1963).

96. Ibid.

97. United Press International, Washington, D.C., March 25, 1963.

98. "Han'guk-ŭi chŏngchi kyŏngchejŏk hyŏnsil-kwa elite-ŭi kwajae," *Chŏngkyŏng yŏn'gu*, vol. 1, no. 6 (Seoul, July 1965).

99. *The Washington Evening Star* (March 21, 1963).

100. *Dong-A Ilbo* (March 19, 20, 22, and April 4, 1963).

101. Bank of Korea, *Economic Statistics Yearbook*, 1967, table 1, pp. 2-3.

102. Ibid.

103. *Korea Annual, 1964,* p. 291.

104. Ibid., p. 290.

105. Economic Planning Board, *First Five Year Economic Development Supplementary Plan* (Seoul, 1964).

106. *Korea Annual, 1964*, p. 201.

107. *Dong-A Ilbo* (September 19, 1963).

108. *The Korean Republic* (August 23, 1963).

109. *Minju konghwa-dang sa nyŏn sa*, p. 127.

110. Ibid., pp. 76-77, 106, and 563; Minju konghwa-dang, *Kyŏngrang-ŭl hech'iko: Minju konghwa-dang i nyŏn-sa* (Seoul, 1964), p. 45; *The Korean Republic* (August 30, 1963).

111. *The Korean Republic* (August 13, 1963).

112. *Taehan Min'guk sŏnko-sa*, p. 491.

113. Cho Il-mun, "Chŏngch'i chagŭm-ŭi yironkwa hyŏnshilchŏk koch'al," *Sassanggye* (February 1970), pp. 45-70.

114. *Minju konghwa-dang sa nyŏn-sa*, p. 146.

115. *Taehan Min'guk sŏnko-sa*, pp. 491 and 627.

116. "Sahoë sip'yŏng," *Sassanggye* (October 1963), pp. 88-89.

117. *Dong-A Ilbo* (May 5, 1967). This article compares statistics for the 1963 and 1967.

118. Eighty-eight of the DRP's seats were won in the district elections, and twenty-two additional seats were apportioned from the forty-four proportional seats on the basis of the percentage of district seats won.

119. *Taehan Min'guk sŏnko-sa*, p. 491.

120. *Dong-A Ilbo* (September 5, 1963); *Han'guk Ilbo* (December 28, 1960).

121. Kim Kwan Bong, p. xviii.

122. *The New York Times* (August 1, 1965).

123. *Chosŏn Ilbo* (December 23, 1964).

124. *Dong A Ilbo* (January 11-14, 1965).

125. "3.24 (sam isipsa) tansi ŭi taehaksaeng ŭi chŏngchi'i ŭisik," *Sae kyoyuk*, no. 120: 39-45 (October 1964).

126. *Dong-A Ilbo* (April 11, 1961).

127. *Han'guk Ilbo* (April 28, 1961).

128. J. Mark Mobius, "The Japan-Korea Normalization Process and Korean Anti-Americanism," *Asian Survey* (April 1966), p. 244.

129. *Han'guk Ilbo* (June 8, 1964).

130. Kim Kwan Bong, p. 79.

131. "Five Point Communique" (with Foreign Minister Yi Tong-won), *The Korean Republic Weekly* (October 7, 1964).

132. *Korea Annual 1967*, p. 165.

133. *Kyunghyang Shinmun* (January 10, 1964).

134. Shin Sang-ch'o, "Kunsa tokjaeka namginkŏt," *Sassanggye* (September 1963), p. 72; Han Sŏk-hŏn, "Han-il hoëdamŭl chipŏ ch'iura," *Sassanggye* (September 1963), p. 50.

135. *Minju konghwa-dang sa nyŏn-sa*, p. 228.

136. Ibid., p. 236.

137. Kim Kwan Bong, p. 153.

138. O Sso-paek, ed., *Haebang isipnyŏn: Charyop'yŏn* (Seoul, 1965), p. 183.

139. *The New York Times* (June 7 and 15, 1964).

140. *Kyunghyang Shinmun* (September 23, 1964).

141. See Lee Chong-Sik, "Korea, Troubles in a Divided State," *Asian Survey* (January 1965), p. 27; *Dong-A Ilbo* (September 23, 1964).

142. Mobius, p. 241.

143. *Dong-A Ilbo* (June 23, 1965).

144. The Korean Federation of Christian Churches had issued a statement in April that "The anti-Japanese struggle is not simply a patriotic act, but . . . a solemn order of God that we have to carry out." *Chosŏn Ilbo* (April 20, 1965).

145. *Minju konghwa-dang sa nyon-sa*, p. 260.

146. Ibid., p. 292.

147. *Dong-A Ilbo* (June 22, 1965).

148. *Chosŏn Ilbo* (June 24, 1965).

149. *Dong-A Ilbo* (March 8, 1966); *Han'guk Ilbo* (March 8, 1966).

150. See Joungwon A. Kim, "Korean Participation in the Vietnam War," *World Affairs* (April, May, June 1966), p. 34.

151. *Korea Annual, 1968*, p. 188; and *Korea Annual, 1969*, p. 202.

152. *Korea Annual, 1969*, p. 197.

153. This kickback system is well-known among Korean business circles and is a more-or-less open secret. It is mentioned in Cole and Lyman, p. 186: "Undoubtedly there was also some collection of payoffs for individuals and for the government's party in connection with the approval of guarantees for these loans; the DRP needed political funds for the election in 1967 and subsequent campaigns." See also Kim Yŏng-sam, "P'yŏng hwajŏk hyŏngmyŏng-ui p'ilyŏnsŏng," *Sassanggye* (December 1969), p. 90, and *Korea Week* (November 6, 1969).

154. *Korea Annual, 1969*, p. 197.

155. *Korea Annual, 1968*, p. 184.

156. United States Operations Mission to Korea, 1969, as cited in Cole and Lyman, p. 135.

157. *Tonghwa nyŏn'gam, 1967*, p. 715.

158. Interview with Washington correspondent of a major Korean newspaper.

159. Cole and Lyman, p. 89.

160. *Chung'ang Ilbo* (August 29, 1966).

161. *Dong-A Ilbo* (August 19, 1966).

162. Paige, *The Korean People's Democratic Republic*, p. 24.

163. *Taehan Min'guk sŏnko-sa*, p. 415.

164. Kenneth G. Clare, et al., *Area Handbook for the Republic of Korea* (Washington, D.C., 1969), pp. 304, 320.

165. *Korea Annual, 1969*, p. 192; Bureau of Statistics, Economic Planning Board, *Han'guk kyŏngche t'ŭkpyŏl pogo* (Seoul, August 1970).

166. *Dong-A nyŏn'gam, 1969*, p. 963.

167. Economic Planning Board, *Major Economic Indicators*, March 1969.

168. *Han'guk kyŏngche t'ŭkpyŏl pogo*.

169. U.S. Department of Agriculture, Economic Research Service, *The Far East and Oceania Agricultural Data Book* (Washington, D.C., May 1967), p. 22; Bank of Korea, *Economic Statistics Yearbook 1967* (Seoul, 1968), p. 146.

170. Hong Song Chick, *The Intellectual and Modernization*, p. 193.

171. Cole and Lyman, p. 226.

172. National Assembly Legislative Research Bureau, "Reference Sources," August 28, 1969.

173. *Taehan Min'guk sŏnko-sa, 1968*, p. 583.

174. Mitsu Haru Masaki, "Daitoryo Senkyo Kankoku no Seijo," *Kokusai Mondai*, no. 88: 10-17 (July 1967); *Taehan Min'guk sŏnko-sa*, p. 583.

175. *Taehan Min'guk sŏnko-sa*, p. 544.

176. See Cho Soon Sung, "Korea: Election Year," *Asian Survey* (January 1968), p. 36.

177. *Taehan Min'guk sŏnko-sa*, pp. 544 and 755.

178. See Cole and Lyman, p. 226, written by two economists who see legitimacy through economic development as a central thesis of contemporary Korean development. Note also Cho Soon Sung, "Korea; Election Year," p. 36.

179. Y.C. Han, "Political Parties and Political Development in South Korea," *Pacific Affairs*, 42:457 (Winter, 1969-70).

180. *Chosŏn Ilbo* (May 26, 1968).

181. *Dong-A Ilbo* (May 27, 1968).

182. *Dong-A Ilbo* (January 7, 1969).

183. *Tonghwa nyŏn'gam*, 1972, p. 87.

184. "Onŭl-ŭi maekpak," *Shindong-a* (October 1969), pp. 80-84; *Dong-A Ilbo* (September 12 and 15, 1969).

185. Seoul radio broadcast, July 25, 1969.

186. *The New York Times* (August 21, 1969).

187. *Tonghwa nyŏn'gam*, 1972, p. 87.

188. Chung'ang sŏnko kwalli wiwŏnhoë (Central Election Control Commission), announcement, October 20, 1969.

189. *Korea Week* (November 6, 1969).

190. *Korea Annual, 1972*, pp. 162-163.

191. *Korea Annual, 1972*, p. 169, and interview with the minister of health and social affairs. Chung Hi-sŏp, July 29, 1968.

192. *Han'guk kyŏngche t'ŭkpyŏl pogo*

193. *Korea Annual, 1972*, pp. 113-114.

194. Ibid., p. 5.

195. Chang Tok-jin, "Pulshil kiŏp chŏngni-ui simal," *Shindong-a* (October 1969), pp. 99-108.

196. Yi Ch'ae-ju, "Pulshil kiŏp chŏngni-rŭl pipan handa," *Shindong-a* (October 1969), pp. 109-121.

197. "Pulshil kiŏp chŏngni-wa kumyung pulshil unyong," *Shindong-a* (September 1969), pp. 185-190.

198. *Tonghwa nyŏn'gam 1972*, p. 277.

199. *Korea Annual, 1972*, p. 162.

200. Ibid., pp. 162-163.

201. Lyman and Cole, p. 176.

202. *Korea Annual, 1972*, pp. 111, 135.

203. *The Korea Times* (May 5, 1970).

204. Kim Chi-ha, "O chŏk," *Sassanggye* (May 1970), pp. 231-248. Kim Chi-ha is the pen name for Kim Yŏng-il.

205. *Tonghwa nyŏn'gam*, 1972, p. 89. Anti-Communist Law, article 4, section 1.

206. Yi Yŏl-mo, "Kyŏngche sŏngchang-man nŏkko salsu ŏpda," *Sassanggye* (May 1970), pp. 38-55; Chu Won-hyŏk, "Chŏlhak ŏbnŭn kŏsa-ŭi haengbang," *Sassanggye* (May 1970), pp. 14-22; Cho Yŏng-pŏm, "Koëdol-ŭl pŏsŏnan kyŏngche sŏngchang-ŭi model," *Sassanggye* (May 1970), pp. 60-70.

207. *Korea Annual, 1972*, p. 164.

208. *Tonghwa nyŏn'gam* 1972, p. 301.

209. *Korea Annual, 1972*, p. 214; Cole and Lyman, pp. 34, 135.

210. Lee Chung-Myun, "Some Aspects of Land Utilization in Korea: With Reference to Irrigation Projects," *Koreana Quarterly* (Autumn 1966), p. 46.

211. *Korea Annual, 1972*, p. 26.

212. *Dong-A Ilbo* (April 29, 1971).

213. *Korea Annual, 1972*, p. 27.

214. *Dong-A Ilbo* (May 5, 1967 and April 24, 1971).

215. *Korea Annual, 1972*, based on information from the Ministry of Agriculture and Forestry.

216. *Dong-A Ilbo* (April 29, 1971).

217. *Korea Annual, 1972*, p. 27.

218. See Lee Chae-Jin, "South Korea: Political Competition and Government Adaptation," *Asian Survey* (January 1972), p. 40.

219. Princeton Lyman, "Korea's Involvement in Vietnam," *Orbis*, 12:563-581 (Summer 1968).

220. *Korea Annual, 1964*, p. 301; *Korea Annual, 1972*, pp. 211-212.

221. C.J. Lee, "Labor Movement and Political Development in Korea," paper delivered to the Conference on Industrialization of Korea, August 1971 (Seoul).

222. *Korea Annual, 1972*, p. 113.

VIII. Institutionalizing the New System in North Korea, 1961-1971: Reformation of Elites, Resocialization of the Masses and the Search for Legitimacy

1. *Fourth Congress Documents*, p. 48.

2. Ibid., p. 50.

3. Kim Il Sung, *The Selected Works of Kim Il Sung*, II, 1-37.

4. Kim Il Sung, *Kim Il-sŏng sŏnjip*, VI, 283.

5. Ibid., p. 287.

6. Kim Il Sung, *The Selected Works of Kim Il Sung*, II, 18.

7. *Tōitsu Chōsen nenkan*, 1968, p. 553.

8. Ibid.

9. *Nodong Shinmun* (February 24, 1960).

10. Kim Il Sung, *Kim Il-sŏng sŏnjip*, I, 35.

11. Ibid., VI, 295.

12. *Pukhan ch'ongkam*, pp. 166, 167.

13. *Nodong Shinmun* (May 13, 1964).

14. Shinn Rinn-Sup, et al., *Area Handbook for North Korea* (Washington, D.C., 1969), p. 106.

15. Kim Il Sung, *The Selected Works of Kim Il Sung*, II, 112-116.

16. *Minju Chosŏn* (January 19, 1966).

17. Kim Il Sung, *The Collected Works of Kim Il Sung*, II, 375 ff.

18. Shinn Rinn-Sup, p. 277.

19. *The New York Times* (July 12, 1961); *The Washington Post* (July 13, 1961).

20. South Korea was soon to learn this bitter lesson when it followed U.S. advice and concentrated resources in the textile area, where it had the most obvious competitive advantage, only to have the United States retaliate by imposing quotas on South Korean textiles after all extensive modern manufacturing facilities had been built, many with American loans which would still have to be repaid, and textile products had become South Korea's major export product.

21. *Nodong Shinmun* (April 11, 1963).

22. Official statistics of the U.S.S.R. See Joungwon A. Kim, "The 'Peak of Socialism' in North Korea: The Five and Seven Year Plans," *Asian Survey* (May 1965), p. 263.

23. *Nodong Shinmun* (October 28, 1963).

24. *Chōsen Shiryo* (July 1964), pp. 7-24.

25. *Nodong Shinmun* (September 7, 1964).

26. Ibid.

27. Kim Il Sung, *The Selected Works of Kim Il Sung*, II, 527, and 542.

28. *Nodong Shinmun* (October 28, 1963).

29. *Pukhan ch'ongkam*, pp. 123, 125, 146, 194.

30. Joungwon A. Kim, "The 'Peak of Socialism' in North Korea," pp. 267, 269.

31. *Minju Chosŏn* (January 19, 1966).

32. *Nodong Shinmun* (June 2, 1965); *Minju Chosŏn* (June 22, 1966).

33. *Nodong Shinmun* (August 12, 1966). Emphasis added.

34. *Tōitsu Chōsen nenkan, 1968*, p. 460.

35. *Pukhan ch'ongkam*, p. 36.

36. Kim Il Sung, *The Selected Works of Kim Il Sung*, II, 519; *Chosŏn chung'ang nyŏn'gam, 1963* (Pyongyang, 1964), pp. 184-185.

37. See B.C. Koh, "North Korea: Profile of a Garrison State," *Problems of Communism*, 17.18-27 (January-February, 1969).

38. *Nodong Shinmun* (January 17, 1965).

39. *Pukhan hyŏnhwang*, p. 87.

40. *Peking Review* (September 3, 1965); see Robert R. Simmons, "China's Cautious Relations with North Korea and Indochina," *Asian Survey* (July 1971), pp. 629-644.

41. *Peking Review* (May 13, 1966).

42. *Pukhan hyŏnhwang*, p. 87

43.   *Nodong Shinmun* (October 6, 1966); *Yearbook on International Communist Affairs, 1966* (Stanford, Calif., 1966), p. 346.

44.   *Pravda* (October 13, 1966).

45.   *Pyongyang Times* (October 13, 1966).

46.   Ibid.

47.   Ibid.

48.   Ibid.

49.   *Pukhan yoram* (Survey of North Korea), Seoul, 1968, p. 178.

50.   Cyril E. Black, "Revolution, Modernization, and Communism," in Cyril E. Black and Thomas P. Thornton, eds., *Communism and Revolution* (Princeton, 1964), p. 7.

51.   *Nodong Shinmun* (January 7, 1969).

52.   Lee Chong-Sik, "Kim Il-sŏng of North Korea," *Asian Survey* (June 1967), p. 381.

53.   *Kŭlloja* (May 25, 1967).

54.   Shinn Rinn-Sup, et al., p. 274.

55.   *Yearbook on International Communist Affairs, 1968*, pp. 434-435; Kim Ilpyong J., "The Mobilization System in North Korean Politics," *Journal of Korean Affairs*, 2:8 (April 1972); Kim Il Sung, "Report to the Fifth Congress," *The Pyongyang Times* (November 3, 1970).

56.   *Nodong Shinmun* (October 5, 1967).

57.   *Brief History of the Revolutionary Activities of Comrade Kim Il Sung*, ed. the Party History Institute of the Central Committee of the Workers' Party of Korea (Pyongyang, 1969), p. 261.

58.   Ibid.; see "Lord and Master," *Far Eastern Economic Review* (November 14, 1970), p. 5.

59. Speech by Kim Kuk-hun to the Fifth Party Congress, *Nodong Shinmun* (November 4, 1970).

60. Ibid.

61. Ibid.

62. *Nodong Shinmun* (February 15, 1968).

63. *Nodong Shinmun* (August 12, 1966).

64. *Nodong Shinmun* (November 3, 1970).

65. Ibid.

66. Initially reported by a North Korean defector to the South, No Kwan-pong, in a Seoul radio broadcast on April 17, 1969, and later confirmed by the absence of these individuals from public view and the use by other persons of these titles.

67. *Nodong Shinmun* (November 3, 1970).

68. Pyongyang domestic radio broadcast, April 23, 1968.

69. *Brief History of the Revolutionary Activities of Comrade Kim Il Sung*, p. 270.

70. *Pukhan hyŏnhwang*, p. 87.

71. *Nodong Shinmun* (February 24, 1969).

72. "On Some Theoretical Problems of the Socialist Economy," *Nodong Shinmun* (March 4, 1969).

73. *Minju Chosŏn* (November 18, 1969).

74. See breakdown of North Korean population by age-groups, United States Department of the Army, *Communist North Korea* (Washington, D.C., February 1971), p. 75.

75. *Nodong Shinmun* (November 3, 1970).

76. *Pukhan hyŏnhwang*, p. 217.

77. *Nodong Shinmun* (November 3, 1970).

78. Ibid.

79. Changes between 1961 and 1970 based on a comparison of the lists in *Chosŏn nodongdang chaesa-ch'a chuyo munhŏnjip*, and *Nodong Shinmun* (November 14, 1970).

80. Changes between 1966 and 1970 based on a comparison of the lists in *Yearbook on International Communist Affairs, 1968*, pp. 434-447, and *Yearbook on International Communist Affairs, 1969*, pp. 529-543, with *Nodong Shinmun* (November 14, 1970).

81. *Nodong Shinmun* (November 3, 1970).

82. *The New York Times* (November 22, 1970).

83. "Man of the Month," *Kukche munje* (May 1971), p. 74.

84. Ibid.

85. Based on the writer's count of the backgrounds of the ranking party members as of 1968, as listed in *Pukhan ch'ongkam*, pp. 1019-1057.

86. *Nodong Shinmun* (November 3, 1970).

87. "Changes in North Korea's Power Structure," *Journal of Korean Affairs* (April 1971), p. 35; Foreign Broadcast Information Service, Asia and Pacific Supplement, October 19, 1971; *The New York Times* (March 22, 1969); Robert A. Scalapino, statement before the subcommittee on Asian and Pacific Affairs, House of Representatives Foreign Affairs Committee, June 10, 1971; *Korean Workers' Party Biographical Study* (Seoul, 1967), pp. 265, 267.

88. *The Revolutionary Front* (August 21, 1970).

89. *Brief History of the Revolutionary Activities of Comrade Kim Il Sung*, p. 3-7; The "General Sherman" was a privately-owned American ship

which, in 1866, sought to explore the Taedong River, which runs from the Yellow Sea on Korea's west up to Pyongyang. The local Koreans, who had never before seen a ship of its kind or Caucasian people, attacked it in much the way that any rural community of today would attack a spaceship of Martians. The ship was set on fire and the entire crew killed. See Han Woo-Keun, pp. 364-370.

90. *Korean Workers' Party Biographical Study*, p. 281.

91. See Suh Dae-Sook, *The Korean Communist Movement*.

92. Report of the Control Committee, speech by Kim Kuk-hun to the Fifth Party Congress, *Nodong Shinmun* (November 4, 1970).

93. *Nodong Shinmun* (November 4, 1970).

94. *Nodong Shinmun* (November 14, 1970).

95. *Sunday Sketch* (November 2, 1969).

96. *Nodong Shinmun* (November 3, 1970).

97. *Tonghwa nyŏn'gam*, 1971, p. 247.

98. See B.C. Koh, "Anatomy of a Revolution: Some Implications of the Fifth KWP Congress," *Journal of Korean Affairs* (October 1971), p. 30

99. *Dong-A Ilbo* (October 16, 1971).

100. *Dong-A Ilbo* (February 28, 1968).

101. *Dong-A Ilbo* (November 4, 25, 26, 29, 1968); *Tonghwa nyŏn'gam, 1969*, p. 88.

102. Pyongyang radio broadcast, April 17, 1969.

103. *Nodong Shinmun* (May 1, 1968).

104. *Pukhan ch'ongkam*, p. 190.

105. *Pukhan hyŏnhwang*, p. 212.

106. *Pukhan ch'ongkam*, pp. 125, 146.

107. *Yearbook on International Communist Affairs, 1968*, p. 443.

108. Havana Domestic Television Service, March 1, 1967.

109. North China News Agency, September 9, 1966.

110. *The New York Times* (August 22-23, 1968).

111. *Chiptan pangwi ch'eche mit ch'ong pyŏngnyŏk* (Seoul, November 1971), pp. 3-4.

112. *The Military Balance, 1971-1972* (London, 1971), pp. 47-48.

113. *The New York Times* (April 16, 1969).

114. *Pravda* (May 17, 1969).

115. *Minju Chosŏn* (June 21, 1969).

116. *Yearbook on International Communist Affairs, 1970*, p. 620.

117. *Kongsankwŏn charyo*, no. 12:229 (December 1970); *Nodong Shinmun* (November 3, 4, 5, 1970).

118. *Dong-A Ilbo* (July 15, 1972), citing Annual Report of Bureau of Intelligence and Research (U.S. Department of State), July 14, 1972; North China News Agency, September 7, 1971 (Peking).

119. *Nodong Shinmun* (February 4, 1971).

120. *Pukhan hyŏnhwang*, p. 22.

121. *Pukhan ch'ongkam*, pp. 283, 286.

122. See S.Y. Liang, "The 'Negro' of Japan," *Atlas* (December 1968); David Conde, "Behind the Korean Schoolhouse in Japan," *Eastern*

Horizon (February 1967), pp. 45-48; Richard H. Mitchell, *The Korean Minority in Japan* (Berkeley, 1967).

123. Oh Ki Song, "An Analysis of Recent North Korean Propaganda Material," *Journal of Korean Affairs*, 1.4:33 (January 1972).

124. Ibid.

125. *The New York Times* (July 5, 1967).

126. *Korea Times* (March 20, 1971).

127. *India Express* (February 9, 1971).

128. *Washington Post* (April 17, 1971).

129. *The New York Times* (October 15, 1971).

130. J.K. Lee and Donald Wellington, "North Korea's Trade with the West: 1956-68," *Journal of Korean Affairs* (April 1971), p. 25.

131. *Nodong Shinmun* (November 5, 1970).

IX. Summary and Conclusions

1. See Hong Sŏng-chik, "Taehaksaeng-un muosul saeng'gakhakko itna?" p. 122; Hong Sung Chick, *The Intellectual and Modernization*; and Hahm Pyong Choon, "Politics of Melancholy: The Recent Experiences of the Korean Polity."

2. *Pukhan hyŏnhwang*, pp. 278-279; *Kyunghyang Shinmun* (July 12, 1972). These figures are based on South Korean calculations.

3. *Kyunghyang Shinmun* (October 18, 1972).

4. *Kyunghyang Shinmun* (November 22, 1972).

5. *Kyunghyang Shinmun* (December 23, 1972)

6.   *Korea Annual, 1969*, p. 109.

7.   *Korea Annual, 1972*, p. 130.

8.   *People's Korea* (January 24, 1973).

9.   *Nodong Shinmun* (December 12, 1972); *People's Korea* (December 20, 1972).

10. *Nodong Shinmun* (December 28, 1972); *People's Korea* (January 3, 1973).

11. *People's Korea* (January 24, 1973).

12. Ibid.

BIBLIOGRAPHY

Allen, Richard C. [pseud.]. *Korea's Syngman Rhee: An Unauthorized Portrait*. Rutland, Vermont, C.E. Tuttle Co., 1960.
———"South Korea: The New Regime," *Pacific Affairs* 34.1:54-57 (Spring 1961).

Baik Bong. *Kim Il Sung Biography*, vols. 1-3. Tokyo, Miraisha, 1969-70.
Bank of Korea, Research Department. *Chosŏn kyŏngche nyŏnbo, 1948* (Korean economic yearbook, 1948). Seoul, Bank of Korea, 1948.
———*Chosa wŏlbo* (Monthly report), December 1961.
———*Economic Statistics Yearbook, 1967*. Seoul, Bank of Korea, 1968.
———*Economic Statistics Yearbook, 1968*. Seoul, Bank of Korea, 1968.
———*Kungmin sodŏk nyŏnbo, 1968* (National income statistics, 1968). Seoul, Bank of Korea, 1968.
Berger, Carl. *The Korea Knot: A Military-Political History*. Philadelphia, University of Pennsylvania Press, 1964.
Black, Cyril E. "Revolution, Modernization, and Communism," in Cyril E. Black and Thomas P. Thornton, eds. *Communism and Revolution*. Princeton, 1964.
Bland, J.O.P. *Li Hung-chang*. London, 1917.
Bradner, Stephen. "Korea: Experiment and Instability," *Japan Quarterly* (October-December 1961), vol. 8, no. 4.
Brief History of the Revolutionary Activities of Comrade Kim Il Sung, ed. The Party History Institute of the Central Committee of the Workers' Party of Korea. Pyongyang, Foreign Languages Publishing House, 1969.
Briggs, Walter. "The Military Revolution in Korea: Its Leader and Achievements," *Koreana Quarterly* (Summer 1963), vol. 5.
Burchett, Wilfred G. *Again Korea*. New York, International Publishers, 1967.
Bureau of Statistics, Economic Planning Board, Republic of Korea. *Korea Statistical Yearbook, 1962*. Seoul, Dong-A Publishing Company, 1962.

————*Han'guk kyŏngche t'ŭkpyŏl pogo* (Special statistical report on Korea). Seoul, August 1970.

Chae ch'il-hoë Taehan Min'guk t'onggye nyŏn'gam (Seventh statistical yearbook of the Republic of Korea). Seoul, 1960.

Chae ohoë kukhoë imsi kukhoë sokkirok (Minutes of the fifth National Assembly regular session), no. 29. Seoul, Kukhoë sammuch'o, 1949.

Chae samhoë kukhoë imsi hoëŭi sokkirok (Minutes of the Third National Assembly temporary session), no. 1 and no. 2, May 21, 1949. Seoul, Kukhoë sammuch'o, 1949.

Chae yukhoë kukhoë chŏngki hoëŭi sokkirok (Minutes of the sixth National Assembly regular session), no. 11, January 21, 1950 and no. 48, March 9, 1950. Seoul, Kukhoë sammuch'o, 1949.

Chang Chun-ha. "Kanŭng ch'ŏngsunŭn yangcha t'angnyuro" (From the Kanung River's clean waters to the muddy Yangtze River), *Sassanggye* 8.12: 252-267 (December 1960).

Chang Myŏn. "Chang Myŏn p'yŏn" (On Chang Myon) in Yi Pŏm-sŏk, et al. *Sasil-ŭi chŏnburŭl kisulhanda* (Report of all the facts: unpublished behind-the-scenes secrets as told by the former main players). Seoul, Hŭimang ch'ulp'an-sa, 1966, pp. 382-383.

Chang Pok-sŏng. *Chosŏn kongsan-dang p'ajaeng-sa* (History of factional rivalry in the Korean Communist Party). Seoul, Taeryuk ch'ulp'an-sa, 1949.

Chang Taek-sang, in Yi Pŏm-sŏk, et al., *Sasil-ŭi chŏnburŭl kisulhanda* (Report of all the facts: unpublished behind-the-scenes secrets as told by former main players). Seoul, Himang ch'ulp'an-sa 1966.

Chang Tok-jin. "Pulsil kiŏp chŏngni-ŭi simal" (Cause and outcome of an unsound enterprise structure), *Shindong-a* (October 1969), pp. 99-108.

"Changes in North Korea's Power Structure," *Journal of Korean Affairs* 1.1:34-35 (April 1971).

Chayu-dang chung'ang tangbu sŏnchŏn wiwŏnhoë. *Minju-dang-ŭi punpa naemak* (Inside story of factionalism in the Democratic Party). Seoul, Chayu-dang chung'ang tangbu sŏnchŏn wiwŏn-hoë, 1959.

Chi Hon-mo. *Choëhuŭi paekbŏm* (The last of Paekbŏm). Seoul, Han'guk kunsa yŏn'gu-hoë, 1960.

Chingbo munhŏn piko (Supplementary book of records), vol. 161, pt. 1.

Chiptan pangwi ch'eche mit ch'ong pyŏngnŏk (Collective defense organization structure and total military forces). Seoul, Kukpangpu, November 1971.

Cho Il-mun. "Chŏngch'i chagŭm-ŭi yironkwa hyŏnshilchŏk koch'al" (Observation on theory and practice with regard to political funds), *Sassanggye* (February 1970), pp. 45-70.

Cho Soon Sung. "Korea: Election Year," *Asian Survey* (January 1968), pp. 29-41.

Cho Yŏng-pŏm. "Koëdol-ŭl pŏsŏnan kyŏngche sŏngchang-ŭi model" (Out-of-kilter economic development model), *Sassanggye* (May 1970), pp. 60-70.

Ch'oë Sŏng-puk. "Pyongyang nampuk hyŏpsang-ŭi insang" (Impressions of the Pyongyang North-South negotiations), *Shinch'ŏnji* (May 1948), pp. 62-71.

Choë Tan-yŏng. "Han'guk-ŭi chŏngdang-kwa chŏngch'i chagŭm" (Korean political parties and political funds), *Chŏngkyŏng yŏn'gu* (March-April 1965), pp. 239-246.

Ch'ŏn Kwan-u, in *Dong-A nyŏn'gam, 1967* (Asia yearbook, 1967), Seoul, Dong-A Ilbo-sa, 1967.

Chŏngbo-kuk Oëmu-pu (Investigation bureau, ministry of foreign affairs). *Pukhan isipnyŏn* (North Korea's twenty years). Seoul, Ministry of Public Information, 1965.

Ch'ŏngyan yukpŏp p'yŏnch'an wiwŏnhoë. *Yukpŏp chŏnsŏ* (Complete six codes). Seoul, 1961.

Chōsen Shiryo.

Chōsen Sōtakafu Tōkei nempō (Annual statistical report of the Government-General of Chōsen). 1910, 1914, 1942, and 1943.

Chosŏn chung'ang nyŏn'gam (Korean central yearbook). Pyongyang, Chosŏn nodong-dang ch'ulp'an-sa. 1949, 1951-52, 1959, 1961, and 1963.

Chosŏn haebang nyŏnbo, 1946 (Korean liberation yearbook, 1946). Seoul, Minuin sokwan, 1946.

Chosŏn haebang nyŏnbo ch'ulp'anbu. *Chosŏn haebang ilnyŏn-sa* (One year history of liberated Korea). Seoul, Chosŏn haebang nyŏn-bo ch'ulp'anbu. 1946.

Chosŏn Ilbo.

Chosŏn Inminbo

Chosŏn minjujui inmin konghwaguk ch'oëgo chaep'anso (The Supreme Court of the D.P.R.K.). *Michaegukjŭi kanch'ŏp*

424

Pak Hŏn-yŏng, Yi Sung-yŏp, to tang-ŭi Chosŏn minjujŭi inmin konghwaguk chŏngkwŏn chŏnpok ŭnmo-wa kanch'ŏp sakŏn kongp'an munhŏn (Trial documents on the conspiracy incident of the American imperialist spies Pak Hŏn-yŏng and Yi Sung-yŏp and their clique's scheme to overthrow the political power of the D.P.R.K.). Pyongyang, Chosŏn minjujui inmin konghwaguk ch'oëgo chaep'anso, 1956.

Chosŏn nodong-dang chaesam-hoë chuyo taehoë munhŏnjip (Third Congress of the Workers' Party of Korea). Pyongyang, Oëguk-nun ch'ulpan-sa, 1965.

Chosŏn nodong-dang chung'ang wiwŏn-hoë jiksok tang'yŏksa yŏn'guso. *Hangil ppalchisan ch'amkajadŭl-ŭi hoësang-ki* (The reminiscence of the participants of the anti-Japanese struggle), vols. 1–4. Pyongyang, Nodong-dang ch'ulpan-sa, 1961.

Chu Sock Kyon. "Why American Aid Failed," *Koreana Quarterly* 4.1:81–93 (Autumn 1960).

Chu Won-hyŏk. "Chŏlhak ŏbnŭn kŏsa-ŭi haengbang" (Tracing the undertaking of a great task without a philosophical foundation), *Sassanggye* (May 1970), pp. 14–22.

Chung, Kiwon. "The North Korean People's Army and the Party," *The China Quarterly* (April-June, 1963), pp. 105–124.

Chung'ang Ilbo.

Clare, Kenneth G., et al. *Area Handbook for the Republic of Korea.* Washington, D.C., United States Government Printing Office, 1969.

Cole, David C. and Princeton N. Lyman. *Korean Development: The Interplay of Politics and Economics.* Cambridge, Mass., Harvard University Press, 1971.

Conde, David. "Behind the Korean Schoolhouse in Japan," *Eastern Horizon* (February 1967), pp. 45–48.

Connelly, John W., Jr. "Report on Economic Provisions of the Constitution of the Republic of Korea." Memorandum prepared for Mr. Morris Wolf, General Counsel, EDA, Washington, D.C., March 24, 1954.

Democratic People's Republic of Korea. Pyongyang, Foreign Languages Publishing House, 1958.

Development of the National Economy and Culture of the People's Democratic Republic of Korea, 1946–1959. Washington, D.C., Joint Publications Research Service, no. 4148, October 31, 1960.

Documents of the Fourth Congress of the Workers' Party of Korea. Pyongyang, Foreign Languages Publishing House, 1961.

Dong-A Ilbo.

Dong-A Ilbo-sa. *Dong-A nyŏn'gam, 1969* (Dong-A yearbook, 1969). Seoul, Dong-A Ilbo-sa, 1969.

The DRP Bulletin 1.10:25-28 (December 1966).

Economic Planning Board, Republic of Korea. *Summary Draft of the Five Year Plan (1962-1966).* Seoul, Economic Planning Board, 1961.

——*First Five Year Economic Development Plan.* Seoul, Economic Planning Board, 1964.

——*First Five Year Economic Development Supplementary Plan.* Seoul, Economic Planning Board, 1964.

——*Major Economic Indicators.* Seoul, Economic Planning Board, 1969.

Education and Culture in the DPRK. Pyongyang, Foreign Languages Publishing House, 1953.

"Election Results for the People's Committees of Northern Korea," *Izvestia* (November 16, 1946), as tr. in *Soviet Press Translations.* Seattle, Washington, Far Eastern Institute, University of Washington (December 14, 1946).

Fairbank, John K. and Edwin O. Reischauer. *East Asia: The Great Tradition.* Boston, Houghton Mifflin Co., 1960.

Fairbank, John K., Edwin O. Reischauer and Albert M. Craig. *East Asia: The Modern Transformation.* Boston, Houghton Mifflin Co., 1965.

Far East Stars and Stripes Weekly.

First Part of the Report of the United Nations Temporary Commission on Korea. New York, General Assembly, Official Records, 3rd sess., supp. 9, A/575, 1948.

"Five Point Communique" (with Foreign Minister Yi Tong-won), *The Korean Republic Weekly* (October 7, 1964).

Gendai Chōsen jinmei jiten (Contemporary Korean who's who), ed. Asian Bureau, Ministry of Foreign Affairs. Tokyo, Kaiko shinbo-shu, 1962.

Government-General of Chōsen. *Annual Report (Chosen Sotakafu tokei nempo)*, 1912-1913, 1921-1922, 1922-1923, 1934-1935, 1942, 1944. Seoul.

Government-General of Tyosen. *Annual Report on Administration of Tyosen*, 1937-1938. Keizyo (Seoul), December 1938.

Grajdanzev, Andrew J. *Modern Korea: Her Economic and Social Development under the Japanese*. New York, Institute of Pacific Relations, 1944.

———"Korea Divided," *Far Eastern Survey* (October 10, 1945), pp. 281-283.

"Habarosuku ya-ei gakkō no jōkyō" (Condition of the field school in Khabarovsk), *Gaiji geppō* (November 1942), pp. 85-86.

Haebang sipnyŏn (Ten years of liberation). Seoul, Himang chipan-sa, 1956.

Hahm Pyong Choon. "Politics of Melancholy: The Recent Experiences of the Korean Polity." Unpublished paper prepared for the Peace Corps.

Hahn Bae-ho and Kim Kyu-taik. "Korean Political Leaders (1952-1962): Their Social Origins and Skills," *Asian Survey* (July 1963), pp. 305-323.

———*Intergroup Conflicts and Political Decision-Making in Korea*. Seoul, Social Science Research Institute, Yonsei University, 1965.

Han Chae-dok. *Kim Il-sŏng-ŭl kobalhanda* (I accuse Kim Il Sung). Seoul, Nae-oë munhwa-sa, 1965.

Han Chŏng-il. *Han'guk chŏngch'i haengchŏng'rŏn* (The theory of Korean politics and administration). Seoul, Pak Yŏng-sa, 1969.

Han Im-hyŏk. *Kim Il-sŏng tongji-ŭi wihan Chosŏn kongsan-dang ch'anggon* (Establishment of the Korean Communist Party by Comrade Kim Il Sung). Pyongyang, Choson nodong-dang ch'ulp'an-sa, 1961.

Han Nae Bok. "April Anniversary in Korea," *Far Eastern Economic Review* (May 4, 1961), pp. 208-211.

———"Readjusting the Rate," *Far Eastern Economic Review* (February 23, 1961), pp. 335-337.

Han Sŏk-hŏn. "Han-il hoëdamŭl chipŏ ch'iura" (Throw away the Korean-Japanese talks), *Sassanggye* (September 1963), p. 50.

Han Sol-ya. *Hero General Kim Il Sung*. Tokyo, Chosen chin-sha, 1962.

Han T'ae-su. *Han'guk chongdang-sa* (History of Korean political parties). Seoul, Sint'aeyang-sa, 1961.

———*Hyŏndae Han'guk chŏngchiron* (The theory of contemporary Korean politics). Seoul, Hoëmun ch'ulp'an-sa, 1968.

Han T'ae-yun. "Kungmu chŏngnikun" (The theory of the prime minister system), *Sassanggye* (October 1960), pp. 30–37.

Han Un-sa. "Chaldoë kapnida" (Everything is going well). Seoul, Tongsŏ munhwa-sa, 1968.

Han Woo-Keun. *The History of Korea*, tr. Lee Kyung-shik and ed. Grafton K. Mintz. Seoul, Eul-yoo Publishing Co., 1970.

Han, Y.C. "Political Parties and Political Development in South Korea," *Pacific Affairs* 42:446–464 (Winter 1969–70).

Han'guk chŏngjaeng-sa (History of the Korean war). Seoul, 1967.

Han'guk chung'ang chŏngbo-pu, ed. *Pukkwe hyŏnhwang* (The situation in North Korea). Seoul, Han'guk chung'ang chŏngbo-pu, March 1971.

Han'guk hyŏngmyŏng chaep'an-sa (History of the Korean Revolutionary Court), vols. 1–4, ed. Han'guk hyŏngmyŏng chaep'an-sa p'yŏnchan wiwŏnhoë (The editorial committee of the Korean Revolutionary Court). Seoul, Han'guk hyŏngmyŏng chaep'an-sa, 1962.

Han'guk Ilbo.

Han'guk kunsa hyŏngmyŏng-sa (History of the Korean military revolution). Seoul, Kukka chaegon choëgohoëŭi Han'guk kunsa hyŏngmyŏng sa ch'ulp'an wiwŏnhoë, 1962.

Han'guk nyŏn'gam (Korea yearbook). Seoul, Han'guk nyŏn'gam pyŏnchan'hoë, 1961.

Han'guk unhaeng chosabu. *Kyŏngchae tonggye nyŏnbo* (Economic statistics yearbook). Seoul, Han'guk unhaeng chosabu, 1963.

"Han'guk-ŭi chŏngchi kyŏngchejŏk hyŏnsil-kwa elite-ŭi kwajae" (Political and economic reality and the elite in Korea), *Chŏngkyŏng yŏn'gu* (July 1965).

Handbook of Korea. Seoul, Office of Public Information, 1955.

Hang'il mujang t'ujaeng chŏnjŏkchi-rŭl ch'ajo-sŏ (Visiting the battlefields of the anti-Japanese armed struggle). Pyongyang, Nodong-dang ch'ulp'an-sa, 1960.

Hanil hoëdam paeksŏ (White paper on the ROK-Japan talks).

Hapdong nyŏn'gam (Hapdong yearbook). Seoul, Hapdong tong-shin-sa, 1961, 1964.

Hatano Kenishi, ed., *Chūgoku kyōsanto 1937 nen shi* (History of the Chinese Communist Party, 1937). Tokyo, 1938.

Headquarters, Japanese Garrison Army in Korea, *Boto tobatsushi* (Record of subjugation of insurgents), appendix, table 2. Seoul, 1913.

Henderson, Gregory. *Korea: The Politics of the Vortex*. Cambridge, Mass., Harvard University Press, 1968.

Henning, Charles N. "Korea: Looking Forward to an Altered Political and Economic Status," *Foreign Commerce Weekly* (January 1, 1944), p. 8.

"Hokuman chiku kyōsan-hi kenkyō jiken" (An incident involving the arrest of a Communist bandit in northern Manchuria), *Gaiji geppō* (November 1943), pp. 125-131.

Holubnychy, Vsevolod. "Soviet Economic Aid to North Korea," *Bulletin of the Institute for the Study of the U.S.S.R.* 4.1:19 (January 1957).

Hong Chŏng-in. "Kunchŏng-ŭi ponsilkwa kuŭi chuii" (The nature of the military government and its aims), *Shinch'ŏnji* (December 1946), pp. 8-15.

Hong Sung Chick. "Taehaksaeng'un muosul saeng'gak hakko itna?" (What are the university students thinking?) *Sassanggye* (April 1962).

―――*The Intellectual and Modernization: A Study of Korean Attitudes*. Seoul, Social Research Institute, Korea University, 1967.

Hong Soon-il. "On Current Political Phenomena," *Korean Affairs* 2.1:95-104 (1963).

Hŏnpŏp kahunan haesŏl (Exposition of the constitution). Seoul, 1962.

Hwang Hyŏn. *Maech'ŏn yarok* (Unofficial record of Maech'ŏn). National History Material Series. Seoul, Shin chi-sa, 1955.

Hŭngsadan-sa pyŏnchan wiwŏnhoë. *Hŭngsadan osipnyŏn-sa* (Fifty year history of the Hungsadan). Seoul, Taesŏng munhwa-sa, 1964.

Hurst, James Willard. *Law and the Conditions of Freedom in the Nineteenth Century United States*. Madison, Wisconsin, University of Wisconsin Press, 1956.

Hyŏn Sang-yun. "Sam-il undong-ŭi hoë-sang" (Recollection of the March First movement), *Shinch'ŏnji* 1.2:230-237 (March 1946).

Im Ch'un-ch'u. *Hang'il mujang t'ujaeng shiki-rŭl hoësang hayŏ* (Recollecting the times of the anti-Japanese struggle). Pyongyang, Chosŏn nodong-dang ch'ulp'an-sa, 1960.

The Independent.

India Express.

Inmin chŏnggwŏn-ŭi suripkwa kuŭi konggohwarŭl wihan (Establishment of the people's regime and the struggle of the Korean Workers' Party for its consolidation). Pyongyang, Chosŏn nodong-dang ch'ulp'an-sa, 1958.

Inmul Han'guk-sa (A history of Korean notables), ed. Inmul Han'guk-sa pyonchan-hoë. Seoul, Paku-sa, 1965.

Ivanov, P. "Elections in Northern Korea," *Pravda* (November 2, 1946), as tr. in *Soviet Press Translations*. Seattle, Washington, Far Eastern Institute, University of Washington (December 14, 1946).

Japan External Trade Organization. *How to Approach the China Market.* Tokyo, Press International, Ltd., 1972.

Japanese Ministry of Foreign Affairs. *Gendai toa jinmei-kan* (Current Asian biography). Tokyo, Toho kankyu-sho, 1950.

Japanese Ministry of Home Affairs, Security Division. *Tokkō Geppō* (Special Police monthly report). Tokyo, June 1945.

Japanese Ministry of Internal Affairs. *Tokkō Geppō* (Higher police report). Tokyo, June 1945.

Kang In-sŏp. "Yuksa p'algi seng" (The eighth graduating class of the military academy), *Shindong-a* (September 1964), pp. 170-198.

——— "Minjudang chŏngkwŏn ch'oëhu-ŭi nal" (The last day of the democratic regime), *Shindong-a* (May 1965), pp. 100-101.

Karshinov, L.N. *Socialist Industrialization in the Korean Democratic People's Republic.* Moscow, International Relations, 1960. trans. Glenn D. Paige.

Kibon chŏngbo: pukkwe chuyo inmul (Basic intelligence: important personalities of the North Korean puppet), ed. Han'guk chung'ang chŏngbo-pu. Seoul, Han'guk chung'ang chongbo-pu, March 1971.

430

Kim, C.I. Eugene and Kim Ke Soo. "The April 1960 Korean Student Movement," *The Western Political Quarterly* (March 1964), pp. 83–92.

Kim Ch'ang-sun. *Yŏksa-ŭi chŭng'in* (History's witness). Seoul, Han'guk asea pankong yonmaeng, 1936.

———*Pukhan siponyŏn-sa* (A fifteen-year history of North Korea). Seoul, Chimungak, 1961.

Kim Chi-ha. "O chŏk" (Five thieves), *Sassanggye* (May 1970), pp. 231–248.

Kim Chin-hak and Han Chŏl-yong. *Chaehŏn kukhoë-sa* (History of the constitution-making assembly). Seoul, Sinjo ch'ulp'an-sa, 1954.

Kim Chong Hoon. "The Rise and Fall of the Liberal Party in Korea:1951–1960." Unpublished M.A. thesis, George Washington University, 1961.

Kim Chŏng-pom and Kim Tong-un. *Haebang chŏnhu-ŭi Chosŏn chinsang* (The actual situation in Korea before and after liberation). Seoul, Chosŏn chŏngkyon yŏn'gu-so, 1945.

Kim Chun-yŏn. *Tongnip nosŏn* (The path of independence). Seoul, Sisasinpo-sa, 1947.

Kim Il Sung. *Modun munje haegyŏreso chungsim kokirŭl t'unt'unhi t'ŭrŏ chapko kŭe yŏgyanggŭl* (In solving all problems let us grasp the central link and concentrate all our forces there). Pyongyang, Korean Workers' Party Press, 1959.

———(Kim Il-sŏng). *Kim Il-sŏng sŏnjip* (The selected works of Kim Il Sung), vols. 1–6. Pyongyang, Chosŏn nodong-dang ch'ulp'an-sa, 1960–63.

———*The Selected Works of Kim Il Sung*, English ed. Pyongyang, Foreign Languages Publishing House, 1965.

———"The Struggle for Consolidation of the Party," at the Third Party Congress of 1956, in *Chosŏn nodong-dang chaesamch'a taehoë chuyo munhŏnjip* (Third Congress of the Workers' Party of Korea). Pyongyang, Oëguk-nun ch'ulp'an-sa, 1965.

———"Report to the Fifth Congress," *The Pyongyang Times* (November 3, 1970).

"Kim Il-sŏng chaggun pudae-wa Chosŏn wiyonggyun-ŭi chunggyon kanbu chwadam-hoë" (Discussion of the main staff of the Kim Il Sung company and Korean volunteer corps), *Shinch'ŏnji* (March 1943), pp. 230–237.

Kim, Ilpyong J. "The Mobilization System in North Korean Politics," *Journal of Korean Affairs* 2.1:3-15 (April 1972).

Kim, Joungwon Alexander. "North Korea's Economic Progress, 1946-1963." Monograph reproduced by the United States Department of State. Washington, D.C., 1964.

——"The 'Peak of Socialism' in North Korea: The Five and Seven Year Plans," *Asian Survey* 5:225-269 (May 1965).

——"Korean Participation in the Vietnam War," *World Affairs* (April, May, June 1966), pp. 28-35.

——"Soviet Policy in North Korea," *World Politics* 22:237-251 (January 1970).

——"The Politics of Predevelopment," *Comparative Politics* 5.2: 211-235 (January 1973).

Kim Koo (Kim Ku). *Paekbŏm ilji: Kim Ku chasŏjŏn* (Memoirs of Paekbŏm: autobiography of Kim Koo). Seoul, Koryŏ sonbong-sa, 1947.

Kim Kwan-bong. *The Korea-Japan Treaty Crisis and the Instability of the Korean Political System*. New York, Praeger, 1971.

Kim Kyŏng-rae. "Chŏnhyangja-nya, ani-nya? " (Is he converted or not?), *Sassanggye* (October 1963), pp. 102-110.

——"Chŏnhwanjŏm-ŭi sum chŏngdangdŭl" (Political parties at turning point), *Sassanggye* (December 1963), pp. 49-50.

Kim Kyu-sik. "The Asiatic Revolutionary Movement and Imperialism," *Communist Review* 3.3:137-147 (July 1922).

Kim Sam-kyu. *Konnichi no Chōsen* (Korea today). Tokyo, Kawade Shobo, 1956.

——"Senri no koma undōno haikei" (Background of the Flying Horse movement), *Korea Review* 3:4-5 (September 1959).

Kim Sang-hak. *Development of Socialist Industry in the DPRK*. Pyongyang, Foreign Languages Publishing House, 1958.

Kim Sang-hyŏp, et al. "Minju chŏngch'i ch'oëhuŭi kyodubo" (The last beachhead of democratic politics), *Sassanggye* (May 1960), pp. 26-39.

Kim Sang-cho. "Naegak chaekimjae-ŭi palso pyongchil hako itda" (The developmental situation of the cabinet system), *Sassanggye* (December 1960), pp. 46-51.

Kim Se Jin. "Military Revolution in Korea." Ph.D. dissertation, University of Massachusetts, 1966.

——*The Politics of Military Revolution in Korea*. Chapel Hill, N.C., The University of North Carolina Press, 1971.

432

Kim Sŏk-yŏng. *Panmunjŏm* (Panmunjom). Seoul, Shin munhwa-sa, 1972.

Kim Sŏk-yun. *Kyŏngmudae-ŭi pimil* (The secrets of Kyung Mu Dai [presidential residence]). Seoul, Pyongjin munhwa-sa, 1961.

Kim Sŭng-shik, ed., *Chosŏn nyŏn'gam, 1947* (Korean yearbook, 1947). Seoul, Chosŏn tongshin-sa, 1946.

Kim, V.A. *Gosudarstvennyi stroi Koreiskoi Narodno-Demokraticheskoi Respubliki.* Moscow, Gosudarstvennoe Izdatel'stvo Iuridicheskoi Literatury, 1955.

Kim, Warren Y. *Fifty-Year History of Koreans in America.* Reedley, Calif., Kim Charles Ho, 1959.

Kim Wŏn-su. "Shinmun tongshin kiŏp kyŏng'yŏng shiltae chosa boko" (Survey of newspapers, news agencies, and their management), *Soŭl Taehakkyo shinmun yŏnkuso hakpo* (Seoul National University research studies on newspapers). Seoul, Soŭl Taehakkyo, 1965.

Kim Yŏng-sam. "P'yŏng hwajŏk hyŏngmyŏng-ŭi p'ilyŏnsŏng" (Necessity for peaceful revolution), *Sassanggye* (December 1969), pp. 86–91.

Kim Yŏng-su. "Minju konghwa-dang sajŏn chojik" The advance organization of the Democratic Republican Party), *Shindong-a* (November 1964), pp. 168–173.

"Kin Nichisei no katsudō jōkyō" (General condition of the activities of Kim Il Sung), *Tokkō gaijo geppō* (November 1944).

Kin Nichisei Senshu (The selected works of Kim Il Sung), vol. 1. Japanese ed., Kyoto, Sanichi shobo, 1952.

Koh, B.C. "North Korea: Profile of a Garrison State," *Problems of Communism* 17:18-27 (January-February 1969).

———"Anatomy of a Revolution: Some Implications of the Fifth KWP Congress," *Journal of Korean Affairs* (October 1971), p. 30.

Koha sŏnsaeng chŏnki p'yonch'an wiwŏnhoë p'yŏn, *Koha Song Chin-u sŏnsaeng-chŏn* (The biography of teacher Song Chin-u). Seoul, Tong-a ilbo-sa, 1965.

Kongsankwŏn charyo, no. 12 (December 1970).

Korea Annual, ed. Hapdong News Agency. Seoul, Hapdong. 1964, 1965, 1967, 1968, 1969, 1972.

Korea Flaming High (Seoul, Office of Public Information, 1960), vol. 4.

Korea Times.

Korea Week.

Korean Government-General, High Court, Prosecutor's Bureau, "Ro Unkyō chōsasho" (Interrogation of Yŏ Un-hyŏng) in *Chōsen shisō undō chōsa shiryō* (Korean Thought Movement investigation materials), no. 2:12 (Seoul, March 1933).

The Korean Republic.

Korean Workers' Party Biographical Study. Seoul, Han'guk chung'ang chŏngbopu, 1967.

Koreana Quarterly.

Koryŏ taehakkyo minjok munhwa yŏn'guso, *Han'guk munhwa-sa taekae* (Comprehensive series of Korean cultural history), vol. 2: *Chŏngch'i Kyŏngchae-sa* (History of politics and economics). Seoul, Ko tae minjok munhwa yŏn'guso ch'ulp'an-bu, 1965.

Ki Cha-pung, "Kim Ku" (Kim Koo), in Yin Sun-buk, et al., *Chongkae yahwha* (The evening story of the political world). Seoul, Hongja ch'ulp'an-sa, 1966, pp. 22-59.

Kukhoëbo, vol. 1, no. 1 (National Assembly report). Seoul, Kukhoëbo, n.d.

Kukhoë sipnyŏ (A ten year history of the National Assembly), ed. Taehan Min'guk kukhoë minŭiwon samuchŏ. Seoul, Taehan Min'guk minŭiwon samuchŏ pupchae chŏsaguk, 1958.

Kukhoë tongil yŏn'gu t'ukpol wiwŏnhoë, *Tongil paksŏ* (Unification white paper). Seoul, Kukhoë tongil yŏn'gu t'ukbol wiwŏnhoë, 1967.

Kukhoë tosŏkwan ippŏp chosaguk, *Kukhoë tosŏkwan ippŏp chosaguk chamgosŏ* (National Assembly library of research on legislation reference work). Seoul, August 28, 1969.

Kŭlloja.

Kwanbo (Gazette).

Kyŏngche paksŏ (Economy white paper), ed. Kyŏngche kaeŭewon. Seoul, Han'guk unhaeng chosabu, 1963.

Kyŏngcherok taesajŏn (Encyclopaedia of economics). Seoul, Pomyŏng-sa, 1964.

Kyŏngrang-ŭl hech'iko: Minju konghwa-dang i nyŏn-sa (Two year history of the DRP: overcoming obstacles), ed. Minju konghwa-dang. Seoul, 1964.

434

"Kyōsan shugi senjin Pak Hŏn-yŏng no taiho ni kansuruken"
(Concerning the arrest of Korean Communist Pak Hŏn-yŏng),
Japanese Ministry of Foreign Affairs Archives, Library of
Congress microfilms, Reel S. 403.
Kyunghyang Shinmun.

Lauterbach, Richard E. *History of the American Military Govern-
ment in Korea.* Korean ed. Seoul, Kukche shinmun-sa, 1948.
Lee, C.J. "Labor Movement and Political Development in Korea."
Paper delivered at the Conference on Industrialization of
Korea. Seoul, August 1971.
Lee Chae-jin. "South Korea: Political Competition and Govern-
ment Adaptation," *Asian Survey* (January 1972), pp. 38-45.
Lee Chong-Sik. *The Politics of Korean Nationalism.* Berkeley,
Calif., University of California Press, 1963.
———"Land Reform, Collectivisation and the Peasants in North
Korea," *The China Quarterly*, no. 14: 65-81 (April-June
1963).
———"Korea, Troubles in a Divided State," *Asian Survey* (January
1965), pp. 25-32.
———"Kim Il-song of North Korea," *Asian Survey* (June 1967),
pp. 374-382.
Lee Chung-Myun. "Some Aspects of Land Utilization in Korea:
With Reference to Irrigation Projects," *Koreana Quarterly*
(Autumn 1966), pp. 44-62.
Lee Hahn-Been. *Korea: Time, Change, and Administration.*
Honolulu, East-West Center Press, 1968.
Lee, J.K. and Donald Wellington. "North Korea's Trade with the
West: 1956-68," *Journal of Korean Affairs* (April 1971),
pp. 25-33.
Lee Won Sul. "The Impact of the United States Occupation Policy
on the Socio-Political Structure of South Korea, 1945-1948."
Ph.D. dissertation, Western Reserve University, 1961.
Legislative Reference Service, National Assembly Library, Republic
of Korea, *Special Report*, August 27, 1969.
Letter to Dr. Robert Oliver, October 21, 1945. Personal collection
of Dr. Robert Oliver, State College, Pennsylvania.
Letter from Syngman Rhee to Robert T. Oliver, July 28, 1948.
Personal collection of Dr. Robert Oliver, State College,
Pennsylvania.

Liang, S.Y. "The 'Negro' of Japan," *Atlas* (December 1968).
"Lord and Master," *Far Eastern Economic Review* (November 14, 1970), p. 5.
Lyman, Princeton. "Korea's Involvement in Vietnam," *Orbis* 12: 563-581 (Summer 1968).

Ma Han. *Han'guk chŏngch'i-ŭi ch'ongpipan* (A complete criticism of Korean politics). Seoul, Chongku ch'ulp'an-sa, 1960.
"Man of the Month," *Kukche munje* (Journal of international studies), May 1971, p. 74.
Mao Tse-tung. *Selected Works*, vol. 1. English ed. Peking, Foreign Languages Publishing House, 1953.
McCune, George M. "Essential Unity of the Korean Economy," *Korean Economic Digest* (January 1946).
———"Korea's Postwar Political Problems." Secretariat Paper no. 2, Institute of Pacific Relations, Tenth Conference, New York, 1947.
———*Korea Today*. Cambridge, Mass., Harvard University Press, 1950.
McKenzie, F.A. *The Tragedy of Korea*. London, Hodder and Stoughton, 1908.
Meade, E. Grant. *American Military Government in Korea*. New York, King's Crown Press, Columbia University, 1951.
The Military Balance, 1971-1972. London, Institute for Strategic Studies, 1971
Military Revolution in Korea, ed. Secretariat of the Supreme Council for National Reconstruction. Seoul, Dong-A Publishing Co., 1961.
Minju Chosŏn.
Minju Han'guk hyŏngmyŏng ch'ŏng-sa (History of the Korean democratic revolution), ed. Minju Han'guk hyŏngmyŏng ch'ŏng-sa p'yŏnch'an wiwŏnhoë. Seoul, Minju Han'guk hyŏngmyŏng ch'ŏng-sa p'yŏnch'an wiwŏnhoë, 1961.
Minju Han'guk hyŏngmyŏng-sa (History of the Korean democratic revolution), ed. Minju Han'guk hyŏngmyŏng-sa p'yŏnch'an wiwŏnhoë. Seoul, Minju Han'guk hyŏngmyŏng-sa ch'ulp'an wiwŏnhoë, 1962.
"Minju-jŭi wa kunsa hyŏngmyŏng" (Democracy and the military revolution), *Sassanggye* 9:4 (June 1961).
Mitchell, Richard H. *The Korean Minority in Japan*. Berkeley, University of California Press, 1967.

Mitsu Haru Masaki. "Daitoryo Senkyo Kankoku no Seijo" (Presidential election and political situation in Korea), *Kokusai Mondai*, no. 88:10-17 (July 1967).

Mobius, J. Mark. "The Japan-Korea Normalization Process and Korean Anti-Americanism," *Asian Survey* (April 1966), p. 244.

Mun Hong-ju. "Uri nara hŏnpŏp-sa" (Our nation's constitutional history), *Chŏngkyŏng yŏn'gu* (July 1965), pp. 11-23.

Mun Myŏng-ho. "Yaebiyŏk changsŏngdŭl" (Retired generals), *Shindong-a* (December 1967), pp. 132-152.

Nae-oë munje yŏn'guso (Internal and External Affairs Institute). *Pukkwe-ŭi p'apol t'u-jaeng-sa* (History of factional struggles in the North Korean puppet). Seoul, 1962.

Naemupu t'ongkaeguk, Chae sahwae Taehan Min'guk t'onggye nyŏn'gam (Fourth statistical yearbook of the Republic of Korea). Seoul, Naemupu, 1957.

Nam Chae-hi. "Chŏngdang unyŏng-kwa tangchaejŏng" (Operation and financing of the political party), *Chŏngkyŏ yŏn'gu* (February 1967), pp. 132-137.

"Nation's First Referendum Approves New Constitution," *Korean Report* 2:3 (November-December 1962).

National Assembly Legislative Research Bureau. "Reference Sources." Seoul, August 28, 1969.

The New York Times.

Newsweek.

Nodong Shinmun.

O Chae-sik. *Han'guk kŭnse wiinŏn* (Biographies of great contemporary Korean men). Seoul, Haengjon shinmun-sa, 1948.

O Sso-paek, ed. *Haebang isipnyŏn* (Twenty years of liberation). Seoul, Haengjon sinmun-sa, 1965.

———*Haebang isipnyŏn: Charyop'yŏn* (Twenty years of liberation: source edition). Seoul, Saemun-sa, 1965.

O Ŭng-hwan. "Korich'ae chŏngni" (Readjusting usurious rates), in O Sso-paek, ed., *Haebang isipnyŏn*. Seoul, Haengjon sinmun-sa, 1965.

Office of the Overseas Minister. *Takumu tōkei, 1939* (Statistics of colonies, 1939). Tokyo, 1939.

Oh Che-do. "The Communist Plot Against Korea." Manuscript, August 8, 1959.

Oh Ki Song. "An Analysis of Recent North Korea Propaganda Material," *Journal of Korean Affairs* 1.1:25-41 (January 1972).

Oliver, Robert T. *Syngman Rhee: The Man Behind the Myth*. New York, Dodd Mead and Company, 1954.

Om Hang-sŏp. *Kim Ku Sŏnsaeng hyŏltu-sa* (History of the bloody struggle of teacher Kim Koo). Seoul, International Cultural Association, 1946.

"Onŭl-ŭi maekpak" (Today's pulse), *Shindong-a* (October 1969), pp. 80-84.

Paek Nam-ju, ed. *Hyŏngmyŏng chidoja Pak Chŏng-hŭi-ron* (Discussion of the revolutionary leader Park Chung Hee). Seoul, Kaccho ch'ulp'an-sa, 1969.

Paige, Glenn D. "The Communist System: The North Korean Party State." Draft, 1964.

———*The Korean People's Democratic Republic*. Stanford, Calif., Hoover Institute of Stanford University, 1966.

Pak Il-kyŏng. "Han'guk chŏngbu hyŏng taeŭi pyŏnchŏn" (Changes in the form of the Korean government), *Chŏngkyŏng yŏn'gu* 1.7:78-91 (August 1965).

Pak Mun-ok. *Haengchŏng-hak* (Public administration). Seoul, Pak Mun-sa, 1962.

Pak Tong-un. *Pukhan t'ongchi kiguron* (The theory of the organization of North Korean rule). Seoul, Asea munche yŏnguso, 1964.

Palmer, Spencer J., ed. *Korean-American Relations*, vol. 2. Berkeley, University of California Press, 1963.

Pang In-hu. *Pukhan Chosŏn nodong-dang-ŭi hyŏngsŏng kwa palchŏn* (The formation and development of the Korean Workers' Party of North Korea). Seoul, Asea munje yŏn'guso, 1967.

Park Chung Hee (Pak Chŏng-hui). *The Country, The Revolution and I*. Seoul, Hollym Corp., 1962.

———*Our Nation's Path*. Seoul, Dong-A Publishing Co., 1962.

Pauley, Edwin W. *Report on Japanese Assets in Soviet-Occupied Korea to the President of the United States*, June 1946 (Unclassified November 8, 1949).

438

Peking Review (September 3, 1965 and May 13, 1966).

People's Korea.

"Personalities and Chronology." Unclassified secret document.

The Philadelphia Inquirer.

Pigulevskaia, E.A. *Koreiskii narod v bor'be za nezavisimost' i demokratiiu.* Moscow, Akademii Nauk U.S.S.R., 1952.

Political Survey of the DPRK, 1945-1960. Pyongyang, Foreign Languages Publishing House, 1960.

Postwar Rehabilitation and Development of the National Economy in the Democratic People's Republic of Korea. Pyongyang, Foreign Languages Publishing House, 1957.

Pravda.

Pukhan ch'ongkam (General book on North Korea), ed. Pukhan nyŏn'gam kanhaeng wiwŏn-hoë. Seoul, Kongsankwŏn munje yŏn'guso, 1968.

Pukhan yoram (Survey of North Korea). Seoul, 1968.

Pukkwe hyŏnhwang (Situation of the North Korean regime). Seoul, Chosŏn chung'ang chŏngbo-pu, March 1971.

Puknodang chae i-ch'a chŏndang taehoë hoëuirok (The minutes of the North Korean Workers' Party Second Congress). Pyongyang, Puknodang ch'ulp'an-sa, 1948.

"Pulshil kiŏp chŏngni-wa kumyung pulshil unyong" (Unsound enterprise structure and unsound operation of finance), *Shindong-a* (September 1969), pp. 185-190.

Pusan Ilbo.

Pye, Lucian W. *The Spirit of Chinese Politics.* Cambridge, Mass., M.I.T. Press, 1968.

The Pyongyang Times.

Reeve, W.D. *The Republic of Korea:A Political and Economic Study.* London, Oxford University Press, 1963.

The Revolutionary Front.

Rhee, Syngman (Yi Sŭng-man). *Tongnip chŏngshin* (The spirit of independence). Seoul, 1904. First published in San Francisco in 1908.

———*Japan Inside Out.* London, John Long, Ltd., 1942.

Robinson, Richard D. "Korea—Betrayal of a Nation." Unpublished manuscript, 1947.

Rudolph, Philip. *North Korea's Political and Economic Structure.* New York, Institute of Pacific Relations, 1959.

"Sahoë sip'yŭng" (Comments on society), *Sassanggye* (October 1963), pp. 88-89.

Sakamoto, Akira. *Report on the State of Public Order.* October 1945.

"Sam-il undong-ŭi hoë-sang" (Recollection of the March First movement), *Shinch'ŏnji* 1.1:28-29 (March 1946).

"3.2.4 [sam isipsa] tansi-ŭi taehaksaeng-ŭi chŏngch'i ŭisik" (Political awareness of the university students on March 24), *Sae Kyoyuk*, no. 120:39-45 (October 1964).

Sarafan, Bertran D. "Military Government: Korea," *Far Eastern Survey* (November 1946), pp. 349-352.

Scalapino, Robert A., ed. *North Korea Today.* New York, Praeger, 1963.

Scalapino, Robert A. and Lee Chong-Sik. "The Origins of the Korean Communist Movement," *The Journal of Asian Studies* 20.1:9-31 (November 1960), 20.2:149-167 (February 1961).

Secret Report of H. Merrill Benninghoff, Foreign Service Officer, Political Advisor to the Secretary of State on Political Movements in Korea, September 29, 1946. Unclassified secret document.

Seoul Shinmun.

Shabshina, F.I. *Narodnoe vosstanovlenie 1919 goda v Korei.* Moscow, Izdatel'stvo Akademii Nauk, 1952.

———*Ocherbi noveishei istorii Korei: 1945-1953.* Moscow, Godussarstvennoe Izdatel'stvo Politicheskoi Literary, 1958.

Shchetinin, B.V. "Voznikovenie narodnykh komitetov v severnoi Korei," *Sovetskoe Gosudarstvo: Pravo* no. 4:67-72 (1947).

Shin Hung-u, "Ri shōban o kataru" (Speaking about Syngman Rhee), Korean Government-General, High Court, Prosecutor's Bureau, Thought Section, *Shisō ihō* (Thought report series), no. 16 (September 1938).

Shin Sang-ch'o. "Kunsa tokjaeka namginkŏt" (Remedies left behind by military dictatorship), *Sassanggye* (September 1963), p. 72.

Shinn Rinn-Sup, et al. *Area Handbook for North Korea*. Washington, D.C., United States Government Printing Office, 1969.

Shisō ihō, no. 4:135 (Tokyo, September 1935).

Simmons, Robert R. "China's Cautious Relations with North Korea and Indochina," *Asian Survey* (July 1971), pp. 629–644.

Smolensky, V. "The Situation in Korea," as tr. in *Soviet Press Translations*. Seattle, Washington, Far Eastern Institute, University of Washington, March 15, 1947.

Sŏ Chŏng-chu. *Yi Sŭng-man Paksa chŏn* (Biography of Dr. Syngman Rhee). Seoul, Samp'al-sa, 1949.

Sŏ Pyŏng-jo. *Chukwonjaŭi chŭng'on: Han'guk taeŭi chŏngch'i-sa* (Testimonies of the sovereign: a history of representative government in Korea). Seoul, Moŭm ch'ulp'an-sa, 1963.

Sohn Jae-Souck. "The Role of the Military in the Republic of Korea." Paper presented to the International Sociological Association at Evian, France in 1966.

Sŏl Kuk-hwan. "Nampuk hoëdamg suhaengki" (Records of the North-South conference), *Shinch'ŏnji* 4–5:72–81 (May 1948).

Sŏn Chang-mu. *Yikŏsi chinsang ida* (This is the truth). Seoul, Chinmyŏng munhwasa, 1966.

Song Kŏn-ho. "Chŏngch'i chagŭm-kwa chaepŏl" (Political funds and plutocracy), *Chŏngkyŏng yŏn'gu* (March-April 1965), pp. 247–255.

Sŏul taehakkyo. *Sŏul taehakkyo shinmun yŏnguso hakpo* (The bulletin of the Institute of Mass Communications of Seoul National University), vol. 2. Seoul, Sŏul taehakkyo shinmun yŏnguso, 1965.

Statistics Bureau, Ministry of Home Affairs. *Chae sa-hoë Taehan Min'guk t'onggye nyŏn'gam* (Fourth statistical yearbook of the Republic of Korea). Seoul, 1957.

———*Chae ch'il-hoë Taehan Min'guk t'onggye nyŏn-gam* (Seventh statistical yearbook of the Republic of Korea). Seoul, 1960.

Stone, Irving F. *The Hidden History of the Korean War* (New York, Monthly Review Press, 1952).

Strong, Anna Louise, "I Saw the North Koreans" (Los Angeles, July 16, 1950).

Suh Dae-sook, "North Korea: Emergence of an Elite Group," in Richard F. Starr, ed., *Aspects of Modern Communism* (Columbia, S.C., University of South Carolina Press, 1965).

———*The Korean Communist Movement, 1918-1948* (Princeton, N.J., Princeton University Press, 1967).

Sunday Sketch.

Supreme Commander for the Allied Powers, *Summation of Non-Military Activities in Japan and Korea, 1946-47*, no. 1 (October 1945), no. 2 (November 1945), no. 3 (December 1945).

Survey of Korea, comp. Military Intelligence Service, War Department General Staff (Washington, D.C., June 15, 1943).

Taehan Min'guk chŏngdang-sa [History of political parties of the Republic of Korea], ed. Chung'ang sŏnko kwalli wiwŏn-hoë [Central election control committee] (Seoul, 1964).

Taehan Min'guk sŏnko-sa [History of elections in the Republic of Korea], ed. Chung'ang sŏnko-sa kwalli wiwŏn-hoë [Central election control committee] (Seoul, 1964).

Taehan Min'guk t'onggye nyŏn'gam, 1960 [The statistical yearbook of the Republic of Korea, 1960] (Seoul, Naemubu t'ongkaeguk, 1960).

Taehan nyŏn'gam, 1952 [Korea yearbook, 1952] (Seoul, Taehan t'ongshin-sa, 1952).

Taehan nyŏn'gam 1955 [Korea annual] (Seoul, Taehan nyon'gam-sa, 1955).

Taekunch'al-ch'ŏng susaguk (Bureau of major investigations). *Chwa-ik sagŏn sillok* (True record of the leftist incident), vol. 1. Seoul, 1964.

Time.

Toitsu Chōsen nenkan, 1968. Tokyo, Toitsu Chōsen shimbun-sha, 1968.

Tonghwa nyŏn'gam (Tonghwa yearbook). Seoul, Tonghwa t'ongshin-sa. 1967, 1971, 1972.

Trud (May 24, 1947), as tr. in *Soviet Press Translations*, 2:70-74. Seattle, Washington, Far Eastern Institute, University of Washington (August 1947).

Truman, Harry S. *Memoirs.* vol. 1: *Year of Decisions.* vol. 2: *Years of Trial and Hope.* Garden City, New York, Doubleday and Company, 1955.

Tsubōe Senji. *Hokusen no kaihō jūnen* (North Korea's ten years of liberation). Tokyo, Nikkan todotsushinsha, 1956.

442

―――*Nansen no kaihō jūnen* (Ten years of Korea's liberation). Tokyo, Nikkan rodo tsushin-sa, 1956.

―――*Chōsen minzoku tokuritsu undōhisi* (Secret history of the Korean people's independence movement). Tokyo, Nikkan roedo tsushin-sha, 1959.

United Korean Committee in America. *Korean Liberty Conference*. Washington, D.C., United Korean Committee in America, 1942.

United Nations. *Report of the United Nations Commission for the Unification and Rehabilitation of Korea*, General Assembly official records: 6 sess., suppl. 12 n. A/1881. New York, 1951.

United Nations Document A/575, vol. 1, 3 sess., suppl. 9.

United Nations Document A/AC, 18/31.

United Nations Document A/AC, 19/30.

United Nations Document A/AC, 19/80.

United Nations General Assembly. Resolution 195 (III), December 12, 1948.

United States Army Area Handbook for Korea. Washington, D.C., 1964.

United States Armed Forces in Korea, *South Korean Interim Government Activities*, no. 27. December 1947.

United States Army Forces in Korea, HQ XXIV Corps, G-2 Section. *The National Society for the Rapid Realization of Independence*. Unclassified document, July 1, 1946.

―――*Republic of Korea, Economic Summation*, no. 36. November-December, 1948.

United States Army Military Government in Korea. *Summation of Activities*, nos. 6,7,8,9,12,13,14,15,16,18,27,36 (1945-1948).

United States Department of Agriculture, Economic Research Service. *The Far East and Oceania Agricultural Data Book*. Washington, D.C., Government Printing Office, May 1967.

United States Department of the Army. *Communist North Korea*. Washington, D.C., Department of the Army, February, 1971.

United States Department of State. *Department of State Bulletin* (December 30, 1945, March 7, 1948, January 23, 1950).

―――*Korea's Independence*. Far Eastern Series, no. 18 (October 1947).

———*The Conferences at Malta and Yalta.* Washington, D.C., Government Printing Office, 1960.

———*North Korea:A Case Study in the Techniques of Takeover.* Washington, D.C., Government Printing Office, 1961.

———*A Historical Summary of United States-Korean Relations.* Washington, D.C., Government Printing Office, 1962.

———*American Foreign Policy: Current Documents, 1961.* Washington, D.C., Government Printing Office, 1965.

Vaintsvaig, N.K. and V.V. Lezin. *Koreiskaya Narodno-Demokratisheskaya Respublika* (The Democratic People's Republic of Korea). Moscow, Academy of Sciences of the U.S.S.R., 1964.

Vinocour, Seymour M. "Syngman Rhee: Spokesman for Korea (June 23, 1951–October 8, 1952): A Case Study in International Speaking." Ph.D. dissertation, Pennsylvania State College, 1953, appendix.

The Voice of Korea.

The Washington Evening Star.

The Washington Post.

Weems, Benjamin B. *Reform, Rebellion, and the Heavenly Way.* Tucson, Arizona, The University of Arizona Press, 1964.

Whiting, Allen S. *China Crosses the Yalu: The Decision to Enter the Korean War.* New York, Macmillan, 1960.

Wolfstone, Daniel. "The Generals Strike," *Far Eastern Economic Review* (May 25, 1961), p. 348.

Wu Pyŏng-kyu. "Kundae naeŭi inkan kwŏn kewajihwa" (Human relations and command in the military), *Sassanggye* (November 1960), pp. 254–263.

Yamana Mikio. *Chōsen sotoku-fu shusei no kiroku* (The last period of the Korean Government-General). Tokyo, Chuo nikkan, 1956.

Yearbook on International Communist Affairs. Stanford, Calif., Hoover Institute Press. 1966, 1968, 1969, 1970.

Yi Ch'ae-ju. "Pulshil kiŏp chŏngni-rŭl pipan handa" (Comment on the unsound enterprise structure), *Shindong-a* (October 1969), pp. 109–121.

Yi Chŏl-chu. *Pukŭi yaesulin* (North Korea's artists). Seoul, Kemong-sa, 1965.

Yi Ki-ha. *Han'guk chŏngdang paltal-sa* (History of Korean political party development). Seoul, Ŭihoe chŏngshi-sa, 1961.

Yi Man-gyu. *Yŏ Un-hyŏng sŏnsaeng t'ujaeng-sa* (History of the struggle of the Honorable Yŏ Un-hyŏng). Seoul, Minju munhwa-sa, 1946.

———*Chosŏn kyoë-yuk-sa* (History of Korea's education). Seoul, 1950.

Yi Pŏm-sŏk, et al. *Sasil-ŭi chŏnburŭl kisulhanda* (Report of all the facts: unpublished behind-the-scenes secrets as told by the former main players). Seoul, Hŭimang, ch'ulp'an-sa, 1966.

Yi Puk. *Kim Il-sŏng wijo-sa* (Counterfeit record of Kim Il Sung). Seoul, Sampal-sa, 1950.

Yi Pyŏng-do, et al., eds. *Haebang isipnyŏn* (Twenty years of liberation). Seoul, Haebang ch'ulp'an-sa, 1965.

Yi Sŭng-man taet'ŏngyŏng-ŭi tamhwajip (A collection of statements by President Syngman Rhee). Seoul, Ministry of Public Information, 1951.

Yi Tong-chun. *Hwansang kwa hyŏnsil* (Fantasy and fact). Seoul, Tongpang tongshin-sa, 1961.

Yi Tong-hwan. "Chŏngch'i chagŭmŭi amnyŏk" (Pressure of political funds), *Sassanggye* (March 1960), pp. 68–79.

———"Kkekkutthan ŭnhaeng-ŭl mandŭlja" (Let's make the banks clean), *Sassanggye* (July 1960), pp. 166–173.

Yi Tong-su, in O Sso-paek, ed., *Haebang isipnyŏn* (Twenty years of liberation). Seoul, Haengjon sinmun-sa, 1965.

Yi Wŏn-sun. *Ingan Yi Sŭng-man* (The human Syngman Rhee). Seoul, Sint'aeyang-sa, 1965.

Yi Yŏl-mo. "Kyŏngche sŏngchang-man nŏkko salsu ŏpda" (We cannot live by economic development alone), *Sassanggye* (May 1970), pp. 38–55.

Yi Yu [pseudonym for the political editor of a well-known South Korean newspaper]. "Korea's Political Dilemma," unpublished manuscript. New York, 1965.

Yim, Louise. *My Forty Year Fight for Korea.* New York, A.A. Wyn, Inc., 1951.

Yim Sun-buk, et al. *Chŏngkae yahwa* (Evening tales from the political world). Seoul, Hongcha ch'ulp'an-sa, 1966.

Yŏ Un-hong. *Yŏ Un-hyŏng*. Seoul, Chongha-gak, 1967.

Yong Nam Ilbo.

Yu Chin-o. *Minju chŏngchiae-ŭi kil* (The way to democratic politics). Seoul, 1963.

Yu Hyŏk-in. "Pak Taet'ongnyŏng-ŭl umjigi-nun salamdŭl" (The people who move President Park), *Shindong-a* (October 1964), pp. 158-159.

Yu Sŭng-t'aek. "Kim Chang-yong-ŭi choëhu" (The last of Kim Chang-yŏng), in O Sso-paek, ed., *Haebang isipnyŏn: Kirok p'yŏn* (Twenty years of liberation: chronological edition). Seoul, Saemun-sa, 1965, pp. 455-488.

GLOSSARY

An Chae-hong　安在鴻

An Ho-sang　安浩相

An Sin-ho　安信好

Chang Ha-il　張河一

Chang Myŏn　張勉

Chang Pyŏng-san　張平山

Chang Si-u　張時雨

Chang Taek-sang　張澤相

Chang To-yŏng　張都瑛

Chang Tŏk-su　張德秀

Chayudang　自由党

Chidojado　指導者道

Cho Bong-am　曺奉岩

Cho Man-sik　曺晚植

Cho Pyŏng-ok　趙炳玉

Cho So-wang　趙素昂

Cho Yŏng　趙英

Ch'oĕ Chang-ik　崔昌益

Ch'oĕ Ch'ol-hwang　崔鐵煥

Ch'oĕ Chong-hak　崔鍾學

Ch'oĕ Hyŏn　崔賢

Ch'oĕ Yŏng-kŏn　崔庸健

Cholla　全羅

Cholla-do　全羅道

Cholla-namdo　全羅南道

Cholla-pukdo　全羅北道

Ch'ŏllima Movement　千里馬運動

Chŏn Chin-han　錢鎮漢

Ch'ŏndokyo　天道教

Chŏng Chun　鄭瀋

Chŏng Chun-t'aek　鄭準澤

Chŏng Il-yong　鄭一龍

Ch'ongsan-li　青山里

Chosŏn　朝鮮

chu-ch'e　主体

Chu Yŏng-ha　朱寧河

Chung Il Kwon　丁一權

Ham Tae-yŏng　咸台永

Hamgyong-pukdo　咸鏡北道

Hamgyong-namdo　咸鏡南道

Han Ik-su　韓益洙

Han Il Mu　韓一武

Han Sang-tu　韓祖斗

Han'guk chung'ang chŏngbopu
　　　　　韓國中央情報部

Han'guk Minju-dang　韓國民主党

Hŏ Chong-suk　許貞淑

Ho Chong　許政

447

Kim Yong-tae 金龍泰
Kim Young Sam 金泳三
Ko Hyŏk 高赫
kun 郡
kungminban 國民班
Kungmin-ŭi-dang 國民의党
kuyŏk 区域
Kwŏn O-chik 權五稷
Kyungmudae 景武台
Kyongsang-do 慶尚道
Kyongsang-namdo 慶尚南道
Kyonsang-pukdo 慶尚北道

Lee Chul-seung 李哲承
li 里

Masan 馬山
Minjudang 民主党
Minju chŏnsŏn 民主战線
Mu Chŏng, see Kim mu-chŏng
myon 面

Nam Il 南一

O Chae-yŏng 吳濟永
O Chi-sŏng 吳致成

O Chin-u 吳振宇
O chŏk 五賊
O Ki-sŏp 吳湛燮

Pak Ch'ang-ok 朴昌玉
Pak Chŏng-ae 朴正愛
Pak Hŏn-yŏng 朴憲永
Pak Il-u 朴一禹
Pak Kŭm-ch'ŏl 朴金喆
Pak Sa-hyŏn 朴士賢
Pak Sŏng-ch'ŏl 朴成哲
Pak Sun-ch'ŏn 朴順天
Pak Ŭi-wan 朴義琓
Paksa 博士
Pang Ho-san 方鎬山
Panmunjŏm 板門店
Park Chung Hee 朴正熙
Poguk kigŭm silhaeng wiwŏnhoë 報國記念実行委員會
Pusan 釜山
Pyŏn Yŏng-t'ae 卞榮泰
Pyongan-namdo 平安南道
Pyongyang 平壤

Rhee Hyo-sang 李孝祥
Rhee Syngman 李承晚
Sam-il 三一
Shin Ik-hi 申翼熙

Shinhan-dang 新韓党
Shinkanhoë 新幹會
Shinmin-dang 新民党
Shinpunghoë 新風會
Silla 新羅
Sŏ Chae-p'il 徐載弼
Sŏ Ch'ŏl 徐哲
Sŏ Min-ho 徐珉濠
Sok San 石山
Song Chin-u 宋鎮禹
Song Yo-chan 宋堯讚
Songdo 松島

Taegu 大邱
Taehan 大韓
Taehan tongnip ch'oksŏng
   kungmin-hoë 大韓独立
       促成國民會
tong 洞
Tonghak 東学
Tongji-hoë 同志会
Tongnip ch'oksŏng chung'ang
   hyŏp-hoë 独立促成
       中央協会

won 員
wŏnae chayudang 院内自由党

wŏnoë chayudang 院外自由党

Yang Hyŏng-sŏp 梁亨燮
Yang Kye 楊界
yangban 兩班
Yi 李
Yi Chŏng-chon 李青天
Yi Chong-ok 李鐘玉
Yu Chu-ha 李舟河
Yi Han-lim 李翰林
Yi Hyo-sun 李孝淳
Yi In 李仁
Yi Kang-guk 李康國
Yi Ki-pung 李起鵬
Yi Kwŏn-mu 李權武
Yi P'il-kyu 李弼圭
Yi Pŏm-sŏk 李範奭
Yi Sang-cho 李相朝
Yi Shi-yŏng 李始榮
Yi Song-un 李松雲
Yi Sŭng-yŏp 李承燁
Yi Wan-yŏng 李完用
Yi Yu-min 李維民
Yi Yun-yŏng 李允榮
Yim Ch'un-ch'u 林春秋
Yo Un-hyŏng 呂運亨
Yosu 麗水

Yu Chin-o　俞鎮午　　Yun Kong-hŭm　尹公欽
Yu Chin-san　柳珍山　　Yun Po-sŏn　尹潽善
Yun Chi-yŏng　尹致暎

INDEX

456

BOOKS PUBLISHED UNDER THE AUSPICES OF
THE RESEARCH INSTITUTE ON COMMUNIST AFFAIRS*

Diversity in International Communism, Alexander Dallin, ed., in
collaboration with the Russian Institute, Columbia University
Press, 1963.

Political Succession in the U.S.S.R., Myron Rush, published jointly
with the RAND Corporation, Columbia University Press, 1965.

Marxism in Modern France, George Lichtheim, Columbia University
Press, 1966.

Power in the Kremlin, Michel Tatu, Viking Press, 1969, was first
published in 1967, by Bernard Grasset under the title *Le Pouvoir
en U.R.S.S.,* and also in England by William Collins Sons and Co.,
Ltd. in 1968.

The Soviet Bloc: Unity and Conflict, Zbigniew Brzezinski, revised
and enlarged edition, Harvard University Press, 1967.

Vietnam Triangle, Donald Zagoria, Pegasus Press, 1968.

Communism in Malaysia and Singapore, Justus van der Kroef,
Nijhoff Publishers, The Hague, 1968.

Radicalismo Cattolico Brasiliano, Ulisse A. Floridi, Istituto
Editoriale Del Mediterraneo, 1968.

Stalin and His Generals, Seweryn Bialer, ed., Pegasus Press, 1969.

Marxism and Ethics, Eugene Kamenka, Macmillan and St. Martin's
Press, 1969.

Dilemmas of Change in Soviet Politics, Zbigniew Brzezinski, ed.
and contributor, Columbia University Press, 1969.

*The U.S.S.R. Arms the Third World: Case Studies in Soviet Foreign
Policy,* Uri Ra'anan, the M.I.T. Press, 1969.

* As of January 1975 the Research Institute on International
Change.

Communists and Their Law, John N. Hazard, University of Chicago Press, 1969.

Fulcrum of Asia, Bhabani Sen Gupta, Pegasus Press, 1970. (Sponsored jointly with the East Asian Institute.)

Le Conflict Sino-Sovietique et l'Europe de l'Est, Jacques Levesque, Les Presses de l'Universite de Montreal, 1970.

Between Two Ages, Zbigniew Brzczinski, Viking Press, 1970.

The Czechoslovak Experiment, Ivan Svitak, Columbia University Press, 1970.

Communist China and Latin America, 1959–1967, Cecil Johnson, Columbia University Press, 1970. (Sponsored jointly with the East Asian Institute.)

Communism and Nationalism in India: M. N. Roy and Comintern Policy in Asia, 1920–1939, John P. Haithcox, Princeton University Press, 1971.

Les Regimes politiques de l'U.R.S.S. et de l'Europe de l'Est, Michel Lesage, Presses Universitaires de France, 1971.

The Bulgarian Communist Party, 1934–1944, Nissan Oren, Columbia University Press, 1971. (Sponsored jointly with the Institute on East Central Europe.)

American Communism in Crisis, 1943–1957, Joseph Starobin, Harvard University Press, 1972.

Sila i Interesi: Vanjska Politika SAD, Radovan Vukadinovic, Centar za Kulturnu Djelatnost Omladine, Zagreb, 1972.

The Changing Party Elite in East Germany, Peter C. Ludz, The M.I.T. Press, 1972.

Jewish Nationality and Soviet Politics, Zvi Gitelman, Princeton University Press, 1972.

Mao Tse-tung and Gandhi, Jayantanuja Bandyopadhyaya, Allied Publisher, 1973.

The U.S.S.R. and the Arabs, the Ideological Dimension, Jaan Pennar, Crane, Russak, and Co. (New York) and Christopher Hurst (London), 1973.

Moskau und die Neue Linke, Klaus Mehnert, Deutsche Verlags-Anstalt, 1973.

Bukharin and the Bolshevik Revolution: A Political Biography, 1888–1938, Stephen F. Cohen, A. Knopf, 1973.

The Soviet Volunteers: Modernization and Bureaucracy in a Public Mass Organization, William E. Odom, Princeton University Press, 1973.

The Origins of the Cultural Revolution. I: Contradictions Among the People 1956–1957, Roderick MacFarquhar, Columbia University Press, 1974.

French Communism, 1920–1972, Ronald Tiersky, Columbia University Press, New York, 1974.

HARVARD EAST ASIAN MONOGRAPHS

18.   Frank H.H. King (ed.) and Prescott Clarke, *A Research Guide to China-Coast Newspapers, 1822–1911*

19.   Ellis Joffe, *Party and Army: Professionalism and Political Control in the Chinese Officer Corps, 1949–1964*

20.   Toshio G. Tsukahira, *Feudal Control in Tokugawa Japan: The Sankin Kōtai System*

21.   Kwang-Ching Liu, ed., *American Missionaries in China: Papers from Harvard Seminars*

22.   George Moseley, *A Sino-Soviet Cultural Frontier: The Ili Kazakh Autonomous Chou*

23.   Carl F. Nathan, *Plague Prevention and Politics in Manchuria, 1910–1931*

24.   Adrian Arthur Bennett, *John Fryer: The Introduction of Western Science and Technology into Nineteenth-Century China*

25.   Donald J. Friedman, *The Road from Isolation: The Campaign of the American Committee for Non-Participation in Japanese Aggression, 1938–1941*

26.   Edward Le Fevour, *Western Enterprise in Late Ch'ing China: A Selective Survey of Jardine, Matheson and Company's Operations, 1842–1895*

27.   Charles Neuhauser, *Third World Politics: China and the Afro-Asian People's Solidarity Organization, 1957–1967*

28.   Kungtu C. Sun, assisted by Ralph W. Huenemann, *The Economic Development of Manchuria in the First Half of the Twentieth Century*

29.   Shahid Javed Burki, *A Study of Chinese Communes, 1965*

30.   John Carter Vincent, *The Extraterritorial System in China: Final Phase*

31.   Madeleine Chi, *China Diplomacy, 1914–1918*

32.   Clifton Jackson Phillips, *Protestant America and the Pagan World: The First Half Century of the American Board of Commissioners for Foreign Missions, 1810–1860*